Color and the Computer

Color and the Computer

Edited by H. John Durrett

Interactive Systems Laboratories
San Marcos, Texas

ACADEMIC PRESS, INC.
Harcourt Brace Jovanovich, Publishers

Boston Orlando San Diego
New York Austin London Sydney
Tokyo Toronto

ACADEMIC PRESS, INC.
Orlando, Florida 32887

United Kingdom Edition published by
ACADEMIC PRESS INC. (LONDON) LTD.
24-28 Oval Road, London NW1 7DX

Library of Congress Cataloging-in-Publication Data

Color and the computer.

Includes index.
1. Color computer graphics. I. Durrett, H. John.
T385.C548   1986   006.6   86-17344
ISBN 0-12-225210-1 (alk. paper)

87 88 89 90   9 8 7 6 5 4 3 2 1
Printed in the United States of America

Contents

Contributors

Numbers in parentheses refer to the pages on which the authors' contributions begin.

Michael A. Andreottola (221), *American Ink Jet Corporation, Woburn, Massachusetts*
Anthony J. Aretz (151), *Department of Behavioral Science and Leadership, United States Air Force Academy, Colorado*
Paul T. Breen (171), *Applied Technology Department, The MITRE Corporation, Burlington Road, PO Box 208 MS E140, Bedford, Massachusetts 01730*
H. John Durrett (ix, 241), *Interactive Systems Laboratories, PO Box 1409, San Marcos, Texas 78666*
Arvin S. Glickman (189), *Brown University, Providence, Rhode Island 02902*
Donald P. Greenberg (83), *Program of Computer Graphics, Cornell University, Ithaca, New York 14853*
Nancy E. Jacobs (285) *Indiana University, Bloomington, Indiana 47405*
Daniel L. McShan (189), *University of Michigan Medical Center, Ann Arbor, Michigan*
Robin M. Merrifield (63), *Display Systems Engineer, Boeing Commercial Airplane Co., Seattle, Washington*
Gary W. Meyer (83), *Department of Computer and Information Science, University of Oregon, Eugene, Oregon*
P.E. Miller-Jacobs (171), *Sperry Corporation, Waltham, Massachusetts 02154*
Harold H. Miller-Jacobs (171), *Applied Technology Department, The MITRE Corporation, Burlington Road, PO Box 208 MS E140, Bedford, Massachusetts 01730*
Gerald Murch (1), *Information Display Division, Tektronix Laboratories, Tektronix, Inc., Wilsonville Industrial Park, PO Box 1000 M/S 63/489, Wilsonville, Oregon 97070*
Judy M. Olson (205), *Department of Geography, 315 Natural Science, Michigan State University, East Lansing, Michigan 48824*
John M. Reising (151), *Wright Patterson Air Force Base, 5435 Gander Road, South Dayton, Ohio 45424*
Robert F. Sapita (115), *Department 285, The Foxboro Company, Foxboro, Massachusetts 02035*
Christopher Schmandt (255), *Architecture Machine Group, Massachusetts Institute of Technology, 77 Massachusetts Avenue, 9-516, Cambridge, Massachusetts 02139*
Louis D. Silverstein (27), *Corporation Technology Center, Sperry Corporation, Phoenix, Arizona 85026*
Wanda Smith (101), *Hewlett-Packard Company, 19447 Prune Ridge, Palo Alto, California*

Howard A. Spielman (267), *Digital Equipment Corporation, Marlborough, Massachusetts*

D. Theron Stimmel (241), *Interactive Systems Laboratories, PO Box 1409, San Marcos, Texas 78666*

Marie E. Wigert-Johnston (139), *Marketing Informations Systems, AT&T Communications, 131 Morristown Road, Rm B-164, Basking Ridge, New Jersey 07920*

Preface

The wide availability of color displays now makes the use of color for information display routine. Unfortunately, what is also routine is the use of every possible color on a single display. This is frequently accompanied by inconsistent use of color in and between displays. The cumulative effect of such practices is to reduce a valuable means of information coding to an annoyance or a device that causes people to make mistakes.

This book began to take form when the editor was shown a sample of color displays that were used for command and control systems, maps, organizational charts, and spreadsheets. Each had been the result of a substantial effort in design and implementation. Each shared inconsistent, incompatible, or distracting uses of color. The creators were clearly unaware of the characteristics of color, how color is perceived by people, and the extensive research that would indicate how color could be most effectively used.

The design and implementation of computer systems to be used by people have, in the past five years, moved beyond what was convenient for the programmer to implement or what made the fewest demands on hardware resources. We are now in a period of system design in which designers and implementers are increasingly aware that *people* see, hear, and respond to the information presented by computers. And, like it or not, people must be considered in the design and implementation process if the best performance or greatest market is to be reached.

This book brings together a substantial collection of fundamental information on color, color displays, and color perception as it relates to the use of color video displays for the presentation of computer generated information. It is not concerned with the presentation of images in color, but rather with the *coding* of text, numbers, graphics, and images using color.

The book is organized into chapters that can generally be read alone. However, there are two major areas of coverage. The first, Chapters 1–5, provides the fundamental knowledge necessary to understand the capabilities and limitations of display systems in presenting information in color and of people in processing and responding to that information. The second part, Chapters 6–16, focuses on the use of color in specific computer-based applications.

In Chapter 1, Jerry Murch provides the basic knowledge and vocabulary that will allow the non-specialist to understand both color and human perception. Lou Silverstein, in Chapter 2, integrates this knowledge with substantial research gained from extensive studies in the field of human factors. Robin Merrifield, in Chapter 3, presents the art and science of generating color on a video display from an engineer's perspective. In Chapter 4, Gary Meyer and Don Greenberg present the interrelationship between what people can see and what displays can show. They show how two uniform color spaces can be used to select color scales to encode variation in other physical dimensions. These chapters constitute a broad look at color, what it is, how we perceive it, how it can be effectively used, and how we can make it occur on a video display.

Wanda Smith provides a concise recapitulation of Chapters 1 through 4 in a straightforward question and answer format in Chapter 5. (*If pressed for time and quick answers are desired, read Chapter 5 first!*)

The remaining chapters present knowledgeable experts who have successfully used color displays in major areas of broad interest. Some of this material has never been collected together in a single work, and much is not available except in obscure technical papers or previously classified documents. These chapters present a variety of color display applications from the perspectives of leaders in various specialties. The following briefly lists the focus of these chapters:

6   Robert Sapita introduces one of the most pervasive uses of color displays for process control and monitoring in a range of manufacturing and service industries.

7   Marie Wigert-Johnston shows how to use color to enhance planning and decision-making for long-distance telephone networks.

8   John Reising and Anthony Aretz explore the emerging use of color displays to replace or enhance traditional cockpit instrumentation.

9   Paul Breen and Harold and P.E. Miller-Jacobs present a survey of color display applications in military command, control, and communication applications.

10   Daniel McShan and Arvin Glickman illustrate the development of color coding techniques for the presentation of medical images.

11   Judy Olson shows the how and why of using color in the computer generation of maps and other cartographic materials.

12   Michael Andreottola takes a look at the complexity of and technology for generating non-photographic color hard copy from computer displays.

13   John Durrett and Theron Stimmel summarize the extensive research examining the use of color in displays to increase learning and performance.

14   Christopher Schmandt presents alternative techniques for displaying text on color displays that accommodate the capabilities and limitations of human perception.

15   Howard Spielman presents a historical overview of the development and use of charts and graphs using color.

16   Nancy Jacobs provides a guide to the selection and use of business graphics systems.

All told, this is a substantial collection of information to guide the designer, implementer, or user of color display systems.

This book took longer to produce than anyone expected. It was a difficult subject to organize and present. Many people and organizations have helped to bring together this material. I particularly want to thank the organizations that employ each of the authors for the support of their work and the excellent editorial staff of Academic Press. Specific recognition goes to Debbie Wilson who entered the first draft into the word processor and to Michelle Friesenhahn who took an assorted collection of computer files, figures, and pictures and delivered them to the publisher in record time. I acknowledge the financial support of Interactive Systems Laboratories for this quixotic enterprise. Finally, thanks to my wife, Tricia, for her strength, and to Cabot-Ann, Devon, and Ashley for helping Daddy get the book finished.

H. John Durrett

Color and the Computer

1 Color Displays and Color Science

Information Display Division
Tektronix Laboratories
Tektronix, Inc.
Wilsonville, Oregon

Introduction

Perception is, very simply, the differentiation of figures from their backgrounds. This means that the figure must in some way differ from the background in order to be discriminated from it. In the visual world, color differences provide the means for this figure-ground separation: The outline of objects as well as the internal contours of objects are formed as edges created by differences in color. Computer-generated images are no different. Both visual displays and printed hard copy consist of figures—lines, edges, shapes—that are differentiated from the background on the basis of color.

Although the term *color* is generally used to describe object attributes such as redness and greenness, the term actually extends to neutral colors (black, gray, etc.) as well. An object that exhibits a specific hue, such as red or green, has a *chromatic color;* an object that stands out from its background on the basis of lightness, such as black or gray, has an *achromatic color*. Figures may be perceived solely on the basis of a hue difference, a lightness difference, or both. Chromatic as well as achromatic colors may also exhibit varying levels of brightness ranging from dark to very bright. The stimulus that allows formation of percepts consists of contours and edges created by differences in lightness, brightness, and hue.

The way the individual perceives color appears to be the result of at least seven factors:

COLOR AND THE COMPUTER
Copyright © 1987 by Academic Press, Inc.
All rights of reproduction in any form reserved.
ISBN 0-12-225210-1

1

1. A physical characteristic of the object itself—the capacity to reflect and absorb certain wavelengths of light.
2. The properties of the light source illuminating the object.
3. The medium through which the light travels as well as the distance it travels through the medium.
4. The properties of the surrounding objects or area.
5. The biochemical state of the eye and visual system at the time of stimulation.
6. The transmission characteristics of the receptor cells and neutral centers.
7. The subject's previous experience with the object or the sensation.

The objective of this chapter is to outline the manner in which colors are produced on printed hard copy and on a visual display. The emphasis is on the description of color from a perceptual point of view and on the production of color from a physical point of view.

The Perception of Achromatic Color

When the light source illuminating an object—such as the sun or an incandescent bulb—contains all of the wavelengths to which the human eye is sensitive and the object reflects all those wavelengths equally, the color of the object is achromatic. That is, the object appears white, black, or some intermediate level of gray. The amount of light reflected largely determines the lightness of the object; objects reflecting 80% or more of the light appear white while those reflecting 3% or less appear black. Various levels of gray are represented by intermediate reflectances. Consider, for example, a black, a white, and a gray automobile. Each reflects different amounts of light and, therefore, takes on a specific achromatic color. If the total amount of light illuminating the cars is increased, the lightness stays the same but the brightness increases. The white car stays white but becomes much brighter—perhaps even dazzling. Thus, lightness is a property of an object itself, while brightness depends upon the amount of light illuminating the object.

Often lightness (white-black) and brightness (bright-dark) are perceptually distinguishable; however, under certain conditions the separation of the two is difficult. For instance, increases in lightness are often coupled with increases in brightness. To make matters even more difficult, the two terms are often used interchangeably in colloquial language. In fact, they are often confused in the psychological literature as well. Even observers carefully trained in the distinction between brightness and lightness often interpret changes in brightness for lightness differences.

For an achromatic hard copy printing system in which the reflectance of the surface and hence its lightness can be varied, it is necessary to develop a lightness scale in which the different degrees of lightness appear evenly spaced throughout the continuum of lightness levels. For example, a system with five levels of gray could be derived by showing many samples to a number of observers and asking them to select a gray that appears perceptually halfway between black and white. Next, the observers select a second lightness that subdivides the white and the previously selected midgray. Finally, a third lightness is chosen that bisects the midgray and black. This procedure can be reiterated to increase the number of levels of lightness to the point where the observer is no longer able to discriminate between levels.

In developing a lightness scale for a hard copy, the illumination is held constant while the reflectance of the surface is varied. Although the exact scale obtained depends upon illumination, the measurement technique employed, and the type of surface, in general, lightness appears to increase as a logarithm of reflectance. As the reflectance of the surface increases, the increase in lightness away from black is initially very rapid— small reflectance changes produce large lightness changes. In fact, most scales locate the middle gray point at a reflectance of 10–25% (Judd & Wyszecki, 1975). The apparent lightness of an object, however, is also largely dependent upon the reflectance values of surrounding objects and the overall level of illumination, so that a general scale of lightness is difficult to establish.

In general, an increase or decrease in illumination has little perceptual effect upon the relative lightness of areas of differing lightness on a hard copy. As the percentage of light reflected from different areas remains unchanged with variations in illumination, the ratios of reflected light also remain the same. An increase in illumination makes everything appear brighter, but the contrast between elements remains constant. On a hard copy, just as with the cars mentioned previously, it is the ratios of reflected light that determine lightness.

The situation for a visual display is more complex. As the electrical signal to the display is increased, a change in both lightness and brightness occurs. The images vary from black to white and from dark to bright. The amount of light reflected from areas of different lightness is roughly the same. When the illumination is increased, an equal amount of light is added to all areas of the display. Conversely, decreasing the illumination increases the contrast as an equal amount of light is removed from all areas.

The amount of light emitted by a display is usually expressed as *luminance* and measured in fot Lamberts (fL). This is a measure of energy that has been corrected to correspond to the visual system's differential sensitivity to wavelength. The human eye is most sensitive to light in the 555 nanometer (nm) range (a yellowish green) with decreasing sensitivity toward the spectral extremes. The luminance of a display, then, is a measure of combined lightness and brightness. Unfortunately, the measure provides only an approximation of the eye's sensitivity so luminance only roughly correspondes to perceived brightness.

In addition to the confounding of lightness and brightness on a visual display, the increase in light output or luminance from the display is not a linear function of applied energy. Figure 1-1, graph (a), plots the applied voltage against luminance in foot Lamberts. Clearly, the luminance changes disproportionately with voltage. In Figure 1-1, graph (b), voltage and luminance are plotted on a logarithmic scale. The slope of the resulting relationship is called the gamma of the display. For monochrome (black-and-white) displays a fairly high gamma level (2. 8 to 3. 0) is desirable so that the dark levels of the display appear a deep black. For a chromatic display, however, such a steep gamma would produce severe color distortions as luminance is increased or decreased. As a result, it is necessary to modify the signals to each of the display's three guns—a procedure known as *gamma correction*.

For a visual display, then, the number of discernible lightness levels or gray levels depends upon the display's gamma and contrast. Contrast, in turn, depends upon illumination.

For the eye to be able to discriminate a lightness difference between two adjacent but not contiguous patches, a luminance difference of about 7% is required. Contiguous panels are perceived as different lightnesses when the difference is only 2% (Laycock & Chorley, 1981).

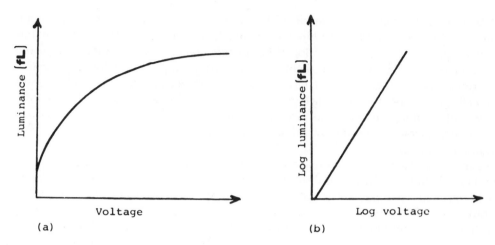

Figure 1-1 Increase in luminance from display not a near function of applied energy.
a) applied voltage against luminance in foot Lamberts.
b) voltage and luminance plotted on logarithmic scale.

A monochromatic display with a gamma of 2.8 and a contrast ratio of 20 to 1 can have a maximum of about 64 discernible steps when the bisection method described earlier is used.

The Perception of Chromatic Color

Objects in the visual environment that reflect or emit distributions of wavelengths in unequal amounts are said to be *chromatic*. Figure 1-2 shows the distribution of wavelengths reflected by the surface of a ripe tomato illuminated by sunlight. The abscissa of the graph indicates the range of wavelengths to which the human eye is sensitive. The tomato reflects most of the visible light striking it but does so in differing amounts. More long wavelengths (600 nm and above) are reflected than short wavelengths which, in turn, tend to be absorbed by the surface. It is the preponderance of long wavelengths

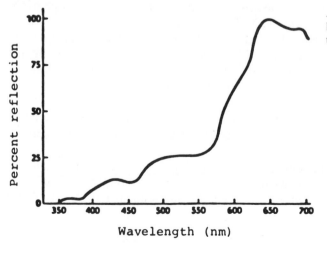

Figure 1-2 Distribution of wavelengths reflected by surface of ripe tomato illuminated by sunlight.

in the energy distribution that is responsible for the perceptual experience of the tomato's chromatic color and the primary basis upon which an observer assigns the names to color experiences.

The willingness to say that an object is a particular color derives from the physical attributes of the dominant wavelengths, the intensity of the wavelengths, and the number and proportion of reflected waves. The identification also depends upon a multitude of learning variables, such as previous experiences with the object and the association of specific sensations with color names. The sensation is also affected by the context in which the color occurs and by the characteristics of the surrounding area or the colors of other objects. The study of the physical attributes of chromatic objects is always compounded by the experiences of the observer with colors in general—because the perception of color is a subjective or personal experience, many of its aspects can be described only in terms of the subject's report of his or her perceptions. These color sensations vary along the psychological dimensions of hue, saturation, lightness, and brightness.

Hue

It has long been known that the color sensations reported by an observer with normal color vision vary as a function of the wavelength of the stimulus. This holds true for the range of wavelengths falling between approximately 380 and 700 nm. The sensations reported by observers exposed to these various wavelengths are known as *hues*. An example of research into the nature of hue is the study by Murch and Ball (1976). Subjects were presented with circles of light, each of which was made up of a single, narrow band (10 nm) of wavelength (monochromatic light) ranging between 450 and 650 nm. They were asked to identify the resulting sensations for each stimulus using the terms blue, green, yellow, and red. This was accomplished by having the observers characterize each stimulus with four numbers corresponding to the amount of blue, green, yellow, and red perceived to be present in that particular target. The results of the study showed that for the range of wavelengths between 450 and 480 nm, the predominant sensation was blue. Green best characterized a fairly broad range of wavelengths extending from 500 to 550 nm, while yellow was concentrated in a narrow range around 570 to 590 nm. Wavelengths over 610 nm were categorized as red. Perhaps the most interesting observation is that most of the colors were characterized by two or more categories. A 500 nm stimulus, for example, was given an average rating of 6.3 for green, 2.2 for blue, .8 for yellow, and .1 for red.

The best or purest colors—defined here as the maximum magnitude estimate for one color name and a minimal value assigned to the other three names—would indicate pure blue at about 470 nm, pure green at 505 nm, pure yellow at 575 nm, and no clear wavelength associated with pure red.

Another way of approaching the relationship between hue perception and wavelength is to establish the amount of increase or decrease in the wavelength of a comparison stimulus that is perceptually different than a standard stimulus of fixed wavelength. Bedford and Wyszecki (1958) reported a study with Professor Wyszecki serving as the single observer. Although a considerable amount of variation between observers is usually noted in such experiments on hue discrimination (Wasserman, 1978), most observers show a pattern similar to Wyzecki's. That is, they are insensitive to (unable to discriminate well) changes in extremely long and short wavelengths. Conversely, at several points in the visual spectrum, discrimination is very good. A change of about 2 nm produces a noticeable shift in hue from a standard set to 420 nm, 480 nm, or 580 nm. Hue discrimination is poorer in the range of 440 to 450 nm and 500 to 540 nm.

Hue, then, is the basic component of color and is primarily responsible for the specific color sensation. While the color names or hues evoked by different portions of the visual spectrum show a close relationship to certain wavelengths, it should be remembered that hue is a psychological variable, and wavelength a physical one. Although all individuals with normal color vision would name a sector of the visual spectrum red, disagreement would occur in deciding which was the reddest red or at what point red becomes orange. These differences probably reflect varying experiences with color as well as intrinsic differences in the color mechanisms of each individual's visual system.

Saturation

A pure monochromatic light source that evokes the sensation of a single hue is seldom encountered. The light reflected or emitted by different objects is multichromatic; that is, it contains a number of different wavelengths, such as the energy distribution of the tomato shown in Figure 1-2.

If an observer starts with a narrow band of wavelengths, he or she will be able to identify a dominant hue. This dominant hue remains the same even with an increase in the width of the band of wavelengths. Increasing the band width causes the sensation to be modified; however, the hue becomes less distinct or clear, and we say then that the hue is less saturated. *Saturation* is most closely related to the number of wavelengths contributing to a color sensation. The narrower the band of wavelengths (e. g., 510 to 512 nm) the more highly saturated the resulting color sensation. Similarly, the wider the band of wavelengths, the less saturated will be the resulting color (e. g., 510 to 590 nm).

Conceptually, it is possible to envision a scale of saturation extending from a pure hue, such as red, through less distinct variants of the hue, such as shades of pink, to a neutral gray in which no trace of the original hue is noticed. A measure of saturation

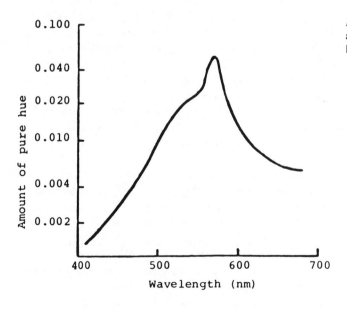

Figure 1-3 Amount of pure hue added to neutral color before the hue becomes detectable.

discrimination can be obtained by starting with a neutral color and determining the amount of a pure hue that must be added to the neutral color in order for the hue to be detectable. Figure 1-3 shows the results of such a study. The abscissa indicates wavelength while the ordinate shows the amount of the pure hue that must be added to the neutral color in order for it to be recognized. Obviously, substantial differences exist in our capacity to detect the presence of color along a scale of saturation. The largest amount of color required before discrimination occurred was for a 570 nm stimulus. This corresponds to a greenish yellow, which in fact appears to be a less distinct color than those produced by other monochromatic lights.

Saturation, then, depends upon the relative dominance of a pure hue in a color sample. Saturation decreases as the band of wavelengths in a color is increased or as the amount of a neutral color added to the pure hue increases. While this general principle holds for all hues, the change in saturation is not the same for all chromatic colors. Yellow appears initially to be less saturated than any other pure hue and desaturates quickly as the wavelength distribution is broadened or as neutral colors are mixed with it.

Lightness

Lightness, it will be recalled from the earlier discussion, refers to the gamut of achromatic colors ranging from white through gray to black; a range often referred to as *gray level*. By definition, achromatic colors are completely desaturated, as no trace of a hue is present. Combining an achromatic color with a specific hue produces a desaturated hue with the level of saturation depending upon the relative amounts of achromatic color and hue. The lightness of the combination will depend upon the lightness of the achromatic color. Therefore, combining white with red, for example, produces a desaturated pink that is lighter than the same hue combined with gray or black. Just as with achromatic colors, the lightness of the mixed color will depend upon the reflectance of the surface under consideration: the higher in reflectance, the lighter the color.

As might be anticipated from the discussion of saturation, monochromatic colors do not appear to be equal in lightness. That is, some hues appear lighter than others, even though their reflectances are the same. If observers are presented with a series of monochromatic lights of equal luminance and asked to rate them in terms of lightness, a relationship similar to that shown in Figure 1-3 results (Kaiser, Comerford, & Badinger, 1976). A monochromatic color with a wavelength of 570 nm appears much lighter than all other wavelengths with the level of lightness decreasing rapidly as the extremes of the visible spectrum are approached. This means that a color made up of a yellow combined with an intermediate gray will appear lighter than a blue-green of the same luminance combined with gray.

Brightness

Increasing the level of illumination of both achromatic and chromatic colors produces a qualitative change in appearance along the dimension of dark to bright. As with achromatic colors, the separation of lightness and brightness often proves difficult as brighter colors invariably appear lighter (Davidoff, 1974).

Consider the situation in which a series of equal reflectance surfaces, each of which reflects a very narrow band of wavelengths, is illuminated by a broad band light source (i.e., one containing all visible wavelengths). Starting with a very low level of illumination and progressively raising the level, the observer first perceives the surfaces as gray. A further increase in intensity allows dark and desaturated hues to become discernible with those wavelengths in the middle of the spectrum (around 555 nm) visible at lower intensity levels. Thus, as the intensity is raised, a broader and broader range of hues appears with the extreme long and short wavelengths visible only at the higher intensities. As noted earlier, this differing sensitivity to wavelength is used in the calculation of luminance.

Note that the terms luminance and brightness are used to describe the visual effects of intensity variation. These terms are not equivalent, as brightness is a perceptual experience and luminance is a standardized measurement based on some components of the perceived brightness.

Interaction of Color Attributes

Increases in intensity produce at least two changes in the appearance of the colors. Clearly the colors become brighter and brighter, but they also appear to increase in saturation as well. Stevens (1975) reports that the increase in saturation as the intensity of the illumination grows or the luminance of the emitted light is raised, reaches a maximum at different levels for each color. Yellow, although never reaching the degree of saturation of the other hues, obtains maximum saturation at a higher level of illumination than the rest of the visible hues, such as orange and green. Interestingly, a high level of intensity is also required for deep red to appear at its most saturated level.

Beyond the point of maximal saturation, still further increases in intensity produce higher levels of brightness but a reduction in saturation. Eventually, the brightness level becomes dazzling, but the hues appear washed out and approach a luminescent white.

Besides changes in saturation and brightness, increases in intensity of a monochromatic color produce further modification in appearance. In a now classic study, Purdy (1937) asked subjects to adjust the wavelength of one-half of a circular field to match the wavelength shown in the other half. He then lowered the intensity of the adjustable portion of a field by a fixed amount and asked the observers to readjust the wavelength of this field so that the two halves, although differing in brightness, showed the same hue. Such measurements were taken over the range of wavelengths from 450 to 660 nm. Figure 1-4 shows the result, which indicates the amount of change in the wavelength of the variable field required to make both fields match in hue after the luminance of the variable field half was lowered. For example, if both halves had a wavelength of 520 nm, a drop in intensity required a change in the variable field of 20 nm (to 540 nm) to make the halves once appear to have the same hue. The changes in hue as luminance changes, known as the *Bezold-Brucke Effect*, are often very large, reaching over 30 nm for a deep red. Perhaps of the greatest interest, however, is that for three wavelengths no change in the wavelength of the variable half of the field was required to maintain a match. These three wavelengths were 470, 505, and 572 nm. These numbers should be familiar as they are essentially the same wavelengths judged as the purest blue, green, and yellow respectively in the color-naming study of Murch and Ball (1976).

The basic perceptual attributes of color—hue, saturation, lightness, and brightness—apply to color produced by any medium. Thus, these principles are the same for printed copy, in which the physical characteristics of the color are determined by inks and dyes, and for the colors of a visual display, in which the colors result from visible light emissions of phosphors.

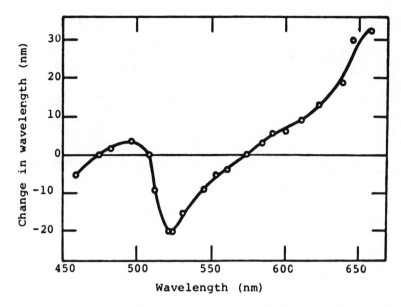

Figure 1-4   Amount of change in wavelength of variable field required to make both fields match in hue after luminance of variable field half was lowered.

Color Mixture

Having considered the visual appearance of achromatic and chromatic colors, the discussion now turns to the production of color—the combination or mixture of colors.

Subtractive Color Mixture

The color of a surface depends upon the capacity of the surface to reflect some wavelengths and absorb others. When a surface is painted or dyed with a particular pigment, a new reflectance characteristic is created based on the capacity of the pigment or dye to absorb some wavelengths and reflect others. A surface painted yellow, for example, might reflect wavelengths above 570 to 580 nm while absorbing most of the longer and shorter wavelengths. Figure 1-5, graph (a), diagrams the energy distribution of a yellow pigment. Consider another surface painted cyan (blue-green) so that wavelengths of 440 to 540 nm predominate. This energy distribution is shown in Figure 1-5, graph (b). If we were to mix both pigments and paint them on a surface, the resulting color would be green. The mixture of cyan and yellow produces green because the yellow pigment absorbs all of the short wavelengths (500 nm and below) and some of the middle band of wavelengths (500 to 550 nm). The cyan pigment absorbs all of the long wavelengths (560 and above) and some of the middle wavelengths (500 to 550 nm). The energy distribution of the mixture is shown in Figure 1-6. Thus, the yellow absorbs those wavelengths evoking the sensation of blue while the cyan absorbs those wavelengths evoking yellow. Between these two extremes, a band of wavelengths is "left over" that evokes the sensation of green. This type of color mixture is called *subtractive color mixture* because bands of wavelengths are subtracted or cancelled by the combination of light-absorbing materials.

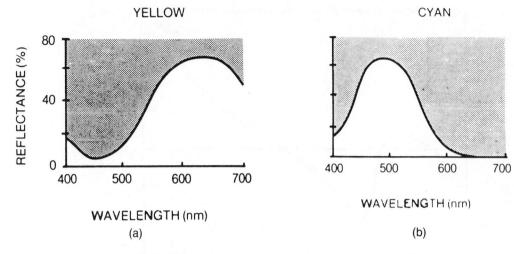

Figure 1-5   Subtractive color mixing.
a) Diagram of energy distribution of a yellow pigment.
b) Diagram of energy distribution of a cyan pigment.

If a third pigment is added to the mixture of yellow and cyan—one that absorbs the band of middle wavelengths, such as a magenta or violet—the surface would appear black because all of the light falling upon it would be absorbed. By this process of eliminating parts of the reflectance distribution through varying the amounts of each pigment, intermediate hues can be created. In the previous example, the resulting green would not be very light, since much of the illumination falling on the surface is absorbed. The mixture of two pigments produces a reflectance surface that absorbs more light than either pigment alone.

A palette of only two pigments, a red and a blue, each with fairly broad reflectance distributions, can create all the intermediate hues by varying the proportion of each pigment. The problem, however, is that the resulting hues will not be very light. Adding a third, fourth, or fifth pigment to the palette helps markedly by increasing the overlap

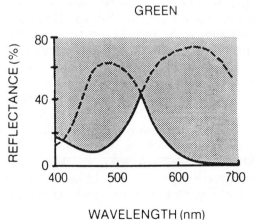

Figure 1-6   Diagram of energy distribution of mixed yellow and cyan pigments.

Color	Subtractive Combination
Red	Yellow + Magenta
Green	Cyan + Yellow
Blue	Magenta + Cyan
Yellow	Yellow
Cyan	Cyan
Magenta	Magenta
White	—
Black	Yellow + Cyan + Magenta

Table 1-1   Minimum palette of 8 colors from 3 primaries.

in the reflectance distributions of each so that lighter mixtures emerge when they are combined. In fact, the minimal number of pigments required is three. These are often referred to as the *primary colors of subtractive color mixture*. An artist, of course, would use many more pigments in order to increase the purity and lightness of the colors produced by various mixtures.

Printed color copy, then, is produced by the subtractive combination of inks or dyes. In most applications, the three primaries used are yellow, cyan (blue-green), and magenta. As shown in Table 1-1, all possible combinations of these three provide a minimum palette of eight colors. Often pure black is included as a fourth color simply because the three primaries that produce the best chromatic color usually do not produce the best black.

To extend the hard copy palette beyond eight colors requires that different levels of the colors occur in each mixture. Two reflective levels of each primary increase the palette to twenty colors. An alternative means of extending the color gamut is to employ a technique known as *halftoning* in which colors are placed on the paper as tiny dots that can vary in either frequency or size. Pure red, for example, would require the highest dot frequency (i.e., 200 dots per inch) while a desaturated pink would result when the dot frequency was reduced to 120 dots per inch. In this technique, the resulting hue occurs as a result of the *additive mixture* of red and the white of the paper.

Additive Color Mixture

Colors can be mixed in another fashion in which bands of wavelengths are added to one another. In fact, this method of *additive color mixture* forms the underlying principle by which the visual system "mixes" colors. Additive color mixture is also the means by which color is produced on a color display, and we will use the functional principles of a visual display to describe this system of color mixture.

The surface of a typical color display is made up of hundreds of tiny dots of phosphor. Phosphors are compounds that emit light when bombarded with electrons, the amount of light given off depends upon the strength of the electron beam. The phosphors on the screen are in groups of three (triads), with one phosphor emitting long wavelength light (red), one emitting middle wavelength light (green), and the third emitting short wavelength light (blue). To display a red object on the screen, for example, all the red phosphors forming the outline and the interior of the object are made to emit light. A green or blue object would be produced in the same manner.

Intermediate hues to red, green, and blue are produced by making two or more of the three phosphors in a triad emit light simultaneously. Because the phosphor dots are very small, the output of the three members of the triad fuses together when viewed from a distance. The result is a field of color that appears homogenous.

When the energy distribution of a typical blue phosphor and the energy distribution of a typical green phosphor are additively combined, the mixture consists of a broader band of wavelengths, which means that the mixture will be less saturated than the blue or green alone. When the energy distribution of a red phosphor is combined with the energy distribution of a green phosphor, the resulting hue of the mixture will be yellow. The exact color of the yellow would depend upon the relative intensities of the red and green phosphors. Increasing the amount of red while decreasing the green would move the color toward orange. Conversely, increasing the intensity of the green would shift the mixture toward a yellow-green. The mixture of two phosphors does not necessarily produce more energy in the wavelength region corresponding to the perceived hue. In fact, the mixture of two single wavelength monochromatic lights can be adjusted to match a yellow for which no energy is present in the emission spectra of either of the phosphors. Basically, the perceived color on a visual display depends upon the ratio of intensities of the primary phosphors. The perception of the color in the eye follows a similar principle in which the relative response of the three types of color receptors determines the experienced color. As a result, it is possible to produce equivalent color sensations from very dissimilar physical sources. Two colors that appear identical despite differing physical structure are called *metameric* colors.

All three phosphors together produce a very broad distribution containing all of the visible wavelengths which, of course, evokes the sensation of white. Varying the intensity or gray level of the three phosphors produces differing levels of lightness. Because one is able to mix most hues, as well as the achromatic colors, by additively combining red, green, and blue, these are called the *primary colors of additive color mixture.*

If an observer considers the visual spectrum of hues as a circle, he or she can locate the three primary colors as points on the circumference of the circle. The upper panel of Figure 1-7 shows this conceptualization.

Mixture colors are produced by varying the proportions of the three primaries. White, denoted by the "w" in the center of the circle, is created when all three primaries are equally represented in the mixture. Increasing the amount of one primary while simultaneously decreasing the other two results in various degrees of saturation of the predominant primary. The broken line in the upper panel of Figure 1-7 indicates various levels of saturation for green ranging from a fully desaturated white (w) to the pure hue at "green." An intermediate mixture, such as greenish yellow, can be produced by increasing the green and red (with a greater increase in green) while decreasing the blue. Varying levels of saturation of the greenish yellow are indicated by the dotted line. Notice, however, that a pure yellow—a point on the circumference of the circle—cannot be produced by combining some proportion of the three primaries. Thus, the hues between red and green, for example, will fall on the solid line connecting the red and green primaries and will be less saturated than any of the primaries alone.

Obviously, the total number of colors that can be produced on a display depends upon the number of steps of gray level obtainable for each phosphor. If the electron gun can be stepped over four levels (2 bits), the resulting palette has 64 colors. Some systems currently available are capable of 256 steps of gray from each gun (8 bits),

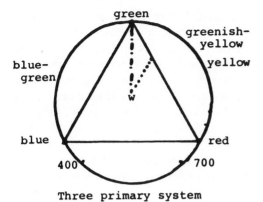

Three primary system

Figure 1-7 Visual spectrum of hues as a circle.

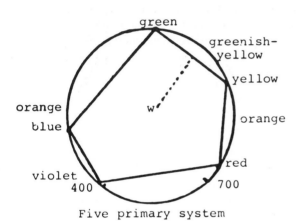

Five primary system

resulting in a formidable palette of over 16 million unique combinations. Obviously, the eye is not capable of discriminating many of the small changes in color so that the viewable palette has many fewer colors. Under optimal conditions, a total of about 3 million discriminable colors can be produced in a visual display; that is, colors that are recognizably different when placed adjacent to one another. The palette shrinks to about 7000 when colors located at different screen areas must be immediately recognized as different from one another.

The obtainable level of saturation for additively mixed colors can be extended by increasing the number of primaries, as shown in the lower panel of Figure 1-7. With five primaries, the greenish yellow is closer to the spectrum and thus more saturated than the same hue produced by red and green. The color television industry experimented with four or five primaries but concluded that the improvement in color did not offset the increase in the expenses of production of such receivers. Visual displays followed this lead.

Colorimetry

The principles underlying the additive mixture of three primaries are indicated in Figure 1-7. When actual mixtures are made with a set of real monochromatic lights or actual phosphors, the resulting diagram takes on a different shape, with the exact shape depending upon the wavelengths of the primaries used. Figure 1-8 shows the diagram resulting from a color mixture study conducted by Wright (1969). Observers viewed a small, centrally divided circular field. One-half of the field was illuminated by a test color while the other half contained a variable mixture of three primaries. Wright's primaries were a blue of 460nm, green of 530 nm, and red of 630 nm. The task of the observers was to vary the proportions of the three primaries so that an exact visual match to a color sample was produced. This can be stated formally with the equation:

$$T \equiv p(R) + p(G) + p(B)$$

which reads: The test sample (T) is visually the same as (≡) the additive mixture of a proportional (p) amount of each of the primary colors of red (R), green (G), and blue (B).

The diagram in Figure 1-8, called a *chromaticity diagram,* has the visual spectrum as the outer boundary. The three primaries (460, 530, and 650 nm) are connected by straight lines to form a right triangle. For each sample, the proportional amounts of red, green, and blue required for a match was measured. The amount of red (R) is given on the horizontal axis (r) and the amount of green (G) is shown on the vertical axis (g). The diagram can only show two of the three dimensions of a mixture because

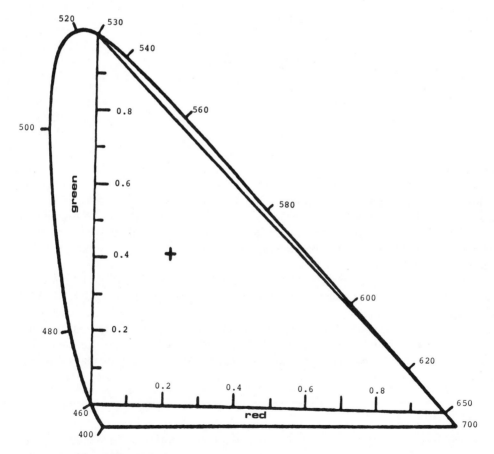

Figure 1-8 Chromaticity diagram.

it is printed as a flat surface, but because the mixtures are given as proportions, the blue contributions can be found by subtraction. Thus, for white the proportions are $(.22)R$, $(.43)G$ and:

$$B = 1.0 - (.22 + .43) = .35.$$

Just as with the diagram in Figure 1-7, all points within the triangle can be produced by an additive combination of the three primaries. All areas outside the triangle, which include all parts of the visual spectrum except for the primaries themselves, cannot. In the matching experiment conducted by Wright, the test colors were pure, monochromatic lights. With the exception of the three primaries themselves, none of the test colors could be matched by an additive combination of the primaries since they lie outside the mixture triangle. To obtain a match, the observer needed to add a certain amount of one of the primaries to the test color in order to desaturate it. For example, a match to a 500 nm test light (T_{500}) would consist of a specific proportion of the 650 nm red primary added to the test color. Expressed in terms of the matching formula, the match is:

$$.55B + .95G \equiv T_{500} + .50R \qquad \text{or}$$
$$T_{500} \equiv -.50R + .95G + .55B.$$

The diagram in Figure 1-8 is constructed by drawing the spectral colors around the mixture triangle, with the distance of the spectral colors from the triangle calculated from the amount of the desaturate needed to perfect the match.

Obviously, an additive mixture of three monochromatic lights will always be less saturated than a corresponding spectral color. The actual color of a mixture plotted in such a diagram can be found by drawing a straight line from white through the position of the color to the spectrum. The hue of the mixture will be that of the color located at the point of intersection with the spectrum, with points along the line representing various levels of saturation of that hue. Thus, a line from white to 500 nm would be comprised of various levels of saturation for a cyan hue.

Figure 1-9 shows a diagram based on color matches by Guild (1925–1926). In this case, the primaries were 436, 547, and 700 nm. The resulting diagram leaves a large number of colors outside the triangle, meaning that these cannot be mixed by additive combination of the three primaries. On the other hand, the spectral colors between 547 and 700 nm *can* be mixed, as the hypotenuse of the triangle falls along the spectrum. This means, for example, that a more saturated yellow can be mixed with Guild's primaries than with Wright's, but a much less saturated cyan. Guild's match to a 500 nm test light would be:

$$T_{500} \equiv -2R + .5G + .5B.$$

The treatment of the fundamentals of colorimetry given here has been cursory. The interested reader should consult the definitive work by Wyszecki and Stiles (1982).

In 1931, a special committee of the Commission Internationale de l'Éclairage (CIE)—an international study group for specification and study of light and illumination—met to develop a standard chromaticity chart. A major goal was to provide a means of numerical specification of additive color mixture. The problem was that diagrams such as those of Wright and Guild could specify only color mixtures made by the combination of a specific trio of primaries.

To overcome this limitation, the committee decided to utilize a concept developed by Maxwell (see Wyszecki & Stiler, 1982) a number of years before in which a set of

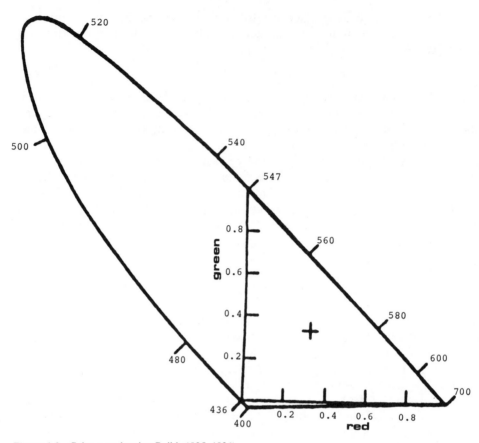

Figure 1-9 Color matches by Guild (1925–1926).

imaginary primaries was determined that encompassed the entire visual spectrum. The imaginary primaries do not exist as physical colors but are mathematical abstractions. Yet it is possible to indicate the position of any real primaries, and the colors that can be mixed by their additive combination, within this space. Because the imaginary primaries do not exist as real colors, they have been given the names X, Y, and Z, with the amount of the X imaginary primary shown on the horizontal axis (x,) and the Y imaginary primary given on the vertical axis (y). Again, the value of Z can be found by subtraction. The colors obtainable with either Guild's or Wright's set of primaries can be plotted in the CIE diagram by connecting them with straight lines. This is shown in Figure 1-10. All colors in the overlapping area of the two triangles can be mixed by either set of primaries. The important point is that a color which plots at the same place in the diagram—that is, has the same x and y values for both sets of primaries—will be the same color, even though it is mixed with different primaries.

Figure 1-11 shows the positions in the chromaticity chart of the primary phosphors used in most color displays (P22 phosphor set). Again, all the colors within the triangle can be produced by the additive combination of the three phosphors while those beyond the triangle's boundaries cannot be achieved. Of course, the actual number of colors along each axis will depend upon the number of gray level steps of each electron gun. The position of the three phosphors in the chromaticity diagram is away from the

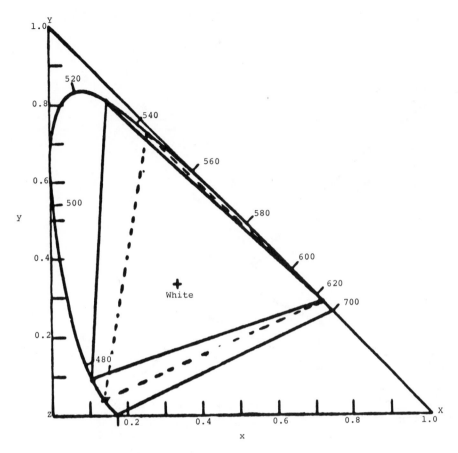

Figure 1-10   CIE diagram of Guild's & Wright's set of primaries.

boundary of the visual spectrum as they are not monochromatic colors. Each phosphor emits a band of wavelengths and as a result produces a color that is less saturated than a spectral color of the same hue. Of the three, red is the closest to a monochromatic source with the concentration of energy around 620 nm. Clearly, the gamut of colors in the real world is considerably larger than the range that can be portrayed on a displayed simulation of the world.

Two widely used definitions of white (D6500 and 9300) are also indicated on Figure 1-11. These two specific proportions of the three primaries refer to a combination which approximates the color temperature (in degrees Kelvin) of a blackbody radiator. The actual color coordinates of these two whites do not fall exactly on the line demarking the color temperature of a blackbody radiator but rather upon an associated line referred to as the daylight locus. The level of deviation from the blackbody radiator is expressed in units of Minimum Perceived Color Differences (MPCD). The white mixture approaching D6500 is usually used as the reference white for color television while visual displays frequently use the 9300 value. This latter mixture contains a higher proportion of blue and is felt by most viewers to produce a better white under the fluorescent illumination found in most work places.

The 1931 CIE (x,y) system has a number of characteristics that render it useful for

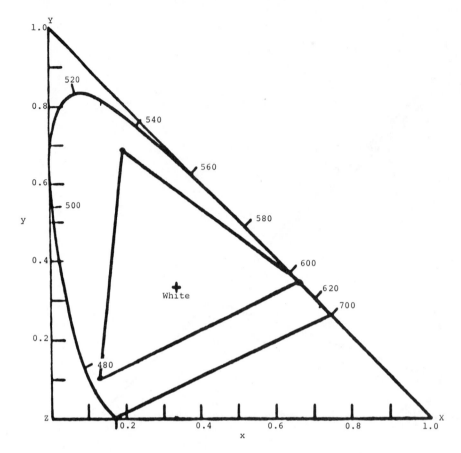

Figure 1-11   Positions in chromaticity chart of primary phosphors.

the description of color hard copy and color displays. An obvious strength is the fact that colors that are produced by one set of primaries can be matched to those of another set by adjusting them to produce the same CIE coordinates. Thus, a pink of $x = .600$ and $y = .380$ will be the same pink, given the same illumination, irrespective of the primaries producing the mixture. Further, the system of imaginary primaries uses the visual sensitivity curve—the variation in visual sensitivity to wavelength—as the Y value. Luminance expressed in cd/m² corresponds to the magnitude of Y in a given mixture (1 foot Lambert = 3.426 cd/m²).

Despite some obvious strengths, the 1931 CIE system has some drawbacks. The most serious of these is that the size of the distance between two points on the CIE diagram tells nothing about the magnitude of the perceived color difference. From a perceptual perspective the CIE space is nonuniform. Figure 1-12 depicts data collected by MacAdam (1942) in which the least amount of change in color required to produce a noticeable difference in hue and saturation is shown for samples taken from throughout the CIE space. Two important aspects of these data need to be noted. First, the amount of change varies considerably for various parts of the diagram. Large changes were required in the top areas that correspond to green while very small differences were

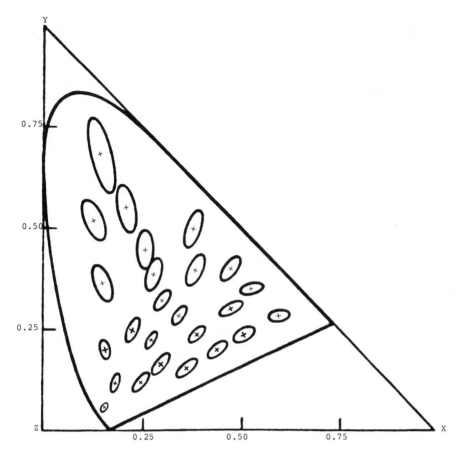

Figure 1-12 Least amount of change in color required to produce difference in hue and saturation.

detectable in the lower portion corresponding to blue. Additionally, the elliptic shape of the measures indicates that the nonuniformity varies along the axis of the diagram.

Recently, a transformation of the CIE 1931 color space has been adopted which produces a more uniform color space. This color space, known as the 1976 CIE *Uniform Color Space* is shown in Figure 1-13. The color triangle for the typical display phosphor set is shown on the diagram. Associated with the diagram is a color difference formula, (ΔE CIE $L^*u^*v^*$), which attempts to scale the magnitude of color differences. With some exceptions, the formula has been reasonably effective in scaling the perceptible differences between colors on displays (Murch, 1983; Snyder, 1982).

Color Description Systems

The complexities of the relationship between hue, lightness, saturation, and brightness, and the intracacies of color mixture require the development of descriptive systems that attempt to model these relations. The goal of such systems is to provide a means of characterizing color samples in some orderly way so that relations between colors can be clarified. From a practical point of view, such systems aid in the specification of particular colors for use in art and industry by providing a numerical index for color.

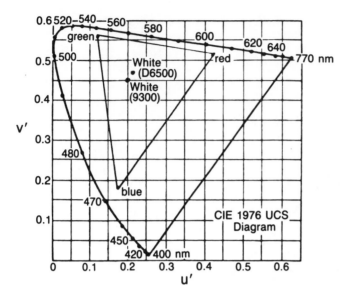

Figure 1-13 CIE Uniform Color Space.

The systems described here do not represent an exhaustive list; rather, they characterize those most widely used for hard copy and displays.

Hard Copy Descriptive Systems

In 1905, an artist named Alfred Munsell introduced the first version of a color description system, *The Munsell System,* which has undergone a number of modifications in the ensuing years. Munsell was motivated by the lack of clarity and distinction between colors afforded by the wide variety of names assigned to different sensations. He drew the analogy to music, pointing out that just as an orderly system relates pitch, intensity, and duration of tones for musicians, so should the artist have a means of relating hue, lightness, and saturation (Nickerson, 1976). Munsell's goal was to provide interrelated scales of hue, lightness, and saturation in which the size of the perceptual change in each dimension was spaced in equal steps.

In the current version published by the Munsell Color Company, the system consists of an ordered array of color swatches that vary in hue, lightness (called "value"), and saturation (called "chroma"). The lightness scale consists of nine shades of gray, visually equally spaced and bounded by white and black. Hue is represented by a circular order in which a total of 40 steps divides the circle into equal units. The dimension of saturation relates the scales of hue and lightness with a maximum of 16 gradations. The Munsell system reflects a number of the relationships previously discussed in that the maximum level of saturation and the lightness level assigned to the purest hues is not the same for all hues. Figure 1-14 diagrams a three-dimensional representation of the system— a so-called "color solid."

The outer circumference of the distorted globe indicates the relative position of the hues with the point of farthest protrusion representing the maximally obtainable lightness for the particular hue. The central axis presents the range of achromatic colors with white at the top. The cutaway panel shows a collection of samples for a specific yellow (denoted 5Y). The single swatch on the far right of this panel, marked 9/14, indicates the lightest (9) and most saturated (14) sample of the hue (5Y). Thus, this sample may

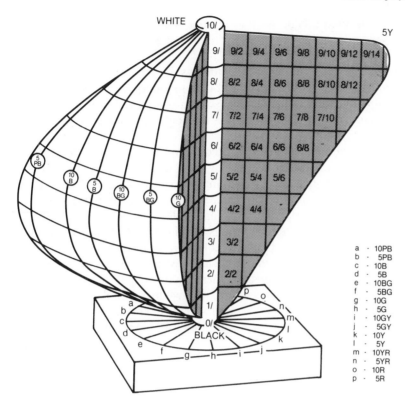

Figure 1-14   Three-dimensional representation of a color.

be characterized as 5Y/9/14. Moving horizontally toward the central axis, variations in saturation (9/12, 9/10, 9/8, etc.) are indicated with hue and lightness held constant. Vertical columns specify levels of lightness (9/6, 8/6, 7/6, etc.) with hue and lightness constant while diagonal excursions demark changes in both lightness and saturation for the specific hue under construction.

As indicated, the Munsell system succeeds to a degree in incorporating a number of features of color appearance. The observation that some hues are always less saturated than others and that differences in lightness exist between hues is incorporated into the system. However, it fails to take other aspects into account, most notably the effect of brightness and associated changes in hue and saturation as brightness increases or decreases. Furthermore, the influence of contrast is not represented (the variance in the appearance of a color as a result of surrounding colors).

A somewhat different approach to color description is taken in the *Natural Color System* developed by Härd and Sivik in Sweden (1981) as an outgrowth of the theory of color vision advanced by Hering. This system places emphasis on qualitative variations in color sensation rather than on equally spaced visual scales as in the Munsell system.

The underlying concept in the Natural Color System is that all colors can be described in terms of three pairs of mutually exclusive polar coordinates: black-white, red-green, and yellow-blue. "Mutually exclusive" here means that a given color can display some aspect of one of each pole of a pair (i.e., whitish-reddish-yellowish) but never both poles of one pair simultaneously (i.e., whitish-reddish-greenish). In other words, certain unique colors can appear as mixtures of one another but others cannot. Thus, the sensation of reddish yellow can occur but not the color reddish green or the color yellowish blue.

Just as with the Munsell system, the Natural Color System includes a consideration of intrinsic lightness and saturation differences and fails to incorporate brightness and contrast effects. Additionally, the Natural Color System describes color relations in terms of mutually exclusive colors. Such a concept is unusual and requires some careful consideration of the logical consequence of relating colors. Such systems offer the possibility of providing the critical link between hard copy and display color despite the fact that color is produced in such different ways by each medium.

While both systems provide a means of specifying the appearance of colors, each emphasizes a slightly different element of color. The Munsell system attempts to provide a psychophysically valid set of scales relating the qualitative differences between colors.

The purpose of both the Munsell system and the Natural Color System is to provide a means of expressing the relationships between colors in an orderly fashion. Their usefulness has been greatly expanded by the publication of the CIE *x, y* coordinates for most of the samples. In the Munsell system, these values constitute the *Munsell Renotation*. Similar work has been carried out by the Swedish Color Center, which has compiled the CIE specifications for 16,000 color samples. The critical importance of these specifications is the link between the description of the appearance of a color and the mixture relations of colors.

Visual Display Descriptive Systems

An obvious approach to a descriptive system for visual displays is to indicate colors in terms of the additive relations of red, green, and blue. The resultant *RGB System* specifies a trio of values ranging from 0 to 1 or 0 to 100% for each of the three primaries. The color relationships that result form a cube as shown in Figure 1-15. Some examples are indicated in the figure. The RGB system is a simple and direct approach to the problem of color description that incorporates the principles of additive color mixture; that is, the user specifies color directly in terms of the electrical activity that the specification will induce.

For individuals understanding the nuances of additive color mixture, the RGB System is comfortable. But most people are more familiar with subtractive color mixture in which a combination of blue and yellow produces green. That red and green should

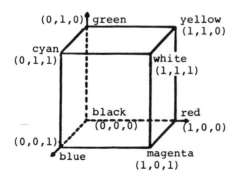

Figure 1-15 Color relationships of additive colors result in cube.

yield yellow is not obvious. Even for those individuals with a clear understanding of additive color, the location and proper specification of colors within the interior of the cube, when some real value for all three primaries is required, proves difficult. Imagine selection of a medium brown, for example. The greatest difficulty is encountered when a color of proper hue and brightness has been located and a shift in saturation is desired. Such a shift would require a disproportionate change in all three values.

The second widely used system of color description for visual displays is a direct application of the perceptual relations of hue, lightness, and saturation. A conceptual diagram of the version of the *HLS System,* developed by Tektronix, Inc., is shown in Figure 1-16. The hues are conceptualized as a circle surrounding the midpoint of the lightness scale. The hues are arranged so that complementary colors are located across from each other on a circle. Hue specification is in degrees starting with blue at 0° and following a spectral order around the circle (magenta = 60°, red = 120°, yellow = 180°, green = 240°, and cyan = 300°). Lightness and saturation are expressed as percentages along a continuum ranging from 0 to 100%. Thus, a cyan of medium lightness and intermediate saturation would be specified as 300°, 50%, 75%.

The strength of the HLS system lies in the reliance on perceptual attributes and the ensuing relationships between colors. The conceptual similarity to the Munsell system is also obvious. Again, the inexperienced user will have difficulty locating colors in the interior of the model. Whereas a change in saturation given appropriate hue and lightness was problematic for the RGB system, it is brightness that creates difficulty for the HLS system. An attempt to increase brightness is inexorably linked to a change in saturation.

Recently, a third notational system, the *Color Naming System (CNS),* has been proposed (Berk, Brownstone, & Kaufman, 1982). The goal of the system is to capitalize on common English names for colors. A basic set of seven generic names (red, orange, brown, yellow, green, blue, and purple) along with white, black, and gray is used. A total of thirty-one hue names are derived by using adjacent hue names together to indicate a hue halfway between two generic hues (i. e., yellow-green) and the suffix *ish* to denote quarter-way hues (i. e., yellowish green). Five lightness levels can be specified (very dark, dark, medium, light, and very light) and four saturation levels (grayish, moderate, strong, and vivid). A complete specification might read "light, grayish, yellowish green." Although this proposal capitalizes on familiar names, the names may have very different connotations for different people. The relationship between brightness and saturation is not clearly distinguished, as terms such as "moderate" or "medium" could be equally applied to saturation or brightness.

Including brown as a generic hue name in the CNS system solves the specification

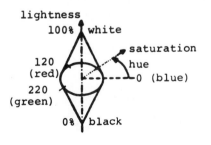

Figure 1-16 Conceptual diagram of HLS system.

difficulty encountered in RGB and HLS. Yet, because brown is very dark orange, the distinction between dark brown and very dark orange is not intuitively obvious. The authors of the system suggest ways of limiting these ambiguities; however, these reduce the simplicity of the model. Finally, the total number of specifiable colors is 627 while many graphic displays offer palettes of 4,096 and up.

Linking Hard Copy to Displays

Without doubt, the capabilities of color copiers will be expanded to increasingly larger color palettes. Since hard copy color is by and large subtractive while display is additive, no obvious algorithm exists to translate from one medium to the other. Now colors are related between display and hard copy by a look-up table that, due to the limited color copying capability, contains only a few entries. In many cases, no attempt to relate the colors is made at all.

The communality of hard copy and display copy will require a common notation system. The most obvious candidates for such a descriptive system are the CIE Uniform Color Space and the Munsell system. Each of these has specific advantages and disadvantages. The Uniform Color Space, for example, is widely recognized as an accepted color metric world wide while the Munsell System is best known in North America. The Munsell System was designed to describe reflective surfaces which creates a number of difficulties in its application to emissive displays: More colors can be produced on todays color displays than are nomiclated in the Munsell System. In contrast, the Uniform Color Space does encompass all realizable colors in either hard copy or displayed copy, but it was developed for emitted light.

Summary

This chapter has attempted to review the basic processes that produce color on a visual display and a printed hard copy. The emphasis has been on a description of the experience of perception in which colors are experienced in terms of hue, saturation, lightness, and brightness. The principles of subtractive color mixture were discussed with reference to hard copy and additive color mixture with reference to visual displays. An overview of colorimetry as it applies to displays sets the stage for the elaboration of color-interface-models-descriptive systems that enable the user to locate and specify colors on a display and hard copy.

The computer and its associated devices have opened up a new world for the description of psychophysics of color perception. Never before have such versatile media existed for the production of color. With the computer as a research tool, science can explore new horizons of color perception and, in turn, make color generation via computer an effective and usable tool. As the following chapters illustrate clearly, both uses of computer driven color displays are taking place.

References

Bedford, R. E., & Wyszecki, G.Wavelength discrimination for point sources. *Journal of the Optical Society of America*, 1958, *48*, 129–135.

Berk, T., Brownstone, L., & Kaufman, A.A new color-naming system for graphics languages. *IEEE CG&A*, 1982, May 37–44.

Chorley, R. A., & Laycock, J. Human factors considerations for the interface between an electro-optical display and the human visual system. *Displays*, July 1981, *4*, 304–314.

Commission Internationale de l'Éclairage Proceedings. Cambridge University Press, Cambridge, 1931.

Davidoff, J. The psychological relationship between lightness and saturation. *Perception and Psychophysics,* 1974, *16,* 79–89.

Guild, J. The colorimetric properties of the spectrum. *Philosophical Transactions of the Royal Society of London,* 1925–1926, *230A,* 149–187.

Härd, A., & Sivik, L.NCS—Natural Color System: A Swedish standard for color notation. *Color,* 1981, *6,* 128–129.

Jameson, D., & Hurvich, L. Perceived color and its dependence upon focal, surrounding, and preceding stimulus variables. *Journal of the Optical Society of America,* 1959, *49,* 890–898.

Judd, D., & Wyszecki, G. *Color in business, science, and industry.* New York: John Wiley, 1975.

Kaiser, P. K., Comerford, J. P., & Bodinger, D. M. Saturation of spectral lights. *Journal of the Optical Society of America,* 1976, *66,* 818–826.

MacAdam, D. L. Visual sensitivity to color differences in daylight. *Journal of the Optical Society of America,* 1942, *32,* 247–274.

Murch, G. M. Brightness and color contrast of information displays. *Digest of Technical Papers, SID,* 1983, *14,* 168–169.

Murch, G. M., & Ball, S. The feasibility of direct magnitude estimation as a quantitative method in the study of complementary afterimages. In H. J. Geissler and V. Zabrodin (Eds.), *Advances in Psychophysics.* Berlin: Veb Verlag, 1976.

Nickerson, D. History of the Munsell color system, company and foundation: Part I. *Color Research and Application,* 1976, *1,* 7–10.

Purdy, D. M. The Bezold-Brucke phenomenon and contours for contrast hue. *American Journal of Psychology,* 1937, *49,* 313–315.

Snyder, H. Perceived color contrast as measured by achromatic contrast matching. Symposium on Self-luminous Displays, Inter-Society Color Council and the Society for Information Display, Charlotte, N.C., 1982.

Stevens. Psychophysics, Wiley Interscience, New York, 1975, 15.

Wasserman, G. S. *Color Vision: An Historical Introduction.* New York: John Wiley, 1978.

Wright, W. D. *The Measurement of Colour.* (4th ed.) New York: Van Nostrand, 1969.

Wyszecki, G., & Stiles, W. S. Color Science, 2nd Ed., Wiley Interscience, New York, 1982, 27.

2 Human Factors for Color Display Systems: Concepts, Methods, and Research

LOUIS D. SILVERSTEIN
Corporate Technology Center
Sperry Corporation
Phoenix, Arizona

Abstract

Recent advances in display technology have made the use of multicolor displays feasible for a variety of applications. While color displays offer increased capability and a number of potential advantages for display design, the effective use of color requires an understanding of the human factors involved in multicolor presentations. Moreover, human performance considerations will have a significant impact on display hardware requirements. The present chapter provides the structure for a human factors analysis of color display systems. A hierarchical approach has been adopted which subdivides the analysis into major levels: visual factors, perceptual factors, legibility/readability considerations, operator performance, and operator impact. Principal determinants of color display effectiveness are identified and detailed at each level, and areas requiring further investigation are discussed. The goal is to provide the reader with an organized, working knowledge of human factors considerations for color display systems.

Introduction

Recent advances in display technology have made the use of multicolor display feasible for a variety of applications. Color offers a number of distinct advantages for display design. First are the obvious aesthetic benefits of color, supported by the general preference for color over monochromatic presentations. Second, color has the potential for greatly increasing information coding capability and flexibility and for reducing visual search time on complex displays. A third advantage is derived from the addition of color contrast, which can increase symbol visibility and reduce display brightness requirements.

Despite the increased capability and potential advantages afforded by color displays, the effective use of color requires an understanding of the human factors involved in multicolor presentations. Moreover, the requirements of the display user will have a significant impact on display system hardware. The present chapter provides the structure for a human factors analysis of color display systems. Principal determinants of color display effectiveness are identified and detailed. Limitations due to insufficient data in certain areas, or interactions among important factors that have not been thoroughly investigated, are also discussed. The goal is to leave the reader with an organized, working knowledge of human factors considerations for color display systems.

Organizational Structure for Color Displays

A great number of complex, interacting factors determine the effectiveness of a color display system. Many of these factors characterize visual displays in general, while others are specifically related to the production and use of color. It is difficult, if not unwise, to isolate and consider color apart from a general framework of considerations for visual display systems.

Figure 2-1 depicts a hierarchical structure for human factors analysis of color display

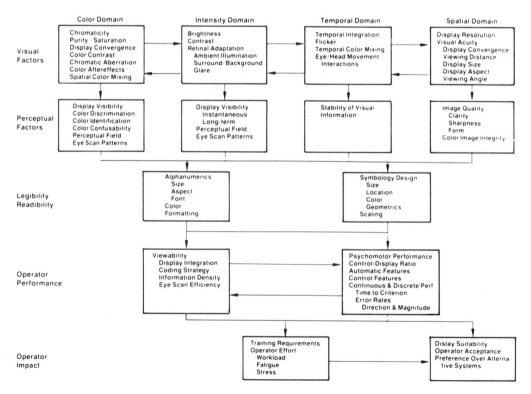

Figure 2-1   Hierarchical human factors analysis for color display systems.

systems. At the top of the hierarchy are critical visual and perceptual factors. Analysis at these two levels can be further subdivided into the domains of color, intensity, temporal, and spatial functions. As one proceeds down through levels of the hierarchy, increasingly complex and integrated functions of both the display system hardware and the human operator come into play. Factors comprising a given level of this hierarchy have a potentially constraining influence on lower functional levels. For example, the visual requirements of the display user must be satisfied before legibility/readability factors can be considered or, in fact, for a color display even to be a viable concept in a given area of application.

Within this framework, specific factors most important for color visual displays are emphasized to provide a reasonable assessment of the impact of color above and beyond general requirements for visual display systems.

Visual and Perceptual Factors

The visual and perceptual determinants of color display effectiveness may be considered together since, in effect, the visual image transmitted by the display and received by the human visual system is the direct object of visual perception. The display user will bring to bear a history of experience and learning that will influence the perception of displayed information. If visual factors involve the transfer of visual information from display to human receiver, then perceptual factors involve the processing of that information to interpret and integrate the image. For most practical purposes, visual and perceptual factors are intimately related in their influence on color display effectiveness.

The separation of visual and perceptual factors into four domains—color, intensity, temporal, and spatial functions—requires similar qualification. While it is useful and convenient to consider these as separate functional domains, as Figure 2-1 indicates, interactions exist among them.

Color Domain

The description of a color visual stimulus is generally based on the translation from the physical qualities of light to three fundamental psychophysical attributes and their corresponding perceptual correlates (Burnham, Hanes, & Bartleson, 1963; Graham, 1965; Wyszecki & Stiles, 1967). On the display or transmitting side of the system, the physical light stimulus is characterized in terms of its spectral distribution and radiance. For the display observer, these physical qualities correspond to the psychophysical attributes of dominant wavelength, excitation purity, and luminance. Finally, these psychophysical attributes are major correlates of the perceptual experience of hue, brightness, and saturation, respectively. The basic relationships between the physical, psychophysical, and perceptual aspects of color are summarized in Table 2-1. It is worthwhile remembering that color is not a direct property of an object or of physical energy, but the perceptual experience of the human observer. Factors that determine a color response are principally the (a) energy characteristics of the visual stimulus, (b) general level and quality of adaptation of the sensing observer, (c) the size and duration of the stimulus, (d) number, size, and energy characteristics of the other objects in the field of view (e) absorption characteristics of the ocular media, and (f) binocular interactions (Burnham et al., 1963).

Color Specification.   No system of color specification has ever taken into account all the factors that determine a color response. However, color specification for most dis-

DISPLAY (PHYSICAL)	OBSERVER/PHOTOMETRIC INSTRUMENT (PSYCHOPHYSICAL)	OBSERVER (PERCEPTUAL)
DISTRIBUTION OF VISIBLE SPECTRAL ENERGY - The variation of the spectral concentration of a radiometric quantity within the range of visible wavelengths.	DOMINANT WAVELENGTH - The wavelength of the spectrum color that, when additively mixed in suitable proportions with a specified achromatic color, yields a match with the color considered.	HUE - The attribute of color perception denoted by blue, red, green, yellow, purple etc.
	EXCITATION PURITY - The ratio of two lengths on a chromaticity diagram. The first length is the distance from a specified achromatic color to the color sample; the second length is the distance along the same direction as the first and running from the achromatic point through the color sample and to the edge of the chromaticity diagram.	SATURATION - The attribute of a color perception determining the degree of its difference from the achromatic color perception most resembling it.
RADIANCE OF VISIBLE SPECTRAL ENERGY - The radiant intensity per unit area of an extended source, as the source is projected to a perpendicular plane from which observations are made.	LUMINANCE - The luminous intensity of an extended source, as the source is projected to a perpendicular plane from which observations are made.	BRIGHTNESS - The attribute of a color perception permitting it to be classed as equivalent to some member of the series of achromatic perceptions ranging from very dim to very bright or dazzling.

Table 2-1 Fundamental physical, psychophysical, and perceptual correlates of color (adapted from Wyszecki & Stiles, 1967).

play devices is typically best accomplished by application of the chromaticity system established by the Commission Internationale de l'Éclairage (CIE), which permits a replicable description of any color through a set of chromaticity coordinates (Judd, 1951; Wyszecki & Stiles, 1967). The basic color space, shown in Figure 2-2, was established in 1931 and relates to a set of color matching functions obtained under standard observing conditions. The 1931 standard observer is based upon a 2-degree, foveally-fixated circular field with dark surround and moderate luminance (Wyszecki & Stiles, 1967).

The basic CIE color space has several extremely useful properties for specifying and describing colors for modern electronic displays. First, the general appearance of any realizable color can be represented by its measured chromaticity coordinates. Second, the dominant wavelength and excitation purity of a color sample can be estimated from the color diagram. Figure 2-3 shows how the dominant wavelength can be obtained by projecting a line from an achromatic reference through the coordinates of the color sample to the boundary of the color gamut. The dominant wavelength can be read directly from the spectrum locus for spectral colors or specified as the complementary wavelength for projections falling on the locus of nonspectral colors. Excitation purity is determined from this same line by calculating the ratio between the distance from the achromatic reference to the coordinates of the color sample and the total distance from the reference to the gamut boundary. Excitation purity can range from zero for an achromatic sample to one for a spectrally pure color. A third property of special importance is that additive mixtures of colors represented by any two points always lie on a straight line connecting them. In turn, these straight lines always lie on the boundary of the color gamut or within it, and the results of all possible additive light

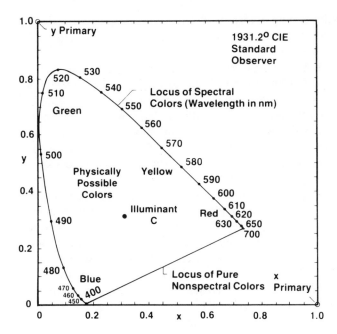

Figure 2-2 The basic CIE chromaticity diagram.

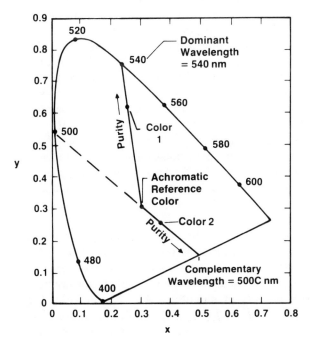

Figure 2-3 Dominant wavelength and purity specification with the basic CIE chromaticity diagram (after Farrell & Booth, 1975. Permission for reprint courtesy of Boeing Aerospace Company).

mixtures that match any given point can be determined. Given this property, the chromaticity diagram is extremely useful for defining stimulus gamuts, or for present purposes, color capability of display systems.

Luminance is factored out of the two-dimensional chromaticity diagram, but one of the tristimulus weighting functions (y) is the photopic luminosity function (Wyszecki & Stiles, 1967). The luminance of a color sample can be determined from the tristimulus value, which is weighted by this function (Y), or alternatively, luminance can be measured and specified directly by photometric measurement of the color sample. The specification of the chromaticity coordinates (x, y) and luminance (Y) of any color sample provides a complete, replicable description of that sample (Judd, 1951; Wyszecki & Stiles, 1967).

Deviations from standard observing conditions render color description in terms of the CIE system less accurate. In 1964, the CIE provided a large-field standard observer using a test field size of 10 degrees (Wyszecki & Stiles, 1967). It is generally recommended that the 1931 system be used for field sizes of 4 degrees or less and the 1964 system for field sizes larger than 4 degrees (Wyszecki & Stiles, 1967). While color image sizes for electronic color displays will often be small, no standard exists for very small color fields subtending less than 1 degree of visual angle. In addition, many of the factors that determine color perception and color discrimination ability are not represented in the CIE system. For complex displays and viewing conditions, color specification in terms of CIE chromaticity coordinates should be interpreted cautiously and with the knowledge that other factors will influence the effective color performance of the display (Silverstein & Merrifield, 1981). The impact of many of these factors are discussed in subsequent sections of this chapter.

The recognition that color discrimination performance was not uniform across the 1931 color space led to transformations such as the CIE 1960 and 1976 Uniform Chromaticity Scales, in which equal distances within a color space correspond more closely to equivalent perceptual differences (CIE, 1978; Wyszecki & Stiles, 1967). The complexity of the color fields generated on color information displays coupled with the general confounding of chrominance and luminance prompted other sources to attempt the definition of new color spaces for electronic color displays (Galves & Brun, 1975; Martin, 1977). Limitations of these attempts are dealt with elsewhere (Silverstein & Merrifield, 1981) but the need remains for better color difference formulations that are more applicable to color display systems. Currently, the CIE recommends the use of the CIE L*u*v* method of estimating color differences, which is based upon the newer 1976 Uniform Chromaticity Scale with associated color difference equations (CIE, 1978). The utility of color difference metrics for selecting high contrast sets of colors and for assessing the impact of display color sets on operator performance has received extensive coverage in two papers by Carter and Carter (1981; 1982). An algorithmic approach to display color and modeling and color selection, based upon the CIE L*u*v* color difference metric, has recently been described by Silverstein, Lepkowski, Carter, and Carter (1986).

The application of the CIE system for describing the color capability of a display system is relatively straightforward. Figure 2-4 shows the color triangle for a shadow-mask cathode ray tube (CRT) display plotted on CIE 1931 coordinates. The corners of the triangle are defined by the chromaticity coordinates of the three phosphor primaries, and the triangle itself represents the boundary of potential colors for the color CRT under consideration. The display is capable of producing any color either on or within the triangular region by appropriate mixtures of luminous output from the primaries.

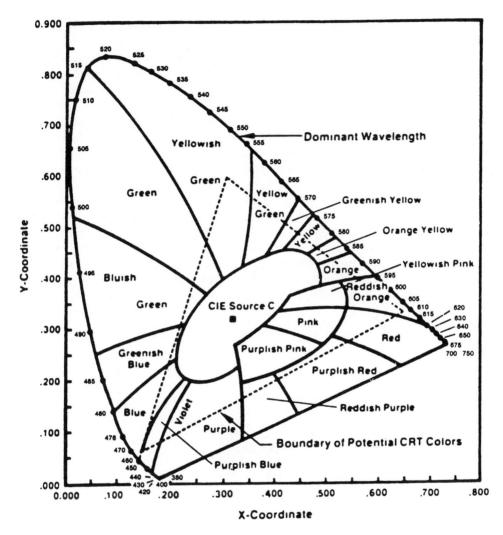

Figure 2-4 Color capability for a shadow-mask color CRT with filtered P22 (Red, Blue) and P43 (Green) phosphors (after Silverstein & Merrifield, 1981).

However, because the CIE chromaticity system is based upon trichromatic proportions with luminance factored out of the two-dimensional diagram, transformations are required to determine the proportional luminous outputs for each of the primaries to achieve a desired color mixture (chromaticity). The chromaticity coordinates for secondary display colors can be obtained by converting the chromaticity (x, y) and luminance for each of the primaries back into tristimulus values (X, Y, Z), summing the respective tristimulus values across primaries, and reconverting into chromaticity coordinates (Wyszecki & Stiles, 1967). Alternative, nomographic methods are available that do not require such conversions and are particularly convenient for manipulating colorimetric quantities for display systems (Silverstein & Merrifield, 1985).

The range of colors available for a color CRT display system is also dependent on methods of beam current modulation. For a shadow-mask type of display, the basis of color synthesis is a spatial additive process. As Figure 2-5 illustrates, color mixture or synthesis occurs by juxtaposition of small primary color fields that cannot be individually resolved by the observer. For example, simultaneous activation of juxtaposed red and green phosphor dots produces a perceived color that is equivalent to a red-green mixture. The color may be yellow or orange in appearance, depending on the luminance of each of the individual components. Because component luminance is primarily a function of CRT beam current, the method of beam current modulation is a major determinant of display color capability. Amplitude modulation provides the greatest flexibility in color synthesis because primary luminance levels can be individually selected for each secondary or mixture color. Time-modulated systems are somewhat more limited since fixed beam currents or primary luminance levels can only be switched on or off in time. Color range for a time-modulated system can be extended by appealing to temporal color synthesis, as the visual system will integrate rapidly alternating chromatic stimuli to produce a color that is a mixture of the time-varying components (Burnham et al., 1963). In this manner, a time-modulated system can produce both a yellow and an orange; for example, by synchronized presentation of red and green components for yellow and alternating yellow and red presentations to produce orange. It should be noted that, undesirable visual effects can result from temporal color synthesis. The

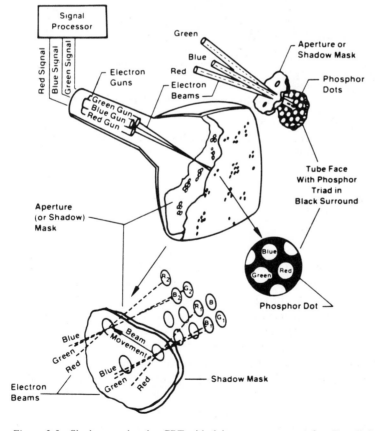

Figure 2-5   Shadow-mask color CRT with delta gun geometry (after Farrell & Booth, 1975. Permission for reprint courtesy of Boeing Aerospace Company).

nature of such effects and their impact on display acceptability are discussed in a subsequent section of this chapter on temporal factors.

Color Differentiation.   The utility of a color-coded information display depends upon effective color differentiation. Characteristics of the display hardware, color-coded presentation format, and display observer affect the ability to distinguish between display colors. Table 2-2 summarizes the principal factors influencing color discrimination and the general directions of their effects.

Wavelength, purity, and luminance.   The first three factors are primarily determined by the display hardware and have been discussed with respect to color specification. In general, as the wavelength separation between display colors increases, the ability to discriminate accurately between them increases accordingly (Haeusing, 1976; Krebs, Wolf, & Sandvig, 1978; Silverstein & Merrifield, 1981). Color purity shows a similar relationship: increases in the purity of display colors maximizes the perceptual distance between them. Changes in the luminance of a colored image cause changes in perceived hue and saturation. As luminance increases, perceived saturation increases and color perception improves. Increments in color display luminance or brightness generally result in enhanced color perception and color discrimination (Farrell & Booth, 1975). Color images may appear achromatic at extremely low or high luminance levels, but the absolute levels where chromatic perception is lost depends upon the image size and the nature of the surrounding field (Burnham et al., 1963). For color display purposes, good color perception and color discrimination can be achieved within the range of 1 to 100 fL.

Color stimulus size.   The size of a color field can have dramatic effects on color perception. Perception improves up to field sizes of 10 degrees (Wyszecki & Stiles, 1967). Field size considerations for color information displays have the most impact for small symbols. Smaller fields appear less saturated and sometimes appear shifted in hue rel-

Factor	▲ Factor	Ability to Distinguish Colors
Wavelength separation	⬆	⬆
Color purity	⬆	⬆
Brightness	⬆	⬆
Color stimulus size	⬆	⬆
Brightness adaptation level	⬆	⬇
Number of colors		⬇
Display background		
Light		⬆
Dark		⬇
Color stimulus location		
Central		⬆
Peripheral		⬇
Type of discrimination required		
Relative - comparative		⬆
Absolute - identification		⬇
User population characteristics	⬆	
Age		⬇
Color vision anomalies		⬇

Table 2-2   Principal factors affecting the ability to distinguish between display colors.

ative to larger targets (Burnham et al., 1963; Farrell & Booth, 1975). The ability to discriminate between colors, particularly along the blue-yellow continuum, is also reduced for small fields. In general, color symbols or fields subtending less than 15 minutes of visual arc impair color perception and discrimination. For reliable discrimination along the blue-yellow continuum, a field size of 20 arc minutes should be considered as a minimum. Small field correction factors have recently been incorporated into color difference equations and have resulted in improved color difference estimates (Silverstein & Merrifield, 1985; Silverstein et al., 1986).

Brightness adaptation level. The general level of brightness adaptation of the display observer varies as a function of display image luminance, display background luminance, and the luminance of the visual field surrounding the display. If the observer's adaptation level is primarily the result of emitted and reflected luminance from the display, then color perception will increase as adaptation level increases. Chromatic sensitivity increases up to adaptation levels of approximately 100 fL (Burnham et al., 1963). Color discrimination ability increases as image and surround luminance are synchronously incremented.

Number of displayed colors. The number of colors used for information coding will strongly affect color discrimination (Semple, Heapy, Conway, & Burnett, 1971). As the number of colors increases, color discrimination becomes more difficult and tighter color control is required (Krebs et al., 1978; Silverstein & Merrifield, 1985). Thus, increased color set size affects display hardware in terms of color production capability and the stability or control of produced colors. Recommendations on the number of usable colors for display coding purposes have been found to be in the range of three to seven colors (Haeusing, 1976; Kinney, 1979; Krebs et al., 1978; Silverstein & Merrifield, 1981, 1985; Teichner, 1979).

Display background. The effects of display background are related to the adaptation level of the observer and the luminance contrast of the display under consideration. Color symbols presented on a light background or surround are perceived as more saturated than the same colors presented on a dark background (Farrell & Booth, 1975; Pitt & Winter, 1974). The increased chromatic sensitivity resulting from surround lightness generally facilitates color discrimination.

Color stimulus location. The region of the retina stimulated by a visual input has dramatic effects on color perception (Hurvich, 1981; Kinney, 1979). Figure 2-6 shows the distribution of rod and cone receptors throughout the retina. It is apparant that the density of cone receptors, those capable of appreciating and differentiating color, falls off rapidly in the periphery. The area of direct viewing, the fovea, encompasses the central 1 to 2 degrees of visual angle and contains only cone receptors. Color perception and visual acuity are greatest in the fovea, and both deteriorate with eccentricity from this central region. The color zones of the retina are not symmetrical: blue-yellow sensitivity extends farther into the visual periphery than red-green sensitivity (Hurvich, 1981; Kinney, 1979). Figure 2-7 shows the results from a study by Kinney (1979) which illustrates the decreases in correct color judgments (red-green-blue-yellow) that occur for a one-degree color stimulus located at varying degrees of eccentricity from the fovea. It has been suggested that color can be used effectively for display coding up to 10 or 15 degrees into the visual periphery.

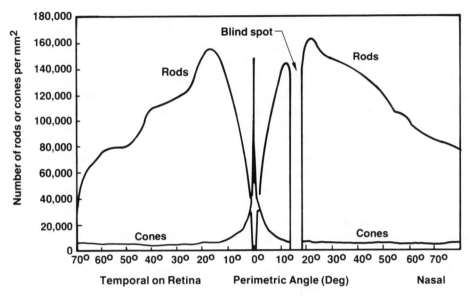

Figure 2-6   Distribution of rod and cone visual receptors throughout the retina (after Pirenne, M. H. Vision and the Eye. *London: Chapman and Hall LTD, 1967*).

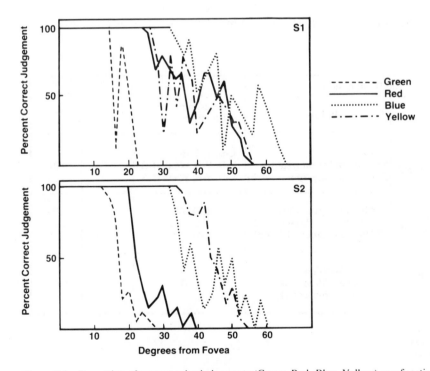

Figure 2-7   Proportion of correct color judgements (Green, Red, Blue, Yellow) as a function of retinal position for two subjects (after Kinney, 1979. Permission for reprint courtesy of the Society for Information Display).

Performance demands.   The type of color discrimination performance demanded from an observer has a significant effect on the ability to distinguish display colors. Furthermore, the type of performance required is determined by the display application and the method of color coding employed. Absolute color discrimination involves the recognition and identification of singularly presented color samples. Relative or comparative color discrimination requires the detection of differences amongsimultaneously presented color samples. The number of discriminable colors and the accuracy and reliability of color judgments are considerably greater for comparative situations than for situations requiring absolute color judgments (Haeusing, 1976; Krebs et al., 1978). This basic performance difference holds regardless of whether reflective surface colors, point-source signal lights, or electronic display-generated colored images are the targets. For operational color displays, a repertoire of three to four colors is realistic where absolute color judgments are required, while the number may be effectively be expanded up to six or seven colors for applications where comparative discrimination is the primary performance requirement (Haeusing, 1976; Silverstein & Merrifield, 1981).

Visual characteristics of the user population.   The last factors to be considered are user population characteristics. Color vision varies to some extent as a function of the age of the observer. Rapid improvement has been reported for color discrimination up to approximately 25 years of age, followed by a gradual decline which becomes more pronounced around age 65 (Burnham et al., 1963).Changes in ocular pigmentation with age and progressive reductions in the transmittance of the ocular media result in decreased contrast sensitivity and particular losses in sensitivity to short wavelength light. Table 2-3 shows the incidence of various color vision deficiencies in the population. In situations where a nonredundant color code is used to convey critical information, the type and frequency of color vision deficiencies may become a serious consideration.

Preferred Designation		Color Discriminations Possible*	Incidence in Population (percent)	
By Number of Components	By Type		Male	Female
Trichromatism (3) (normal or color weak)	Normal Protanomaly (red weak) Deuteranomaly (green weak)	L-D, Y-B, R-G L-D, Y-B, Weak R-G L-D, Y-B, Weak R-G	— 1.0 4.9	— 0.02 0.38
Dichromatism (2) (partial color blindness)	Protanopia (red blind) Deuteranopia (green blind) Tritanopia (blue-yell blind)	L-D, Y-B L-D, Y-B L-D, R-G	1.0 1.1 0.002	0.02 0.01 0.001
Monochromatism (1) (total color blindness)	Congenital Total Color Blindness (cone blindness)	L-D	0.003	0.002

*L-D = Light-Dark
 Y-B = Yellow-Blue
 R-G = Red-Green

Table 2-3   Incidence of color vision deficiencies for males and females (adapted from Judd & Wyszecki, 1963).

Determining Display Color Specifications. It should be apparent that color specification and color differentiation pose difficult problems for the human factors specialist and display designer. The broad range of variables involved, as well as the interactions and trade-offs between them, contributes to the complexity. For any given color display application, the most potent factors affecting color effectiveness are often difficult to isolate and the trade-offs between them are seldom obvious. Operational and economic constraints further complicate matters. At present, there are no analytical tools sufficient to solve all of these problems and provide realistic color display requirements for varied applications (Silverstein & Merrifield, 1985). Available analytical techniques and guidelines will generally have to be supplemented with visual testing tailored to the particular display hardware and application.

One example of an applied test methodology can be drawn from a set of studies by Silverstein and Merrifield (1981) involving color and luminance specifications for a shadow-mask color CRT used in commercial avionics. The objective was to develop an effective color repertoire for use in ambient environments ranging from .1 fc to 8000 fc. Operational display formats were to consist of raster background fields up to 5.5 degrees of visual arc and varied stroke-written symbols of small angular subtense. In the initial step, a preliminary color repertoire was developed through analytical techniques. A computer color model was used to facilitate the attempt to maximize the perceptual dispersion among colors, within the constraints imposed by the display hardware. The initial color set contained seven stroke colors, four of which were also used for the larger raster fields.

Visual testing to verify and/or modify the selected colors and to determine luminance requirements was conducted in three phases. Pilots and engineering personnel, all screened for color vision deficiencies, served as subjects. The visual task employed a comparative, forced-choice color-naming task that best represented the partially redundant use of color coding on the operational flight displays. A criterion of 95% correct color discrimination for each color was adopted as acceptable.

In the first test phase, raster chromaticity and luminance requirements for 5.5 degree raster fields of red, green, amber, and cyan were determined. Testing was conducted under simulated sunlight viewing conditions estimated at 8000 fc for the particular displays under consideration. The second test phase, also conducted under 8000 fc of ambient illumination, was designed to determine chromaticity and luminance requirements for seven stroke-written symbol colors. Diamond-shaped symbols of approximately 20 minutes of visual arc were used as targets and were presented on either a blank background or a background consisting of one of the raster colors specified in the first test phase. Raster luminance was fixed at previously determined levels, and stroke symbol luminance was manipulated in increments of stroke/raster contrast ratio. Figure 2-8 shows the locations of the seven stroke colors in CIE 1931 coordinates and the directional shifts in chromaticity due to ambient illumination of the display. Figure 2-9 illustrates the test pattern generated on the CRT display, as well as a summary of test conditions. The basic test results for the second test phase are shown in Figure 2-10. Color discrimination performance increased up to a stroke/raster contrast ratio of approximately 5.0, but beyond that point additional increments in stroke luminance offered no significant improvements in performance. Figure 2-10 also reveals that criterion performance for the seven colors was not reached simultaneously. During the last phase of test, criterion color discrimination performance at a stroke/raster contrast ratio of 5.0 was verified under low-ambient viewing conditions (.1 fc).

An examination of subject comments and color confusions led to two modifications

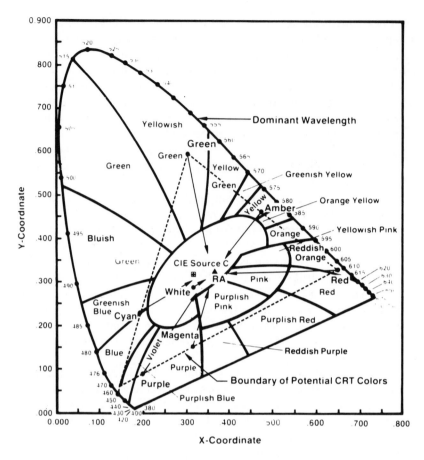

Figure 2-8   Shadow-mask display colors located in CIE 1931 coordinates. The point marked RA designates the chromaticity coordinates of reflected ambient illumination. Directional vectors show color shifts due to 8000 fc of ambient illumination (after Silverstein & Merrifield, 1981).

of the color repertoire. Purple was eliminated from use as a stroke color due to its relatively low luminance and lack of clarity for small images. A disproportionately high number of red-magenta confusions was of concern due to the use of red as a warning cue. As a result, magenta was shifted slightly closer to blue along the red-blue chromatic axis. Table 2-4 provides chromaticity and luminance specifications for the final, verified color repertoire. The end product of this test program, which contributed significantly to the new generation of commercial avionics displays premiered on the Boeing 757/767 airliners, may be examined in the color photographs found in Chapter 8.

Intensity Domain

The visual and perceptual factors of the intensity domain are primarily related to display brightness and contrast. These two factors are major determinants of display visibility, visual acuity of the observer, and the general operational utility of all display systems. The ambient viewing environment, in terms of its effects on both the display and the observer, has a very significant impact in this area. Luminance and contrast requirements

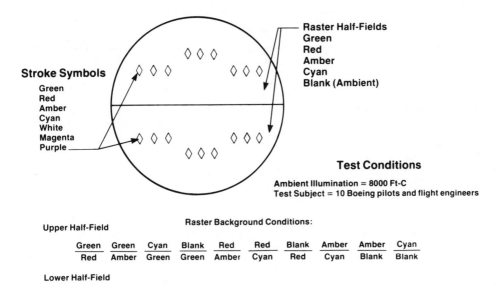

Raster Half-Fields
Green
Red
Amber
Cyan
Blank (Ambient)

Stroke Symbols
Green
Red
Amber
Cyan
White
Magenta
Purple

Test Conditions

Ambient Illumination = 8000 Ft-C
Test Subject = 10 Boeing pilots and flight engineers

Upper Half-Field

Raster Background Conditions:

Green	Green	Cyan	Blank	Red	Red	Blank	Amber	Amber	Cyan
Red	Amber	Green	Green	Amber	Cyan	Red	Cyan	Blank	Blank

Lower Half-Field

Figure 2-9   Color test pattern and summary of experimental test conditions for visual verification testing of shadow-mask color display (after Silverstein & Merrifield, 1981).

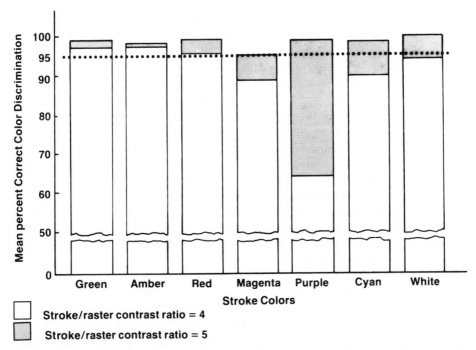

Stroke/raster contrast ratio = 4
Stroke/raster contrast ratio = 5

Figure 2-10   Stroke-written color discrimination performance (averaged across color raster and reflected ambient backgrounds) as a function of stroke/raster contrast ratio (adapted from Silverstein & Merrifield, 1981).

Color	Chromaticity Coordinates				Primary	Percent Primary Luminance			Primary Luminance Level (fL)		
	X	Y	U	V							
Green	.3000	.5900	.1266	.3734	G R B	100	0	0	30.0	0	0
Red	.6530	.3230	.4689	.3479	G R B	0	100	0	0	14.0	0
Amber	.4678	.4631	.2455	.3646	G R B	83.3	88.6	0	25.0	12.4	0
Cyan	.1923	.2067	.1509	.2434	G R B	64.0	0	100	19.2	0	5.1
Magenta	.3205	.1488	.3093	.2154	G R B	0	100	100	0	14.0	5.1
Purple	.2046	.0881	.2243	.1449	G R B	0	22.1	100	0	3.3	5.1
White	.3147	.2740	.2225	.2905	G R B	100	100	100	30.0	14.0	5.1
Green Raster	.3000	.5900	.1266	.3734	G R B	100	0	0	5.8	0	0
Red Raster	.6530	.3230	.4689	.3479	G R B	0	100	0	0	2.7	0
Amber Raster	.4678	.4631	.2455	.3646	G R B	83.3	88.9	0	4.8	2.4	0
Cyan Raster	.1923	.2067	.1509	.2434	G R B	64.0	0	100	3.7	0	.97

Table 2-4 Chromaticity and luminance specifications for a verified color repertoire (after Silverstein & Merrifield, 1981).

for color displays can be expected to be somewhat different from those for monochromatic displays. The additions of chromatic contrast and the visual demands of color discrimination performance are probably most responsible for these differences.

Color Display Luminance and Contrast Considerations.   Luminance and contrast recommendations for color CRT displays are available from several sources (Haeusing, 1976; Krebs et al., 1978; Silverstein, 1982). Actual requirements for a given color display application will be dependent upon many factors, most of which have been discussed in relation to color differentiation. However, few studies have provided data relevant for a range of ambient operating conditions. The data in Table 2-4 indicate luminance requirements for seven CRT-generated colors using both large- and small-size color images. While these requirements reflect actual performance data gathered under both low and high ambient viewing conditions, they are somewhat dependent on the particular shadow-mask CRT and contrast-enhancement filter that were tested. It is important to remember that the chromaticity of display colors, as well as luminance contrast, changes as a function of ambient illumination. The luminance data in Table 2-4 can be converted to a contrast measure by considering that the test display produced a background luminance of 98.5 fL under the specified 8000 fc illuminant.

The data in Figure 2-11 provide a comparison of luminance and contrast requirements for monochromatic CRTs versus a shadow-mask color display. The curve shown for the monochromatic CRT is adapted from a study by Knowles and Wulfeck (1972) that examined luminance and contrast requirements for several high-contrast monochromatic CRTs. The curves for the shadow-mask CRT were obtained with the same system and color specifications described previously (Silverstein & Merrifield, 1981). All of the curves in Figure 2-11 were obtained with relatively complex display formats and rep-

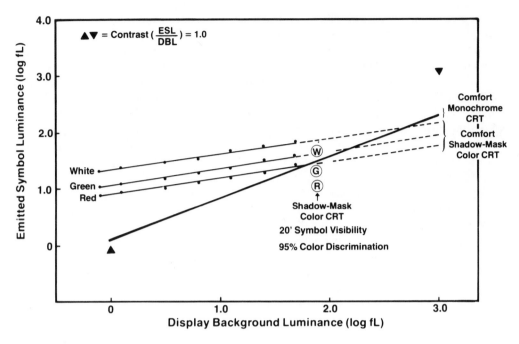

Figure 2-11   Monochromatic and color CRT display luminance and contrast requirements (monochromatic data adapted from Knowles & Wulfeck, 1972).

resent operator-selected display brightness levels for comfortable viewing. For the color display, all colors were presented simultaneously as part of a color-coded presentation. Data from Table 2-4 are also plotted for comparison purposes, since it generally has been found (at least for monochromatic displays) that observers select higher display luminance levels for comfortable viewing than are actually required for minimum visual performance (Knowles & Wulfeck, 1972).

The most immediately apparent difference between the color and monochromatic displays is the discrepancy in the slopes of the functions relating display background luminance and emitted symbol luminance. The slopes for the color display are less steep, suggesting that observers prefer higher symbol luminance and contrast at lower levels of display background luminance. At high levels of display background luminance, the curves for monochromatic and color displays intersect until finally the luminance for color symbols falls below selected levels for the monochromatic displays. Of the several possible explanations for the slope differences between the two types of displays, perhaps the most obvious involves two components. First, at low levels of display background luminance the eye adaptation level and relatively dark display background are not optimal for color perception, and observers compensate by increasing color symbol luminance. Second, at higher levels of display background luminance color perception is facilitated, and the added benefit of chromatic contrast reduces the demand for luminance contrast.

Effects of Ambient Illumination on Display-Generated Colors.   Ambient illumination incident upon a color display causes changes in both the luminance contrast and the chromaticity of displayed information. Incident illumination is reflected from display phosphors and combines with diffuse and specular reflections from other display surfaces to produce a background luminance with a specific chromaticity. Emitted symbol luminance and display background luminance summate to determine total symbol luminance. The luminance contrast of the display is then directly proportional to emitted symbol luminance and inversely proportional to display background luminance. A consequence of the summation of emitted symbol luminance and display background luminance, each possessing a specific chromaticity, is that the chromaticity of the displayed colors shifts toward the chromaticity of the background. In terms of CIE x-y coordinates, the resulting display color will lie on a straight line between the locations of the color and the background. The exact position on this line is dependent upon the luminous proportions of the combining chromaticities.

Display background luminance and chromaticity are functions of physical display characteristics as well as the intensity and color temperature of the illuminant. Background chromaticity will typically fall somewhere within the bounds of the display color space defined by the system primaries. For a three-primary system and a broad-band source of illumination, such as daylight, a relatively achromatic background is generally produced, and resulting display color shifts due to ambient illumination affect color purity more than dominant wavelength. Figure 2-8 illustrates the effects of an 8000 fc. illuminant of 5250 degrees Kelvin on the seven shadow-mask display colors described previously.

Temporal Domain

Temporal domain factors have their major effects on the stability of visual information. Display refresh rates and information update rates must be adequate to prevent the perception of intermittency in the time-varying visual input. Flicker can produce distracting and fatiguing effects, as well as biases in apparent brightness and color perception (Brown, 1965).

Color Effects on Flicker Sensitivity.   The regeneration rates required to preclude observable flicker on a CRT display are primarily functions of image size, luminance, retinal position, and phosphor persistence (Brown, 1965; Farrell & Booth, 1975; Gould, 1968; Semple et al., 1971). Color *per se* has a minimal impact on refresh rate requirements when other factors are held constant (Brown, 1965; DeLange, 1958; Kelly, 1971). Figure 2-12 shows that flicker sensitivity is independent of wavelength at photopic levels of retinal illuminance. For most color display applications, regeneration rates in the range of 60 to 80 Hz will be sufficient for preventing display flicker (Farrell & Booth, 1975; Gould, 1968; Semple et al., 1971). References cited for this chapter contain in-depth coverage of flicker-related factors.

Considerations for Temporal Color Mixing.   In the previous section of this chapter on color specification, the relative merits of amplitude-modulated and time-modulated color display systems were discussed. The extension of color capability for a time-modulated system by appealing to temporal color synthesis was described as leading to potentially undesirable visual effects. The nature of such effects are temporal in origin. Temporal color synthesis requires the alternation of chromatically different stimulus components (Burnham et al., 1963). The components may or may not differ in luminance, but for most display applications the components will differ substantially in luminance. Chromatic modulation may be apparent at low alternation or regeneration rates; however,

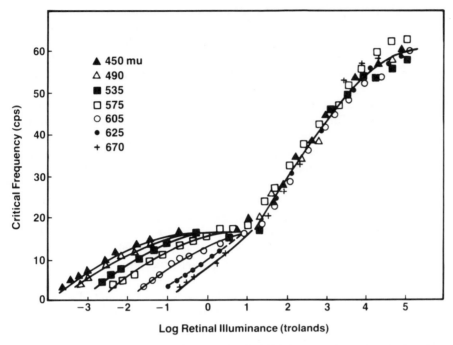

Figure 2-12   Flicker sensitivity as a function of retinal illuminance and wavelength of a color stimulus (after Hecht & Shlaer, 1936. Reproduced from The Journal of General Physiology, *1936,* 19, *pp. 956–979, Figure 3, by copyright permission of the Rockefeller University Press).*

luminance differences between components can produce brightness flicker at rates higher than those required to prevent flicker for colors produced by additive spatial synthesis alone. The effect can be described as a simultaneous reduction in the modulation amplitude and frequency fundamental of the temporally synthesized color. In this manner, both flickering and stable colors can be generated on the same display.

A more serious consequence of temporal color synthesis can result from the interaction of alternating chromatic components with saccadic eye movements and eyeblinks. Rapid changes in position of the eyes allow for the possibility that the alternating chromatic components will stimulate different positions on the retina. In such cases, the two components may be seen as spatially separated images of differing color rather than a single, chromatically fused image.

Spatial Domain

The factors in this functional domain are important determinants of image quality. Spatial resolution and visual acuity are limiting factors for all visual displays, and the impact of color on spatial functions requires careful consideration. For color display systems employing spatial color synthesis, such as shadow-mask CRTs, spatial alignment, or convergence of the color components, has a major impact on perceived color as well as image quality.

Visual Acuity and Resolution As a Function of Color.   Because the eye exhibits significant chromatic aberration, it might be expected that visual resolution and acuity vary as a function of color. On the contrary, with the exception of the short wavelength (blue) portion of the spectrum, fine detail can be seen about equally well in monochromatic lights of differing wavelength and equivalent photopic luminance (Brindley, 1970; Green, 1968; Riggs, 1965). These findings are generally consistent with basic studies on the spatial modulation transfer of the eye for chromatic stimuli (Green, 1968; Van Nes & Bouman, 1967).

Two relatively recent investigations have attempted to measure contrast sensitivity for red, green, and achromatic sinusoidal gratings under viewing conditions more or less representative of a display environment. Nelson and Halberg (1979) used broad-band spectral filters to simulate red and green phosphors of broad spectral emission. The results from this study, shown in Figure 2-13, indicated no differences in contrast sensitivity as a function of color for the two observers tested. The authors concluded that, under normal viewing conditions, no significant differences in the acquistion of spatial information should be expected for red, green, or achromatic displays of equal resolution. The second study by Verona (1978) used small CRT displays equipped with either a narrow-band red (P22), narrow-band green (P43), or a white (P45) phosphor. No differences in spatial contrast sensitivity were found between the phosphors tested.

Several additional studies have commented on the deleterious effects of short wavelength stimuli on visual acuity (Jones, 1964; Mitchell & Mitchell, 1962; Myers, 1967). It has been found that the normal emmetropic eye focuses blue images in the front of the retina, and accommodative adjustments may not be sufficient to bring blue images into clear focus. Older display users may have additional focus problems, since with increasing age the eye becomes presbyopic or characterized by a restricted range of visual accommodation (Southall, 1961). Furthermore, the photopic luminance of short wavelength emissions from most display media is low, and visual acuity is to a great extent a function of luminance and contrast (Riggs, 1965). For these reasons, the display of saturated blue images of small angular subtense is generally not recommended.

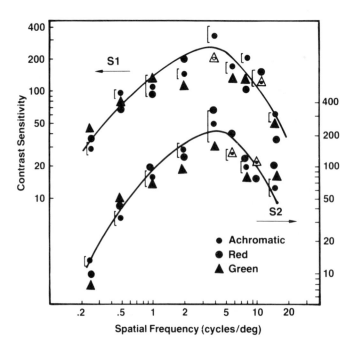

Figure 2-13 Contrast sensitivity measures for two subjects (S1, S2) as a function of spatial frequency for red, green, and achromatic grating patterns (after Nelson & Halberg, 1979. From Human Factors, *1979, 21, pp. 225–228, Figure 1. Copyright 1979, by the Human Factors Society, Inc., and reproduced by permission).*

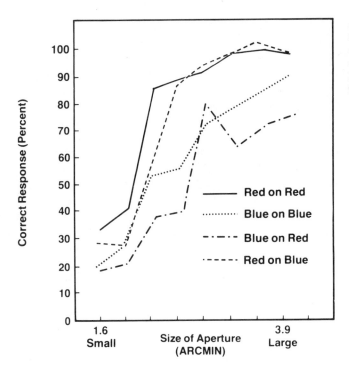

Figure 2-14 Visual acuity as a function of target and background color. Responses are correct in-dentification for orientation of Landolt Ring Apertures (adapted from Myers, 1967).

Figure 2-14 shows the result of an acuity investigation by Myers (1967) that combined blue and red acuity targets with backgrounds of blue or red. Red targets yielded a higher percentage of correct identifications of Landolt ring gaps than blue targets, and color targets presented on the same color background generally produced superior performance. Presumably, the failure of color contrast to enhance visual acuity in this investigation resulted from chromatic aberration due to the extreme wavelength separation of the two colors used.

Measured changes in visual accommodation to actual color display presentations have been unavailable until recently. Murch (1982) measured observers' accommodative responses to a shadow-mask color CRT display equipped with P22 phosphors. Measurements were taken for the display primaries (red, green, blue), as well as the mixture colors yellow, cyan, magenta, and white. As would be expected, maximum variations in accommodation occurred between the red and blue primaries with the other display colors falling within this range. Most importantly, the estimated depth of focus for the colors tested revealed that with the exception of the blue primary, all of the color images displayed could be resolved without the need for reaccommodation. It was suggested that a desaturation of the blue primary would improve its viewability and eliminate the need for accommodative readjustments within display presentations containing blue symbols (Murch, 1982). Alternatively, if blue symbols are required, a large amount of green can be mixed with blue without the resulting color perception being changed from blue (Haeusing, 1976; Silverstein & Merrifield, 1981).

Color Image Integrity.   Since color mixture with any type of spaital-additive color display, such as a shadow-mask CRT, is essentially accomplished by spatial color mixing at the retina of the eye, the convergence or alignment of the separate color images at the display face affects the perceived color of composite images. Misconverged beams can result in a loss of color purity as well as shifts in hue and produce color fringes on the borders of symbol elements.

Symbol edges or borders can reveal prominent color fringes when convergence is inadequate. For example, a stroke-written yellow line may appear as a homogeneous yellow color with optimal convergence, as a yellow line with red and green borders or fringes when convergence is marginal, or separate red and green lines with no perception of the intended yellow color when misconvergence is severe. Unfortunately, few data exist to substantiate guidelines for acceptable convergence limits on color displays. There is some evidence that the threshold for perception of color fringes occurs in the range of approximately 1 minute of visual arc separation between green and red lines. Higher values have been found for green-blue and red-blue combinations (Silverstein & Merrifield, 1985). The threshold for detection of image separation is certainly dependent upon a number of factors: image subtense, luminance and line width of individual components, component chromaticity, color and luminance of the display background, and the observer's eye adaptation level. The upper threshold for the perception of the desired color is considerably higher than the fringing threshold but should be dependent on the same factors (Silverstein & Lepkowski, 1986). Somewhere between these limits, observers establish criteria as to what constitutes an acceptable color image.

Snadowsky, Rizy, and Elias (1966) examined misregistration in color additive displays using a three-color projection technique. Misregistration was defined as the degree or percent misalignment from the perfectly registered image and was thus dependent upon line width. Time required to correctly identify color-coded alphanumerics was recorded, and it was found that performance deteriorated with increases in misregistration. The most marked performance decrements were found above 67% misregistration, although it has been suggested that misregistration not exceed 33% for operational displays. Convergence requirements for color additive information displays should be based on image line width or percent misregistration criteria and also should take into account the display viewing distance. Acceptable limits in the range of 33 to 67% misconvergence appear to be realistic for most applications.

Legibility/Readability Considerations

Symbol legibility and display readability are functions of a number of complex parameters, as is the case with most human factors considerations. General design objectives for alphanumeric and geometric symbols produced on electronic information displays are available from several good sources (Farrell & Booth, 1975; Gould, 1968; Semple et al., 1971; Shurtleff, 1980). The intent of this section is to provide an assessment of the impact of color on existing guidelines for symbol characteristics.

Symbol Size

In a previous section it was indicated that, with the exception of short wavelength images of high purity, visual acuity and spatial contrast sensitivity are relatively independent of color for most practical applications. Minimum size requirements for color symbols are thus primarily dictated by the relationship between image size and color perception. The recommended minimum symbol heights presented in Table 2-5 are adapted in part from previous size recommendations for color symbols (Krebs et al., 1978). Table 2-5 shows that size requirements are scaled according to (a) critical nature

Type of Information Displayed	Comparative Color Discrimination (2-7 Colors)	Absolute Color Identification (2-4 Colors)	Symbol Luminance
Critical Data Variable Position	$\geq 20'$	$\geq 20'$	≥ 1 fL
Critical Data Fixed Position	$\geq 16'$	$\geq 20'$	≥ 1 fL
Non-Critical Data	$\geq 12'$	$\geq 16'$	≥ 1 fL

*Symbol heights expressed in minutes of visual ARC

Table 2-5   Recommended minimum symbol sizes for color information displays.

of the data, (b) static or dynamic nature of the symbols, and (c) type and range of color discrimination performance demanded by a particular color-coding application. The minimum symbol luminance level of 1 fL reflects the lower end of the luminance range for good color perception. Of course, operational luminance and contrast levels will depend on characteristics of the display and ambient operating environment. When considering symbol sizes for CRT displays, it is worth remembering that symbol dimensions are often specified with reference to the center of symbol construction elements (e.g., strokes or dots) since element widths vary with display luminance. As a result, effective symbol dimensions will often be somewhat larger than actually specified.

Symbol Color

The color in which symbols are presented does appear to have some effect on symbol legibility. However, the effects that have been found are not always consistent, and symbol luminance and color are often confounded. Figure 2-15 shows the results of a study, reported by Meister and Sullivan (1969), that examined the relative legibility of seven colors as a function of symbol size. The data indicate the speed at which alphanumerics can be read as a function of symbol color and size. White, yellow, and red symbols were read at the highest rates, while blue symbols revealed an obvious performance decrement. Performance for all colors improved with symbol size. The results from a similar study, reported by Shurtleff (1980), are presented in Figure 2-16. These data reveal that symbol identification accuracy was best for white and for colors near the center of the spectrum (green, yellow). Slight decrements in identification accuracy were found for alphanumerics displayed in blue and red, the spectral extremes.

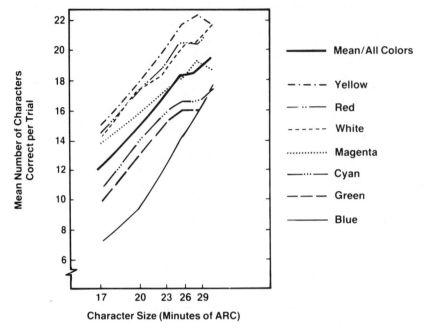

Figure 2-15 Performance in reading individual color-coded alphanumerics as a function of size and color (adapted from Meister & Sullivan, 1969).

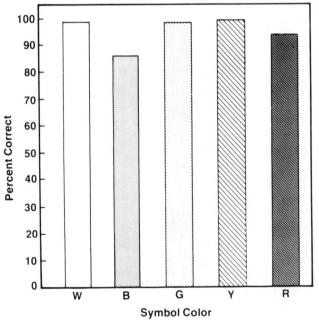

Figure 2-16 Symbol identification accuracy as a function of color (after Shurtleff, 1980. Figure reproduced by permission).

Again, blue yielded the poorest performance. Rates of symbol identification for these colors followed the same general pattern as the accuracy data. Comparisons with studies investigating color symbol legibility in which color and luminance were not confounded have revealed a marked agreement in the amount of impairment for blue symbols (Shurtleff, 1980).

In general, symbol color *per se* has a limited impact on legibility. While there is evidence that colors from the spectral extremes adversely affect legibility, the data are most consistent with respect to short wavelengths. Small blue symbols of high purity should be avoided. Inherent luminance variations of display colors should be considered when selecting a color repertoire for alphanumeric and graphic symbols.

Color Contrast and Readability

Data relating color contrast to display readability have been conspicuously lacking until very recently. In many of the studies from which such relationships could potentially be derived, color contrast and luminance contrast have been confounded and no quantitative estimates of color contrast have been employed. Since color contrast can enhance target visibility and discrimination between visual targets, it might be expected to contribute to display readability as well.

One relevant study by McLean (1965) investigated the effects of color contrast at fixed levels of luminance contrast on a dial scale reading task. The results, shown in Figure 2-17, indicate that color contrast facilitated reading time at intermediate values of luminance contrast. The failure to find that color contrast enhanced performance at all levels of luminance contrast may be due to the fact that color contrast *per se* was not quantified and the amount of color contrast varied across levels of luminance contrast.

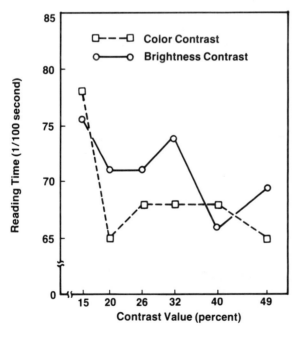

Figure 2-17 Dial scale reading time as a function of brightness contrast and color contrast (after McLean, 1965. From Human Factors, *1965, 7, pp. 521–526, Figure 4. Copyright 1965, by the Human Factors Society, Inc., and reproduced by permission*).

A more systematic approach is needed to quantify the relationship between display readability and color contrast as well as the relative contributions of luminance contrast and chrominance contrast to readability. Fortunately, just such an approach has been adopted in the recent work by Lippert (1986), in which a quantitative color difference formulation was found to reliably predict the speed of reading strings of numeric symbols. Future work should expand the use of quantitative color difference formulations that permit contrasting images to be broken down into estimated differences in hue, brightness, and saturation (CIE, 1978; Wyszecki & Stiles, 1967).

Operator Performance

The performance of the color display user is affected to some degree by all of the factors considered in previous sections. A careful inspection of the hierarchical structure of Figure 2-1 should reveal the logic of interrelationships among performance variables. Assuming that a particular color display provides suitable image brightness and chromatic differentiation and that the display's temporal and spatial characteristics offer a stable, readable presentation, it is now important to consider how and when the color coding of displayed information can be used to best advantage.

Color coding has been shown to have both positive and negative effects on operator performance (Christ, 1975; Krebs & Wolf, 1979; Krebs et al., 1978; Teichner, 1979). The nature and complexity of the operator's task, the manner in which color is functionally related to the task, and the operating environment are all major determinants of color coding effectiveness (Krebs & Wolf, 1979; Krebs et al., 1978). Color may also be used for reasons of aesthetics and pictorial realism. Aesthetic and functional applications of color coding may differ in their requirements and influence on operator performance.

A color-coded information display offers the most potential for enhancing performance in certain operational situations. Table 2-6 summarizes the conditions under which color coding will prove most beneficial. In general, the utility of color as a coding dimension increases as the complexity of the display and of the operator's task increase. Color can also provide benefits in situations where symbol legibility may become degraded by environmental conditions. Additionally, the methods of coding used for a particular color display system can have a significant impact on display hardware as well as operator performance.

- Unformatted displays
- High symbol density
- Operator must search for relevant information
- Symbol legibility may become degraded
- Color code is logically related to operator's task
- Information requirements and/or operator work load are high

Table 2-6 Summary of display situations where color coding can be most beneficial (adapted from Krebs et al., 1978).

Methods of Color Coding

There are many possible ways in which color can be used as an information coding dimension. Color can provide a unique source of information. It can also be combined with other coding dimensions to increase the amount of information that can be displayed or enhance the effectiveness of multiple codes. Table 2-7, adapted from an extensive review and analysis of color coding research for visual displays by Christ (1975), delineates the major methods of information coding and the relative efficiency of color for each method compared to achromatic codes. Before a discussion of performance effects, the types of displays and coding options require description.

Unidimensional Displays. For this type of display, information elements differ from one another in terms of a single dimension or attribute; for example, color, brightness, size, shape, location, or any other single dimension. The dimension selected for a unidimensional code may have as many levels as are operationally feasible; however, only the selected dimension may vary. All other dimensions are held constant.

Multidimensional Displays. Most complex information displays require a combination of a number of coding dimensions to convey specific information. The use of multiple codes provides a great deal of flexibility and, depending on the particular display application, can increase the amount of information that can be displayed or enhance the discriminability of information elements. For example, alphanumeric, color, and position coding might be combined effectively in some situations. Virtually any stimulus attributes can be combined in a multidimensional display.

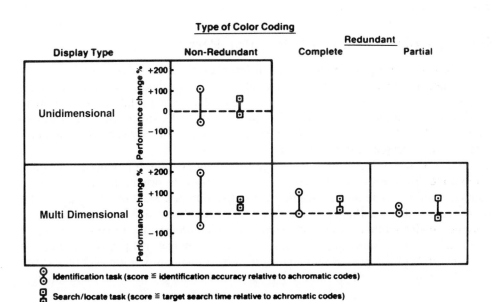

Table 2-7   Relative efficiency of several uses of color coding compared to achromatic codes (adapted from Christ, 1975).

Nonredundant Coding.   In this method of coding, dimensions or attributes must vary independently of one another. Unidimensional displays are, by defintion, coded in a nonredundant fashion since only one dimension conveys information. However, for a multidimensional display nonredundant coding implies independence of attributes. For example, a multidimensional display with nonredundant color and shape codes might consist of all possible combinations of the colors red, green, and blue with circular, square, and triangular shapes. The codes are independent in the sense that knowledge of one of the attributes of a display element (e.g., its color) provides no information as to its other attribute (shape). Each dimension of a nonredundant code conveys unique information not contained in other dimensions.

Redundant Coding.   Multidimensional displays may be characterized by the degree of correlation between coding dimensions. Nonredundant coding is defined by independence, or zero correlation between dimensions. When some degree of correlation exists between coding dimensions, redundancy is implied. Complete redundancy occurs when the correlation between dimensions is perfect, such that knowing the value of one dimension completely determines the value on other dimensions. If the correlation between dimensions is greater than zero but not perfect, then partial redundancy exists. A multidimensional display combining numeric and color codes provides a good example of redundant coding. If the numeric code consists of the digits 1 to 6 and the color code consists of six diffeent colors, the unique assignment of one of the six colors to each of the six digits would produce complete redundancy. Knowing either the digit or the color would provide complete information. However, if only three colors were used and each color was assigned to two of the six digits, then the color code would be only partially redundant with the numeric code. Knowledge of the color of a symbol would constrain the range of possible numeric values, thus providing only partial information as to the exact numeric value.

Effects of Color Coding on Operator Performance

Table 2-7 shows the range of performance differences obtained when color is used as a coding dimension in a variety of coding applications. The data reveal the maximum and minimum gains (or losses) in performance for color coding relative to achromatic codes when visual target identification and search/locate tasks are considered. It should be understood that these data, representing the compilation of a large number of methods, must be interpreted only as general range effects.

The studies on which Table 2-7 is based generally support the following conclusions for symbol identification tasks: (a) color is superior to size, brightness, and shape as a unidimensional target feature, but inferior to alphanumeric symbols; (b) color is superior to size and shape within nonredundant, multidimentional displays and equivalent with respect to alphanumerics; (c) completely redundant color added to an achromatic, multidimensional display facitiates identification performance; (d) partially redundant color and natural color representation have little effect on identification accuracy. With respect to search/locate tasks, Table 2-7 reveals that color generally has a facilitative effect.

One very important consideration in the use of color is that color can interfere with identification and search performance for achromatic attributes of information elements (Christ, 1975). Performance decrements of this sort are relevant only to multidimensional displays and suggest that color be used judiciously in complex display presentations. Irrelevant and unnecessary color should be avoided at all costs.

Symbol Density.   Color is at least as effective as any other coding dimension for reducing visual search time on complex displays. The relative advantages of color coding for search/locate task performance increase as display symbol density increases and as the number of nontarget symbols differing in color from target symbols increases (Christ, 1975). Figures 2-18 and 2-19 show the results of a study by Kopala (1979) that examined the effects of symbol density and method of display coding on performance for a complex, threat situation display embedded in a fighter aircraft simulation. The experimental task required pilots to fly a mission scenario and monitor the threat display in order to respond to specific questions. Questions related to displayed targets involved searching, counting, and comparison operations. Figure 2-18 reveals that redundant color coding had a facilitative effect by reducing the response time to the target questions. The relative advantages of color for reducing response times were almost constant across density levels. However, the pattern of response errors shown in Figure 2-19 indicates that performance with the color-coded display improved relative to shape coding as symbol density increased.

The data in Figure 2-20 illustrate the effects of symbol density, color coding, and knowledge of the target color on visual search time. In this study by Green and Anderson (1956), facilitation of visual search performance with a color-coded display relative to a monochromatic display increased with symbol density. Knowledge of the target color also had a marked effect on search performance. When the target color was not known to the searcher (i.e., color was irrelevant), performance with the color display was inferior to searching without color.

Carter (1982) recently revealed several important findings regarding visual search

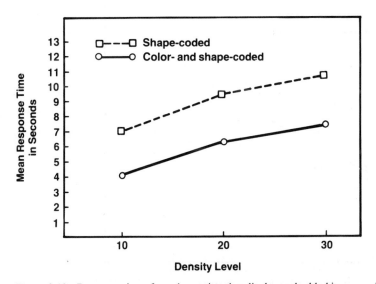

Figure 2-18   Response times for a threat situation display embedded in a complex fighter aircraft simulation. Times are shown as a function of type of coding and symbol density (after Kopala, 1976. From *Proceedings of the Human Factors Society*, 1979, pp. 397–401, Figure 4. Copyright 1979, by the Human Factors Society, Inc., and reproduced by permission).

56   Louis D. Silverstein

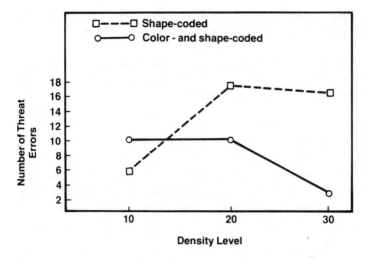

Figure 2-19 Simulated threat situation display errors as a function of type of coding and symbol density (after Kopala, 1979. From *Proceedings of the Human Factors Society*, 1979, pp. 397–401, Figure 5. Copyright 1979, by the Human Factors Society, Inc., and reproduced by permission.

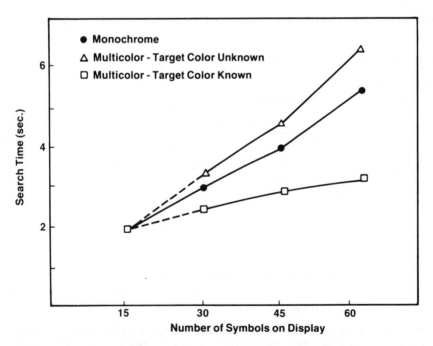

Figure 2-20 Time to locate targets as a function of color coding, symbol density, and knowledge of target color (after Green, B. F., & Anderson, L. K. Color coding in a visual search task. *Journal of Experimental Psychology*, 1956, 51, pp. 19–24. Copyright (1956) by the American Psychological Association. Reprinted by permission of the author).

with color-coded displays. First, search time on color-coded displays increases approximately linearly as the number of display items of the target's color increases from one to all of the items on the display. Second, search time also increases with the number of items not of the target's color, (i.e., background items), if the color of target and background items is sufficiently similar. Third, given a significant color difference between target and background items, the number of background items has no effect on search performance.

Irrelevant Use of Color.   Although the systematic, task-related use of color coding can facilitate operator performance, color coding is not always advantageous. Adding color to a basically monochromatic presentation in such a way that color is irrelevant or not functionally related to the operator's task performance was illustrated in Figure 2-20, in which search time for a redundant color-coded display with an unknown target color was shown to be inferior to a monochromatic display (Green & Anderson, 1956).

A more direct assessment of the impact of relevant versus irrelevant color coding on task performance has been reported by one study of simulated aircraft displays (Krebs & Wolf, 1979). In this study, a set of displays was coded in one of four ways: (a) monochromatic symbology—no color; (b) a three-color code to group similar items— color used as an organizer; (c) a three-color code assigned at random to different symbol elements—color :rrelevant, meaningless; and (d) a three-color code to provide a unique cue (e.g., the color red) for monitoring out-of-tolerance conditions while concurrently performing a two-dimensional manual tracking task that varied in difficulty. A combined performance score reflecting both tracking accuracy and detection speed was computed for comparing the different coding schemes. The results, shown in Figure 2-21, indicate

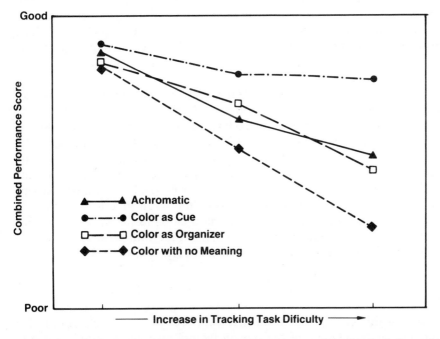

Figure 2-21   Relative effects of task difficulty on performance of simulated piloting tasks as function of different methods of color coding after Krebs, Wolf, & Sandvig, 1979. Permission for reprint courtesy of the Society for Information Display.

that the best performance was obtained when color was used as a cue, and the worst performance occurred under conditions of irrelevant color coding. In addition, the difference between these two applications of color increased as the task became more difficult. The monochromatic and color-as-organizer conditions had equivalent effects on task performance.

Operational Benefits of Redundant Coding Methods.   Several important operational benefits are derived from the redundant coding of color information displays. Most prominent is the preservation of information in the event of partial display or color component failure. In this situation, coding redundancy permits a failure mode of monochromatic presentation without any loss of essential information. Color shifts as a function of display instabilities and aging also have a minimal impact on operator performance when color coding is used redundantly. Finally, color vision deficiencies in the user population are of less concern when all displayed information is available through multiple codes.

Operator Impact

A color information display may or may not produce significant performance advantages over a well-designed monochromatic display in a particular application. However, regardless of measured performance, display users exhibit a general preference for color over monochromatic presentations. In the extensive review of research that was referenced in previous sections, five studies included subjective preference ratings and questionnaire responses regarding color (Christ, 1975). In all cases, there was a strong preference for color displays. Operators reported that they felt more secure with color coding, that color displays are more natural and improve their ability to detect details, and also that color displays are less monotonous and produce less eye strain and fatigue. Pilots have been found to be highly consistent in their preference for color in electronic aircraft displays and tend to select vivid, highly saturated colors for display coding (Beyer, 1971; Silverstein & Merrifield, 1981).

Many questions regarding the impact of color on display operators remain unanswered. While the appeal of color is almost uniform across applications, measured performance often does not support the benefits of color coding information displays. Yet the explanations offered by operators in defense of their preference for color are generally plausible. Is it possible that past research has not always measured the most appropriate aspects of performance? Have objective performance evaluations of the relative benefits of color been obtained under too restricted a range of operational conditions? Perhaps the performance measures previously used have been too insensitive to detect subtle differences in the way operators use color-coded information displays. A satisfactory reconciliation between preference and performance awaits future research. For the present, operators' preferences for color in information displays remain a valid criterion.

Summary

The central theme of this chapter has been that the effective use of color in display systems requires an understanding of the human factors involved in multicolor presentations. The goal has been to provide an overview of human factors concepts, methods, and research relevant to color displays. To this end, the most important issues bearing upon the application of color have been subdivided into major analytical levels.

These levels form a hierarchy that includes visual factors, perceptual factors, legibility/readability considerations, operator performance characteristics, and the subjective impact of color on the display operator. All of these factors must be considered in order to achieve the objective of a more effective man-machine interface through the incorporation of color in information displays.

Advances in display technology will continue, and along with new developments comes an increasing burden to fully understand the interactions between display and observer. This has never been more true than with the recent emergence of full-color electronic display systems. Given such an understanding, the capabilities offered by computer-generated color display systems are limited only by our imaginations.

References

Beyer, R. A limited study of the trade-off between luminance and color coding in electronic aircraft displays. *AGARD Conference Proceedings on Guidance and Control Displays*, No. 96, Paris, France, 1971.

Brindley, G. S. *Physiology of the Retina and Visual Pathway*. Baltimore: Williams and Wilkins, 1970.

Brown, J. L. Flicker and intermittent stimulation. In C. H. Graham (Ed.), *Vision and Visual Perception*. New York: John Wiley, 1965.

Burnham, R. W., Hanes, R. M., & Bartleson, C. J. *Color: A Guide to Basic Facts and Concepts*. New York: John Wiley, 1963.

Carter, R. C. Visual search with color. *Journal of Experimental Psychology: Human Perception and Performance*, 1982, *8*, 127–136.

Carter, E. C., & Carter, R. C. Color and conspicuousness. *Journal of the Optical Society of America*, 1981, *71*, 723–729.

Carter, R. C., & Carter, E. C. High contrast sets of colors. *Applied Optics*, 1982, *21*, 2936–2939.

Christ, R. E. Review and analysis of color-coding research for visual displays. *Human Factors*, 1975, *17*, 542–570.

Commission Internationale de l'Éclairage. *Recommendations on Uniform Color Spaces, Color Difference Equations, Psychometric Color Terms*. Supplement No. 2 to CIE Publications No. 15, 1978.

DeLange, H. Research into the dynamic nature of the fovea-cortex systems with intermittent and modulated light. I. Attenuation characteristics with white and colored light. *Journal of the Optical Society of America*, 1958, *48*, 777–784.

Farrell, R. J., & Booth, J. M. *Design Handbook for Imagery Interpretation Equipment*. Seattle: Boeing Aerospace Company, 1975.

Galves, J., & Brun, J. *Color and Brightness Requirements for Cockpit Displays: Proposal to Evaluate Their Characteristics*. Paris: Thomson CSF Electron Tube Group, Lecture No. 6, AGARD Avionics Panel Technical Meeting on Electronic Displays, 1975.

Gould, J. D. Visual factors in the design of computer-controlled CRT displays. *Human Factors*, 1968, *10*, 359–376.

Graham, C. H. Some basic terms and methods. In C. H. Graham (Ed.), *Vision and Visual Perception*. New York: John Wiley, 1965.

Green, B. F., & Anderson, L. K. Color coding in a visual search task. *Journal of Experimental Psychology*, 1956, *51*, 19–24.

Green, D. G. The contrast sensitivity of the colour mechanisms of the human eye. *Journal of Physiology*, 1968, *196*, 415–429.

Haeusing, M. Color coding of information on electronic displays. *Proceedings of the Sixth Congress of the International Egronomics Association*, 1976, 210–217.

Hurvich, L. M. *Color Vision*. Sunderland, Mass.: Sinauer Associates, 1981.

Jones, M. R. Color coding. *Human Factors*, 1964, *4*, 355–365.

Judd, D. B. Basic correlates of the visual stimulus. In S. S. Stevens (Ed.), *Handbook of Experimental Psychology*. New York: John Wiley, 1951.

Kelly, D. H. Theory of flicker and transient responses. Uniform fields. *Journal of the Optical Society of America*, 1971, *61*,, 537–546.

Kinney, J. S. The use of color in wide-angle displays. *Proceedings of the Society for Information Display*, 1979, *20*, 33–40.

Knowles, W. B., & Wulfeck, J. W. Visual performance with high contrast cathode-ray tubes at high levels of ambient illumination. *Human Factors*, 1972, *14*, 521–532.

Kopala, C. J. The use of color-coded symbols in a highly dense situation display. *Proceedings of the Human Factors Society,* 1979, 397–401.

Krebs, M. J., & Wolf, J. D. Design principles for the use of color in displays. *Proceedings of the Society for Information Display,* 1979, *20,* 10–15.

Krebs, M. J., Wolf, J. D., & Sandvig, J. H. *Color Display Design Guide.* Office of Naval Research Report ONR-CR213-136-2F, 1978.

Lippert, T. M. Color-difference prediction of legibility performancefor CRT raster imagery. *Society for Information Display Technical Digest,* 1986, 86–89.

McLean, M. V. Brightness contrast, color contrast, and legibility. *Human Factors,* 1965, *7,* 521–526.

Martin, A. The CRT/observer interface. *Electro-Optical Systems Design,* June, 1977.

Meister, D., & Sullivan, D. J. *Guide to Human Engineering Design for Visual Displays.* Contract No. N00014-68-C-0278, Engineering Psychology Branch, Office of Naval Research, 1969.

Mitchell, R. T., & Mitchell, R. R. Visual acuity under blue illumination. *IEEE Transactions on Human Factors in Electronics,* March 1962.

Murch, G. M. Visual accommodation and convergence to multichromatic information displays. *Society for Information Display Digest,* 1982, 192-193.

Myers, W. S. *Accommodation Effects in Multicolor Displays.* AFFDL-TR-67-161, Air Force Flight Dynamics Laboratory, Research and Technology Division, Air Force Systems Command, Wright-Patterson Air Force Base, Ohio, 1967.

Nelson, M. A., & Halberg, R. L. Visual contrast sensitivity functions obtained with colored and achromatic gratings. *Human Factors,* 1979, *21,* 225–228.

Pitt, I. T., & Winter, L. M. Effect of surroundings on perceived saturation. *Journal of the Optical Society of America,* 1974, *64,* 1328–1331.

Riggs, L. A. Visual acuity. In C. H. Graham (Ed.), *Vision and Visual Perception.* New York: John Wiley, 1965.

Semple, C. A., Heapy, R. J., Conway, E. J., & Burnett, K. T. *Analysis of Human Factors Data for Electronic Flight Displays,* Air Force Flight Dynamics Laboratory, Technical Report AFFDL-TR-70-174, 1971.

Shurtleff, D. A. *How to Make Displays Legible.* La Mirada, Calif.: Human Interface Design, 1980.

Silverstein, L. D. Human factors for color CRT displays. *Society for Information Display: Seminar Lecture Notes,* 1982, *2,* 1–41.

Silverstein, L. D., & Lepkowski, J. S. The perception of primaryarea spatial distribution in color information displays. *Society for Information Display Technical Digest,* 1986, 416–419.

Silverstein, L. D., Lepkowski, J. S., Carter, R. C., & Carter, E. C.Display color modeling and algorithmic color selection.*Proceedings of the SPIE: Advances in Display Technology VI,* 1986, 26–35.

Silverstein, L. D., & Merrifield, R. M. The Development and Evaluation of Color Display Systems for Airborne Applications: Phase I - Fundamental Visual, Perceptual, and Display System considerations. Technical Report DOT/FAA/PM-85-19, July 1985.

Silverstein, L. D., & Merrifield, R. M. Color selection and verification testing for Airborne color CRT displays. *Proceedings of the Fifth Advanced Aircrew Display Symposium,* Naval Air Test Center, September 1981.

Snadowsky, A. M., Rizy, E. F., & Elias, M. F. Symbol identification as a function of misregistration in color additive displays. *Perceptual and Motor Skills,* 1966, *22,* 951–960.

Southall, J. P. C. *Introduction to Physiological Optics.* New York: Dover, 1961.

Teichner, W. H. Color and information coding. *Proceedings of the Society for Information Display,* 1979, *20,* 3–9.

Van Nes, F. L., & Bouman, M. A. Spatial modulation transfer in the human eye. *Journal of the Optical Society of America,* 1967, *57,* 401–406.

Verona, R. W. Contrast sensitivity of the human eye to various display phosphor types. *Society for Information Display Digest,* 1978, 60–61.

Wyszecki, G., & Stiles, W. S. *Color Science - Concepts and Methods, Quantitative Data and Formulas.* New York: John Wiley, 1967.

Biography

Louis D. Silverstein received the B. S. degree in psychology and the M.A. and Ph.D. (1977) degrees in Experimental Psychology/Psychophysiology from the University of Florida. He was subsequently awarded a postdoctoral fellowship to pursue two years of advanced research and studies at the University of Wisconsin, focusing on psychophysiological aspects of human performance. Dr. Silverstein has worked as a human factors specialist for Rockwell International and was a research scientist in the Crew Systems Research Group at the Boeing Company for three years. He has worked as a principal scientist at General Physics Corporation, and at present, is doing research at the Sperry Corporation in Phoenix.

Dr. Silverstein has worked on a number of significant applied human performance problems, most recently concentrating on the development of effective color display systems for both airborne and ground-based operations. He has interests in all aspects of human performance, with major emphasis on applied vision and audition, cognitive processing, performance measurement methodology, and operator workload measurement.

Dr. Silverstein is a member of the American Psychological Association, the Society for Psychophysiological Research, the Society for Information Display, the Society of Engineering Psychologists, and the Human Factors Society.

3 Visual Parameters for Color CRTs

ROBIN M. MERRIFIELD
Display Systems Engineer
Boeing Commercial Airplane Co.
Seattle, Washington

Color Space

Color is that characteristic of visible radiant energy by which an observer can distinguish between two fields of views of different spectral composition (Wyszecki & Stiles, 1967). Figure 3-1 shows a simplified schematic diagram of the organization of color in terms of its salient visual parameters—hue, saturation, and luminance. *Chromaticity* is the quality of light expressing hue and saturation characteristics. Chromaticity can be conceptualized as a plane in color space and is typically definable by one of a number of chromaticity coordinates. The chromaticity system most currently used by color CRT investigators is the 1931 Commission Internationale de l'Éclairage (CIE) chromaticity diagram shown in Figure 3-2 (see color insert). This system is derived from two degree standard observer data and organized such that $x + y + z = 1$. The z chromaticity coordinate value is implied on the 1931 CIE diagram. Luminance is considered constant (white = black, yellow = brown).

In the 1931 CIE system, hue is indicated by the wavelength of the central frequency of a color. The perimeter of the 1931 CIE diagram from 380 through 700 nanometers is called the *spectrum locus* and includes all fully saturated spectral hues. All colors located on any line between the spectral locus and neutral energy white ($x = 0.33$, $y = 0.33$) have the same central frequency of spectral wavelength and differ in chromaticity by their level of saturation or colorfulness. The bottom perimeter of the CIE diagram is a locus of non-spectral colors sometimes referred to as the *line of purples*. Hues along the line of purples have no spectral wavelength and are characterized in

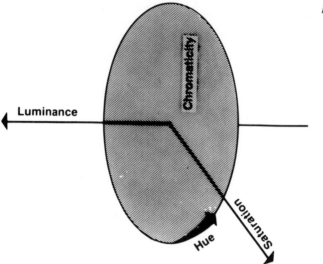

Figure 3-1   Color space.

hue by a complimentary wavelength found by extending a line from the line of purples through neutral energy white to the spectrum locus. Colors on the spectrum locus and line of purples represent the most saturated hues the human can perceive. Neutral energy white is the zero saturation level for all colors.

The 1931 CIE chromaticity system has several properties useful to color CRT engineers. Phosphors are usually specified in terms of their 1931 chromaticity coordinates. Colors generated by a combination of phosphor excitations can be easily resolved into 1931 CIE chromaticity coordinates due to characteristics of the systems geometric construction. The system does not, however, provide a perceptually uniform chromaticity space from which the perception of chromaticity difference can be derived. Nor does it take into account the effects of luminance on color perception.

In recognition of this problem, the CIE provisionally adopted the 1960 CIE-UCS (Uniform Chromaticity Scale) based on research by MacAdam, 1937 (Figure 3-3). This chromaticity system provides a more perceptually uniform chromaticity space and was chosen by the CIE because of the simplicity of the transformations that produce it from

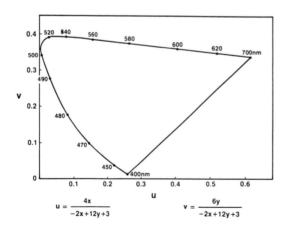

Figure 3-3   1960 CIE-UCS diagram.

$$u = \frac{4x}{-2x + 12y + 3} \qquad v = \frac{6y}{-2x + 12y + 3}$$

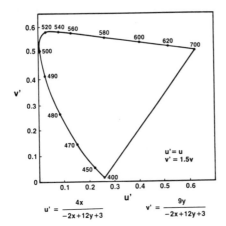

Figure 3-4 1976 CIE-UCS diagram.

$$u' = \frac{4x}{-2x+12y+3}$$

$$v' = \frac{9y}{-2x+12y+3}$$

the 1931 CIE chromaticity diagram (CIE, 1977). Further research produced the 1976 CIE-Uniform Chromaticity Scale (CIE-UCS), presently considered to be the most perceptually uniform chromaticity space available for self-luminous sources (Figure 3-4). The single difference between this system and the 1960 CIE-UCS system is its v'-axis transformation.

Color Modeling

The wide compendium of colors available from a self-luminous device such as a shadow-mask CRT is derived from the selective addition of specific luminance levels of the three CRT primaries—green, red, and blue *(G, R, B)*. The color modeling task of the CRT engineer is to relate the visual parameters of the color generating device to a mathematical model capable of predicting the luminance and chromaticity of a generated color from the CRT primary values. The luminance value of a CRT-generated color is simply the summation of the luminance levels of the CRT primaries involved. To predict the resultant chromaticity of a CRT-generated color, however, requires an algorithm which relates CRT primary luminance and chromaticity values to the chromaticity systems previously discussed.

If we construct a triangle in color space bound by the chromaticity coordinates of the three CRT primaries *(G, R, B)*, such a triangle will contain all colors the CRT is capable of generating (Figures 3-5). By definition, the blue-green axis of the triangle and its extension is a plot of colors real and imaginary where red = 0. If we assume an equiluminous point E (where $G = R = B$) and connect the G and B ventices through E to the red-blue and red-green axis one derives points where red equals 50%. Connecting these points forms a line that intersects red = 0 at the focus for all lines where red is constant, r_f. By performing this geometric derivation for all three primaries, the focus of lines of constant primary values for each primary can be determined (g_f, r_f, b_f). These points form a line known as an alychne along which colors of zero luminance lie. Any parallel to the alychne and bound by the zero and 100% constant lines of a primary represents linear intercept directly proportional to the luminance contribution of the primary—a luminance nomograph (Fink, 1955).

An interesting and highly useful property of the 1931 CIE diagram is that through

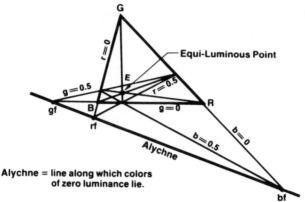

Figure 3-5   Construction of the alychne.

Equi-Luminous Point

Alychne = line along which colors
of zero luminance lie.

projective geometry, the *x* axis is constructed to be an alychne. By locating the *x* and *y* coordinates of the red and green CRT primaries on a 1931 CIE diagram as shown on Figure 3-6, a triangle is formed that includes all colors the CRT is capable of generating.

The focus of lines of constant luminance for red and green primaries (r_f and g_f) can readily be derived by projecting the line on the color triangle which represents that primary at zero luminance value (for red, the green-blue axis, etc.). A nomographic representation of the luminance contribution of red and green primaries can be constructed by creating lines parallel to the CIE diagram *x*-axis and bound by the zero and 100% constant lines of the primaries. The percentage blue primary component is simply the remainder since $R + G + B = 100\%$. Using this nomographic color mix model, the chromaticity of any color generated by CRT primaries of known luminance and chromaticity values can be graphically located in 1931 CIE *x* and *y* coordinates.

With equal ease, any color can be resolved into the percentage contribution of each CRT primary required to generate the desired color. The effect of background addition on CRT-generated colors can also be computed by resolving the reflected background into equivalent primary luminance values, summing these with the primary luminance

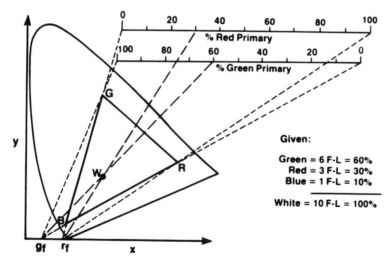

Given:

Green = 6 F-L = 60%
Red = 3 F-L = 30%
Blue = 1 F-L = 10%

White = 10 F-L = 100%

Figure 3-6   Nomographic color mix model.

values of the CRT-generated color and recombining the resultant luminance values through the nomographic mix model.

Discrimination

Developing a perceptually uniform model of color to predict the magnitude of perceived color difference between two color stimuli has long been recognized as an urgent industry problem. In a perceptually uniform color space, an identical distance between points representing two luminous sources always represents an identical difference in visual impression (Martin, 1977). In this manner, the distance between points in color space becomes a numerical expression of *discrimination*.

Discrimination, the operators ability to perceive a difference between colors, must take into account: (a) the luminance and chromaticity difference between stimuli sources, (b) the ambient environment acting upon the generated stimuli, (c) the adaptation environment which determines the level of accommodation of the eye, and (d) the information field size or solid angle subtended by the information at the distance viewed.

In 1976, CIE adopted a uniform color space which takes into account several of the factors related to discrimination. This color space model, called 1976 CIE (L^*, u^*, v^*) and commonly referred to by its abbreviation CIELUV, expresses the color coordinates of each self-luminous source referenced to a nominally white object-color stimulus such as the CIE standard illuminant D_{65}.

CIELUV coordinates:

$$L^* = (116(Y/Y_n)_{1/3}) - 16 \qquad \text{for } Y/Y_n > 0.01$$
$$u^* = 13L^*(u' - u'_n)$$
$$v^* = 13L^*(v' - v'_n)$$

Where Y = object color luminance
Y_n = object color stimulus luminancer
u', v' = 1976 CIE-UCS coordinates for object color
u'_n, v'_n = 1976 CIE-UCS coordinates for object color stimulus

The typical object color stimulus is D_{65} where

$$Y_n = 100$$
$$u'_n = .1978$$
$$v'_n = .4684$$

The three perceptually normalized color parameters shown above provide a three-dimensional model of psycho-colormetric space which can be expressed in rectangular coordinates (L^*, u^*, v^*), and a color difference parameter, ΔE^*, which numerically represents the perceptual difference between two luminous sources:

$$\Delta E^*_{uv} = [(\Delta L^*)^2 + (\Delta u^*)^2 + (\Delta v^*)^2]^{1/2}$$

To be a useful tool for the color CRT engineer, a color space must relate the visual parameters and ambient environment of a CRT to the perception of color difference of the operator. This relationship can be derived by the use of the nomographic mix model and CIELUV formulation if the chromaticity coordinates of the color CRT primaries and the luminance level and chromaticity coordinates of the reflected ambient are known (Figure 3-7).

Using the nomographic mix model, the first three steps shown in Figure 3-7 can be accomplished: (a) Each of the two CRT-generated colors can be defined in luminance

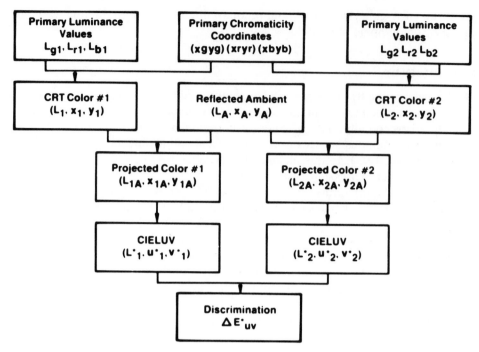

Figure 3-7   Color CRT discrimination derivation.

and chromaticity from the primary luminance levels used to produce them. (b) The reflected ambient of known luminance and chromaticity can be expressed in primary luminance components. (c) The summation of reflected ambient primary luminance components with the primary luminance components of each CRT-generated color can be resolved into the luminance and chromaticity coordinates of the CRT colors are projected in the ambient environment. The last two steps shown in Figure 3-7 are accomplished by transforming the 1931 chromaticity coordinate of each projected color into 1976 CIE-UCS coordinates, transforming the resultant luminance and chromaticity values into CIELUV parameters, and calculating ΔE^*.

One of the most useful applications of color difference or discrimination is for the selection of colors to be used on CRT presentations. The color CRT is quite limited in luminance output when compared to its monochromatic counterpart. This fact, coupled with the rather extreme ambient light environments that some color monitors confront (such as aircraft cockpit applications), requires that discrimination through color selection be a primary design goal. If a monitor application requires only a three color repertoire, blue is shown as a CRT primary rather than a color candidate. For a color CRT under a high ambient environment and with approximately equal beam currents available from each primary, the lowest color difference or ΔE^* values will occur between amber-white-cyan-magenta-red as indicated in Figure 3-8 (Silverstein & Merrifield, 1981). By proper selection of primary mix and color coordinates for secondary colors calculated under worst case ambient conditions, a color repertoire can be developed through analysis where the ΔE^* between each of these five colors is equal. The color repertoire selection will, therefore, be optimized when the following conditions are met:

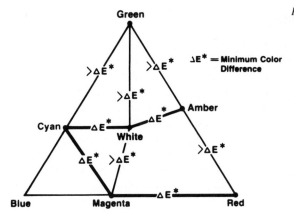

Figure 3-8   Discrimination analysis.

(1)
$$\Delta E^*_{G-A} = \Delta E^*_{A-R} \geqslant \Delta E^*_{Min}$$

(2)
$$\Delta E^*_{A-W} = \Delta E^*_{W-C} = \Delta E^*_{C-M} = \Delta E^*_{M-R} = \Delta E^*_{Min}$$

(3)
$$\Delta E^*_{G-W} = \Delta E^*_{W-M} \geqslant \Delta E^*_{Min}$$

(4)
$$\Delta E^*_{C-G} \geqslant \Delta E^*_{Min}$$

Where
G = Green
A = Amber
R = Red
W = White
C = Cyan
M = Magenta
ΔE^*_{Min} = Minimum color difference

This type of discrimination analysis will result in the lowest possible CRT beam currents providing acceptable discrimination under the ambient conditions of usage. Since tube life is largely a function of primary beam current usage, this type of discrimination analysis will maximize tube life and thereby minimize cost of ownership.

Unfortunately, the CIELUV system and corresponding analysis do not take into account all factors which relate to discrimination. Research from which CIE standard observer data was derived and from which the 1931 CIE chromaticity system was generated was based on a 2-degree information field size. Smaller image field sizes such as character, symbol, and graphic presentation line widths, will require larger color difference values than predicted by CIELUV for adequate discrimination. Nor is the CIELUV color space perceptually uniform for image field sizes less than 2-degrees. Small field sizes that have a significant blue component have significantly lower discrimination than predicted by CIELUV (Silverstein & Merrifield, 1981). Extremely high or low adaptation levels will also significantly change the color difference required for discrimination since the accommodation level of the eye is changed. Further research in these areas is required to resolve these and other discrimination factors into a model of perceptually uniform color space as with as wide a range of applications and environments as the color CRT. These considerations require that the prudent engineer use the CIELUV system as a useful tool rather than an absolute standard for discrimination.

Shadow-Mask CRT Technology

The shadow-mask color CRT assembly consists of three closely spaced electron guns, a shadow-mask, and a three color phosphor screen. Focused electron beans emitted from each primary gun pass through apertures in the metal shadow-mask and impinge upon phosphor dots for each corresponding color. Figure 3-9a illustrated a *delta gun* configuration of a shadow-mask CRT. The three electron guns are arranged in an equilateral triangle, or delta. Each shadow-mask aperture allows the three electron gun beams to project onto an inverted delta or triad of phosphor dots. The angle of incidence of an electron beam as it passes through a shadow-mask aperture determines the color of phosphor dot it excites. Electron beams of a particular gun are blocked by the shadowing of the mask from impinging upon the other two color phosphor dots of each triad. A shadow-mask CRT has a very simple mechanism for selecting color. The three independent guns in the shadow-mask design provide independent control of the luminance of the red, green, and blue phosphors. In this manner, it is possible to reproduce any color within the chromaticity triangle formed by the primary colors.

Several configurations of gun alignments, mask structures, and phosphor arrangements are available. Figure 3-9b illustrates an in-line gun configuration projecting through mask apertures onto a delta-type phosphor dot faceplate. The in-line gun shadow-mask

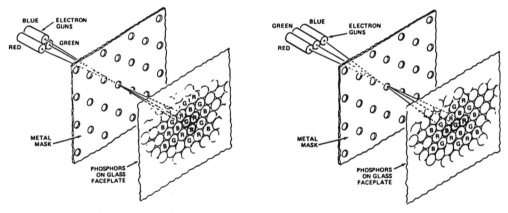

Figure   3-9a   Delta-gun/Delta mask color CRT.   *Figure 3-9b*   In-line gun/Delta mask color CRT.

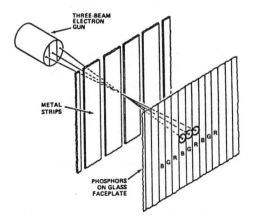

Figure 3-9c   In-line gun/Slotted mask color CRT.

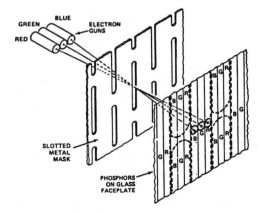

Figure 3-9d   Single lens in-line gun/Metal-strip mask color CRT.

CRT has the three electron guns configured in a closely spaced horizontal line. The mask and phosphor dot geometry are the same as for a delta configuration, however, the in-line gun electron beams excite a horizontal row of the three color phosphor dots through a shadow-mask aperture. In-line gun configurations are currently popular because of the relative ease of converging the electron beams over the display surface. Resolution of in-line gun tubes is typically poorer than delta-gun tubes, however, due to their smaller focus aperture in the tube neck and the aspherical form of the electron beam at the corners of the display surface. Slotted and metal strip aperture masks are also available with in-line gun configurations (Figures 3-9c and 3-9d). These tubes use vertical phosphor strips on the face plate instead of phosphor dots and typically have a higher luminance output than phosphor dot surfaces.

The granularity of a shadow-mask CRT is determined by its *pitch*. The pitch is the distance between mask apertures. Shadow-mask CRTs are available with pitch values ranging from 0.6 down to 0.2 millimeters. Tubes with pitch values below 0.3 millimeters are considered high density shadow-masks. The tube pitch or triad spacing should not be confused with the resolution of the CRT. An electron beam typically projects through several mask apertures. Resolution of the CRT, in most cases, is determined by the electron optics of the tube or video bandwith of the inputs rather than the tube pitch.

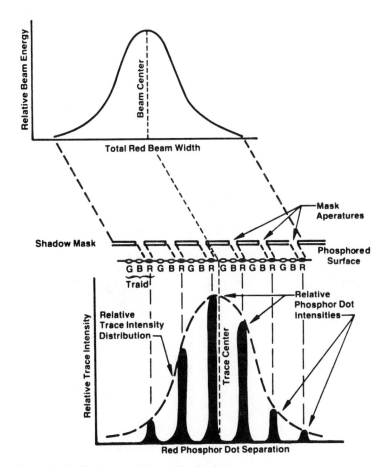

Figure 3-10 Shadow-mask beam distribution.

Shadow-Mask Beam Distribution

Each color gun beam has an energy distribution which is approximately gaussian. A gun beam excites several phosphor dots, each to a luminance level determined by the energy distribution of the beam incident through the shadow-mask apertures. Figure 3-10 shows the electron beam distribution for a red gun beam projected through the shadow-mask. Since the phosphor dot separation is less than the acuity of the eye at typical viewing distances, the eye integrates the phosphor dot intensities into a relative trace distribution or line width that is gaussian in nature. It should be noted that only a small amount of the beam energy of any color gun reaches the phosphor dots. The majority of the beam is blocked or shadowed by the mask.

Guard Band

Phosphor dots of conventional shadow-mask screens circumscribe the beam spot projected through the mask aperture, as shown in Figure 3-11a. The area between the beam spot projection onto the phosphor dot and the outer circumference of the phosphor dot is called the *guard band*. This guard band gives a tolerance reserve for beam mislandings which can occur through the tube assembly fluctuations, influences of magnetic fields, or thermal dislocations of the shadow-mask with respect to the faceplate. If the magnitude of the beam mislanding exceeds the guard band, the beam from one color gun will partially excite phosphor dots of other colors and color purity will be degraded.

Shadow-mask CRTs which are used in high ambient light environments may use black matrix screens. Phosphor dots on black matrix screens inscribe the beam spot projected through the mask aperture, as shown in Figure 3-11b. The black matrix screen has a structure of light absorbing material, such as carbon black, which is coated on the mask area that does not serve as light-emitting area. The mask apertures of a black matrix tube are larger and the phosphor dots are slightly smaller than for a conventional shadow-mask tube having the same guard band. The smaller phosphor dot size of the

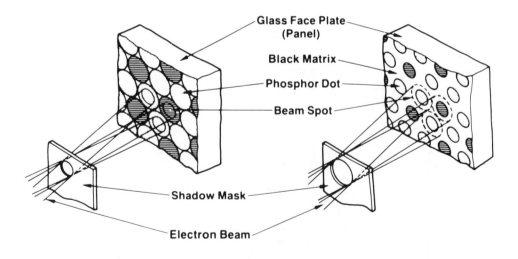

(a) Conventional Screen   (b) Black Matrix Screen

Figure 3-11   Guard band structure of shadow mask color CRT.

black matrix screen results in a slight loss in achievable luminance. The contrast, however, is greatly enhanced by minimizing the ambient reflectivity of non-light-emitting areas.

Doming

During the early stage of operation following CRT turn-on, the shadow-mask is warmed by an electron beam bombardment. The mask frame, because it has a larger heat capacity and is more difficult to warm quickly, exhibits a thermal lag. The mask portion stresses against the frame and causes a phenomenon called *mask doming*. When doming of the shadow-mask occurs, the beam spot projecting through the shadow-mask aperture shifts on the phosphor dot as shown in Figure 3-12. If the shift of the beam spot becomes larger than the guard band, color purity is degraded. After thermal equilibrium of the mask system is reached, the shadow-mask and the frame expand uniformly and the mask aperture shifts on the phosphor dot as shown in Figure 3-12. If the shift of the beam spot becomes larger than the guard band, color purity is degraded. After thermal equilibrium of the mask system is reached, the shadow-mask and the frame expand

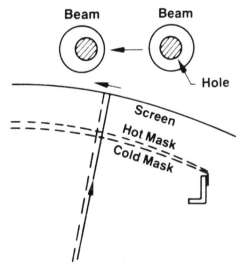

Figure 3-12 Mask doming.

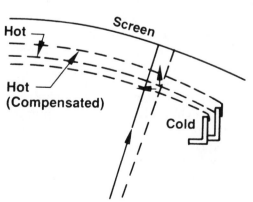

Figure 3-13 Doming temperature compensation.

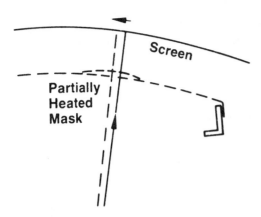

Figure 3-14   Local doming.

uniformly and the mask aperture shifts outward in a radial direction. Bimetal clips of the mask-supporting assembly provides compensation for this mask shift as shown in Figure 3-13. The whole mask assembly moves axially toward the screen by the action of the bimetal clips, and correct beam landing can be maintained.

Doming also occurs when a strong signal is applied to a small area of the shadow-mask, even after thermal equilibrium is reached. This is called *local doming*, and is shown in Figure 3-14. Local doming and the resultant color purity degradation is more pronounced for white and secondary colors where more than one gun is bombarding the mask structure. For raster applications, in most cases, the local doming phenomenon establishes the maximum level of luminance output of a shadow-mask CRT over which color purity can be maintained.

Contrast Enhancement Techniques

Due to several limitations inherent in the shadow-mask tube design, the luminance output of shadow-mask CRTs is quite limited when compared to the family of high luminance monochromatic CRTs available. The luminous efficiency (lm/w) of red and blue phosphors used in color CRTs is low compared to the green and white phosphors used in high luminance monochromatic tubes. The mask structure of the shadow-mask tube blocks most of the beam energy generated by each color gun. Local doming limitations impose still further restrictions on the luminance output of shadow-mask tubes. These factors limit the achievable luminance output of shadow-mask CRTs to about ten to twenty percent of that available on a high luminance monochromatic tube.

To compensate for the luminance bounds and achieve the level of discrimination required for high ambient viewing, several contrast enhancement techniques are employed in a state-of-the-art shadow-mask CRT. The use of black matrix screens discussed earlier enhances contrast by minimizing reflected ambient light. Phosphors are sometimes impregnated with pigments that reflect the light having wavelengths near the emitted light of the phosphors and absorb all other light. Pigmentation lowers phosphor emission somewhat, but the reflectivity of ambient light is also lowered. By prudent selection of a phosphor pigmentation grade, a compromise between luminance output and contrast can be reached which improves contrast ratio and discrimination.

The ambient light reflecting off a display surface is both specular and diffuse in nature. Specular reflectivity or light rays reflecting at specific angles is usually minimized by the use of anti-reflection coatings on the outer surface of the display. Diffuse reflectivity

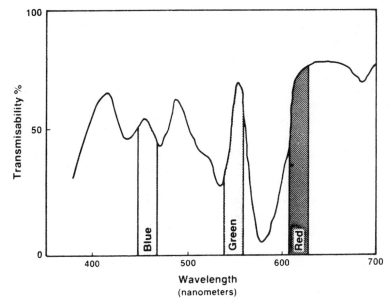

Figure 3-15   Multispectral filter transmissibility.

or light rays reflecting at several angles can be minimized by any one of a family of contrast enhancement filters suitable for color CRT applications.

Angle restrictive filters are available that use a thin non-reflective honeycomb or mesh structure parallel with the line of view of the display.The depth and width of the mesh structure restricts the angles of incidence an ambient light source can enter the filter to a few degrees around the operators line of sight. The primary advantage of this type of filter is the relatively high transmissibility of CRT emitted light. Unfortunately, the reflectivity of ambient light sources within the viewing cone of an angle restrictive filter is also high, and the viewing angle of the display is limited.

Neutral density filters can be used to achieve a high symbol-to-background contrast ratio. Neutral density filters are basically wide spectral band light attenuators. They attenuate ambient light as it enters the filter, and once again attenuate the light reflected off of the display surface. Since the light emitted by the phosphors is only attenuated once by the neutral density filter, the contrast ratio is improved.

Didymium glass filters have been used on several CRT displays employing more than one phosphor. Didymium glass is multispectral in its transmissiblity characteristics, absorbing different amounts of incident light at different spectral wavelengths as shown in Figure 3-15. By selecting phosphors with central frequencies or wavelengths which match peaks of the spectral response curve of didymium glass, a higher contrast can be achieved between CRT emitted light and reflected ambient light than afforded by a neutral density filter.

Convergence

To create secondary colors on the shadow-mask CRT, two guns scan the same mask area simultaneously. If the two resultant trace intensity distributions are perfectly registered on the phosphor surface, the resultant trace is said to be converged. *Miscon-*

vergence is defined as the trace center to trace center misregistration. In the case of a yellow trace made up of red and green beams, small levels of misconvergence will create a yellow trace with a green fringe on one side and a red fringe on the other side. Extreme levels of misconvergence will result in red and green traces with little or no yellow between.

Convergence or beam registration on a delta-gun color CRT is accomplished in two ways. Static convergence adjustments are made at the deflection yoke assembly which provide radial direction movements on each primary beam and a lateral direction movement on the blue beam. These movements achieve convergence at the screen center. Due to the inherent geometry of a delta-gun configuration, the misconvergence of beams as they move away from the screen center is a parabolic function. Correction for misregistration as the beams move away from the tube center is called *dynamic convergence*. Dynamic convergence is accomplished on delta-gun CRTs by introducing correction currents into the convergence coils of the CRT yoke assembly. These corrections are basically parabolic functions synchronized with horizontal and vertical deflection signals. Most of the in-line gun shadow-mask CRTs use self-converging magnetic deflection yokes. These deflection yoke assemblies generate non-linear deflection fields which, by design, correct the beam misconvergences associated with the electron optic geometry of in-line gun tubes. The use of self-converging yokes minimizes or eliminates the need for the sophisticated parabolic correction waveform generation which is required for dynamic convergence on delta-gun tubes.

The current trend of using shadow-mask CRTs as data terminal displays and aircraft instrumentation creates much more stringent convergence requirements than those associated with commercial color TV. As the distance between the viewer and the display surface decreases, the ability of the operator to detect misconvergence increases. Red-green beam misconvergence is the most perceivable of the beam combinations. For line width of one to two minutes of visual arc, as little as one-half minute of red-green beam misconvergence is detectable. Blue-green beam misconvergence, the least perceivable of the beam combinations, is detectable at slightly over a minute of visual arc.

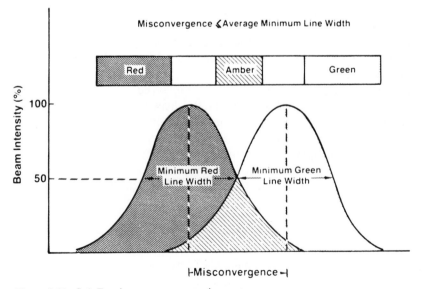

Figure 3-16   S.A.E. misconvergance requirement.

The level of convergence on a color CRT required to preserve the color information presented is largely a function of the CRT minimum line width, the viewing distance, and the spacing between symbol, character, or alphanumeric segments. A well focused shadow-mask CRT is capable of high luminance half-amplitude line widths of 0.3 to 0.8 millimeters. At low luminance levels, line widths can decrease to 0.15 to 0.25 millimeters. As the line widths of the color beams decrease, misconvergence becomes more objectionable due to the decreasing area of the primary beam overlay. The misconvergence requirement proposed by the Society of Automotive Engineering as an airborne electronic display certification criteria, calls for misconvergence to be no greater than the minimum half-amplitude line width of the display (Figure 3-16). Although this level of misconvergence requirement does not result in an aesthetically pleasing presentation, it will preserve the secondary color information at short viewing distances. At long viewing distances where the acuity of the eye subtends an arc greater than a line width, a larger level of misconvergence is tolerable.

Minimum Line Width

A beam occlusion phenomenon occurs on a shadow-mask CRT which the designer or user must take into consideration when establishing minimum line width requirements for a color display. On a delta configuration phosphor surface, the phosphor dots of any one primary are arranged in an equilateral hexagonal pattern. At the vertical axis and ± 60 degrees around the vertical axis, there are areas where no phosphor dots of a specific primary color lie (Figure 3-17). For a tube with 0.3 millimeter pitch between horizontal primary rows, these areas are about 0.15 millimeter wide depending on phosphor dot size.

At low luminance levels where the minimum line widths of the CRT are achieved, the color gun beam centers can be occluded by the areas between phosphor dots. This shadow-mask beam occlusion can cause dramatic shifts in the intended luminance and

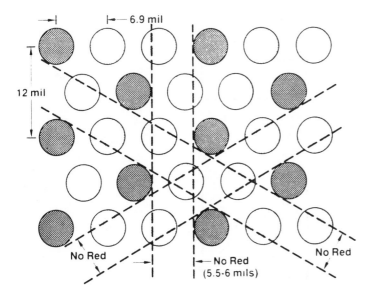

Figure 3-17 Shadow-mask beam occlusion.

chromaticity of colors written at the angles mentioned. As a rule of thumb, the minimum line width of a delta-configured shadow-mask CRT should be no less than two-thirds of the pitch of the phosphor dots. This can be easily accomplished by defocusing the beams to this minimum line width level. However, in some cases, the maximum high luminance line width will be greater than desired at this level of focus (or defocus). On possible solution is to allow the CRT assembly to be sharply focused at high luminance levels and selectively defocus at low luminance outputs. If this technique is employed, the traces should be overfocused at minimum luminance outputs rather than under-focused. Overfocusing or increasing the magnitude of the focus coil potential preserves the slope of the intensity distribution of the trace and results in sharper lines than un-derfocusing allows.

Color CRT Measurement Techniques

Color CRTs, especially shadow-mask tubes, present unique measurement problems to the engineer. Line width, convergence, and stroke or symbol element luminance mea-surements are complicated by the mask structure and phosphor dot matrix. The type of scanning photometer with slit aperture used for monochromatic CRT line width and stroke luminance measurements will not accurately measure these parameters on a shadow-mask tube. If a slit aperture small enough to accurately measure the intensity distribution of a line is used, a plot similar to Figure 10 will result. If a larger slit aperture is used to round off the dot intensities into a relative trace intensity distribution, a degree of uncertainty as to the peak intensity, half-amplitude points, and beam center will be introduced.

A relatively easy and accurate way to circumvent the inaccuracies and uncertainties of slit aperture measurement is to measure the intensity distribution of a single phosphor dot. This can be accomplished by using a photometer with an aperture small enough to inscribe a single phosphor dot. A deflection offset signal of known scale factor which will deflect a primary line across the phosphor dot measured can then be introduced.

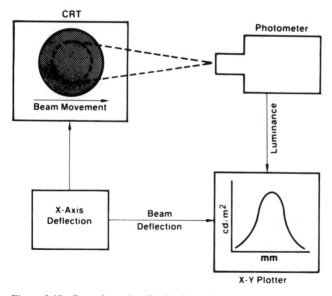

Figure 3-18   Beam intensity distribution measurement.

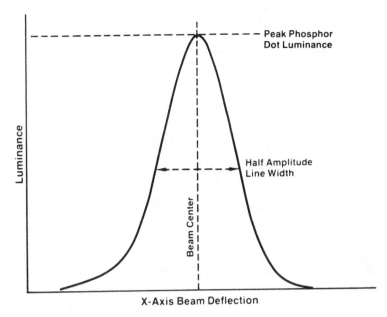

Figure 3-19   Beam intensity distribution parameters.

Connecting the deflection offset signal to the *x*-axis and the photometer output to the *y*-axis of the plotter produces a plot of the beam intensity distribution of the primary color measured (Figure 3-18). Properly scaled, the half-amplitude line width and peak phosphor dot luminance can be read off the plotter sheet (Figure 3-19). Since line width of sport size is asymmetric on many tubes, both *x* and *y* axis lines should be deflected past the phosphor dot measured.

The misconvergence between the three primary beams can be measured using the same technique. If three horizontally adjacent red, green, and blue phosphor dots are measured by scanning a horizontal white line vertically across the phosphor dots with the same deflection offset signal, the vertical misconvergence between the three primaries can be read off the *x-y* plotter sheet. By scanning the same three phosphor dots with a horizontally deflected vertical white line and subtracting the physical distance between dots from the resulting plots, the horizontal misconvergence between the three primaries can be determined. The total misconvergence between any two primary pairs is the square root of the sum of the squares of the horizontal and vertical misconvergence values.

Accurate measurement of the peak luminance of a primary raster or stroke written line on a shadow-mask CRT cannot be taken directly and must be calculated from the peak phosphor dot luminance of the beam intensity distribution. Conceptually, the shadow-mask structure can be considered to be a light filter which attenuates the luminance output by the ratio of the total dot area of any primary divided by the total usable screen area. An approximation of primary raster or stroke line luminance can be derived by multiplying the peak phosphor dot luminance by this ratio. This approximation, however, assumes that the phosphor dot size is uniform across the CRT and does not take into account any edge refraction properties the phosphor dots or filter assembly may exhibit.

A more accurate means of assessing raster or stroke luminance is by use of a

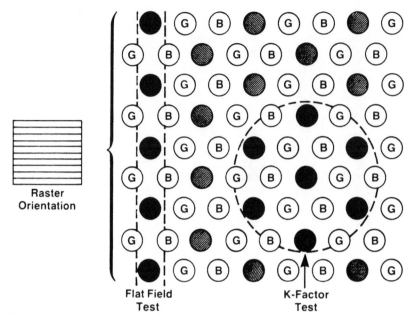

Raster
Orientation

Flat Field
Test

K-Factor
Test

Figure 3-20   K-Factor testing.

K-factor. K-factor is the ratio of raster area luminance to phosphor dot luminance taken by actual measurement, using a flat-field raster (raster with zero line separation modulation). A flat-field raster condition is imposed on the display system by underfocusing a raster field until the primary phosphor dots in a row orthogonal to the raster orientation yield approximately equal luminance. Under these operation conditions, the peak phosphor dot luminance of seven or more phosphor dots are measured in the area of interest by inscribing each phosphor dot with a photometer aperture, and determining the peak of the beam intensity distribution (Figure 3-18). A flat field raster area luminance measurement taken in the same area divided by the average of the seven phosphor dot luminance measurements will yield the K-factor (Figure 3-20). Once the K-factor of the area of interest is derived and the system is refocused, raster or stroke line luminance can be determined by multiplying the K-factor by the peak phosphor dot luminance of a focused beam. Line luminance calculations from K-factor measurements are only reliable for the specific CRT area in which the K-factor measurements are taken. It cannot be assumed that the K-factor will be constant across the usable area of the CRT unless sufficient measurements of the tube have been taken to support this assumption.

References

Commission Internationale de l'Éclairage. *Recommendations on uniform color space, color-difference equations, and psychometric color terms.* Supplement No. 2 to CIE Publication No. 15, 1987.

Fink, D. *Handbook of Color Television Engineering.* 1955.

MacAdam, D. L. Projective transformation of ICI color specifications. *Journal of Optical Society of America,* 1967, *27,* 294.

Martin, A. The CRT/observer interface. *Electro-Optical Systems Design*, June 1977.

Silverstein, L., & Merrifield, R. Color selection and verification testing for airborne color CRT displays. *Fifth Advanced Aircrew Display Symposium*. Patuxent River, MD, 1981.

Wyszecki, G., & Stiles, W. S. *Color Science—Concepts and Methods, Quantitative Data Formulas*. New York: John Wiley, 1967.

4 Perceptual Color Spaces for Computer Graphics*

GARY W. MEYER
Department of Computer and Information Science
University of Oregon
Eugene, Oregon

DONALD P. GREENBERG
Program of Computer Graphics
Cornell University
Ithaca, New York

Abstract

Perceptually uniform color spaces can be a useful tool for solving computer graphics color selection problems. Before they can be used effectively, however, some basic principles of tristimulus colorimetry must be understood, and the color reproduction device on which they are to be used must be properly adjusted. The Munsell Book of Color and the Optical Society of America (OSA) Uniform Color Scale are two uniform color spaces that provide a useful way of organizing the colors of a digitally controlled color television monitor. The perceptual uniformity of these color spaces can be used to select color scales to encode the variations of parameters such as temperature or stress.

Introduction

A perceptually uniform color organization has been sought for years by color scientists attempting to set tolerances on color reproduction techniques, by psychologists probing the psychophysics of vision, and by artists looking for new color harmonies. The idea is to define a color system in which an equal perceptual distance separates all of the colors. For example, the grayscale of the system should provide a smooth transition between black and white. Although such an ideal system has yet to be found, numerous

*Modified from the version that first appeared in *Computer Graphics*, Vol. 14, no. 3, 1980, pp. 254–261. Copyright 1980, Association for Computing Machinery, Inc., reprinted by permission.

proposals have been made for approximately uniform systems. Most of these proposed color organizations are described in terms of the color notation system standardized by the Commission Internationale de l'Éclairage (CIE).

Since color television is based on the CIE color notation system, these uniform spaces can be directly applied to work with digitally controlled color television monitors once the colorimetry and calibration of the monitors is understood. Color collections such as The Munsell Book of Color and the Optical Society of America (OSA) Uniform Color Scale can supplement the color organizations described in Joblove and Greenberg (1978) and Smith (1978) as palettes from which to make color selections. In addition, the perceptual uniformity of these color spaces can be used in such problems as color encoding of information and image data compression.

Color Science and Television Colorimetry

Only the fundamental results of trichromatic color theory and television colorimetry will be presented here. For more detailed information, the reader is referred to Hunt (1975), Judd and Wyszecki (1975), and Wyszecki and Stiles (1982) which are excellent general references on color science and color reproduction. Television colorimetry is discussed in Neal (1973), Wentworth (1955), and Wintringham (1951).

Colorimetry provides a technique for predicting whether two colors match. Tristimulus values X, Y, and Z are computed from the expressions:

$$X = \int_{380}^{780} E(\lambda)\bar{x}(\lambda)d\lambda$$

$$Y = \int_{380}^{780} E(\lambda)\bar{y}(\lambda)d\lambda \qquad (4\text{-}1)$$

$$Z = \int_{380}^{780} E(\lambda)\bar{z}(\lambda)d\lambda$$

where $E(\lambda)$ is the spectral energy distribution of the color and $\bar{x}(\lambda)$, $\bar{y}(\lambda)$, and $\bar{z}(\lambda)$ are the experimentally determined color matching functions (Figure 4-1). The Y tristimulus value is referred to as the luminance of the color and is expressed either as an absolute luminance or as a percent luminous reflectance. Two spectral energy distributions that yield identical Y values will match in brightness. When all three tristimulus values are the same, the two spectral energy distributions will match completely.

When plotted, the locus of possible tristimulus values is found to be bounded by a cone called the cone of realizable color (Figure 4-2). This coordinate system is referred to as 1931 CIE XYZ space. Given that spectral energy distributions of identical shape but different relative height (i.e., a variable intensity light source) arise frequently and that the locus of tristimulus values for these distributions is a straight line through the origin of XYZ space, it is often useful to adopt an alternative notation system in which a color is described by the direction and magnitude of a vector through the origin. The point of intersection of the vector with the unit plane in 1931 CIE XYZ space expresses the direction of the vector (Figure 4-3) and is found from the tristimulus values by:

$$x = \frac{X}{(X + Y + Z)}, \qquad y = \frac{Y}{(X + Y + Z)} \qquad (4\text{-}2)$$

Once the direction of the vector is established, one tristimulus value (typically Y) is all that is required to define the vector's magnitude. A two-dimensional plot of x versus y is known as a chromaticity diagram.

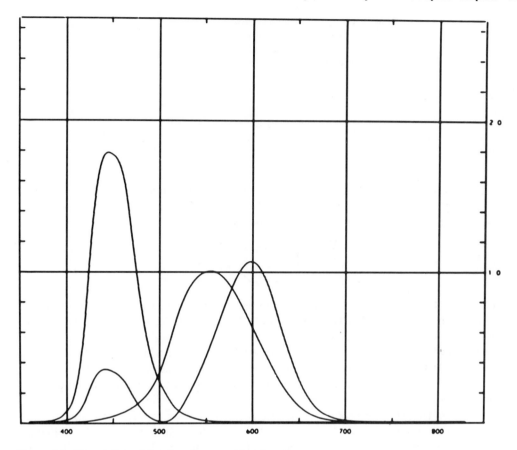

Figure 4-1 From left to right, the color matching functions $\bar{z}(\lambda)$, $\bar{y}(\lambda)$, $\bar{x}(\lambda)$ (tristimulus values of equal-energy spectrum) for the 1931 standard cover.

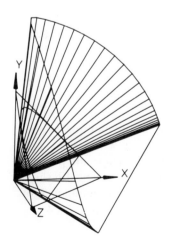

Figure 4-2 Cone of realizable color (drawn to an arbitrary length), unit plane and their curve of intersection in 1931 CIE XYZ space.

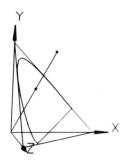

Figure 4-3 Point of intersection between the unit plane and the vector which passes through a particular tristimulus value.

Because color matching has been shown to be a linear process, the laws of linear algebra apply. The transformation between the *RGB* color space of a color television monitor and 1931 CIE *XYZ* space can be expressed as:

$$\begin{bmatrix} X \\ Y \\ Z \end{bmatrix} = \begin{bmatrix} X_R & X_G & X_B \\ Y_R & Y_G & Y_B \\ Z_R & Z_G & Z_B \end{bmatrix} \begin{bmatrix} R \\ G \\ B \end{bmatrix} \tag{4-3}$$

where R, G, and B are each on a range from 0.0 to 1.0 and represent the coordinates of the color in the monitor's *RGB* color space; X, Y, and Z are the coordinates of the color in 1931 CIE *XYZ* space; and X_R, X_G, X_B, Y_R, Y_G, Y_B, Z_R, Z_G, and Z_B are the unknown elements of the transformation matrix. If the directions of the *RGB* basis vectors in 1931 CIE *XYZ* space are known, and the coordinates of a single point are known in both *RGB* space and 1931 CIE *XYZ* space, then the transformation between the two spaces can be fully specified. The chromaticity coordinates of the monitor's phosphors determine the direction of the *RGB* basis vectors in CIE *XYZ* space. The monitor's white point, which occurs when R, G, and B are all equal, can be adjusted as described below so that it has a particular chromaticity and luminance in 1931 CIE *XYZ* space. The algebraic details of the derivation can be found in several sources (Hazeltine, 1956; Neal, 1973; and Wintringham, 1951). The results are:

$$\begin{aligned} X_R &= x_R C_R, & X_G &= x_G C_G, & X_B &= x_B C_B \\ Y_R &= y_R C_R, & Y_G &= y_G C_G, & Y_B &= y_B C_B \\ Z_R &= (1 - x_R - y_R)C_R, & Z_G &= (1 - x_G - y_G)C_G, & Z_B &= (1 - x_B - y_B)C_B \end{aligned} \tag{4-4a}$$

$$C_R = \frac{Y_w}{y_w} \frac{x_w(y_G - y_B) - y_w(x_G - x_B) + x_G y_B - x_B y_G}{D}$$

$$C_G = \frac{Y_w}{y_w} \frac{x_w(y_B - y_R) - y_w(x_B - x_R) - x_R y_B + x_B y_R}{D} \tag{4-4b}$$

$$C_B = \frac{Y_w}{y_w} \frac{x_w(y_R - y_G) - y_w(x_R - x_G) + x_R y_G - x_G y_R}{D}$$

$$D = x_R(y_G - y_B) + x_G(y_B - y_R) + x_B(y_R - y_G) \tag{4-4c}$$

where x_R, y_R, x_G, y_G, x_B, and y_B are the chromaticity coordinates of the monitor's phosphors; x_W and y_W are the chromaticity coordinates of the monitor's white point; and Y_W is the luminance of the monitor's white point. Figure 4-4 shows the shape and position of a typical color television monitor gamut in CIE *XYZ* space. Figures 4-5 and 4-6 show two views of the monitor gamut in a space where the chromaticity and luminance of colors are plotted.

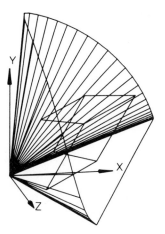

Figure 4-4 Cone of realizable color and color television monitor gamut in 1931 CIE XYZ space.

The intended chromaticity coordinates of the monitor's phosphors (x_R, y_R, x_G, y_G, x_B, y_B) are usually available from the manufacturer. They are measured by using a spectroradiometer to obtain the relative radiance distribution of each phosphor, applying Equation 4-1 to obtain XYZ coordinates for the energy level at which the distributions were measured, and then using Equation 4-2 to obtain the chromaticity coordinates. Since phosphors vary from tube to tube even for manufacturers who tightly control them, the chromaticity coordinates for a particular tube should be measured if precise colorimetric work is intended.

The derivation of Equations 4-3 and 4-4 assumes that the origin of the *RGB* color space is coincident with the origin of 1931 CIE *XYZ*. To insure that this is the case for a color television monitor, one must set the white point by adjusting the individual brightness and contrast controls for each gun so that over the entire dynamic range of the monitor, equal amounts of red, green, and blue always yield a white with the desired chromaticity coordinates (x_W, y_W). This chromaticity can be measured using a spectro-radiometer, but this is impractical. One device for setting the white point is a color comparator (Beintema, 1974; Sanders, Gaw, & Wyszecki, 1968). The operator adjusts the monitor controls while looking through the color comparator to obtain a match between the monitor and a reference white of known chromaticity. The user

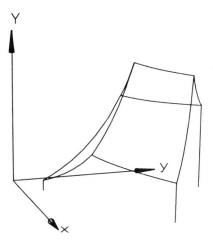

Figure 4-5 Color television monitor gamut in chromaticity—luminance space (1931 CIE Yxy space).

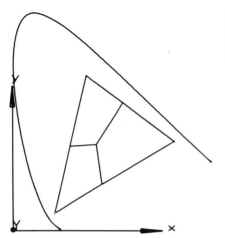

Figure 4-6 Orthographic projection onto xy plane of color television monitor gamut and spectrum locus.

should have normal color vision since abnormal vision can significantly affect the results. A tristimulus colorimeter is another device that can be used to set the white point.

The luminance of the white point (Y_w) can be measured using a photometer. Often this parameter is simply assigned the value 1.0 since most colorimetric work only deals with relative luminances.

Implicit in the derivation of Equation 4-3 is the assumption that R, G, and B vary linearly over their range. For example, the point represented by $R = .5$, $G = .5$, and $B = .5$ must lie equidistant from the point $R = 0$, $G = 0$, $B = 0$ and the point $R = 1.0$, $G = 1.0$, $B = 1.0$. A frame buffer controls the monitor R, G, and B by signal voltages R_{volt}, G_{volt}, B_{volt} (normalized to the range 0.0 to 1.0 in this chapter). If only one of the R_{volt}, G_{volt}, B_{volt} is varied and the others are held at zero, a line is traversed in CIE XYZ space with direction determined by the phosphor chromaticity coordinates. If one of the CIE XYZ coordinates can be measured as this is done, the Yxz coordinates and hence the XYZ tristimulus values can be recorded. RGB values can be found by applying the inverse of Equation 4-3 and the relationship determined between R_{volt}, G_{volt}, B_{volt} and RGB. When a digital photometer is used to measure Y the data produced can be fit with curves of the form:

$$R = (R_{volt})^{\gamma_R}, \qquad G = (G_{volt})^{\gamma_G}, \qquad B = (B_{volt})^{\gamma_B}, \qquad (4\text{-}5)$$

where γ_R, γ_G, and γ_B are almost identical and lie on the range 2.5 to 3.0 depending on the monitor. (Because the radiance and luminance produced by an isolated phosphor are related by a constant, a radiance meter can also be used to find γ_R, γ_G, and γ_B.) Higher order curve fitting techniques that can be applied to this problem are discussed in Cowan (1983). Figure 4-7 shows the nonlinear distribution of points in CIE XYZ space produced by combinations of ten evenly spaced R_{volt}, G_{volt}, B_{volt} values.

The validity of the transformation given by Equations 4-3, 4-4, and 4-5 can be tested by reproducing colors of known chromaticity and relative luminance and comparing them to actual color samples. In making these comparisons, it is important that the color samples are illuminated with light of the same spectral energy distribution as

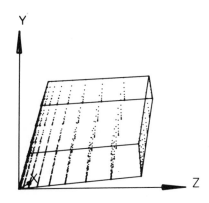

Y

Z

X

Figure 4-7   Nonlinear distribution of monitor colors in 1931 CIE XYZ space produced by equal signal voltage increments.

the light used to illuminate them when their chromaticity coordinates were determined.

One cannot overemphasize the importance of accurately measuring and adjusting such monitor properties as phosphor chromaticity, white point chromaticity, white point luminance, and gamma. If these parameters are not tightly controlled, accurate and consistent color reproduction is impossible.

It must also be remembered that variables held constant during the experiments that led to the laws of tristimulus colorimetry cannot be allowed to vary when these laws are applied. The level of ambient illumination has a significant effect on color perception and is something that can be quite different for an observer viewing an original scene and an observer viewing a reproduction of that scene on a monitor in a dimly lit room. Adjustments to straight colorimetric calculations to account for this have been suggested and are discussed elsewhere (Bartelson & Breneman, 1967; DeMarsh, 1972; Novick, 1969).

Uniform Chromaticity Diagrams

The tristimulus values for the facets of an object that diffusely reflects incident light can be shown to have the same chromaticity but different luminance (when interreflections in the environment are discounted). This indicates that chromaticity specifies the basic color of an object, and comparing chromaticities gives the best indicator of the color difference between two objects. A chromaticity diagram where equal physical distances indicate equal perceptual differences would, therefore, be of significant practical value.

Experiments to quantify the perceptual spacing of the chromaticity diagram for 1931 CIE *XYZ* space have been performed (MacAdam, 1942). Subjects were shown color samples of known chromaticity and luminance (luminance being held constant throughout the experiment) and were asked to match the sample using an adjustable color source. The results are shown in Figure 4-8. Each chromaticity point studied is surrounded by an ellipse proportional in size to the standard deviation by which the match chromaticity varied from the actual chromaticity. These ellipses indicate how quickly a color change is perceived in different parts of the chromaticity diagram. Obviously this chromaticity diagram does not have perceptually uniform spacing.

Attempts have subsequently been made to find a linear transformation from 1931 CIE *XYZ* space to a coordinate system whose chromaticity diagram would have a per-

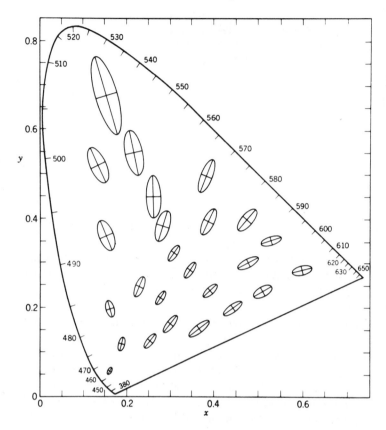

Figure 4-8 Statistical variation of chromaticity matches in different parts of the 1931 CIE chromaticity diagram. For clarity the axes of each ellipse have been enlarged 10 times (from Judd and Wyszecki 1975).

ceptually uniform spacing. Figure 4-9 shows how the ellipses of Figure 4-8 plot on the chromaticity diagram created by one linear transformation which has gained wide acceptance (MacAdam, 1937). A slightly modified version of this transformation was adopted by the CIE in their 1976 standards on uniform color spaces (CIE, 1978) and can be expressed as:

$$\begin{bmatrix} X \\ Y \\ Z \end{bmatrix} = \begin{bmatrix} 2.25 & 0.0 & 0.0 \\ 0.0 & 1.0 & 0.0 \\ 2.25 & -2.0 & 3.0 \end{bmatrix} \begin{bmatrix} U \\ V \\ W \end{bmatrix} \tag{4-6}$$

The shape and orientation of a typical monitor gamut in this space is shown in Figure 4-10. In a chromaticity/luminance space derived from the above space, the monitor gamut plots as shown in Figure 4-11.

Figure 4-9 shows that Equation 4-6 does not completely succeed in producing a chromaticity diagram where the ellipses of Figure 4-8 plot as circles. In fact, it has been determined that no linear or nonlinear transformation exists that would accomplish this. However, by assuming a certain tolerance for the accuracy of the data used to generate the ellipses, a nonlinear transformation has been found that makes the ellipses approach circles (MacAdam, 1971). It is expressed as:

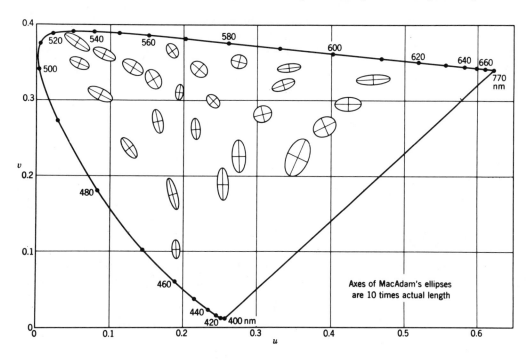

Figure 4-9 Ellipses of Figure 4-8 replotted using transformation of MacAdam 1937 (from Judd and Wyszecki 1975).

$$\xi = 3751a_1^2 - 10a_1^4 - 520b_1^2 + 13295b_1^3 + 32327a_1b_1 - 25491a_1^2b_1 -$$
$$41672a_1b_1^2 + 10a_1^3b_1 - 5227a_1^{1/2} + 2952a_1^{1/4} \qquad (4\text{-}7a)$$

$$\eta = 404b_2 - 185b_2^2 + 52b_2^3 + 69a_2(1 - b_2^2) - 3a_2^2b_2 + 30a_2b_2^3$$

$$a_1 = \frac{10x}{(2.4x + 34y + 1)}, \qquad b_1 = \frac{10y}{(2.4x + 34y + 1)}, \qquad (4\text{-}7b)$$

$$a_2 = \frac{10x}{(4.2y - x + 1)}, \qquad b_2 = \frac{10y}{(4.2y - x + 1)} \qquad (4\text{-}7c)$$

where x and y are the chromaticity coordinates of the color in 1931 CIE *XYZ* space and ξ and η are chromaticity coordinates of the color in a "geodesic" chromaticity diagram. The ellipses of Figure 4-8 are plotted using this transformation in Figure 4-12.

Figure 4-10 Monitor gamut in 1976 CIE UVW space.

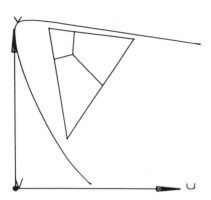

Figure 4-11 1976 CIE UCS chromaticity diagram showing monitor gamut.

The Munsell System

In 1905, Albert H. Munsell published a book and a series of color charts that proposed a color notation system with three dimensions: hue, value, and chroma. His definitions for these terms were:

> *Hue*—"It is that quality by which we distinguish one color family from another, as red from yellow, or green from blue or purple."
>
> *Value*—"It is that quality be which we distinguish a lightcolor from a dark one."
>
> *Chroma*—"It is that quality of color by which we distinguish a strong color from a weak one; the degree of departure of a color sensation from that of white or gray; the intensity of a distinctive Hue; color intensity" (Munsell, 1946).

Although Munsell used a sphere to describe the geometry of his color coordinate system in his original publication, it is more consistent with the organization of *The Munsell Book of Color* (Macbeth, 1979) to think of the notation system in cylindrical

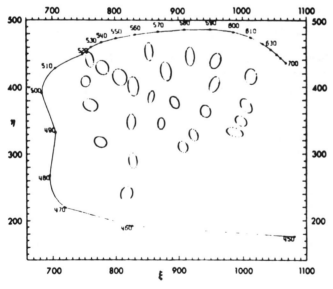

Figure 4-12   Ellipses of Figure 4-8 replotted on geodesic chromaticity diagram (from MacAdam 1971).

coordinates with hue as the angle relative to the cylinder's central axis, value the vertical position, and chroma the radial position.

In addition to labeling colors using hue, value, and chroma, Munsell also wanted a notation system that demonstrated his ideas about color balance. For example, colors that lie at opposite sides of the color solid are "balanced" about the central neutral gray. This example and others like it suggest that there is a psychological nature to his color system; that is, steps along the hue, value, or chroma directions are perceptually equal.

In 1940, the CIE tristimulus values for *The Munsell Book of Color* were measured in terms of CIE illuminant C, and a new study of their perceptual spacing was undertaken. Forty observers made some three million color judgments that resulted in a redesignation of the hue, value, and chroma specification for each color sample (Newhall, 1940). Using this data, Newhall, Nickerson, and Judd (1943) found the relation between a sample's percent luminous reflectance (Y) and value (Λ) to be:

$$Y = 1.2219\Lambda - 0.23111\Lambda^2 + 0.23951\Lambda^3 - 0.021009\Lambda^4 + 0.0008404\Lambda^5 \quad (4\text{-}8)$$

The data for the samples were also plotted on chromaticity diagrams of constant value (and constant luminous reflectance according to Equation 4-8). Smooth curves defining loci of constant hue and constant chroma were drawn on the charts based on the redesignated Munsell samples (Newhall, et al., 1943). The results for value 5/ are shown in Figure 4-13. These loci were extrapolated to the 1/ and 9/ value levels and to the boundary of the object color solid for CIE illuminant C (MacAdam, 1935). In 1954, these extrapolations were extended to the .2/ value level (Judd & Wyszecki, 1956).

If the intersection points of the loci shown in Figure 4-13 are entered into a computer for all Munsell value levels, then the percent luminous reflectance for any Munsell color can be calculated from Equation 4-8, and the chromaticity can be determined by suitable interpolation techniques from the chart data. Furthermore, the color can be reproduced on a digitally controlled color television monitor by using Equations 4-3, 4-4, and 4-5. The percent luminous reflectance is converted to an absolute monitor luminance by using the percent luminous reflectance as a fraction of the maximum luminance with which the monitor can reproduce CIE illuminant C. This maximum luminance can be found by calculating where a color vector with chromaticity coordinates identical to CIE illuminant C intersects the monitor gamut in CIE XYZ space. With the absolute luminance and chromaticity coordinates, tristimulus values XYZ can be found and Equations 4-3, 4-4, and 4-5 applied to find the signal voltages necessary to reproduce the color on the monitor. Figure 4-14 shows "spiders" of constant Munsell value and their position within a typical color television monitor gamut. Each spider arm has constant hue, and the dots on the arm represent equal chroma spacings.

Deciding which Munsell renotation colors are reproducible on the monitor is difficult because the monitor and Munsell color gamuts have irregular shapes and their intersection is not well defined. The monitor gamut as shown in Figure 4-14 is determined by the phosphor chromaticities, the white point chromaticities, and the white point luminance. The Munsell renotation colors are bounded by the object-color solid (or theoretical pigment limit) as determined for CIE illuminant C (MacAdam, 1935) (Figure 4-15). It is of interest to note that the gamut of currently available pigment technology is not only smaller than the boundary of the object color solid but is also smaller in certain areas than the gamut of color television. Hence, a color television monitor can produce Munsell renotation colors that have heretofore only been defined by extrapolation.

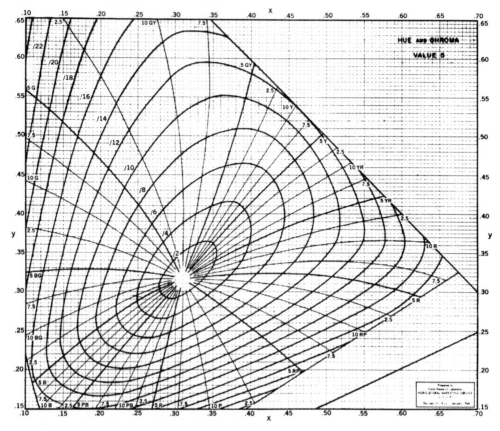

Figure 4-13   1931 CIE chromaticity diagram showing loci of constant Munsell hue and chroma for Munsell colors of constant value 5/ (from Judd and Wyszecki 1975).

Figures 4-16, 4-17, and 4-18 (see color insert) show three slices through Munsell renotation space as produced on a color television monitor. The background of Munsell value 5/ in these displays is within the 5/ or greater range for which the perceptual spacing of the Munsell system was determined. The effect of different backgrounds on the perceptual spacing of the slice shown in Figure 4-16 is shown in Figure 4-19 (see color insert).

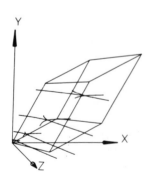

Figure 4-14 "Spiders" of constant Munsell value in 1931 CIE XYZ space and their position relative to the monitor gamut.

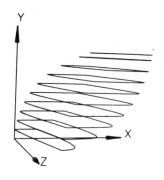

Figure 4-15 Boundary of object color solid for CIE standard illuminant C in 1931 CIE XYZ space.

The Optical Society of America Uniform Color Scale

An inherent problem with any color organization such as The Munsell Book of Color that uses a cylindrical coordinate system is that the spacing between colors changes as two radial lines are followed outwards from the center of the cylinder. For distances between nearest color neighbors to remain constant throughout the color system and to maximize the number of equidistant nearest color neighbors for each color, a space lattice must be used. This is the approach taken in the OSA uniform color scale.

The basic element of the space lattice used in this system is the cubo-octahedron shown in Figure 4-20. A point at the center of the cubo-octahedron has the vertices of the polyhedron as twelve equidistant nearest neighbors. When these polyhedrons are packed together, the result is called a regular rhombohedral lattice. Any point in the lattice is a member of six different linear color scales and seven different color planes.

The research that led to the specification of colors for each lattice point extended over some thirty years. "Judgements of relative magnitudes of color differences exhibited by 128 selected nearest-neighbor pairs of 59 colored tiles were recorded by 49 to 76 observers, all of whom had normal color vision" (MacAdam, 1974). According to available experimental results, 43 of the colors had the same luminous reflectance and uniform chromaticity spacing. Sixteen of the colors were arranged into four sets of four tiles, each set forming a regular tetrahedron in different portions of the tentative color space. The color specificaton that resulted from this data is (MacAdam, 1974):

$$L = 5.9 \, [Y_o^{1/3} - 2/3 + 0.042 \, (Y_o - 30)^{1/3}]$$

$$Y_o = Y \, (4.4934x^2 + 4.3034y^2 - 4.276xy - 1.3744x - 2.5643y + 1.8103)$$

$$g = C \, (-13.7R^{1/3} + 17.7G^{1/3} - 4B^{1/3})$$

$$j = C \, (1.7R^{1/3} + 8G^{1/3} - 9.7B^{1/3}) \tag{4-9}$$

$$C = 1 + \frac{0.042 \, (Y_o - 30)^{1/3}}{(Y_o^{1/3} - 2/3)}$$

$$R = 0.799X + 0.4194Y - 0.1648Z$$

$$G = -0.4493X + 1.3265Y + 0.0927Z$$

$$B = -0.1149X + 0.3394Y + 0.717Z$$

where L, j, and g stand respectively for lightness, yellowness (*jaune* in French), and greenness. X, Y, Z are the tristimulus values of the color (Y being expressed as percent luminous reflectance), and x, y, are the color's chromaticity coordinates. They are based on $D6500$ illumination and the CIE 1964 supplementary observer. The correspondence between the L, j, g coordinates and the vertices of a cubo-octahedron is shown in Figure 4-20. The inverse of this transformation can be accomplished by an iterative numerical technique (MacAdam, 1979). The formulas are valid only when the colors are viewed on a background of 30% reflectance gray and when an L, j, g triplet matches one of the approximately 558 triplets for which the transformation is defined (MacAdam, 1978).

This color space can be reproduced on a color television monitor by use of Equations 4-3, 4-4, and 4-5. It is important to remember, however, that Equation 4-9 is based on the CIE 1964 supplementary observer. This means that the phosphor chromaticity co-ordinates used in Equation 4-4 must be experimentally determined since the chromaticity coordinates available from the manufacturer are based on the CIE 1931 standard ob-server. Figure 4-21 (see color insert) shows a monitor reproduction of a color plane from the OSA Uniform Color Scale.

CIE Uniform Color Spaces

The CIE has recommended two uniform color spaces designated 1976 CIE L*u*v* and 1976 CIE L*a*b* (CIE 1978). In both spaces, two of the dimensions are coordinates on a uniform chromaticity diagram. The third dimension is identical in both spaces and is a simplification of Equation 4-8 for Munsell value:

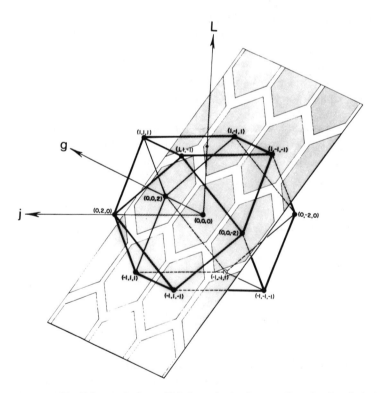

Figure 4-20 Cubo-octahedron which forms basic element of regular rhombohedral lattice. Vertices are labeled with their (L, j, g) notation. Cutting plane depicted corresponds to plane shown in Figure 4-21.

$$L^* = 116\left(\frac{Y}{Y_n}\right)^{1/3} - 16 \qquad \frac{Y}{Y_n} > .008856$$

$$L^* = 903.3 \left(\frac{Y}{Y_n}\right) \qquad \frac{Y}{Y_n} \leq .008856$$

(4-10)

where L* is psychometric lightness, Y is the luminance tristimulus value of the color and Y_n is the luminance tristimulus value of the nominally white color stimulus.

The remaining two dimensions of CIE 1976 (L* u* v*) space are formally defined as:

$$u^* = 13\, L^*(u' - u_n') \qquad v^* = 13\, L^*(v' - v_n')$$

(4-11)

where u', v', u_n', and v_n' are chromaticity coordinates calculated from the U, V, W and U_n, V_n, W_n produced when the inverse of Equation 4-6 is applied to X, Y, Z, and X_n, Y_n, Z_n. X, Y, Z are the tristimulus values of the color to be transformed and X_n, Y_n, Z_n are the tristimulus values of the nominally white color stimulus.

The uniform chromaticity diagram used in CIE 1976 (L* a* b*) space involves a nonlinear transformation from 1931 CIE XYZ space and is based on the cube-root version of the Adams-Nickerson color difference formula. The remaining two coordinates in this space are expressed as:

$$a^* = 500\left[f\left(\frac{X}{X_n}\right) - f\left(\frac{Y}{Y_n}\right)\right],$$

$$b^* = 200\left[f\left(\frac{Y}{Y_n}\right) - f\left(\frac{Z}{Z_n}\right)\right]$$

$$f\left(\frac{X}{X_n}\right) = \left(\frac{X}{X_n}\right)^{1/3} \qquad \frac{X}{X_n} > .008856$$

$$f\left(\frac{X}{X_n}\right) = 7.787\left(\frac{X}{X_n}\right) + \frac{16}{116} \qquad \frac{X}{X_n} \leq .008856$$

$$f\left(\frac{Y}{Y_n}\right) = \left(\frac{Y}{Y_n}\right)^{1/3} \qquad \frac{Y}{Y_n} > .008856$$

$$f\left(\frac{Y}{Y_n}\right) = 7.787\left(\frac{Y}{Y_n}\right) + \frac{16}{116} \qquad \frac{Y}{Y_n} \leq .008856$$

$$f\left(\frac{Z}{Z_n}\right) = \left(\frac{Z}{Z_n}\right)^{1/3} \qquad \frac{Z}{Z_n} > .008856$$

$$f\left(\frac{Z}{Z_n}\right) = 7.787\left(\frac{Z}{Z_n}\right) + \frac{16}{116} \qquad \frac{Z}{Z_n} \leq .008856$$

(4-12)

where X, Y, Z are the tristimulus values of the color to be transformed and X_n, Y_n, Z_n are the tristimulus values of the nominally white color stimulus.

Figures 4-22 and 4-23 show how the monitor gamut of Figure 4-24 looks when transformed into 1976 CIE (L*u*v*) space and 1976 CIE (L*a*b*) space.

Figure 4-22 Monitor gamut in 1976 CIE (L* u* v*) space.

Application of Uniform Color Spaces

The application of uniform color spaces to computer graphics problems must be prefaced with some words of caution. The data on which these uniform spaces are based were obtained under tightly controlled environmental conditions. Some of the parameters held constant include (a) the size of the color samples, (b) the spacing between color samples, (c) the luminance and chromaticity of the background on which the color samples were compared, and (d) the luminance and chromaticity of ambient light in the test environment. To maintain the perceptual uniformity of the space, the settings of these parameters in the final application must match the conditions existing when the data were originally recorded. However, even with this limitation, these uniform spaces are still the best available tools for addressing the problems mentioned below.

When storing or transmitting color images, one should limit the information to no more than the viewer can perceive. Uniform color spaces can be used to decide at what level of resolution the color information should be encoded (Limb, Rubinstein, & Thompson, 1977). The National Television System Committee (NTSC) color television standards incorporate a data compression scheme that has a perceptual basis but that was not derived using uniform color spaces (Fink, 1955). The standard's *YIQ* transmission primaries are allocated band widths based on their relative importance in creating a subjectively acceptable color image. Reconstruction of a full color image from various combinations of the *YIQ* signal components is shown in Figure 4-24 (see color insert).

"False" coloring occurs when the true colors of an image are mapped into another set of colors. Black and white television, which generates images using only *Y* of the *YIQ* signal (Figure 4-24), is an example of each color being mapped to a position on a grayscale. While this is an effective data compression scheme, it makes it impossible to differentiate between colors with the same *Y* value. Often the intent of false coloring is to draw the observer's attention to certain features in an image by maximizing the difference in color between the feature and the surrounding area of the image. Uniform

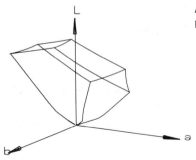

Figure 4-23 Monitor gamut in 1976 CIE (L* a* b*) space.

color spaces can be used to map image colors into a set with maximum perceptual spacing (Booth & Schroeder, 1977; Doucette, 1977).

Color has also been used to encode the variations of parameters, such as temperature or stress. The accuracy with which an observer interprets these images has been questioned (Booth & Schroeder, 1977; Morse, 1979), but they still remain an effective means for showing data trends. For two-dimensional data plots, uniform color spaces such as Munsell or OSA can be used to select color scales. Although this application of uniform color spaces violates many of the restrictions about size and spacing of color samples mentioned earlier, the results can still be quite satisfactory. Figures 4-25 and 4-26 (see color insert) show data being displayed using two different paths through the Munsell color solid. A problem in selecting such color scales from the Munsell and OSA color spaces is that the pigment gamut used to derive these spaces is generally smaller than the gamut of color television and the intersection of the television and pigment gamuts is irregular. This makes it difficult to find color scales that incorporate the most brilliant monitor colors and that lie completely within the area of intersection of the monitor and pigment gamuts. For three-dimensional data presentations only chromaticity can be used to encode the parameter because the length of the color vector in 1931 CIE *XYZ* space is used for the color intensity variations which convey the shape of the object. A uniform chromaticity diagram can be used to select a scale of chromaticity variations with uniform perceptual spacing.

Summary

Uniform color spaces can be a useful tool for solving computer graphics color selection problems. This chapter has presented some relevant uniform color spaces from the color science literature and has shown how these spaces can be applied to computer graphics work with digitally controlled color television monitors. In particular, the Munsell and OSA color organizations were reproduced as new palettes from which to make color selections, and a stress range was encoded using color scales selected from the Munsell color system. Uniform color spaces were also suggested as solutions to problems in image data compression and false coloring.

Although this chapter was primarily concerned with existing uniform color spaces, future uniform color spaces will undoubtedly be defined with the aid of digitally controlled color television monitors. The flexibility and wide color gamut of this medium offer significant advantages over the complex formula and limited color gamut that characterize the pigment technology used in the definition of current uniform color spaces.

References

Bartelson, C. J., & Breneman, E. J. Brightness reproduction in the photographic process. Photographic Science Engineer, July-August 1967.

Beintema, C. D. Whose face is green now? *Broadcast Engineering*, January 1974.

Booth, J. M., & Schroeder, J. B. Design considerations for digital image processing systems. *Computer*, 1977, 15.

Commission Internationale de l'Éclairage. *Recommendations on uniform color space, color-difference equations, and psychometric color terms.* Supplement No. 2 to Publication CIE No. 15, 1978.

Cowan, W. B. An inexpensive scheme for calibration of a color monitor in terms of CIE standard coordinates. *Computer Graphics*, 1983, 17.

DeMarsh, L. E. Optimum telecine transfer characteristics. *Journal of the Society of Motion Picture and Television Engineers*, October 1972.

Doucette, A. R. Color discrimination in digital displays. *Society for Information Display (SID) Digest of Technical Papers,* 1977, 48.

Fink, D. G. (ed.). *Color Television Standards,* New York: McGraw-Hill, 1955.

Hazeltine Laboratories Staff. *Principles of Color Television.* K. McIlwain & C. E. Dean (Eds.). New York: John Wiley, 1956, 549–551.

Hunt, R. W. G. *The Reproduction of Color.* (3rd ed.). New York: John Wiley, 1975.

Interactive Systems Laboratories Staff. *Fourth Quarterly and Final Report: CGG Project 1.* San Marcos, Tex.: Interactive Systems Laboratories, 1983.

Joblove, G. H., & Greenberg, D. Color spaces for computer graphics. *Computer Graphics,* 1978, *12.*

Judd, D. B., & Wyszecki, G. Extension of the Munsell renotation system to very dark colors. *Journal of the Optical Society of America,* 1956, *46,* 281.

Judd, D. B., & Wyszecki, G. *Color in Business, Science and Industry.* (3rd ed.). New York: John Wiley, 1975.

Limb, J. O., Rubinstein, C. B., & Thompson, J. E. Digital coding of color video signals—A review. *IEEE Transactions on Communications,* 1977, *25,* 1349.

MacAdam, D. L. Maximum visual efficiency of colored materials. *Journal of the Optical Society of America,* 1935, *25,* 361.

MacAdam, D. L. Projective transformations of ICI Color specifications. *Journal of the Optical Society of America,* 1937, *27,* 294.

MacAdam, D. L. Visual sensitivities to color differences in daylight. *Journal of the Optical Society of America,* 1942, *32,* 247.

MacAdam, D. L. Geodesic chromaticity diagram based on variances of color matching by 14 normal observers. *Applied Optics,* 1971, *10,* 1.

MacAdam, D. L. Uniform color scale. *Journal of the Optical Society of America,* 1974, *64,* 1691.

MacAdam, D. L. Colorimetric data for samples of OSA color scales. *Journal of the Optical Society of America,* 1978, *68,* 121.

MacAdam, D. L. Private communication, 1979.

Macbeth. Munsell color. *The Munsell Book of Color.* Baltimore, Md.: Macbeth, A Division of Kollmorgen Corp.

Morse, A. Some principles for the effective display of data. *Computer Graphics,* 1979, *13,* 94.

Munsell, A. H. *A Color Notation.* Baltimore, Md.: Munsell Color Company, Inc., 1946.

Neal, C. B. Television colorimetry for receiver engineers. *IEEE Transactions on Broadcast Television and Receiver,* August 1973.

Newhall, S. M. Preliminary report of the OSA subcommittee on the spacing of the Munsell colors. *Journal of the Optical Society of America,* 1940, *30,* 617.

Newhall, S. M., Nickerson, D., & Judd, D. B. Final report of the OSA subcommittee on the spacing of the Munsell colors. *Journal of the Optical Society of America,* 1943, *33,* 385.

Novick, S. B. Tone reproduction from colour telecine systems. *British Kinematography Sound and Television,* October 1969.

Sanders, C. L., Gaw, W., & Wyszecki G. Color calibrator for monitors in television studios. *Journal of the Society of Motion Picture and Television Engineers,* June 1968.

Smith, A. R. Color gamut transform pairs. *Computer Graphics,* 1978, *12.*

Wentworth, J. W. *Color Television Engineering.* New York: McGraw-Hill, 1955.

Wintringham, W. T. Color television and colorimetry. *Proceedings of the IRE,* October 1951.

Wyszecki, G., & Stiles, W. S. *Color Science.* (2nd ed.). New York: John Wiley, 1982.

Acknowledgments

This work benefited from discussions with several people at the Cornell University Program of Computer Graphics. In particular, Christopher Odgers stressed the importance of having the proper equipment to adjust a color television monitor, Richard Gallagher wrote the program used to generate Figures 4-25 and 4-26, Michael Schulman performed the structural analysis dipicted in Figures 4-25 and 4-26, and Bruce Forbes helped draw Figure 4-20. Special thanks are extended to GTE Sylvania for help in measuring the colorimetric properties of our television monitors and to Rensselaer Polytechnic Institute for providing the data that defines the Munsell color system. The Cornell University Program of Computer Graphics is partially funded by the National Science Foundation.

5   Ergonomic Vision

WANDA SMITH
Hewlett-Packard Company
Palo Alto, California

Ergonomics

The recent reduction in the price of computer displays has resulted in their widespread proliferation in business applications as well as in the home. This increase in use, especially in businesses, has resulted in concern over how to maximize the efficient use of displays. This is usually accomplished by optimizing the interactions (visual, mental, manual, and acoustic) of the users with information presented by these displays.

The task of analyzing the interface of people with equipment (such as computer displays) is the primary activity of professionals in the field of human factors engineering, also known as *ergonomics*. The ultimate use of the information generated by these professionals is in its application to the design of products that will be efficient but, at the same time, will minimize risk to the health and well-being of the individual user.

In order to accomplish this objective, these professionals study the interface with devices such as visual displays to evaluate their impact on physical, physiological, and mental processes. Because the primary interaction with computer displays is in the visual processing of screen information, a large amount of study has been conducted on the impact of displays on the visual system. The study of this process has proved especially useful because of user's concerns that displays may cause visual discomfort, stress, fatigue, and/or damage. One of the worst fears voiced pertains to the radioactive emissions, particularly those from the cathode ray tube (CRT)—currently the most commonly used display (Weiss, 1983).

On a less serious scale, there is also a concern that long-term viewing of visual display units at close focal distances causes undue amounts of visual stress, resulting in muscle fatigue of the lens of the eye. Additional concern has been expressed that frequently shifting back and forth between paper and visual displays may produce stress on the mechanisms that control the size of the pupil in the eye. The reasoning behind this claim is that frequent changes in pupil size occur when the eyes alternately view these two different brightness sources and that this ultimately results in pupillary fatigue. However, research has not supported these claims (Smith, 1979; 1980).

Issues like the visual stress claim are becoming such widespread concerns that laws are being introduced (both in Europe and the United States) that will strictly specify the design characteristics of displays and their workstations, limit the maximum number of hours spent viewing displays, and set the number and extent of work breaks during their use.

The recent decrease in the cost of the multicolor display has allowed it, too, to be economically integrated into the business office and the home. As a result, it is also becoming exposed to the same kinds of concerns as the typical single color display (white, green, or yellow).

Changes in Modes of Displaying Information

Since the introduction of displays into the work and home environments, the characteristics of image information to which the human visual system is subjected have significantly changed. In the past, this information was mainly presented in the form of printed characters on paper: usually black characters on a white background. In contrast to this, information presented on computer displays is typically in the form of lighted characters on a dark background: white on dark gray, light green on dark green, or yellow on brown.

Displays with white text images on a dark gray background, or vice versa, are called *achromatic* (colorless) screens. Displays with one color used for images are called *monochromatic*. Information is now being presented in text, as well as graphics, in several colors displayed concurrently on the screen. These displays are commonly referred to as *multicolor* screens.

Some of the differences between these three modes of information presentation that are relevant to visual perception and comfort are (a) contrast between images and the screen background, (b) color, size, spacing, focus, and stability of the images, and (c) glare and reflections from the surface of the screen. These factors significantly contribute to the ability of the user to perceive, read, and interpret information on the screen (Kinney, 1979; McLean, 1965; Robertson, 1982). Incorrect design or adjustment of any of them can lead to complaints of visual discomfort or stress.

There are also other major differences between traditional and current modes of information presentation. Printed material, such as books, can generally be viewed or held in a variety of positions or orientations. In contrast, displays are vertically positioned and are relatively limited by their size and weight. This restricts the user's mobility and can result in a static load on neck and head muscles (Grandjean, Hunting, & Piderman, 1983). In addition, since the location of the information display unit is relatively inflexible due to limited table top space, the general position of the user is also somewhat restricted. Recent advances in design of tilt and swivel mechanisms have reduced this problem. Also, reduction of the size of the display unit itself has allowed it to be more easily repositioned or relocated.

Environmental factors, such as improper levels of light in the office environment, ambient glare caused by reflection of light off surrounding surfaces, long periods spent viewing the visual display unit without rest pauses, and improper design of the workstation can also lead to stress and visual discomfort (Starr, 1982). Personal factors, as well, can adversely affect visual (including color) perception and comfort. These include defective or corrected vision, type of optical aids used, and the age of the individual which can all contribute to visual stress and fatigue.

Concerns and Issues

The purpose of this section is to address some of the design characteristics of the display—multicolor displays in particular—that are of concern to users. The questions most frequently asked by users are presented and answered. Where appropriate, a more detailed discussion of information is included in order to provide the reader with a broad base of understanding of the basic issues from which the question may have originated.

Radiation Emissions

Question.   Are there dangerous radiation emissions from a multicolor CRT?

Answer.   The amount of radiation emission from a multicolor computer CRT is less than that from a fluorescent light or even a rock in a sunlit parking lot.

Discussion.   In order for a device such as a CRT to be sold in most countries, it must meet very strict radiation emission standards. Governmental agencies in Canada, England, and the United States have tested multicolor CRTs and have found the emissions far below that allowed by the specifications, laws, or standards of these countries. These agencies have also issued statements that working with a CRT produces no radiation hazards to people (Weiss, 1983). A comparative analysis of the maximum level of radiation measured on CRTs in the office study done by the National Institute for Occupational Safety and Health (NIOSH) is shown in Table 5-1. Some comparisons

Maximum Measured Radiation Levels Compared with Accepted Standards

Radiation Region	Maximum Level Measured	Occupational Standard
X-Ray	ND*	2.5 mR/hr
Ultraviolet (near)	0.60 uW/cm^2	1000 uW/cm^2
Visible	40 fL	2920 fL
Radiofrequency		
Electric field	ND*	40,000 V^2/m^2**
Magnetic field	ND*	0.25 A^2/m^2**

* Amount too low to be detected.

** Far field equivalent of 10m/w/cm^2.

Table 5-1   Maximum Measured Radiation Levels Compared with Accepted Standards.

between CRT radiation exposure and exposure to other elements in our daily experience follow:

X-ray comparison.   One standard chest x-ray gives a dose of x-radiation 4 times higher than the allowable occupational exposure limit for 1 hour, or 20 times higher than the allowable emission level from a CRT for 1 hour.

Annual exposure comparison.   If a person sat 2 inches from the front of a CRT for 40 hours a week, 52 weeks a year, the annual radiation exposure from a CRT that emitted a "worst case" dose of radiation would be less than $\frac{1}{3}$ the recommended annual exposure limit for the general population. It would be over 30 times less than the annual occupational exposure limit. (A 2-inch viewing distance is obviously unrealistically close, and as one moves farther away from the surface of the screen, the radiation exposure decreases geometrically.)

Color Perception Loss

Question.   Is the temporary loss of the ability to perceive a specific color an indication of visual fatigue?

Answer.   This is a normal response called "color adaptation." Due to its quick recovery rate, it is not generally defined as a type of fatigue. Instead, it is usually defined as a change in sensitivity. Sometimes individuals think that if they experience even a temporary loss in a sensation (like the perception of a certain color), they are experiencing fatigue (of the visual system).

Discussion.   A decrease in the ability of a human system to perform at its previous level is not always an indication of fatigue; however, it is often erroneously defined as such.

A mechanism can lose its ability to respond due to "adaptation" as well as to "fatigue." For example, when you first enter an Italian restaurant, the smell of spices and cheeses is very strong. But as your senses "adapt," the aromas become less noticeable. This does not mean your system is unable to respond to odors in general. If you left the restaurant and then returned several seconds later, you would notice the odors until your senses once again adapted. Also, if a nervous skunk walked into the restaurant (introducing a new smell to the environment), you would probably be very aware of its odor.

The same thing occurs in vision, particularly with colors. If you look intensively and continuously at two colors similar in saturation and brightness (like a desaturated cyan and white), your eye will become adapted to the cyan, and the differences between the two colors will become less obvious. However, if you look away from the screen to an object of a different color for several seconds, the color differences will once again be apparent when you return your gaze to the screen.

Visual Fatigue

Question.   Can viewing a color display for continuous periods result in an undue amount of visual fatigue or stress?

Answer.   Viewing a well-designed computer display should be no more demanding of the visual system than performing a similar task (such as reading a book, writing a report, or performing fine detail assembly) at an equivalent distance, under similar viewing conditions.

Discussion.   Visual fatigue may be manifested by performance or subjective symptoms and/or physiological change. In particular, the functions reported to appear vulnerable to fatigue effects are the focusing system of the eye, retinal sensitivity, reception and perception of visual images in the brain, and muscle efficiency controlling movement and fixation of the eye.

Symptoms of visual fatigue include subnormal clarity due to inability to maintain focus and fixation, hazy and blurred vision, color fringing of objects, image confounding, and double vision. Studies have shown that these symptoms appear to correlate with the appearance of bloodshot eyes, inflamed eyelids, watering eyes, a feeling of tenseness or heaviness of the eye, a burning sensation in the eye, or frequent blinking (Smith, 1980).

These symptoms appear to also occur when the eyes are used for unusually long periods of time, as in the following conditions:

At close viewing range; e.g., reading a book for three hours.

In less than optimum viewing conditions; e.g., driving for a few hours on a very foggy road at night.

In a high glare environment; e.g., snow skiing on a sunny day without sunglasses.

No sleep for several days.

Viewing and interpreting extremely blurry images for an hour or more.

An understanding of the phenomena of visual fatigue is, at best, difficult. One of the reasons for this confusion is that its symptoms vary among individuals, and it is described and defined in a variety of often contradictory ways.

The term *fatigue* can be defined as weariness of an organism due to exertion or as the temporary loss of power to respond due to continued stimulation. It can be characterized as acute, chronic, or task induced. *Acute fatigue* refers to those symptoms produced by brief but tiring work activity with its primary effects in the muscles—it can be relieved by rest. *Chronic fatigue* involves physiological phenomena that are cumulative and, in some instances, may not be alleviated by rest. *Task-induced fatigue* is temporarily induced or produced by working at a particular task for a long time (e.g., fatigue occurring when a person experiences monotony, which can be quickly relieved by changing the task).

One definition of visual fatigue is: a functional, readily reversible physiological effect of prolonged, excessive, or difficult contraction of ocular muscles in an attempt to maintain fine focus. However, *visual fatigue* has appeared to many researchers to be more of a "combination" of ocular muscle fatigue and perceptual fatigue. The former refers to eye movement (fixing and focusing systems); whereas, perceptual fatigue results from prolonged effort in interpreting visual images. Perceptual fatigue may be present with or without eye muscle fatigue, although some of the symptom complex of visual fatigue might be due to the tiring of perceptual effort.

Research conducted on visual fatigue has indicated that it appears to be of the acute or task-induced type. This indicates that it could be caused by work of the muscles and/or by a decrease in mental faculties.

The concept of mental (cognitive) fatigue is, however, confounded with that of visual fatigue. Some of the visual indices of mental fatigue are critical flicker fusion, blink rate, and pupil diameter. Yet visual fatigue has been measured by evaluating these same indices of mental fatigue.

In many cases, other forms of fatigue (and/or stress) are confused with visual fatigue. For example, an individual may actually be experiencing postural stress due to static load on the muscles or a cramped neck position. Muscles in the back of the neck could be pinching nerves that radiate to the forehead, causing a headache. The headache may be attributed to viewing conditions on the computer screen but may, in fact, be due to the position of the chair, leading to poor posture and cramped neck muscles. As shown in Figure 5-1 (see color insert), some recent studies have reported this finding (Grandjean et al., 1983; Starr, 1982). When display terminal users were given properly designed and adjusted furniture, improved environments, and better managed conditions, reports of "visual stress" were significantly reduced.

Multicolor Screen Fatigue

Question.   Can viewing a multicolor screen for a long time result in more visual fatigue than viewing a single-color or achromatic (black and white) screen?

Answer.   Evidence indicates that multicolor screens can reduce many reports of "visual fatigue or stress" from users who have previously viewed information on single-color or achromatic screens. However, the exact causes of the sensations of visual discomfort, stress, and/or fatigue are not yet agreed upon by the scientific community. (See previous discussion.)

Discussion.   If visual fatigue is defined as motor fatigue of the ocular muscles, multicolor displays actually decrease muscular fatigue. Research has shown that, in dense screens, it takes fewer eye scans to locate objects correctly coded in color than those coded by other methods (Luria & Strauss, 1975). This, in turn, can reduce the possibility of exertion (or work) by the muscles that move the eyes laterally and vertically. (The muscles that control eye movement are composed of striated tissue that is susceptible to fatigue. You can experience a "pull" on these muscles if you quickly move your eyes from a far-left position to a far-right position several times.)

Studies defining visual fatigue as perceptual fatigue have shown that assignments of meaning, and thus interpretation, are superior with color over other forms of coding, provided the color coding is done properly (Bishop & Crook, 1961; Cahill & Carter, 1976; Keister, 1981; Kinney, 1979; Newman & Davis, 1962; Robertson, 1982; Schmit, 1977; Shontz, Trumm, & Williams, 1971; Smith, 1963; Thorell, 1983). Figure 5-2 (see color insert) illustrates these conclusions. It shows average search time as a function of average number of eye fixations. Color-coded items resulted in a superior performance.

Visual Distance Changes and Fatigue

Question.   Does frequent switching of visual fixations from a paper to a screen (located at different distances on the desk) result in fatigue of the muscles that control the focusing mechanism of the eyes?

Answer.   Frequent change of large viewing distances is a normal function for the eye to perform. The range of distance changes from a screen (typically located 50 cm from a user) to a paper (30 up to 50 cm from a user) is very small. This does not impose an abnormal or excessive amount of exertion on the muscles of the eye.

Discussion.   The ability of the eye to change viewing distance and yet retain a focused image is dependent upon two types of muscles in the eye: internal and external. Internal muscles control the shape of the lens and the size of the pupil. External muscles of the eye move the eyes to a particular point of interest and keep the eyes in slight motion to insure image retention.

Internal muscles are smooth tissue and are not susceptible to fatigue. External muscles are striated tissue and can be fatigued (Smith, 1980). However, the external muscles will not experience a significant strain from the change in viewing an object from 30 to 50 cm. In addition, almost no exertion is required of these muscles to converge the eyes (direct them inward to allow continued focus of the image) at this distance; therefore, the probability of fatiguing the external muscles is highly unlikely.

Another point that should be made here is that exercise is beneficial for any muscle. In fact, static muscle activity is reportedly more fatiguing than dynamic activity over the same time span. If the exerted muscle force exceeds 10-15% of that muscle's maximum capacity, a static muscle contraction cannot be maintained. Therefore, the effort required to keep eyes still can be more tiring than that to move the eyes.

With visual displays, the visual system is not only changing view from documents to display, but also scanning dynamic text and continuously processing information. Thus, moving the eyes back and forth and inwards (converging) is actually beneficial. Conversely, according to the information above, holding these movements, still would actually result in more fatigue.

If you hold an object at arm's length from your face, cover one eye, and then move the object toward your face and away from it very quickly, you will not notice a sensation of muscle pull in the lens of the eye. This is a very different sensation experienced with types of muscles that "are susceptible" to fatigue.

Alternate Viewing and Fatigue

Question.   Does alternately looking at a dark colored screen and a white document fatigue the eye muscles that control the size of the pupil?

Answer.   There is no evidence that this activity fatigues the pupil.

Discussion.   The size of the pupil is dependent on the overall light in the person's visual field. For example, at the typical viewing distance of a screen in an office (50 cm), the pupil adjusts to the light in the viewing range of the eye, as opposed to only the light emitted from the screen or the light reflected from the documents on the table. Any variations in pupil size caused by viewing dark displays and white paper are extremely small, if detectable at all. Even if extreme variation in pupil size occurred, the muscles that control the pupil diameter (like those that control the shape of the lens) are smooth muscle tissue and are almost impossible to fatigue (Smith, 1980).

Research has demonstrated no performance differences between a very dark screen background or a very light screen background (Kokoschka & Fleck, 1980); however, a preference is often shown for a white background. The reasons for this preference are not clear. One theory is that people are most familiar with seeing print on a white background (paper) and are therefore biased. Another theory is that fewer reflections are perceived on a screen with a white background.

There are disadvantages to using a white background with a CRT. The light background may add more glare to the user's visual environment than a dark screen. In fact, the perception of flicker on positive video (dark images on a light background) is greater than it is on negative video (light images on a dark background). In addition, characters on positive video look smaller (thinner) and may not be recognized as far away as those on negative video. This occurs because of the "blooming" effect of white or colors that are significantly lighter than dark colors. Lastly, for individuals with cataracts, the perception of information on a display is reportedly easier on screens with dark backgrounds.

Brightness Values and Muscle Fatigue

Question.   Does alternately viewing colors of different brightness values result in excessive change in size of the pupil of the eye? If so, will the muscles that control the pupil become fatigued?

Answer.   Changes in character brightness on a screen effect the size of the pupil even less than switching from a dark screen to a white document (see the previous question and answer); therefore, there should be no fatigue of the pupil muscles.

Hue Differences and Muscle Fatigue

Question.   Does the eye continually refocus on different colors? Does this result in fatigue of the muscles that control the shape of the lens of the eye?

Answer.   The lens of the eye changes its shape very slightly to focus on images of different wavelengths. However, as previously discussed, there is no scientific evidence that the muscles controlling the lens are susceptible to fatigue.

Discussion.   The lens of the eye is not "color corrected," and as a result, the different wavelengths transmitted through it do not form a single image at one point inside the eye. Images of short wavelengths (like blue) are focused closest to the front of the eye and long wavelengths (like red) are imaged farthest away, toward the back of the eye (Campbell & Gubisch, 1967; Tansley, 1976). The result is called "chromostereopsis" and the effect is that red objects may look closer than blue objects. Some people are more aware of this phenomenon than others.

Color and Eye Ease

Question.   Which color is "easiest" on the eyes for text or other images?

Answer.   Studies have not yet demonstrated that any one color results in more or less visual fatigue. Any color should be acceptable and comfortable to view as long as there is sufficient contrast to its background.

Studies have demonstrated preferences for certain display image colors. These preferences appear to be a function of several variables, including the geographic location of users, their culture, and/or the advertising to which they are exposed. There are a number of claims that yellow is the best color for display characters because the eyes are most sensitive to its wave length. Actually, if the eyes are adapted to a typically lighted environment, maximum sensitivity is in the green or yellowish green regions of the visible spectrum, regardless of the size of the image on the display. For a dark-adapted eye (working in a very dark office), the eyes are actually more sensitive to colors at the lower end of the visible spectrum, in the blue-green range.

If the eye is most sensitive to green or yellow green, visual performance should be best with these colors. Research does not support this contention. Results of one study of colors on dark backgrounds indicate that reading performance is better on yellow, magenta, cyan, and red than for green and blue (in this order) (Rizy, 1967). However, it is not known if all the colors projected on the display were of equal brightness. If they were not, test subjects could have responded to brightness cues instead of color cues. Results of a more recent study comparing reading of green and orange characters set at the same brightness showed no significant performances (Wichansky, 1985).

Figure 5-3 (see color insert) shows the relationship between performances for the various colors on an eight-color display. When characters are very small, differences in ability to discriminate colors become greater. For example, as shown in Figure 5-4 (see color insert), the reading performance for white, red, yellow, and magenta is much greater than for cyan, green, and blue (Rizy, 1967).

Optimal Number of Colors

Question.   What is the optimum number of colors to present on a display at one time? If more than this number is used, will it result in visual fatigue?

Answer.   For most aplications, between four and seven is the maximum suggested number of colors on a screen at one time. However, in some applications more colors are necessary. These include:

A line graph with more than seven variables,

A split screen with different (un-related) types of data plotted in the different sectors,

A representation of geographic areas (e.g., states in the U.S.),

Realistic simulations or pictorial representations.

There is no indication that the use of colors in general or of many colors will result in visual fatigue; however, degraded performance, frustration, and resulting stress can result if colors are applied unwisely (Phillips & Noyes, 1980).

Color and Distance

Question.   Can images on a multicolor screen be viewed at greater distances than images on a black-and-white screen?

Answer.   In general, information on multicolor screens can be perceived at greater viewing distance than a black-and-white version.

However, if the information is presented in very small images or text, and if the spaces between the images are very narrow, the black-and-white information can be more clearly seen at a greater viewing distance. (This presumes equal quality and brightness of the images on both types of displays.)

Discussion.   In general, the use of color results in a more versatile and flexible system because it allows more placement and viewing possibilities.

Glare and Visibility

Question.   What is the impact of reflections and glare spots on the ability to see colored characters and images?

Answer.   Reflections and glare spots are a source of visual distraction and reduce the contrast of the images on the screen.

Discussion.   This problem is particularly acute with negative video displays (light characters on a dark background). A major impact of glare is that it desaturates the color on a CRT; it is similar to adding white light to the colors of the images. This effect can be so strong that color recognition of yellow and cyan is impaired. Moreover, if the glare source has a dominant color component (like the blue of fluorescent lights), it can shift the adaptation state of the eye. Effectively, this will shift the "white" point of the eye and reduce the ability to distinguish shades of the illuminant color (i.e., blue fluorescents reduce the number of discernible shades of blue). These effects show the importance of using an effective antiglare treatment on color displays.

Treating Glare

Question.   What type of antireflection filter or treatment is best for multicolor screens? How effective are color filters?

Answer.   Several types of screen treatment are available to reduce reflections and glare. Each has its positive and negative impact on color images:

Etched (similar to a sandblasting treatment) screens diffuse the transmitted light and result in a reduction of image resolution (fuzzy, blurry edges).

Woven fiber filters, are usually attached to the front surface of the screen. They can be fragile and collect dust in their interwoven fibers. Visual distortions, such as Newton rings (circular color effects due to light reflections) and moire patterns (repetitive patterns different from surface material) can interfere with color differentiation and perception.

Optically coated, quarter–wavelength filters do not result in visual distortions. They are, however, easily marked by fingerprints which may interfere with color perception.

Both the woven fiber and quarter wavelength filters enhance the apparent contrast of the characters to the screen background by reducing the brightness of the screen. The brightness of the characters may, however, have to be increased. Despite claims made about the advantages of color filters, they have not been shown to significantly reduce reflections.

Glare and Tinted Glasses

Question. Do tinted glasses eliminate visual discomfort or visually distracting glare on the screen surface?

Answer. In spite of the fact that color filters have not demonstrated their ability to significcnatly solve glare problems, tinted glasses have recently been suggested as a way to reduce the discomfort of screen glare. There are serious drawbacks to this recommendation. One is that the tint of glasses can distort the perception of colors. Another is that tinted lenses can reduce the brightness of the illuminated images by as much as 40%. This can further reduce the perception and discrimination of the color.

Discussion. To compensate for the reduction of brightness resulting from the tint of glasses, the user will often increase the brightness of the images. This can result in a blooming effect in which the edges of the characters become blurry.

Brightness and Contrast Controls

Question. Are a separate brightness control and contrast control necessary for multicolor screens?

Answer. Color information is best presented when the effective contrast (the sum of the brightness and color contrast) is maximized (Lippert, Farley, Post, & Snyder, 1981; Mclean, 1965; Tansley, 1976). This can be accomplished best by having a brightness control and a contrast control.

Discussion. Until the last few years, many of the CRT displays had neither brightness nor contrast adjustments. Most of those that did had only brightness controls. In addition, when a control was offered, it was generally located either in the back of the display device or under the casing, requiring adjustment with a tool.Nowmost displays offer at least a brightness control, and many offer a contrast control as well.

This is an important feature because different users have different requirements. People with visual deficiencies benefit from the ability to change brightness and contrast. For example, older people need more light to read characters easily; people with cataracts reportedly perceive information more easily when bright images have a high contrast against a dark background; individuals with color-vision deficiencies can use brightness aided by contrast differences to differentiate colors.

In addition, users in different environments have varied requirements. Some people have their displays next to brightly sunlit windows, while others work in dimly lighted offices. Extreme environments like these require different brightness and contrast adjustments (Laycock & Viveash, 1982).

Light Level and Color

Question. Is there an optimum light level for rooms where multicolor screens are used? Is this different from the light level normally used for single-color or black-and-white screens?

Answer.   In general, the best illumination of a room in which multicolor displays are viewed is about 250 to 400 lux. If it is necessary to have a high illumination level for reading documents or viewing detailed drawings, a separate task light can be used.

Discussion.   The average luminance across the display should be at least 8 fL to allow efficient discrimination in an office of 500 to 1000 lux. If a display like a CRT is used in a very bright room, such as 2600 lux, the ability to discriminate colors is also decreased because of the effect of the bright light on the contrast of the images to the background of the screen. In addition, the white components of ambient light will desaturate the screen colors, making them less easy to recognize. Lastly, reducing the overhead light level in an excessively bright room will improve recognition and discrimination of colors and reduce the number of overhead reflections from the screen.

Summary

Several issues of current concern to users of computer displays have been addressed. Although questions about displays, in general, have been answered, the majority related to multicolor displays. Review of studies conducted on radiation emissions has revealed that the amount of radiation from a CRT display is insufficient to pose a health hazard. Research on symptoms of visual discomfort has led to the conclusion that, in general, this condition appears to be a result of factors other than the design of the images on the screen. The major contributor to this phenomenon appears to be a work environment that does not accommodate the task of viewing information on a computer screen. Factors include improper room illumination, excessive glare, and lack of adjustments in workstation furniture. Improper prescription lenses are an individual factor that has also been shown to be a contributor to visual stress. Multicolor screens (if the colors are correctly assigned) have been shown to enhance the visual and mental processing of the information on the screen by the user. Multicolor displays can, therefore, reduce frustration and stress by improving user performance and satisfaction.

References

Bishop, H. P. & Crook, M. N. Absolute Identification of Color for Targets Presented Against White and Colored Backgrounds. Wright Air Development Division Technical Report (AD 266 403), 1961, 60–611.

Burnham, R. W., & Newhall, S. M. Color perception in small test fields. *Journal of the Optical Society of America*, 1953, *43*, 899–902.

Cahill, M. C., & Carter, R. C. Color code size for searching displays of differenc density. *Human Factors*, 1976, *18*(3), 273–280.

Campbell, F. W., & Gubish, R. W. The effect of chromatic abberration on visual acuity. *Journal of Physiology*, 1967, *192*, 345–358.

Grandjean, E., Hunting W., & Piderman, M. A field study of preferred settings of an adjustable VDT workstation and their effects on body postures and subjective feelings. *Human Factors*, 1983, 25(2), 161–175.

Keister, R. S. Data entry performance on color versus monochromatic displays. *Proceedings of the Human Factors Society 25th Annual Meeting*, 1981, 736–740.

Kinney, J. S. The use of color in wide-angle displays. *Proceedings of the Society for Information Display*, 1979, *20*(1), 33–40.

Kokoschka, S., & Fleck, H. J. *Experimental Comparison of Negative and Positive Screen Images*. Research Report from Institute der Universitat Karlsruhe, 1980.

Laycock, J., & viveash, J. P. Calculating the perceptibility ofmonochrome and colour displays viewed under various illumination conditions. *Displays*, 1982, *3*(2), 88–89.

Lippert, T. M., Farley, W. W., Post, D. L., & Snyder, H. L. *Color Contrast Effects on Visual Performance*. (Technical Report), Virginia, Blacksburg: Polytechnic Institute and StateUniversity, 1981.

Luria, S. M., & Strauss, M. S. Eye movements during search forcoded and uncoded targets. *Perception and Psychophysics*, 1975, *17*, 303–308.

McLean, M. V. Brightness contrast, color contrast, and legibility. *Human Factors*, 1965, *7*, 521–526.

Newman, K. M., & Davis, A. R. Non-redundant colour, brightness and flashing rate encoding of geometric symbols in a visual display. *Journal of English Psychology*, 1962, *1*, 47–67.

Phillips, R. J., & Moyes, L. A comparison of colour and visual texture as codes for use as area symbols on thematic maps. *Ergonomics*, 1980, *23*, 1117–1128.

Rizy, E. R. *Dichroic Filter Specification for Color Additive Display: II Further Exploration of Tolerance Areas and the Influence of other Display Variables*. USAF Rome Air Development Center(RADC-TR-67-513,AD659-346), 1967.

Robertson, P. J. *A Guide to Using Color on Alphanumeric Displays*. IBM Technical Report G320-6296-0, Hursley Park, United Kingdom: International Business Machines, 1980.

Robertson, P. J. *Review of Color Display Benefits*. IBM Technical Report HF056, Hursley Park, United Kingdom: International Business Machines, 1982.

Schmit, V. P. *A Selective Review of Relevant Aspects of Colour Perception for the Application of Colour to Displays*. Royal Aircraft Establishment Technical Memorandum FS 114, Farnborough, Hants, 1977.

Shontz, W. D., Trumm, G. A., & Williams, L. G. Colour coding for information location. *Human Factors*, 1971, *13* 237–246.

Smith, S. L. Legibility of overprinted symbols in multicolored displays. *Journal of English Psychology*, 1963, *2*, 82–96(b).

Smith, W. J. A review of literature relating to visual fatigue. *Proceedings of the Human Factors Society 23rd Annual Meeting*, 1979, 362–366.

Smith, W. J. Physiological correlates of visual fatigue.Unpublished thesis, Stanford University, 1980.

Starr, S. J., Thompson, C. R., & Shute, S. J. Effects of video display terminals on telephone operators. *Human Factors*, 1982, *24*(6), 699–711.

Sundet, J. M. The effect of pupil size variations on the color stereoscopic phenomenon. *Vision Research*, 1972, *12*, 1027–1032.

Tansley, B. W. Psychophysical studies of the contribution of chromatic mechanisms to the visual perception of borders. Doctoral dissertation, University of Rochester, 1976.

Thorell, L. G. Introduction to color vision. *Proceedings of the Society of Photo-optical Instrumentation Engineers*, January 1983, 158.

Weiss, M. M. The video display terminal—Is there a radiation hazard? *Journal of Occupational Medicine*, 1983, *25*(2), 98–100.

Wichansky, A. M. Legibility and User Acceptance of Monochrome Display Phosphor Colors. Work with Visual Displays Conference Proceedings, Stockholm, May 1986, 216–219.

6   *Process Control Using Color Displays*

ROBERT F. SAPITA
The Foxboro Company
Foxboro, Massachusetts

Abstract

Long before computers, video display terminals (VDTs) and fault tolerant system architectures were applied as process management enhancement tools and color utilization was well established in the process industries. In the production of various petrochemicals, refined metals, pharmaceuticals, textiles, paper, and food products, color has been used extensively to identify the products, the processing equipment, and the operational status of the process itself. This chapter reviews these applications with an emphasis on the computer-based human-process interface and the role of color in process monitoring and control.

Introduction

The past seventy-five years have witnessed a remarkable evolution in the design and application of devices to provide an interface between the process operator and the process. From a simple beginning consisting of pressure gauges, sight glass, thermometers, etc., process industries have progressed to sophisticated distributed system architectures containing computers of various capabilities, fiber optics, microelectronic signal transducers, and VDT-equipped consoles. The continual introduction of newer technologies in data acquisition, control, communications, and human-machine interface (HMI) has enhanced the operator's overall ability to monitor and assess process conditions and to initiate control changes. Devices capable of effecting dynamic color changes in response to varying process or system conditions exemplify a typical interface improvement. Improperly applied, however, a potential operator aid can become an impediment to efficient and error-free operation. For example, the color red had fourteen different meanings in the control center at the Three Mile Island Nuclear Power Plant (Malone, Kirkpatrick, et al., 1980).

An objective of this chapter is to assist the display designer in making judicious use of color in process control and management applications. If opportunities to use color were limited or if universally accepted standards existed, the designer could simply state the governing commandments and rules. Unfortunately, such is not the case. While significant interdisciplinary research has provided objectivity in particular areas, many topics remain to be investigated. Consequently, the designer will most likely have to decide when it is appropriate to use color and which colors to use. In the process industries, this decision-making process can be facilitated by some understanding of two areas: (a) process types, control techniques, operator roles, and color-related practices commonly found in the industries and (b) generic and specific color recommendations.

This chapter is divided into four sections. The human-process interface (HPI) section describes process types, control techniques, and operator roles in the process industries. Its objective is to provide the reader with some understanding of the process management and control mission. The section on color applications provides a historical perspective of the use of color in control and noncontrol applications. The process computer graphics section describes some current computer-based color display applications in the industries. The versatility and dynamic adaptability of these systems are explored in both process control and management situations. Finally, the application guidelines section presents procedures recommended for selection and assignment of colors in process control displays.

Human-Process Interface

Considerable emphasis is placed on the human-machine interface (HMI) (formerly the man-machine interface) associated with today's computer-based systems. The majority of computer systems today provides services for people by accepting data, commands, programs, etc., and returning the results through some form of input/output device. This HMI can be a simple terminal or a complex system comprised of various input and output technologies. In addition to this interface, control systems have another interface equally complex—the interface between the process and the control system. Figure 6-1 depicts the three major elements of the process control system. The leftmost area represents the human element; the center, the machine system; and the right side, the process.

The machine-process boundary and the human-machine boundary represent the two major system interfaces. *Human* refers to the plant operations personnel: lead operators, unit and plant supervisors, and maintenance and engineering specialists. *Machine* refers to the control system, such as field-mounted process variable transducers, data transmission paths, control elements, displays, and hand controls. *Process* includes the chemical, physical, electrical, and mechanical activities to be monitored and controlled.

An idealized system would have these interfaces so well designed that they become nearly transparent, resulting in a theoretical human-process interface. Particular attributes of the HMI, including the use of color, should contribute to this trans-

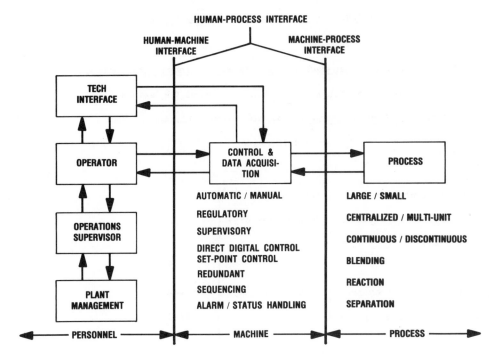

Figure 6-1 Idealized concept of the Human-Process-Interface.

parency and facilitate the operator's primary mission—safe and efficient operation of the process.

The community of users who must interact with the process and the control system is a diverse group. Shift operators, instrument technicians, various types of engineers, supervisors, and managers all view the system as a tool to facilitate their respective job functions. These include the safe day-to-day functioning of the plant equipment, productivity optimization, process fault diagnosis, preventive maintenance, production accounting, and management reporting.

Sheridan (1980), in discussing the human supervisory controller, identified four task headings associated with computerized control systems: (a) planning (b) programming the computer-automated system (c) monitoring the computer system's action including routine operation and abnormality checks and (d) intervening in normal operation when it is necessary to control manually for shutdown, or maintenance. He expanded this categorization into fifteen different human operator tasks (Table 6-1) and noted that the the tasks presuppose three separate computer activities: (a) an off-line computer model used for planning, not necessarily synchronized to the actual plant (b) an on-line computer model, synchronized to the plant and used primarily to aid the operator in thinking through incremental control actions and (c) computerized automation of the plant itself, for performance subordinate control functions, generation of displays, and recording data.

Extensive use of color has been applied to Tasks 9, 12, 13, and 14, in both noncomputerized and computer-based systems. While the color utilization potential is high for Tasks 2 and 7, the practice is currently limited and not often seen in actual control centers. Subsequent sections of this chapter review these applications in further detail.

The Tasks of the Human Supervisory Controller

Per T.B. Sheridan, from Man-Machine Interfaces for Industrial Control,
(Proceedings of the 6th Annual Advanced Control Conference),
published by Control Engineering, Barrington, IL, April 1980.
With permission

1. Models plant characteristics desired (but constrained by physical and economic reality) in his head.

2. Programs the plant characteristics in a computer model and runs tests.

3. Develops procedures and plant control programs interactively with other persons.

   — Planning off-line

4. Commits agreed-upon procedures to his own (and other operators') memory.

5. Programs the actual plant basec on procedures and design.

   — Teaching or programming off-line

6. Exercises plant model in his head (and other operators) to plan actual short-term future control of plant.

7. Exercises plant model in on-line computer to plan short-term future control of plant.

   — Planning on-line — Monitoring

Table 6-1   The tasks of the human supervisory controller. Per T. B. Sheridan, from Man-Machine Interfaces for Industrial Control (proceedings of the 6th Annual Advanced Control Conference), published by Control Engineering, Barrington, IL, April 1980. With permission.

Table 6-1   continued

8. Operates plant: controls and observes
    displays (including plant start-up if
    necessary.

9. Modifies plant model in his head to agree with
    experience.

10. Modifies plant model in computer to agree with
    experience.

11. Uses Steps (9) and (10) to identify behavior
    changes in the plant from that desired or
    expected.

12. Modifies plant parameters on line if
    appropriate.

Teaching or programming on-line   Monitoring

13. Intervenes in automatic control if necessary
    and does manual control.

14. Intervenes in normal operation to do
    maintenance or repair (including plant
    shutdown if necessary)

15. Does other tasks (rests, manages, tends to
    personal tasks, goes home)

Intervening

Machine (Control System)

The machine (control) subsystem links the operator to the process (see Figure 6-1). While it is beyond the scope of this chapter to discuss all the technologies employed, some of the major functions and common practices that typically use color are presented. The following sections are based on the three major functions of the control subsystem:

1. To provide a reliable and accurate machine-process interface.
2. To provide secure automatic process control, surveillance, and manual override capability.
3. To provide interaction capability and observation "windows" for plant personnel at the human-machine interface.

Process-Machine Interface.   Key elements of this interface include measurement transducers (inputs) and valve positioners (outputs) as well as electrical switchgear. The transducers convert physical process conditions like temperature, pressure, fluid flow rates, levels, pH, and component concentrations to electrical signals compatible with the data acquisition components of the system. Similarly, discrete electrical signals representing the status of motors (run/stop) and binary valves (open/closed) are sampled and made available as state information to the control system.

Output signals resulting from the execution of automatic control algorithms or manually inserted commands must also be accommodated by this interface. These signals in analog or digital format, are transformed into control valve positions, angular shaft positions, light intensity, etc. to affect process conditions such as flow rates, temperatures, speeds, and reaction rates. Manipulation of binary devices; for example, motors (run/stop) and valves (open/closed) must also be accommodated at this interface.

Control and Surveillance.   For safe, efficient control of many process variables, closed-loop control systems continuously monitor the value of a particular parameter and initiate action as necessary to maintain its desired value, relieving the operator of the burden.

Figure 6-2 represents a simple block diagram of a negative feedback control loop. The symbols representing the variables and loop components are defined as follows:

r = reference value or set point
b = feedback value
c = controlled variable
m = manipulated variable
u = load variable
e = error or actuating signal
$S1$ = remote/local switch
$S2$ = automatic/manual switch

The controller compares the reference value or set point (r) with the feedback value (b), which is a representative measurement of the controlled varialble (c). Any difference, the actuating signal (e), is used to develop an output (m), which maintains the controlled variable at the reference value. Assuming no set point changes by the operator, differences (e) usually result from load change disturbances (u) within the process.

Analog systems, both mechanical and electrical, and sampled digital systems have been used successfully to synthesize both simple loops and more complex control strategies, such as nonlinear, feedforward, and cascade. Computer-based systems employ

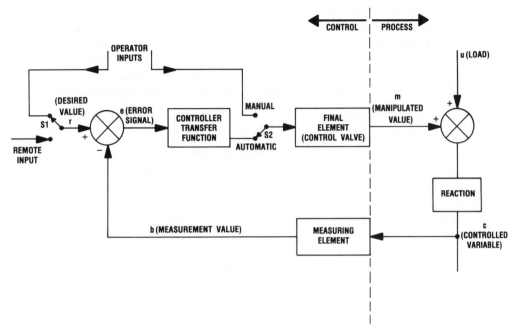

Figure 6-2   Closed loop negative feedback system.

a "shared control" technique—different control transfer functions are implemented as subroutines and used by more than one loop. Individual loops are uniquely characterized at execution time based on stored data base parameters.

Other features of control are worth noting since color is frequently used to represent various operational modes and parameter conditions. For example, an *automatic* or *manual* switch S2 would enable either of these two modes of operation with the decision in direct control of the operator in manual. Another switch (S1) would make possible the selection of the set point source. In *local*, the operator manipulates the set point; in *remote*, the set point could be a computer-calculated value or the output of another loop.

Another type of control capability is batch process automation. Controllers employed in batch process automation are characterized by a multitude, sometimes thousands, of binary devices, such as valves, pumps, and motors, that must be operated as functions of time and logic analyses based on plant conditions and recipe data. While dedicated relays or electronic elements are often used for simple interlocking schemes, distributed programmable controllers (PCs) and computer-equipped systems are necessary for more complex operations. The computers make possible on-line production scheduling, product changeovers, and yield accounting in addition to performing real-time control.

An automatic control technique often employed is initiation of a predefined sequence of equipment manipulations called steps. Before each step is performed, the anticipated effects of all previous steps are confirmed. Any inconsistency detected by the system will automatically initiate suspension or shutdown logic, the choice being a function of predefined decision rules.

In addition to performing different types of automatic control, process control systems maintain surveillance of both process and control system operating parameters. High frequency scanning and analysis of process conditions allow the detection and notification of abnormally high or low absolute values, excessive rates of change, improperly positioned valves, and other process aberrations. Self-checking of the control system extends this monitoring to the detection of any communications, data storage, computational, or similar control system malfunction. This monitoring capability relieves the operations staff of the burden of routinely evaluating an unwieldy quantity of items on a high frequency basis, that is, hundreds of items per second. Audio and visual cues alert the operations staff to any detected abnormality.

Human-Machine Interface.   Characteristics of interest at the human-machine interface can be classified as either functional or ergonomic. This interface must provide an adequate translation function while embracing the known human factors guidelines. As a translator, the system must accurately and efficiently present real time and historical data to the operations staff and also accept data and commands for the control and process subsystems. Design characteristics that can result in psychological stress (perplexing operator error messages, inconsistent cueing, poor response time, etc.) and physiological stress (eye and posture fatigue, environmental extremes like temperature and vibration) must be avoided.

The human-machine interface has evolved along with advances in measurement, control, and computer application technologies. Yesterday's assemblage of meters, controllers, trend recorders, alarm annunciators, pushbuttons, pilot lights, switches, etc., mounted in large panels or wall boards is today emulated by computer driven consoles equipped with visual display units (CRTs and flat panel devices) and associated keyboards, light pens, and touch screens. The combination of visual display units and input devices is called the *visual display terminal* or VDT.

VDTs, like their panel-mounted instruments predecessors, contain five major elements:

1. A real-time display capability of process and control parameters including state information.
2. A historical record containing first and second derivative, accumulative, and sequence of events information.
3. Input devices for making manipulative changes in the process.
4. A schematic representation of process equipment, fluid and energy pathways, and control process connections.
5. An alarm annunciator system.

Color has been extensively used in providing these five elements. Subsequent sections review specific color applications in greater detail.

Process.   The list of industries included in the process control arena represents a diverse range of chemical- and energy-related technologies. Blending, reaction, separation, energy conversion, classification, and distribution are the basis of most industrial processes. It is common to classify these operations as either *continuous* or *discontinuous* processes. This differentiation assists in recognizing potential applications of color in the human-process interface. The words "continuous" and "discontinuous" are also used to distinguish different types of control based on feedback action. Continuous control relates to systems where the feedback signal is continuously being compared with the set point signal. Discontinuous control includes situations where the signals are periodically sampled or where signals must reach a particular value before control is initiated—on/off feedback control systems.

Continuous processes. This classification would imply that, after completion of the start-up phase, the process equipment configuration remains constant relative to energy sources/sinks and material-flow pathways. While the configuration remains constant, the quantitative values associated with the process can change significantly to match product demands, product specification changes, feedstock characteristics, and so on. Examples of continuous process units are distillation towers, boilers, evaporators, and dryers. The physical state, purity, and flow rate of the process components are the controlled variables whose target values are varied by the operator and the control system. It is not unusual for continuous processes to operate for months, sometimes years, between start-up and shutdown.

Discontinuous processes. Processes in this category routinely undergo significant configuration changes as a result of either manual manipulation or automatic control based on Boolean logic, time, programmable procedures, and recipe values. Material and energy pathways are altered as valves and circuit breakers assume either open or closed states. This pathway manipulation enables the addition of ingredients in pre-defined amounts, the checking of interlocks associated with starting and stopping rotating equipment, product analysis, and the regeneration or cleanup of equipment at the con-clusion of a process cycle. These are representative examples of how discontinuous control is applied to batch reactions, blending, catalyst regeneration, fermentation, and power distribution operations. Color is of value to these operations due to the recurring opportunities to display state information.

The majority of process plants contain elements of both continuous and discontinuous processes; for example, filters are routinely cycled out of a continuous fluid stream for regeneration, typically a discontinuous operation. Although some would claim that all processes are discontinuous since they must undergo a transient start-up, shutdown, and occasional product grade change, it is customary to distinguish between these two types of process operations.

Color Applications

Color has been an integral part of the process industry. Its application has been universal, encompassing process, product, operations, and control systems. The ability of color to facilitate identification, search, and qualification tasks has encouraged its use in both noncontrol and control situations. The uses are interrelated, however, since many con-trol-based color associations are derived from noncontrol meanings.

Noncontrol

Color is customarily used to classify or identify products, assist in preventive main-tenance, and improve operational safety, yet few formally recognized standards exist to govern its the use for these applications. Different manufacturers in the same industry often assign contradictory meanings to the same color. Accordingly, it behooves the display designer to search out any applicable standard or customary practice and in-corporate it where feasible in the human-process interface design.

Identification. It is common practice to either color certain products directly with spe-cial dyes or imply the identity by using color-coded containers. This technique minimizes the need for costly analytical apparatus and instrumentation in the storage, distribution, and consumption of the final product. An example of coded products is aviation gasoline. Blue, yellow, and red dyes are used to identify various grades of gasoline that differ in antiknock quality and lead content (ASTM, 1981). Colorless industrial gases such as oxygen, nitrogen, and argon, are stored in color-coded containers (Airco Industrial Gases, 1982; Woodson, 1981). The color code is used along with an attached label to provide redundant identification. Other applicable identification guidelines are identified by the American National Standards Institute (ANSI, 1981) and in military specifications (MIL-STD-161; MIL-STD-172) for process piping and containers. The ANSI standard for the identification of piping systems uses color to indicate contents based on material classifications of inherently hazardous (flammable, toxic, extreme temperature or pressure), low hazard, or fire quenching.

Preventive Maintenance.   Color is a fundamental coding tool for preventive maintenance of process equipment. Various wallboard scheduling schemes rely on color to indicate frequency, priority, and due dates for equipment lubrication, regeneration, special testing (e.g., spectral vibration analysis), and complete overhauls. Particular lubricants are identified by the color of their respective containers. Maintenance technicians merely use red grease guns on red grease fittings, blue on blue, etc. Parts are identified by color to denote function and interchangeability.

Safety.   Color plays a significant role in improving the overall safety in process plants. Signs used in transportation, material handling, and process areas all contribute meaning by their respective shapes, symbols, and colors. Certain components of processing equipment are painted to comply with the *Safety Color Code for Marking Physical Hazards* (ANSI, 1979). This particular code specifies using red to denote danger and stop, orange to identify dangerous parts of machinery, yellow as a cautionary indicator, green to signify safety, and blue to denote non-safety related messages and equipment under repair. Combinations are also given specific meanings; for example, black (formerly purple) on yellow for radiation and black on white for traffic markings. Since the process interfaces often provide a means to monitor and initiate safety-related procedures, the associated displays ought to comply with accepted coding standards. The 1979 ANSI standard contains the fundamental specifications for safety color codes in Munsell and equivalent CIE notations.

Control

Previous sections have reviewed the process industry control systems and the operating tasks performed by plant personnel. It has also been noted that the process industries have become accustomed to using color in various ways. This and subsequent sections explore how color has been specifically applied to the control system with emphasis on the human-machine interface. As an information coding tool, color is most often used to:

1. Provide identifications,
2. Indicate pathway relationships,
3. Relate state and priority,
4. Denote quality.

Identification.   One of the most common identification roles for color has been associated with the recording and presentation of trend data. Recorders capable of multiple traces have often used color to distinguish one trace from another. For observing current values, recorder pen arms are similarly equipped with corresponding colored pointers and scales for parameter identification and value correlation. Computer-based VDT systems have incorporated similar schemes with certain presentation enhancements. The computer-generated displays can present colored areas representing differences, sums, and preferred operating zones. Variable time bases and scales can be operator–selected and distinguished by use of color.

A schematic representation of the process as applied to a paper drawing is referred to as a Process and Instrumentation Diagram (P&ID). Selected portions of such diagrams, called process graphics, have often been incorporated into the HPI design. The graphic panel shown in Figure 6-3 (see color insert) is a typical example of non-computer-based interface. Various process elements such as process fluids, processing equipment, and control interfaces are distinguished by color. Also, like product identification schemes, process components such as steam, cooling water, and intermediate products are identified by colors. Computer-based systems representing an evolution in interface design provide similar capabilities.

For situations where it is customary practice to provide special backup or emergency equipment, such as injection pumps for reactors or fire protection equipment, color has been used to uniquely delineate associated controls, labels, panel segments, and displays. Color also identifies physical parameters like flows, pressures, temperatures, etc.

Pathway Relationships.   Examples of discontinuous processes such as batch, blending, and distribution were cited in previous sections. They were partially characterized by the multiple pathways that were possible for material and energy flow. Colored pilot lamps have frequently been used to indicate valve position (open/closed) and, thus, indirectly to indicate the active flow path. Symbols representing conveyors, power transmission lines, pumps, compressors, etc., have been colored with various techniques to indicate their active/inactive state and thus relate material and energy flow. Computer-generated displays are particularly useful in these situations since they can adapt and modify the display according to the actual process conditions. A unique, active pathway might suggest a correspondingly unique grouping of process measurements (i.e., temperatures, flow rates, etc.) and also establish associations such as what indicator is active with a particular flow path. The objectives are to minimize search time, recognition time, and opportunities for operator selection errors.

State and Priority.   All elements of the human-process system can assume different states—active, inactive, standby, manual, automatic, and alarm, to name a few. "Alarm" is an application category that often uses color as a redundant indicator. Switch position, brightness, flashing, and alphanumeric label changes are typical redundant visual codes. Horns, sirens, and synthesized speech are audible cues associated with changes of state and are the means by which the process paces the operator.

Since the uniquely definable state conditions are numerous in process control systems, it is easy to create situations where a limited choice of colors has too many associated meanings, or too many colors exceed the channel capacity of the operator. This is particularly true during process transients (upsets), which are usually accompanied by the rapid presentation of large amounts of visual information. While color has demonstrated its superiority to other forms of coding in minimizing search time and improving identification performance (Banks & Clark, 1981), it has also been shown that the effectiveness of color as a partially redundant coding variable deteriorates with the increase in the proportion of nontargets of the same color. The advantage became a disadvantage when the proportion exceeded about 0.70 (Banks & Clark, 1981).

In situations where the operator paces the process, such as changing set points, outputs, control strategies, etc., the current status or state of the control scheme must first be observed and recognized. Color is again used as a redundant indicator to facilitate operator actions. As an example, yellow could indicate those parameters adjustable by the operator. Then, if a loop were in automatic, the set point would be displayed in yellow, and a loop in manual would have its output shown in yellow. The ability of the loop display to modify attributes such as color as a function of state is an attractive feature of computer-generated process interfaces.

Quality.   The operations personnel should have a readily available means to ascertain the qualitative "degree of goodness" associated with the current operation of the process. What are the acceptable excursions from the design or operational targets? At what point is the excursion considered abnormal and potentially dangerous to the security of the process? Since the interface often consists of hundreds of analog variables and discrete states, relying exclusively on memory and cognitive skills would place an unreasonable burden on the operating staff. Here again, color has played a significant role in simplifying the process interface. The expression "red line" has migrated from the world of sports cars to refer to any situation where actual conditions exceed recommended maximum or minimum values. Individual instrument displays often utilize colored dials to indicate normal regions in green, cautionary regions in yellow, and danger zones in red. Similarly, computer-generated line charts, referred to as trend displays, often employ color coded zones to highlight past abnormal operations.

Earlier sections discussed the automatic controller and its role in generating output signals to manipulate process equipment (e.g., valves) to achieve the desired value. At times, the force of the load disturbance exerted on the process may exceed the ability of the loop to maintain an ideal match of these two parameters. The resulting difference, called deviation, is a key qualitative indicator to the operator. It is customary practice to create displays with graphical elements, such as bar combinations or bar and pointer combinations, to show the relative magnitudes of the set point, measurement, and corresponding deviation. That portion of the measurement bar that extends above (high deviation) or below (low deviation) the set point indicator can be colored to qualitatively signal normal, abnormal, and dangerous situations. This is especially helpful when the operator must quickly scan and evaluate many parameters during process emergencies.

Computer-based systems often incorporate calculations and logical operations that at times may operate on input data of questionable value. For example, the output signal from a composition analyzer may periodically be replaced with a manually inserted value while the analyzer undergoes routine maintenance and calibration. The fidelity of the system is now compromised by the artificial value, and decisions and control actions based on such values could be inappropriate. Another example of compromised data is values related to functions that are off scan, in alarm, disabled, or clamped. Values such as these, referred to as *dubious values*, can be referenced by many other calculations, control strategies, displays, logs, etc. Often these levels of cascading are complex, and any attempt to display all functions including the sources of dubious values would exceed recommended guidelines concerning display density. Also, illogical groupings might result. For these situations, specific quality tags are propagated to downstream functions and are reference for control and display purposes. Color codes alert the operator to any questionable or dubious upstream conditions.

Process Computer Color Graphics

The application of color graphics in the process industries has become widespread, encompassing all industries and enhancing the presentation of process management, control, engineering, and maintenance information. The acceptance and dependence on color graphics reflect its inherent advantages over other interface techniques. This section explores some particular applications and advantages in further detail.

Emulation

Before any attempt is made to surpass an established system, the fundamental functions and strengths of the existing system must be represented in the "improved" design. Contemporary color graphics represent a culmination of evolutionary developments that began with conventional instrument panels. Initially, monochromatic or achromatic VDTs were used to supplement conventional panels. Despite the handicap of being unable to exploit well-established color coding techniques, such hybrid systems contributed to improved plant performance by using the computer for more sophisticated control, recovery analysis, and production reporting. The lack of color was compensated for in three ways: modifying line quality (dotted, dashed, solid, etc.), changing symbol shapes, and applying alphanumeric labels to various process and control conditions.

The introduction of cost-effective color VDTs enabled the completion of the evolutionary emulation cycle. The interface could now utilize color in ways similar to conventional instrumentation. Scales and graduations could be colored to indicate preferred operating regions. Individual trends could be identified in multiple plot presentations. Abnormal conditions, such as alarms, could be highlighted along with identification of "first cause" and sequence of events. The presentation of start/stop controls for motors could be more natural—matching in form and function the devices that had long ago become industrial pseudostandards. With the emulation completed, the operator could, with an equal degree of success, monitor, appraise, and manipulate the process. Moreover, the computer-generated displays introduced new capabilities that enabled the interface to surpass the performance benchmarks established by conventional displays and facilitate safer, more efficient process operations.

Process Unit Displays

A combined presentation of state, qualitative, quantitative, and pathway information is called a *process unit display*. These displays incorporate emulations of panel instruments such as controllers, meters, switches, etc., along with graphic symbols and constructs representative of process vessels, pumps, valves, etc. Unlike the graphic displays mentioned earlier, the computer-generated displays allow dynamic manipulation of the graphics as a function of process conditions. Also, the pictorial correlation of parameters to process eliminates the need for identification labels and descriptors. Results are a more efficient display, less operator reading, and a clean, uncluttered appearance. The following example based on Figure 6-4 (see color insert) demonstrates the usefulness of color graphics and the superior capability of computer-based systems.

Example.   The primary objective of the standby vaporizer system shown in Figure 6-4 is to maintain a minimum pressure in the gas holder shown in the upper-right corner. The primary source of gas for the holder is another process unit, which is subject to unplanned production interruptions. The vaporizer system represents a backup source that can temporarily satisfy the demand by converting an inventory of liquified gas to the gaseous state. Key components of the system are the liquid and gas storage tanks, steam heat exchanger (vaporizer), pumps with block valves, flow control valves, and associated piping. During periods of high gas demand, both pumps may be required to maintain sufficient liquid flow.

The process unit display represented by Figure 6-4 includes not only a mimic of the process, but also a portion of the control and human-process interface subsystems. The control and HPI systems are indicated by yellow dashed and solid lines. Facsimiles of flow controllers, signal lines, and valve actuators are shown. Simulated pushbuttons for starting and stopping the pumps are included within the boundary of the controller emulations. Alphanumeric and graphic techniques are employed in the controller facsimile. Two cyan bars graphically represent the magnitude of the desired flow rate along with the numerical value. The white bar between the cyan ones similarly represents the current flow measurement shown numerically above the set point. The wide, white bar represents the controller output scaled 0–100%.

A review of Figure 6-4 reveals additional information that demonstrates the capabilities of color in graphic displays. Based on block valve colors, the controller B display, and the subdued presentation of pump B and its associated piping, the operator can determine that only pump A is running. The two levels of redundancy are included: One is an alarm indicator (not shown) that would alert the operator if the pump were not in the desired state implied by the "start" control choice; the other is the absence of controller parameter displays. The resulting display is relatively uncluttered and places emphasis on the equipment in service.

This example demonstrates how an ergonomically recognized shortcoming can be an asset in certain situations. Dark blue symbols and lines are particularly difficult to perceive against a black background (poor contrast ratio). Although they are legible, the operator must make an extra effort to interpret them. The blue-black combination used here produced a more efficient and helpful display by reducing the opportunities for operator distraction and potential manipulative errors.

Process Management Displays

Another category of display types made available with computer-driven VDTs is the *management display*. Here the interest focuses not only on the regulatory control parameters, but also on operating plans, economics, decision-making aids, and process diagnostic tools. These displays are characterized by their ability to depict, in both overview and detail, cause and effect relationships. Real-time values, manually entered production targets, energy costs, and product values plus on-line historical data form the basis for such presentations. The resulting displays facilitate comprehension and evaluation of current and historical operations, plus predictive "what if" scenarios.

Strategic overview displays ought to provide quick answers to questions such as: How well is the unit running? If operation is less than ideal, how severe is the excursion? What effect is this action having on other parameters? What corrective action should be taken first? What is the anticipated effect of a proposed action? Although not inclusive, this list of questions is representative of the concerns that overview displays help address. Pattern recognition aided by appropriate color coding has been the basis for providing symbolic answers to questions such as these.

Danchak (1981), in his work on multivariate displays, provides a detailed discussion on the relative applicability of numerous schemes with emphasis on nine of the most promising overview presentation techniques. One such display, called a "fourfold circular display", uses individual segments to represent five interactive parameters (Figure 6-5). The parameters shown include real-time process variables as well as calculated economic values such as product recovery percentages and energy consumption efficiencies. Each parameter is represented by a 72 degree arc whose radius is scaled to match the value. Ranges are chosen and values normalized to provide an approximate geometric circle when operating at ideal conditions. Excursions are readily recognized by the modified shape and use of color to identify normal, abnormal, and emergency zones within each segment.

Display types commonly used in scientific, medical, and business systems can also be found in process management applications. Color represents a key attribute of these displays either as a quantitative indicator or as an identification aid. The following are some examples:

1. Imaging—pointillistic displays that utilize color to denote quantitative values in the presentation of temperature, density, concentration, and other physical profiles.
2. Surfaces—three-dimension functional plots that assist in understanding the results of linear and nonlinear programming techniques.
3. Charts—pie and bar charts that help convey multivariable relationships regarding energy and raw material consumption, recovery efficiencies, and product distribution ratios.
4. Reports—alphanumeric and graphical techniques suitable for both VDT and hard copy presentation that convey totalized, averaged, maximum and minimum values, and operational state summaries.

Adaptability

Previous sections have cited particular applications and features of computer-driven color graphics. The VDT consoles are capable not only of panel emulation but also of interactive unit and process management displays. These two classes of displays profit from the computer's ability to adapt to dynamic processes. Unlike conventional panels

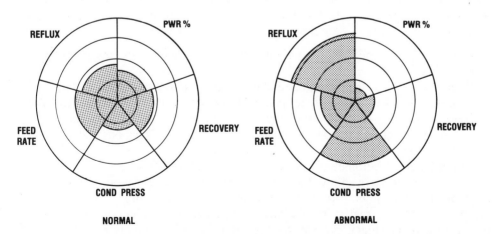

Figure 6-5   Fourfold circular overview display (adopted from Danchak). Reprinted by permission. Copyright © Instrument Society of America 1976. From Instrumentation Technology—October 1976.

and monochromatic displays, the color-based system can present information coded to reflect the current configuration and condition of the process. As an example, an alarming scheme, with computer-assigned priority levels and displays that have modifications based on plant operating status, can help the operator during a major plant upset. The computer's ability to monitor and perform combinatorial and computational analyses can also be applied to predictive alarming. Computer adaptability and color VDT versatility allow situation-dependent displays to facilitate process-operator communication—the idealized human-process interface.

Application Guidelines

Chromatic display technolgy enables the display designer to incorporate aesthetics, realism, and information through coding in the human-process interface. The degree of success depends on its prudent application. Which elements of a display should be colored, color choices, element-color relationships, and color for "looks" or color for "information" are the fundamental issues confronting the designer. Confounding the designer are the contradictory common practices, standards, and recommendations supported by regulatory, military, societal, and industrial organizations, plus cognitive psychologists and physiologists. The designer's freedom is also constrained by equipment capability and project budget. At the risk of adding yet another layer of confusion, this section presents some guidelines and suggestions rather than rules for the application of color.

Display Elements

Earlier portions of this chapter identified different types of displays commonly used for process control and process management, such ascontroller emulations, process graphics (P&ID mimics), trends, and pie and bar charts. Since a particular installation might contain all of these and more, a well-conceived plan must be developed to minimize contradictory meanings and maximize the effectiveness of color as a carrier of information.

The "system color plan" should serve as a guide to the application team for consistent assignment of color to different classes of display elements. Although not inclusive, the following list of classes with associated examples demonstrates the far-ranging scope of display elements that are potential candidates for color coding.

1. Process mimics—equipment symbols, fluid paths (piping), energy paths (piping or wiring).
2. Equipment states—run/stop, open/closed, active/standby, on/off.
3. Process states—fill phase, react phase, drain phase, fluid flowing/not flowing.
4. Process security—critical alarms, warnings, preferred operating regions.
5. Control parameters—set points/targets, measurements, deviations, rates, desired versus actual states.
6. Control states—automatic/manual, on/off control, on/off scan.
7. Physical parameters—flow, temperature, pressure, composition.
8. Economic parameters—recovery, efficiency, cost, inventory.
9. Qualitative tags—real/artificial value, clamped/dubious value, out of range.
10. Identification—steam, coolant, feed, product, 13.8 kilovolts bus.

With so many opportunities available, it is obvious that careful planning is required to avoid diluting the effectiveness of color. Common practice segregates and limits just a few classes to any one particular display type; for example, system status reflecting active communication channels would not be combined in a display with the status of valves, pumps, etc. on the same display.

Colors

Color VDTs employ additive color mixing based on the three additive primaries: red, green, and blue. Simplistic binary control of the three CRT guns enables the display of the primaries, second-order combinations, white, and black. Recent advances in the price/performance ratios of monitors and display controllers have enabled the application of devices that can mix percentages of each primary, resulting in up to 4096 unique choices. Since we intend to use color as an information carrier, the choices for use must be perceptible, distinguishable, and few in number.

A straightforward guideline for the display designer to follow in selecting colors within the visible spectrum is to choose colors that are widely spaced in wavelength. This will facilitate accurate color identification and thus comprehension of the implied coded message. Ten colors that can be identified correctly nearly 100% of the time under good viewing conditions are listed in Table 6-2 (Krebs, Wolf, & Sandvig, 1978).

Synder (1980) and Banks and Clark (1981), whose works represent extensive literature searches on the utilization of color, are in agreement regarding the lack of quantitative

Ten Recommended Colors That Can Be Identified Correctly Nearly

100% of the Time, from Baker and Grether (1954)

as presented by Krebs et al

Dominant Wavelength (nm)	Color Name
430	Violet
476	Blue
494	Greenish-Blue
504	Bluish-Green
515	Green
556	Yellow-Green
582	Yellow
596	Orange
610	Orange-Red
642	Red

Table 6-2 Ten recommended colors. From Baker and Grether (1954) and presented by Krebs et al. (1978).

data that might predict the effects of variable combinations of chromaticity, lumination, chromatic contrasts, and ambient illuminance on the legibility of chromatic displays. Snyder referenced the contributions of Meister and Sullivan (1969) and Rizy (1967), who evaluated the effects of color on reading accuracy. Their results, shown in Table 6-3, indicate good agreement. However, Snyder states:

> Such studies use (1) a stimulus described by either a dominant wavelength or a subjective color label, (2) no measurement of saturation or purity of the stimulus, and (3) a black or achromatic background. That is, there is no quantitative radiometric specification of the stimulus and, most importantly, there are no *quantitative* data known to relate performance to the intrinsic chromatic contrast between one chromatic stimulus and its (different) chromatic background. Where the potential for such data has existed, (e.g., Mclean, 1965), the only "contrast" measure made for various color stimuli was that of luminance contrast. Thus, it is not possible to describe the chromatic contrast in such experiments in any conventional color space system.

Although "quantitative gaps" currently exist regarding the interactive effects of varying color attributes, the significant singular research contributions along with qualitative experience have enabled a pragmatic approach to the application of color in process cóntrol displays. High contrast color combinations are chosen to facilitate search and recognition of alarms and measurements while avoiding those known trouble spots that can produce receptor fatigue. Low contrast situations that hinder legibility are typically avoided for presenting key display elements. The visibility of certain colors, such as blue and red displayed on black, is more dependent on the area of the stimulus than many other colors. Other color selection guidelines for process control applications are worth noting:

Relative Ranking of Different Colors in Alphanumeric Recognition Studies

(lowest ranking indicates best performance)

from Snyder

Color	Meister and Sullivan (1969)	Rizy (1967)
Red	2	1
Yellow	1	2
Magenta	4	3
White	3	4
Cyan	5	5
Blue	7	6
Green	6	7

Table 6-3 Relative ranking of different colors in alphanumeric recognition studies. Snyder, H. L., Human Visual Performance and Flat Panel Display Image Quality, *Technical Report (HFL-80-1/ONR-80-1), Blacksburg: Virginia Polytechnic Institute and State University, July, 1980. This research was sponsored by the Office of Naval Research.*

1. Black is best for backgrounds. Dynamic data displayed in colors that contrast well with black facilitate search and recognition activities. This recommendation may conflict with guidelines associated with many VDT applications such as word processing, EDP, and other situations where 80% of the operators work with hard copy (Cakir, Hart, & Stewart, 1980). Here the luminance ratio should be less than 1:5 between the paper and display.
2. Recommended color combinations include: black on yellow, yellow on black, green on white, orange on black, red on white, cyan on black, blue on white, and white on black.
3. Situations to avoid include: yellow on white, yellow on green, small blue symbols and alphanumerics, pure colors, and colored backgrounds.
4. Where equipment features provide the capability to display third-order color choices, earth tones are suggested for large symbol fills. They provide a more natural image and help provide cold-warm contrast and harmony to the display. Typically lower in luminosity and purity, they will not compete for the operators attention with information in first- and second-order colors.

Quantity

In conjunction with the understanding of which colors used singularly and in combinations are most useful, the designer must consider how many information-bearing colors to use in a given display. Krebs et al. (1978) suggest selecting a maximum of five, and Woodson (1981) lists four coding steps for color. Conover and Kraft (1958) (found in McCormick, 1976) present: "four sets of colors for coding purposes when absolute recognition is required (barring the use of color-blind people). These sets include, respectively, eight, seven, six, and five colors." It is important to recognize that the useful number of colors for coding is substantially fewer than the fifty Munsell colors of varying saturation and brightness identifiable by some highly trained observers (1958) and far fewer than the hundreds displayable on current state-of-the-art devices.

Element-Color Relationship

A sound plan for color association is a key component of the interface design. It provides the fundamental guidelines for classifying with color codes: process, control, and system conditions. For a particular installation it might have to accommodate a wide range of display types, such as instrument emulations, process flow diagrams, and overview displays, and trend them with varying amounts and types of dynamic and static information. The designer should provide adequate time to establish a "project standard" to govern the use of color. While no universally recognized standards exist, numerous pseudostandards have been developed by the user and equipment vendor communities. As a consequence, many contradictions regarding the meaning of particular colors prevail. One industry will use red to indicate "off" or "closed," while another will associate "on" or "open" with red. Both would seemingly conflict with common meanings such as "emergency," "fire," or "out of limits." Long-standing contradictory meanings such as these, along with the numerous opportunities to use color, the limited number of endorsed color combinations, and equipment capabilities, reinforce the need to develop a "project-approved" color application plan. To do otherwise will potentially dilute the effectiveness of color coding in facilitating search and recognition tasks, and diminish a color's ability to convey information.

The Munsell notations for Conover and Kraft's (1958) four color sets follow:

8-color: *1R; 9R; 1Y; 7GY; 9G; 5B; 1P; 3RP*
7-color: *5R; 3YR; 5Y; 1G; 7BG; 7PB; 3RP*
6-color: *1R; 3YR; 9Y; 5G; 5B; 9P*
5-color: *1R; 7YR; 7GY; 1B; 5P*

The results of Smith's investigation of redundant codes (in McCormick, 1976) clearly demonstrate the usefulness of color in improving search and counting tasks when used as a multidimensional stimulus. These tasks dominate situations where the process paces the operator (e.g., alarming, prompting, and sequential events displays). Danchak (1976), in discussing the work of Hitt (1961) regarding abstract coding techniques, reinforces the use of color as a redundant code. Figure 6-6 from Danchak's work relates different coding techniques to operator tasks and identifies where color and blink are most suitably applied. A "check" subtask defines a state or status (on/off, run/stop) while a "read" subtask refers to a variable magnitude such as pressure, temperature, etc. Using color in a redundant fashion lessens the concern regarding the use of color VDTs by individuals with impaired color vision.

For the process-related mimic diagrams, redundancy with shapes is easily achieved. Symbols are typically used to represent pumps, valves, mixers, and other process equipment. A run/stop state can be indicated by using symbols in either outline or solid form. An open valve would be solid (full of fluid) while a closed valve would appear in outline form. Color changes (e.g., red/green) would correspond to position as well as alarms (flashing yellow) when the valve is not in the desired state. Using shape, configuration, and color codings results in a less busy display than one with alphanumeric status labels.

In developing a color association plan, it is suggested that the designer first establish a set of generic meanings for each of the color candidates. By limiting the number of colors, one can effectively aid operators in interpreting the specific meaning. An example of such a generic definition set follows:

		NUMERICS	TEXT	SHAPES	COLOR	BLINK
SEARCH				✓	*	*
IDENTIFY			✓	✓	*	
COMPARE	CHECK		✓	✓	*	
	READ	✓		✓		
VERIFY	CHECK		✓	✓	*	
	READ	✓		✓		
COUNT	CHECK		✓	✓	*	
	READ	✓				

✓ ACCEPTABLE   * REDUNDANT

Figure 6-6   Recommended coding schemes (Per Danchak, with permission © Instrument Society of America 1976, From Instrumentation Technology).

Color	Generic Meaning
White	Dynamic data
Cyan	Static but significant
Blue	Static but of secondary importance
Green	Normal or preferred
Red	Emergency
Yellow	Abnormal, initial alert
Magenta	Secondary dynamic indicator
Orange	Operator entry fields

These assignments are somewhat similar to the pilot lamp color codes recommended for military systems. This coding scheme uses five colors having the following meanings:

Color	Generic Meaning
Red	Inoperative subsystem, error, failure
Red (flashing)	Emergency condition
Yellow	Advisory, cautionary
Green	In Tolerance, ready, function activated
White	Transitory conditions
Blue	Advisory but perferentially avoided

Using the generic definitions as a guide, the specific elements of particular display types can then be coded. The designer will undoubtedly be forced to make some arbitrary decisions regarding what is dynamic versus static, major versus minor headings, etc. Consistency in judgment and willingness to modify the plan are critical as unforeseen conflicts are encountered during the subsequent display design and commissioning phases.

Table 6-4 represents a typical display-element color relationship plan. Although not inclusive of all possible elements found on a typical system, it is representative of the different categories of elements. Elements associated with continuous and batch control, instrumentation emulations, and system configuration status are included. For applications where certain colors have unique meanings, such as reddish purple for radiation hazards, equipment capable of more than six colors should be considered. Magenta would accordingly be reserved for alarms and related radioactivity associations while preserving the meanings of the other familiar colors listed in the plan.

Summary

Although color represents a significant coding technique, it complements many other attributes of a robust display design. Other coding techniques, display loading, and positioning of information are some of the important considerations the designer must accommodate. If a monochromatic display "works," it will surely be improved with well-used color. On the other hand, a poor monochromatic display is rarely salvaged by color.

Color coding in process control applications will be most effective when used:

1. For search and recognition tasks,

Element–Color Plan

Color	Elements
White	Dynamic Alphanumeric Values
	Measurements (Analog Representation)
	Modulating Control Valves
	System Messages (Process Related)
	Active Sequential Step (batch)
	No. 1 Trend Trace (Solid Line)
	No. 2 Trend Trace (Dashed Line)
Cyan	Process Vessels/Equipment (In Service)
	Process Piping (In Service)
	Set Point (Analog Representation)
	Major Labels
	Scales
	Engineering Units
	Future Sequential Steps (Batch)
Blue	Process Vessels/Equipment (Standby)
	Process Piping (Standby)
	Loop Tags
	Tuning Parameters
	Completed Sequential Steps (Batch)
	Minor Labels
	Controller Outlines (off scan/
	off control)
Green	Open Binary Value
	Running Motor
	Preferred Operating Region

Table 6-4   Element—color plan.

Process Control Using Color Displays   137

Table 6-4   continued

Red   Emergency Stop

                                     Closed Binary Valve

                                     Motor Not Running

Yellow   System Alert Messages

                                     Alarms

                                     Abnormal Condition or Operating Region

Magenta   No. 3 Trend Trace (Solid Line)

                                     No. 4 Trend Trace (Dashed Line)

Orange   Controller Outlines

                                     Instrumentation Connections

2. As a redundant code,
   • full redundancy for detection and identification
   • partial redundancy for quality tagging and grouping
3. Sparingly; i.e., avoiding limited functionality,
4. Consistently regarding implied meaning,
5. To simplify the operator interface,
6. Within the plant's established color-application practices and standards.

References

Airco Industrial Gases. *Industrial Gases Data Book*. (AIG-1077R), Murray Hill, N.J.: Airco Industrial Gases, 1982.

ANSI. *Safety Color Code for Marking Physical Hazards*. (ANSI Z53.1), New York: American National Standards Institute, 1979.

ANSI. *Scheme for the Identification of Piping Systems*. (ANSI A13.2), New York: American Society of Mechanical Engineers, 1981.

ASTM. *Standard Specification for Aviation Gasolines*. (ASTM D910-81), Philadelphia: American Society for Testing and Materials, 1981.

Banks, W. W., & Clark, M. T. *Some Human Engineering Color Considerations Using CRT Displays: A Review of the Literature*. EC&G Technical Report (SD-B-81-001), Idaho Falls, Idaho: EC&G,1981.

Baker, B. C., & Grether, W. F. *Visual Presentation of Information*. Technical Report (WADC-TR-54160), Wright Air Development Center, Ohio, 1954.

Cakir, A., Hart, D. J., & Stewart, T. F. M. *Visual Display Terminals*. Toronto: John Wiley, 1980.

Conover, D. W., & Kraft, C. L. *The Use of Color in Coding Displays*. (WADC-TR55-471), Wright Air Development Center, Ohio, 1958.

Danchak, M. M. CRT display for power plants. *Instrumentation Technology*. October, 1976, 29–36.

Danchak, M. M. *Techniques for Displaying Multivariate Data on CRTs with Applications to Nuclear Process Control*. (NUREG/CR-1994), Idaho National Laboratory, 1981.

Hanes, R. M., & Rhoades, M. V. Color identification as a function of extended practice. *Journal of the Optical Society of America*, 1959, *49*, 1060–1064.

Hitt, W. D. An evaluation of five different abstract coding methods - Experiment IV. *Human Factors*, 1961, *3*, 120–130.

Krebs, M. J., Wolf, J. D., & Sandvig, J. H. *Color Display Design Guide*. Honeywell Report (ONR-CR213-136-2F), Minneapolis, Minn.: Honeywell Systems & Research Center, 1978.

McCormick, E. J. *Human Factors in Engineering and Design*. New York: McGraw-Hill, 1976.

McLean, M. V. Brightness contrast, color contrast, and legibility. *Human Factors*, 1965, *7*, 521–526.

Malone, T. B., Kirkpatrick, M., Mallory, K., Eike, D., Johnson, J. H., & Walker, R. W. *Human Factors Evaluation of Control Room Design and Operator Performance at Three Mile Island-2*. (NTIS No. NUREG/CR-1270), Alexandria, Virg.: The Essex Corporation, 1980.

Meister, D., & Sullivan, D. J. *Guide to Human Engineering Design for Visual Displays*, ONR Report under Contract N0014-68-C-0278, 1969.

MIL-STD-161: *Identification of Bulk Petroleum Products and Missle Fuels*, 1985.

Mil-STD-172: *Color Code for Containers of Liquid Propellants*, 1982.

Rizy, F. F. *Dichroic Filter Specification for Color Additive Displays: II. Further Exploration of Tolerance Areas and the Influence of Other Display Variables*. (RADC-TR-67-513), USAF Rome Air Development Center, 1967.

Sheridan, T. B. Theory of man-machine interaction as related to computerized automation. In *Man-Machine Interfaces for Industrial Control, Proceedings of the 6th Annual Advanced Control Conference*, Barrington, Ill.: Technical Publishing Co., 1980.

Smith, S. L. *Display Color Coding for Visual Separability*. Mitre Report (MTS-10), Bedford, Mass.: Mitre Corp., 1963.

Snyder, H. L. *Human Visual Performance and Flat Panel Display Image Quality*. Technical Report (HFL-80-1/ONR-80-1), Blacksburg: Virginia Polytechnic Institute and State University, July 1980. This research was sponsored by the Office of Naval Research.

Woodson, W. E. *Human Factors Design Handbook*, New York: McGraw-Hill, 1981.

7

Color Graphic Displays for Network Planning and Design

MARIE E. WIGERT-JOHNSTON
AT&T Communications
Basking Ridge, New Jersey

Abstract

Color graphics and interactive systems combine to assist the network engineer in planning and designing a telecommunications network. The prototype of such an application is described, illustrating how the two technologies can be introduced into the work environment. An actual account of the steps taken, from data gathering through evaluation, are discussed. Through the experiences of an engineering application, this chapter provides a perspective and a variety of findings that are useful to the design of any color graphics application.

Introduction

The purpose of this chapter is to provide an insight into the area of color in computer graphics as it applies to the planning and design of a telecommunications network. One of the best ways to visualize the planning of a telecommunications network as it is discussed in this chapter is to draw a comparison to a railroad system. Railroad tracks and junctions are referred to as *facilities* and *terminals*, and the stretch of track between two junctions is called a *link*.

The management of a railroad system includes planning for the future so that the correct quantity and type of track will be in place to accommodate the number of railroad cars expected to travel throughout the country. In the same way, facilities must be in place to accommodate the forecast telecommunications demand.

Based on a forecast demand, the planner can analyze the links that have extra capacity

COLOR AND THE COMPUTER

and those that are overloaded or exhausted. With this information, the engineer can make decisions and take appropriate action. Such network planning and design is an important task, critical in fact, to building an efficient communications service.

For the engineer, the process begins with a forecast given by the marketing department. The forecast varies from year to year and represents requirements from business and domestic customers indicating the degree of utilization that will occur between any two points in the network. For example, as new business complexes are built, or as people migrate from one part of the country to another, the demand put on any set of links will increase or decrease.

To build an efficient network, facilities with extra capacity must be more fully utilized, while those being utilized to capacity must be monitored for a possible overload or exhausted condition. Action must be taken if the demand on a facility exceeds its capacity. To balance utilization, the excess demand can be rerouted from the exhausted links to links with unused capacity. In some cases, the option of expanding capacity through new technologies is used. Where necessary, new facilities are constructed.

The engineering department must be sure the network can carry the forecast amount of data and message calls from one point to another. For adequate planning, the following questions must be answered:

1. What will happen when tomorrow's forecast is placed on the existing network?
2. Where do exhausted or overload conditions appear?
3. Where are the candidates for rerouting?
4. Where are expansion and construction necessary?
5. What are the effects on the network of making these decisions?

Color computer graphics are being employed to answer these questions by linking the forecasts and the action proposed to insure the future efficiency and integrity of the network. A color-based graphics system is the decision-support tool that allows the engineer to view a simulated network before and after the forecast demands are introduced. By viewing the effects of the forecast, the engineer can identify areas where action must be taken to solve utilization imbalances. The system further allows the engineer to view the effects of proposed solutions on the network. Using engineering judgment and expertise, the planner can use the information provided in the form of computer-generated color graphics to make quality decisions in a relatively short period of time.

This network planning function in the telecommunications industry resembles the functions of transportation companies, gas and electric suppliers, and package and mail delivery services. This chapter outlines the process of designing, implementing and evaluating a smooth human interface to a color-based system for the engineering planner. It can serve as a model for most resource management systems of this nature.

The chapter is divided into five sections, representing phases in a model that tracks the considerations and guidelines used and the steps taken in the practical application of color to a computer graphics system.

The first section, describing the investigation phase, shares useful information from the literature, seminars, and discussions with others working in this field. Next, the application phase includes the issues surrounding the practical use of this information in a network planning system. In the third section, the preparation phase describes the proper environmental design to accommodate a color-based system. The last two sections include the system introduction and evaluation phases. They describe integration of the system into the present work flow, and evaluation of design decisions.

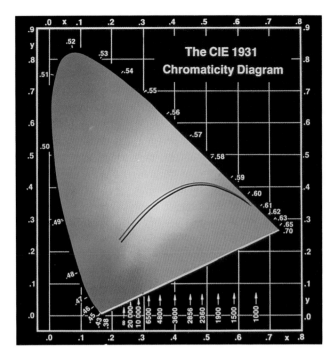

Figure 3-2 1931 CIE chromoticity diagram.

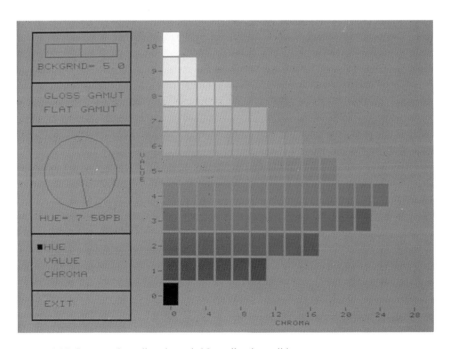

Figure 4-16 Constant hue slice through Munsell color solid.

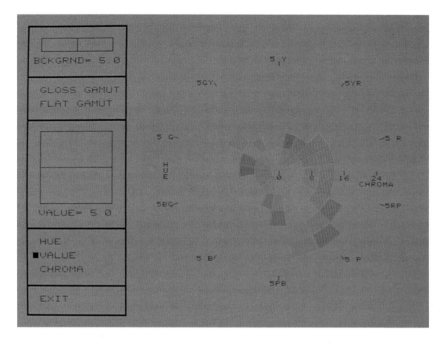

Figure 4-17 Constant value slice through Munsell color solid.

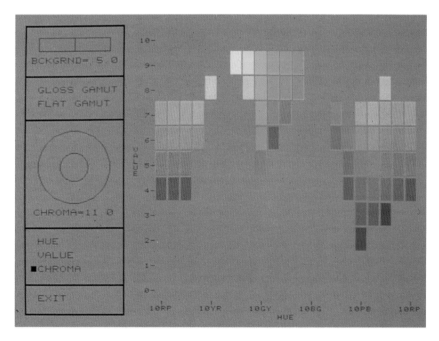

Figure 4-18 Constant chroma slice through Munsell color solid.

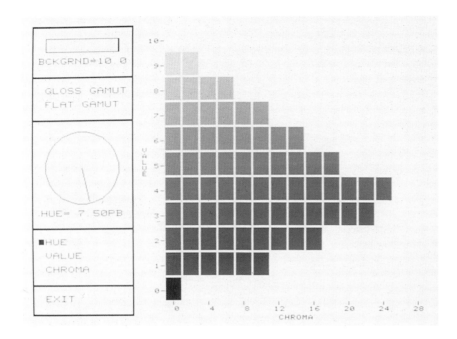

Figure 4-19 Hue slice of Figure 4-16 on background of Munsell value 10/.

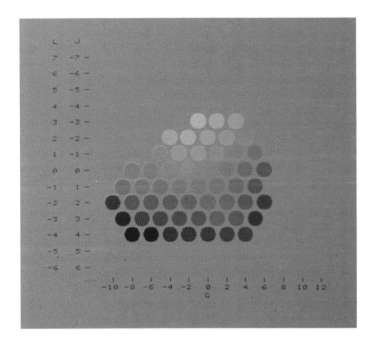

Figure 4-21 Monitor reproduction of the L + j = 0 plane in the OSA committee uniform color space.

Figure 4-24 Full color RGB image (upper left) digitally transformed into YIQ color space and retransformed back into RGB space using only Y (upper right), only YI (lower left), and only YQ (lower right).

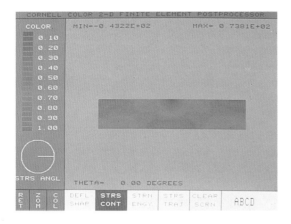

Figure 4-25 A stress variation from compression (top of color scale) encoded as a variation in Munsell value. Color scale goes from 10RP 9/4 (Hue Value/Chroma) at the top to 10RP 2/4 at the bottom.

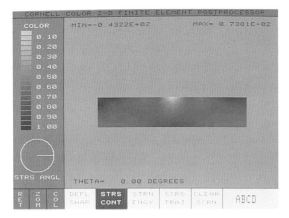

Figure 4-26 Stress distribution of Figure 4.25 encoded by combining two paths through Munsell color space which intersect at the neutral axis. Top half of color scale goes from 5PB 5/12 to the neutral color 5PB 5.5/0. Bottom half of scale goes from this same neutral color (which has equivalent designation 7.5 R5.5/0) to the color 7.5R .5r 6/18.

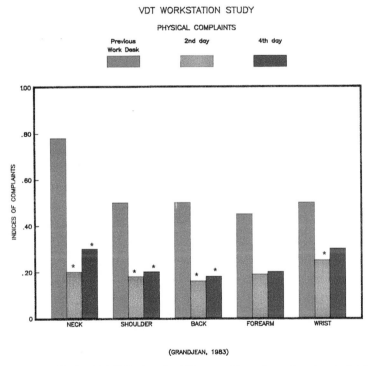

Figure 5-1 Study of VDT Workstation Effects on Discomfort. Results of a field study conducted to determine effects of adjustable furniture on complaints of 65 workers at VDTs (visual display terminals). Complaints were recorded before and after 2 days and 4 days of installation of adjustable furniture (chairs and tables). Complaints of neck, shoulder, back and wrist significantly decreased (p = .05) and are indicated by an asterisk (*) over the appropriate bars. Complaints of visual stress (not plotted in graph) also significantly decreased.

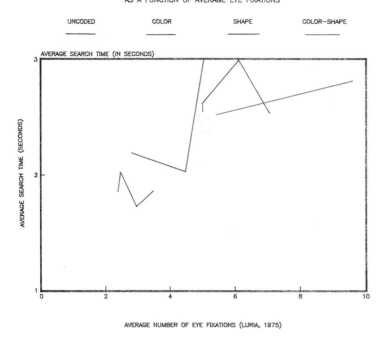

AVERAGE SEARCH TIME

AS A FUNCTION OF AVERAGE EYE FIXATIONS

UNCODED   COLOR   SHAPE   COLOR-SHAPE

AVERAGE SEARCH TIME (IN SECONDS)

AVERAGE SEARCH TIME (SECONDS)

AVERAGE NUMBER OF EYE FIXATIONS (LURIA, 1975)

Figure 5-2 Eye Movement Responses to Targets Coded by Color, Shape, and Uncoded (Adapted from Luria, 1975). Test subjects located targets coded in color with fewer number of eye movements and less search time than when targets were coded by shape, color and shape, or uncoded.

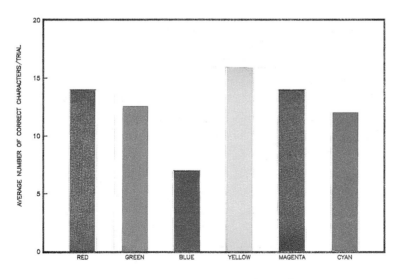

OBSERVER PERFORMANCE AS A FUNCTION OF COLOR

RELATIVE READABILITY OF COLORED CHARACTERS

AVERAGE NUMBER OF CORRECT CHARACTERS/TRIAL

RED   GREEN   BLUE   YELLOW   MAGENTA   CYAN

CRT CHARACTER PHOSPHOR COLOR   (RIZY, 1967)

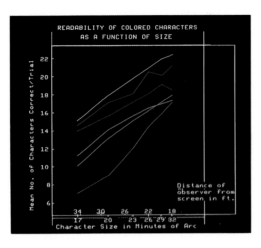

READABILITY OF COLORED CHARACTERS
AS A FUNCTION OF SIZE

Mean No. of Characters Correct/Trial

Distance of
observer from
screen in ft.

Character Size in Minutes of Arc

Figure 5-4 Ability to Read Characters in CRT Display Colors. Comparison of performance in a reading task when viewing characters of different colors on a CRT display with a dark background. The average number of characters correctly read was highest when presented in yellow and least when presented in blue (Adapted from Rizy, 1967).

Figure 6-3 Graphics control panel.

◄*Figure 5-3* Photopic and Scotopic Sensitivity Functions. Shows how visual sensitivity varies as a function of wavelength when the eye is light-adapted and dark-adapted. The light-adapted (photopic) eye is maximally sensitive to light at about 555 nm (nanometers) and the dark-adapted (scotopic) eye is maximally sensitive to light at about 505 nm.

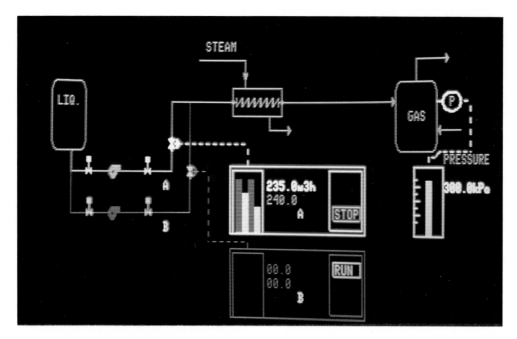

Figure 6-4 Process unit display of standby vaporizer system.

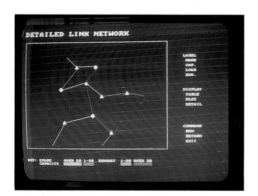

Figure 7-1 Detailed link network.

Figure 7-2 Aggregated network.

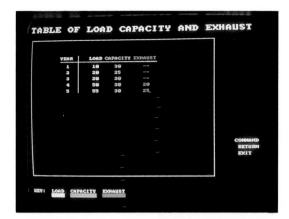

Figure 7-3 Load capacity and exhaust results.

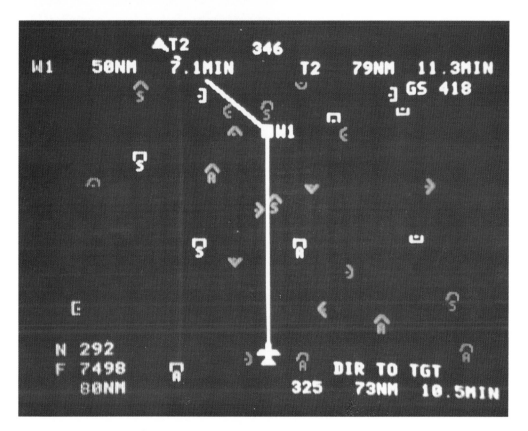

Figure 8-2 Color version of tactical display format.

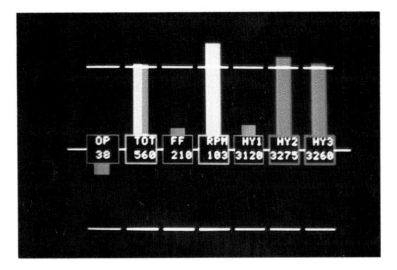

Figure 8-3 Color version of engine display format.

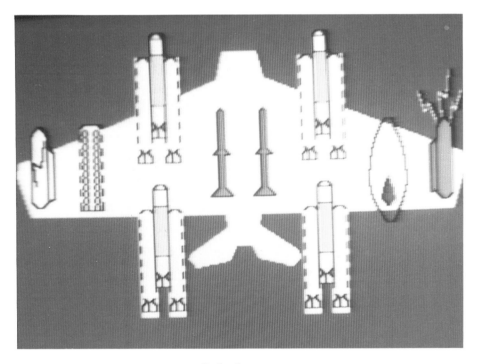

Figure 8-4 Pictorial stores management display format.

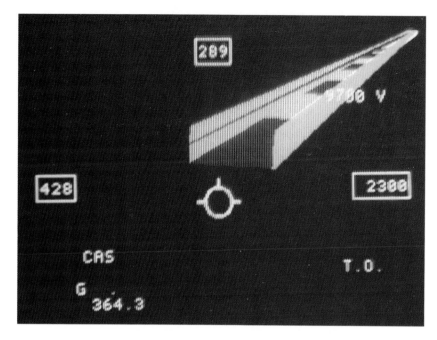

Figure 8-5 Channel-in-the-sky display format.

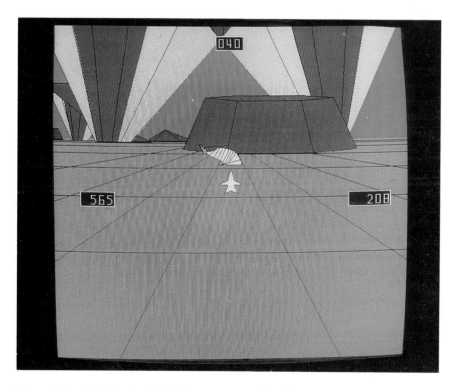

Figure 8-6 Tactical situation display format - perspective view.

Figure 8-16 Color pictorial cockpit.

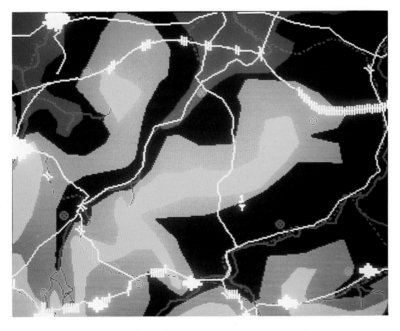

Figure 9-1 Simulated map of moving targets used to verify the effectiveness of tactical attack planning tools. The display shows screened areas (indicated by white bars) along which moving or assembled ground targets can remain hidden from airborne radars.

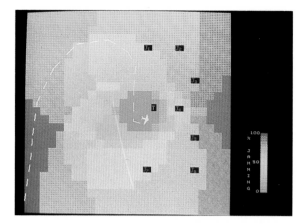

Figure 9-2 Color graphics illustrate the intensity of jamming by an array of jammers against a penetrating aircraft for countermeasures analysis. The color spectrum at right indicates red for the most intense and green for the least intense jamming.

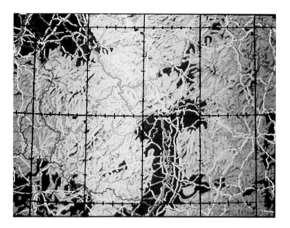

Figure 9-3 Detailed terrain maps made of composite color ''overlays'' from data stored on video discs can be tailored and displayed for different tactical applications.

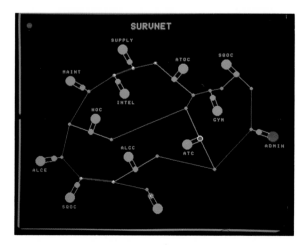

Figure 9-4 This simulation of a survivable network configuration is used to determine network performance under various operating conditions. The object is to develop and demonstrate a computer network capable of continuing communication among distributed processors in case of node or link outage.

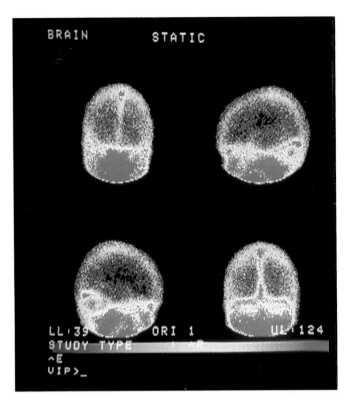

Figure 10-1 Nuclear medicine brain scan with rainbow color spectrum related to measured activity.

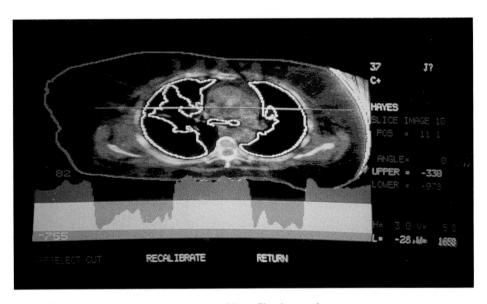

Figure 10-2 Computerized tomography scan with profile plot overlay.

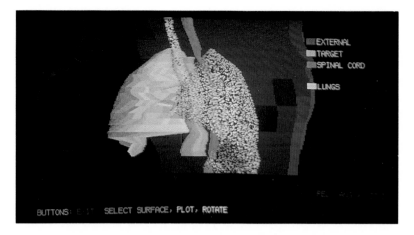

Figure 10-3 Reconstruction of upper thoracic anatomy (anterior-left view.)

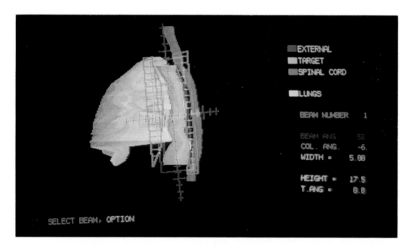

Figure 10-4 External beam portal simulation with blocking.

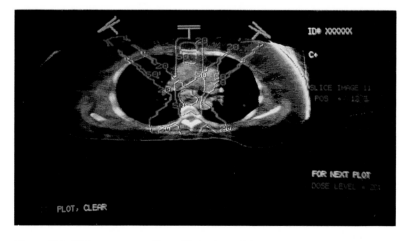

Figure 10-5 CT lung cross-section with isodose plot.

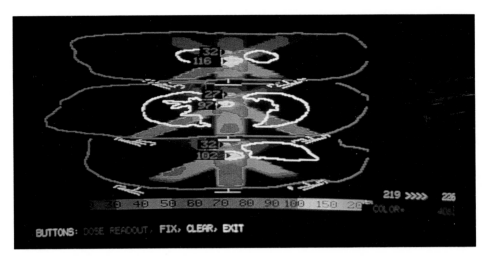

Figure 10-6 Multiple cross-sectional planes with pseudo-color dose assignments.

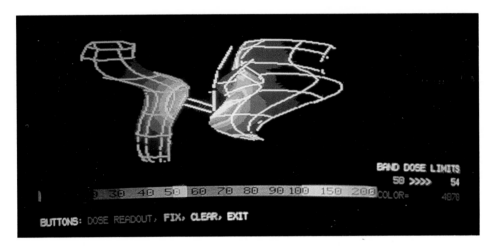

Figure 10-7 Cervical radiation application with pseudo-color dose computed for rectal and bladder surfaces.

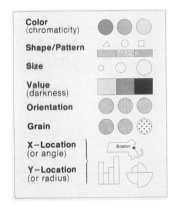

Figure 11-1 The eight visual variables.

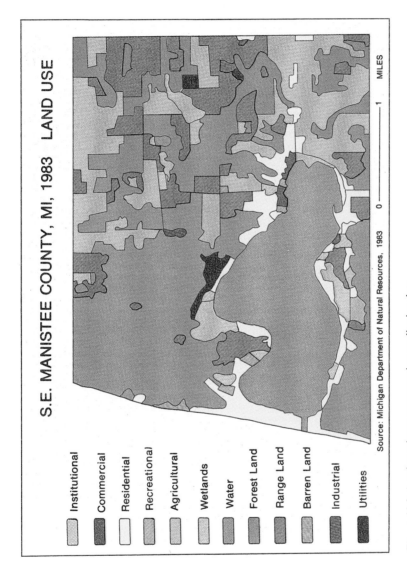

Figure 11-2 A color scheme representing qualitative data.

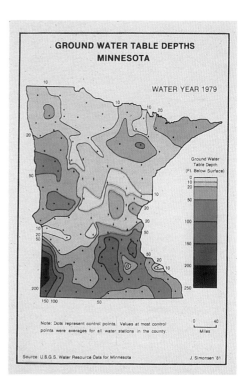

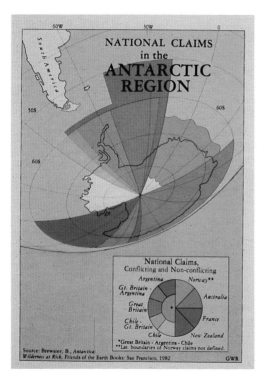

Figure 11-3 A color scheme for qualitative data that includes overlapping categories.

Figure 11-4 Monochromatic use of color in mapping.

Figure 11-5 Double-tone progression.

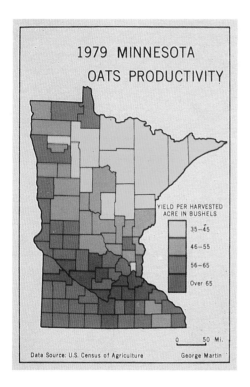

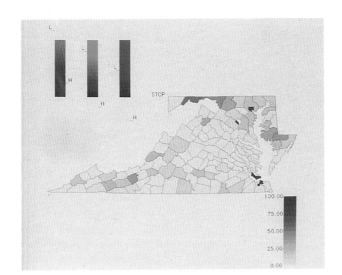

Figure 11-6 Continuously varying scheme.

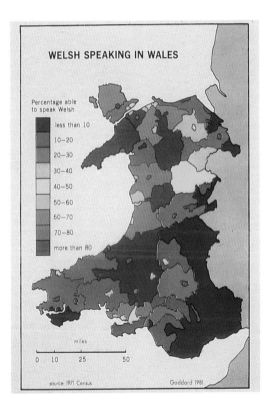

Figure 11-7 Double-ended scheme using greens, yellow, and reds.

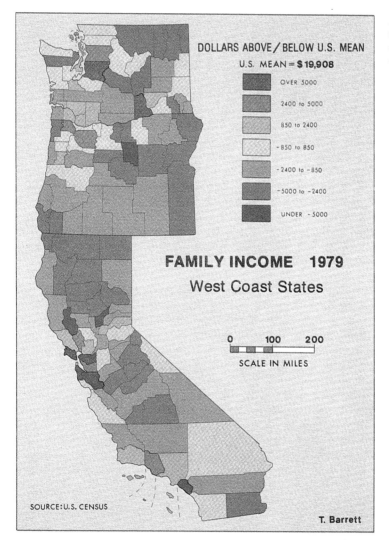

DOLLARS ABOVE / BELOW U.S. MEAN

U.S. MEAN = $19,908

OVER 5000

2400 to 5000

850 to 2400

- 850 to 850

- 2400 to - 850

- 5000 to - 2400

UNDER - 5000

FAMILY INCOME 1979

West Coast States

0   100   200

SCALE IN MILES

SOURCE: U.S. CENSUS

T. Barrett

Figure 11-8 Double-ended scheme designed to accommodate the red-green color blind.

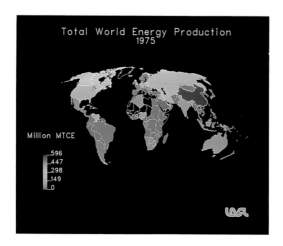

Total World Energy Production
1975

Million MTCE

596
447
298
149
0

Figure 11-9 Double-ended scheme with tones varying continuously.

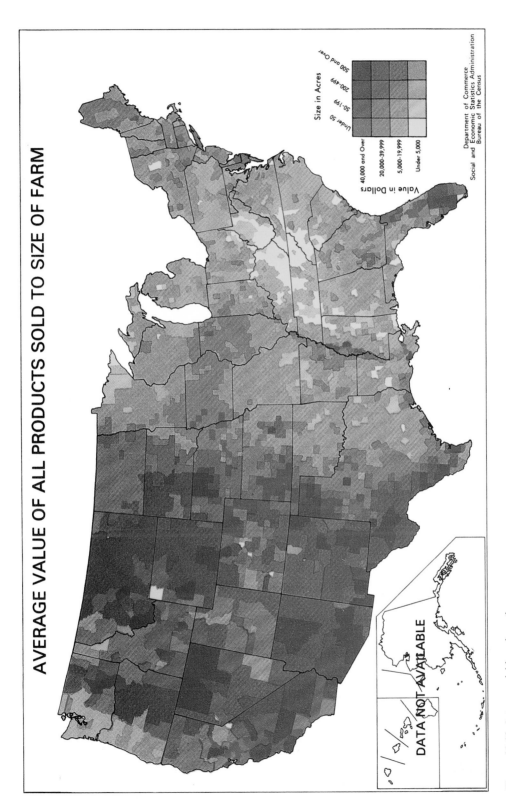

Figure 11-10 A two-variable color scheme.

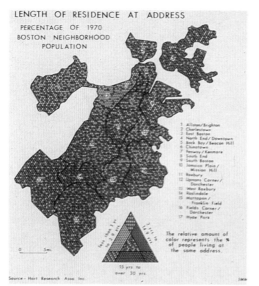

LENGTH OF RESIDENCE AT ADDRESS

PERCENTAGE OF 1970
BOSTON NEIGHBORHOOD
POPULATION

1 Allston/Brighton
2 Charlestown
3 East Boston
4 North End/Downtown
5 Back Bay/Beacon Hill
6 Chinatown
7 Fenway/Kenmore
8 South End
9 South Boston
10 Jamaica Plain/
   Mission Hill
11 Roxbury
12 Uphams Corner/
   Dorchester
13 West Roxbury
14 Roslindale
15 Mattapan/
   Franklin Field
16 Fields Corner/
   Dorchester
17 Hyde Park

The relative amounts of
color represents the %
of people living at
the same address.

Source – Hart Research Assoc. Inc.

Figure 11-11 A three-variable color scheme.

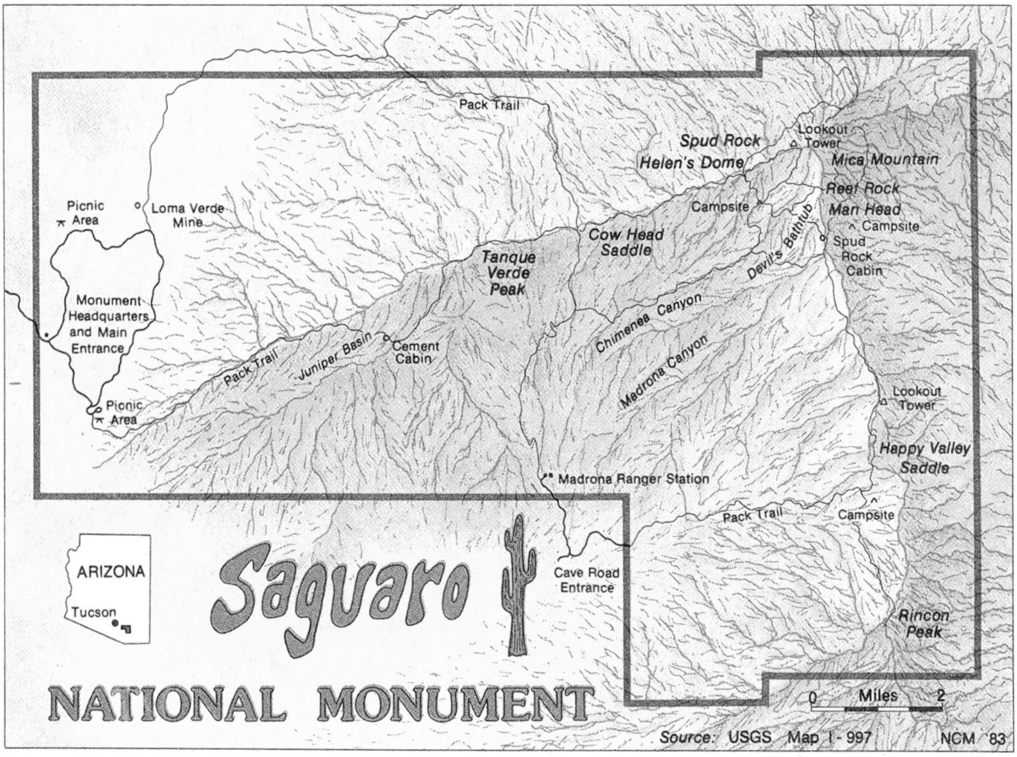

Figure 11-12 Continuous shading scheme for a realistic appearance.

Figure 11-13 Continuous shading superimposed on qualitative categories.

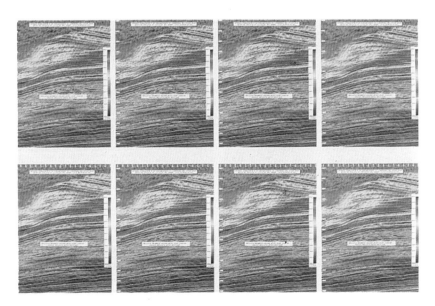

Figure 12-6 Seismic data example.

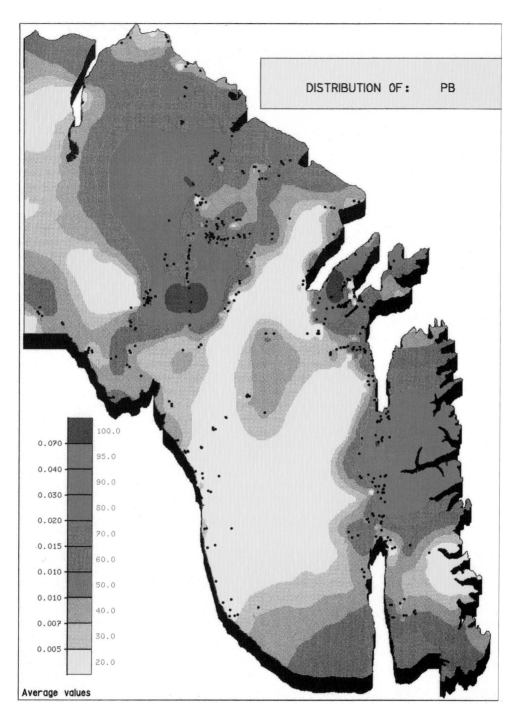

Figure 12-7 Mapping example.

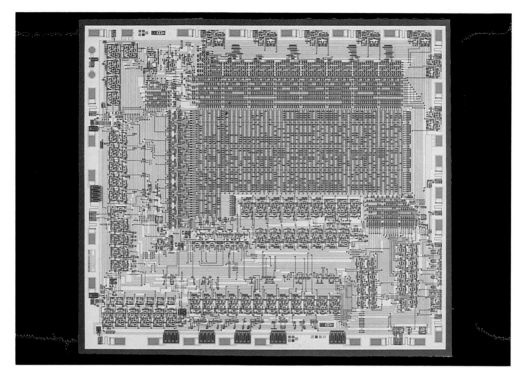

Figure 12-8 Integrated circuit design example.

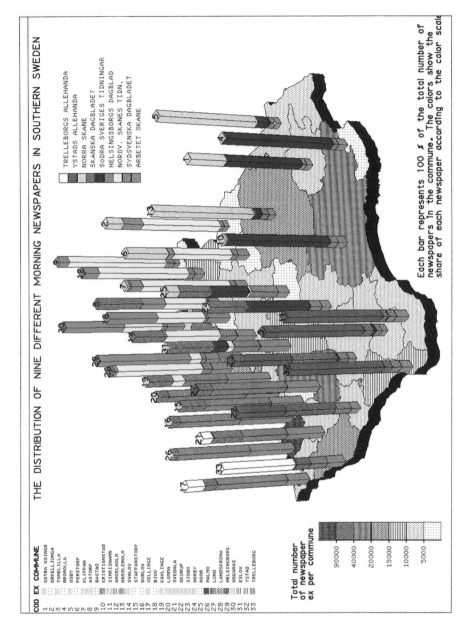

Figure 12-9 Business graphics example.

Figure 12-10 Ink-jet artwork example.

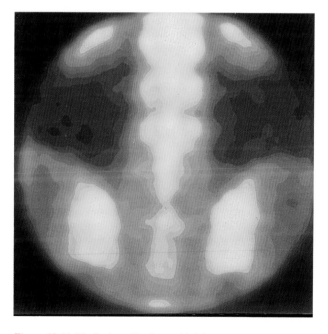

Figure 12-11 Medical applications of ink-jet use.

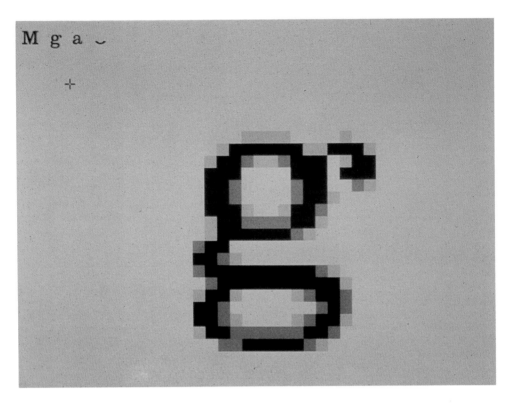

Figure 14-6 Magnified multiple bit character.

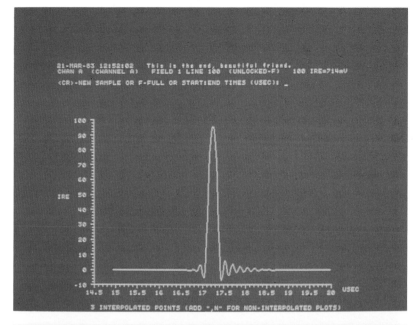

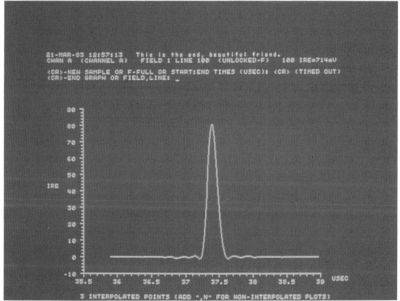

Figure 14-7 Comparison of ringing effects in the luminance scale.

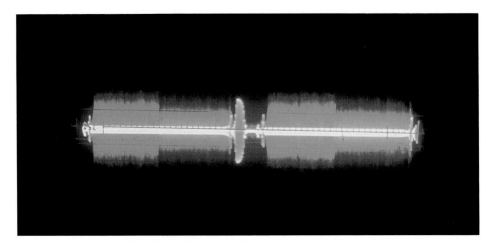

Figure 14-8 Comparison of luminance to chrominance crosstalk.

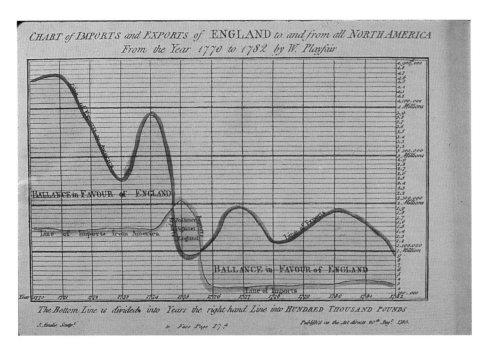

Figure 15-1 Grid chart for imports and exports.

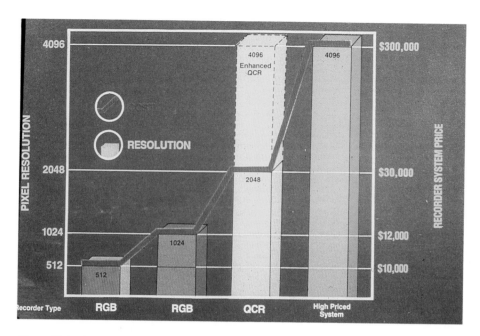

Figure 15-3 Line recorder for film recorders.

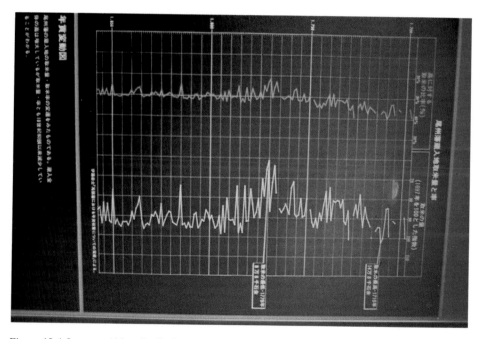

Figure 15-4 Japanese "time-line" chart.

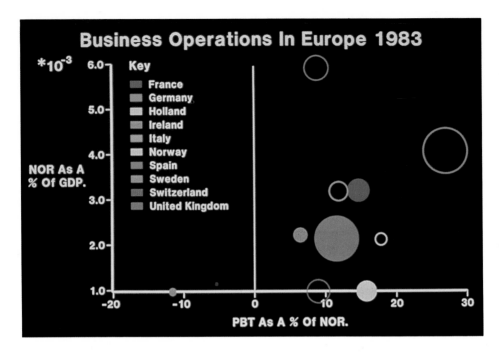

Figure 15-6 Bubble chart for business data.

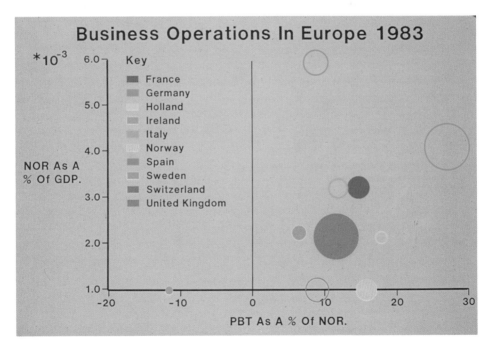

Figure 15-7 Bubble chart for business data.

Investigation

The uniqueness of designing this project required an in-depth investigation to uncover any relevant material on the subject of color and color-based systems. A literature search produced several articles on the subject of color, but few on the subject of computer-generated color. Seminars on the subject and discussion with experts in the field provided information that was more state-of-the-art. As a whole, the investigation revealed a lack of information that could be used specifically to make design decisions relevant to the systems under consideration.

Providing human factors support to the design of any system requires understanding and evaluating the various technological developments as they become available. In the case of color output capability, this includes determining its most efficient uses. In the literature review, four major categories of color as an effective communications tool and several guidelines for application of color emerged.

Categories of Effective Color Use

One of the effective uses of color is to help locate information. While it is possible to communicate information using techniques, such as a key with geometric shapes, color will often convey the information more quickly and reduce search time significantly. It is possible to use geometric shapes along with color to code information, reinforcing the meaning of each code. Such redundant coding can be particularly helpful when users with color vision deficiencies are using the system. If they are unable to recognize a particular color, they can refer to the geometric shape.

The second major category where color can be effective is as a communications method for alerting an operator of a change in status. While monochromatic devices can be used to convey an emergency situation, a color such as bright red or yellow is much more effective in getting attention.

Color can also be used to separate or demarcate information categories. For example, in designing alphanumeric displays, color can facilitate the transfer of information by giving organization to an otherwise confusing set of data. Even a presentation of familiar information such as an input screen can be organized with the use of color—different colors can be used effectively to separate constant fields from variable data.

Finally, color has been found to aid in the retention of information. This can be useful when the information obtained on one display is to be used as an input into a future display.

When color can be an efficient tool to serve one of these four purposes, specific design guidelines should be followed. Adding color to a display will not automatically improve the effectiveness of the material. Color must be applied in a way that facilitates task performance.

Guidelines for Display Design

The following five guidelines were used in designing displays for the network planning and design application:

1. Any color coding must be task related. It is important to carefully analyze the system, both human and the computer components. Decide what the person is expected to do, and design the color coding to facilitate the task. Irrelevant and confusing stimuli retard job performance.

2.   Keep the color coding relevant to the meaning it is conveying. For example, in a display where color is applied to draw attention to a dangerous condition, it is good practice to apply color according to its conventional meaning. In this case, red would reinforce the danger of the situation. This practice will not only save time, but reduce the chance of error.

3.   Keep design consistent. This is important in designing CRT screens for any system, but the availability of color creates a tendency to deviate from this guideline. An effort must be made to apply colors consistently on the various displays used throughout a system. For example, if it is important for operators to know which form number they are looking at when entering data on a CRT, you may decide to highlight this information by using color. If yellow is selected, use yellow to code this form information throughout the series. While this may limit the creativity of the designer, it has a high performance payoff for users who view the system as a single entity.

4.   This guideline follows from human factors literature that suggests the maximum number of colors on a display should be four to seven. Too many colors can introduce clutter and confusion, diluting the positive effects of color.

5.   Finally, some of the most important decisions that have to be made are those dealing with the selection of specific colors from the wide range of possibilities available. With some terminals capable of producing thousands of hues, designers must decide not only if a display element should be red or blue, but which variation of the color should be used.

Making Color Decisions

One of the key objectives in making color decisions is to produce color harmony in each display. To achieve this harmony it is important to understand the composition of color, the three elements that can be varied to make one color different from another. Hue, value, and chroma are the terms often given to these three components. *Hue* describes what we usually refer to as the color of an object such as red, blue, or green. *Value* indicates the lightness or brightness of a color and is often described as light, dark, or washed out. *Chroma* indicates the purity or saturation of a color and is perceived as the degree of departure from gray.

A designer can make colors harmonious by adjustments in hue, value, and chroma. Too many contrasts or too much similarity should be avoided. Increasing the chroma of some colors or the value differences between colors can add contrast for emphasis, and reducing these differences can increase harmony. Becoming proficient with proper color selection requires practice as well as familiarity with some terminal hardware and its method of color generation. In some cases, additional software is needed to give the designer the flexibility of hue, value, and chroma adjustments.

In the network planning application that follows, all five design guidelines were used and found helpful in making design decisions.

Application

One of the beginning stages of a planner's job is an analysis of the network at an aggregate level to locate exhaustions or unused capacity conditions. In Figure 7-1 (see color insert), the conventional meanings of the colors red, green, and yellow parallel the type of information the planner would be seeking. Therefore, exhausted links are color coded red, and links with unused capacity are represented by green. Since it was also important to cover the degrees of exhaustion and capacity, two hues of each color, with variations in saturation and intensity are used to make the distinction.

An interesting problem arose in deciding the appropriate hue of red and green to depict the corresponding degree of exhaustion or capacity. The objective was to order the colors to represent the continuum from maximum capacity to maximum exhaustion.

The key in Figure 7-1 shows a light green to represent maximum capacity, and dark red for maximum exhaustion. The darker greens and lighter reds were used to represent the lesser degrees of these conditions. Originally, the decision was made to use a fully dark green to code maximum capacity, and a washed-out light green to represent least capacity. With traditionally printed maps, this might have been the most meaningful arrangement; however, when viewed on a CRT screen, with light-generated color, the lighter shade appeared brighter and more pronounced than the dark shade. Hence, the shade with more green actually conveyed less capacity while the shade with less green conveyed more capacity. This effect was not found to be true with the degrees of exhaustion. The evaluation following the introduction of the system reinforced the revision made on this configuration.

The alphanumeric, descriptive, and command information that is static and requires no special color coding is set apart from the rest of the display. This is accomplished by setting aside designated areas of the display and using white. In all displays, the same designation is made so that this information can always be easily located.

By selecting an option on the control panel along the right-hand side of the display, the planner can produce a detailed version or breakdown showing the individual links that make up any one of the aggregate links. The color coding convention for aggregate network maps is carried down to the most detailed link level, as represented in Figure 7-2 (see color insert). This prevents confusion from inconsistent coding of capacity and exhaustion information on the aggregate level and the detailed level.

Another option on the control panel produces a display of alphanumeric information in a tabular format. A table such as Figure 7-3 (see color insert) can give quantitative information about any link pictured on a network display.

Planners are also interested in additional information about the links they are analyzing. It is important to know, for example, whether the link is a cable, radio or fiber type. Color conveyed this information through a discreet color for each type of link. In most cases, the colors corresponded to the paper maps used before introduction to the system and were most familiar to the planner.

The color-coded displays convey more information than a desk top full of computer printouts. Color was effectively used to separate information categories, help locate information, and alert the planner to changes in the status of link capacity.

Preparation

The proper workstation environment had to be designed before the system could be turned over to the user organization. Because the system included color producing equipment, analysis of the work location gave particular attention to the lighting conditions as well as the physical layout of the equipment and furniture. Information was gathered to help consider the needs for human efficiency, comfort, and safety. Recommendations were presented to upper management to resolve inconsistencies discovered between the existing and desired conditions.

Lighting was one of the most important aspects in workstation design for a color-based computer system. Problems with the reflection of light and glare on the CRT screen had to be solved. Indirect ambient lighting, with a user-controlled dimmer switch, was a satisfactory solution. Incandescent track lighting, which can be positioned to control glare, replaced the fixed fluorescent type originally available. A room without windows, or with windows that could be completely covered to block out sunlight, was recommended to eliminate problems with sunlight. An antiglare coating bonded to the glass surface of the CRT screen was also recommended. The walls were painted with a dull finish to reduce light reflecting in the room.

As with any work environment that includes CRT viewing, it was important to consider the placement of equipment and furniture. As a result, the workstation was designed with CRT terminals placed so as to minimize eye travel and assist body movements. The selection and placement of furniture emphasized flexibility so that all body sizes could be accommodated. This was accomplished in part by adjustable tables and chairs. Terminals on swivel mounts and movable keyboards and other input devices further improved flexibility of the workstation. Because the environment included large (19-inch diagonal) color CRTs, particular care had to be taken to allow an adequate viewing distance. Proper design of the work environment was found to be an important factor in the acceptance and usefulness of the color-based system.

System Introduction

The system was turned over to the user organization in the form of a prototype during a regularly scheduled taskforce meeting. Engineering planners from all over the country met at a central location to analyze network data and produce a plan for future action. During the taskforce meeting, the system was introduced as a prototype to be used parallel to the existing operational systems. This proved to be a successful approach for insuring that the objects of the taskforce would be met while using the realistic setting to try out the system.

The taskforce participants were introduced to the system through a formal training session. During this session, the concept of the system was explained, and the features were described in terms of their ability to facilitate job functions. The engineers were encouraged to use the color computer graphics as often as possible. They did continue to rely heavily on the existing methods and tools, which primarily involved analyzing computer-generated paper reports.

The initial training session was followed by less formal on-the-job training on an individual basis. Planners operated the equipment and used the system's functions with trainer assistance.

Evaluation

Evaluation was perhaps the most critical phase in developing and introducing this color-based system with all its unique characteristics. The purpose of the evaluation was to determine whether the personnel subsystem functioned as designed and to decide where improvements were needed.

Observations and Interviews

First, feedback from users was obtained directly through comprehensive interviews as well as preinterview observation to obtain firsthand information regarding human interaction with the system. Observation information served as a basis for discussion during the interview session and also to detect unique and unexpected problems. After two weeks of observing, trainers conducted the interviews.

Interview questions were derived from human factors decisions made for the prototype. Color design decisions dealt with choice of colors selected, number of colors used, and use of color to convey qualitative information. Other interview areas involved layout of the work station, the impact of the color graphics system on job satisfaction, and the time, effort, and quality of the work performed.

Several conclusions were drawn from responses in the interview sessions. With the exception of a few problem areas, the evaluation of the displays was positive, a response not unexpected in light of the novelty and attractiveness of color graphics.

Design Data.   Valuable information that could be used to further improve the design was also obtained. One of the reported problems reinforced the already identified need to give further consideration to increasing the differences between the two hues of red and the two hues of green used to identify exhaustion and capacity conditions on network links.

Workstation Layout.   Discussions regarding the layout of the workstation made it evident that the work environment met the majority of the specifications addressed in human factors literature and received approval from most system users. The responses also highlighted some potential problems, such as the digitizing tablet taking up too much of the work surface. This increased efforts to investigate alternative cursor control devices such as a mouse. Some dissatisfaction was expressed with the size of the 19-inch color monitor. Further investigation revealed that the problem was not that the screen was too small, but that at times the information display was congested. Use of the zoom feature was recommended to resolve this condition.

Job Satisfaction.   Users also reported more job satisfaction when they used the computer graphics capability. One user reported, "It was reassuring to visualize the information and see it from a variety of different angles." When users were asked to describe the impact of the use of color computer graphics on the time, effort, and quality of work performed, responses varied. They ranged from "It made the job more complex because it gave a flood of information," to "It simplified the job and made it more fun."

During the interview session, an attempt was made to compare the planner's job before and after the introduction of computer graphics, with the finding that a one-for-one comparison could not be made along the dimensions of time, effort, and quality. Since the prototype was used parallel to the existing and more familiar mode of paper reports, the latter was relied upon much more heavily. Even though a fair comparison could not be made, several planners saw potential benefits of color graphics and were encouraged by the current capabilities of the system.

Field Evaluations

The verbal responses obtained through the interviews constituted a major source of feedback. However, information of a more quantitative nature was needed regarding decisions on the use of color. To get this information, field evaluations were made, including tests designed to indicate potential problems.

Twenty subjects, representative of management and nonmanagement, took part in the field evaluation. All were unfamiliar with the system and the planning process. The evaluative tasks were designed to give further information on, the use of differing hues to depict qualitative information as well as the use of specific colors to print alphanumeric information.

Color Identification.   In the first task, each subject was asked to identify the color of a link one inch or less, pointed to by the tester on the aggregate network display. Results were expected to indicate which network colors (yellow, two hues of red and green) are difficult to identify on a crowded display where links are relatively small. Results are summarized in Table 7-1.

Color	% Correct
Light green	74
Dark red	100
Light red	83
Dark green	98
Yellow	100
Average	91

Table 7-1   Percent of correct responses

The figures in Table 7-1 suggest that something related to the display design caused subjects to perform below a desired 95%–100% level of accuracy. A 95% total average represents the minimum desired for recognizing the particular hue of green or red or yellow on links of one inch or less in length. A higher percentage would be expected if it were not for the fact that detecting the difference in hues (light to dark green and light to dark red) is not critical to grasping the concept behind the coding, and an exploded picture of these short links can be produced by using the "window" function.

Results in a later task suggest that performance (in recognizing hues of red and green) improves as the length of the link is increased and the density of the display reduced.

Meaning and Color Association.   The next task was designed to indicate the color and hue most often associated with each meaning (relative value)—information valuable in evaluating colors for capacity and exhaustion conditions. A display of the index network was presented with the key concealed. Each subject was then given the background information needed to perform the task: that all the links on the map presented pipelines through which a pile of marbles had been rolled and that the pipes were color coded to show those with room left in them and those with no room left in them. The subject was then given a list of four definitions and asked to match each definition with the color that fit the description. The definitions were as follows:

1. There is more room left in these pipes than in any other.
2. There is room left in these pipes, but not as much as in Definition 1.
3. These pipes have just begun to break at the seams because a few too many marbles have been forced into them.
4. These pipes have completely broken at the seams because a large amount of marbles has been forced into them.

The definitions correspond to levels of capacity and exhaust, where Definition 1 represents high capacity, 2 represents low capacity, 3 represents low exhaustion, and 4 represents high exhaustion.

The results presented in Table 7-2 show that the majority of the subjects associated the definition representing high capacity with light green, low capacity with dark green, low exhaustion with light red, and high exhaustion with dark red. This sequencing of colors is identical to the one chosen for the engineering application.

Definition	Light Green	Dark Green	Light Red	Dark Red	Yellow
Definition 1	*39%	22%	4%	4%	*30%
Definition 2	22%	*39%	17%	4%	17%
Definition 3	0	13%	*61%	17%	8%
Definition 4	4%	4%	4%	*74%	13%
	*Highest percent agreement between a definition and a color				

Table 7-2   Percent of times a definition and color were matched

A close look at the percentages shows that the choice of red hues for exhaustion conditions was higher than green hues for capacity conditions. This could be accounted for by the high percentage of yellow matched with Definition 1, which was a capacity definition. A possible reason for subjects associating yellow links with a capacity definition is that the yellow links were perceived as larger (because of their brightness) than red and green links. Subjects might have associated the apparent physical size of these links with the definition, rather than the color itself. Based on these results, the present scheme will be retained with continued monitoring of user feedback.

Color for Alphanumerics.   The task defined to evaluate colors used for alphanumerics was based on a display of a table of numbers. Subjects were asked if any one of the colors was particularly easy to read, and why. This information would be valuable for choosing colors for alphanumeric displays. Results are summarized in Table 7-3.

Color	Easier	More Difficult
Green	19	3
Red	14	4
White	10	10
Yellow	1	19

Table 7-3   Colors found easier and harder to read in alphanumeric displays

Results in Table 7-3 show that the majority of negative responses were made for yellow, and the majority of positive responses were made for green. Conversely, the fewest positive responses were made for yellow, and the fewest negative responses were made for green. The conclusion might be to avoid that particular hue of yellow for alphanumerics. Results also suggest that the particular hue of green will produce a more favorable response than the other colors.

Table 7-3 also shows that red was considered "easier" 3½ times more frequently than it was considered "more difficult." From this finding, at least a preliminary conclusion can be drawn that the red used is likely to produce a favorable response when used on alphanumeric information.

The responses for white were equally divided, 50% positive and 50% negative. Due to the nature of the negative comments (e.g., white is "too harsh," "blurry," and "offensive"), it is recommended that white be avoided for alphanumerics. The similarity between the comments made for white and yellow confirm the warnings given in some of the literature on display design; that is, if a color such as white or yellow appears on a dark background, it has a tendency to "bleed" into the background unless its intensity is reduced.

The negative conditions revealed by this evaluation can be alleviated. It should be noted, however, that some software/hardware changes will be required in order to correct the condition without negative affecting other conditions that are currently satisfactory. Specifically, the ability to create separate color tables for each display without negatively affecting response time will have to be available. The present arrangement, which has the same color scheme for each display, uses the same yellow for the asterisk on the control panel and for the sublink exhaustion figures. The results of this alphanumeric evaluation reinforce the need for this capability to create separate color tables.

Color Preferences.   After performing a number of other evaluation tasks, subjects were asked to report which colors were most difficult to see. Many reported difficulty in differentiating between the hues of green and red. Some complained that the yellow was too "bright" and that the white was too "strong." Another problem was reported in viewing orange and blue lines positioned close to each other. The combination of the two made the line appear purple.

While the results obtained from these evaluations can be explained only in the context of the uncontrolled variables present in the tasks, the data collected have been interpreted as being valuable in the current time frame. The data also have future value where they can be used as a baseline to measure results of additional studies or as a benchmark to mark comparisons of alternative decisions.

Design Modifications

As a result of field evaluations, some of the modifications under consideration are listed below:

1. Remove the slash from the center of the zero character (0), to reduce confusion with other rounded numbers such as 8 and 3.
2. Consider the font features (i.e., options for variable font types) of graphics terminals being evaluated for future use.
3. Provide the capability for separate color tables for each display.
4. Select less intense whites and yellows for alphanumeric information on tables and plots.
5. Allow for alphanumeric labels to displace (rather than overprint) display elements, to increase legibility.
6. Create two hues of green more distinct from one another than those in use for more accurate capacity detection.

Summary

The use of color graphics in this network engineering application added a new dimension to the efficient presentation of data. Careful planning in workstation design, deliberate application of color and presentation of the system in terms of job design and training are key factors in the project's success. Subsequent versions of the system will include enhancements in the areas listed above. Continued research, more entensive testing and user feedback will be used to direct the decisions that are made.

Literature Reviewed

Christ, R. E. Review and analysis of color coding research forvisual displays. *Human Factors*, 1975, *17*, 542–570

Danchak, M. CRT displays for power plants. *Instrumental Technology*, 1976, 29.

Galitz, W. *Human Factors in Office Automation*, Atlanta: Life Office Management Association, 1980.

Joblove, G., Greenburg, D. Color spaces for computer graphics. *Computer Graphics*, 1978, *12*, 20–25.

Krebs, M., Wolf, J. Design principles for the use of color in displays. *Proceedings of the Society for Information Display*, 1979, *20*, 10–15.

Shontz, W. D., et al. Color coding for information location. *Human Factors*, 1971, *13*, 237–246.

Smith, S. Color-coded displays for data-processing systems. *Electrotechnology*, April 1963, 63–69.

Teichner, W. Color and visual information coding. *Proceedings of the Society for Information Display*, 1979, *20*, 3–4.

Toney, E. Human engineering guidelines for color CRT mask design with suggested applications to NASS/TNDS - case 49077-45. Bell Telephone Laboratories, 1980.

Wong, K. W., Yacomelos, N. G. Identification of cartographic symbols from TV displays. *Human Factors*, 1973, *15*, 21–31.

Biography

Marie Wigert-Johnston has worked in the area of Human Factors and computer systems for seven years at American Telephone and Telegraph, where she is a staff manager.

In designing sophisticated computer systems to support the functions of the engineering department, the Human Factors contribution to the project team is provided in four key areas: Analysis, Design, Documentation and Training. Marie's work experiences in these areas have included: performing analyses of user needs and functions, designing input/output CRT displays and hard copy reports, writing user manuals, job aids and training material as well as conducting training sessions. In addition to these functions, her job responsibilities have included research in the area of color computer graphics and its practical application to a network planning system.

The design of CRT screens which include the added dimensions of color and graphics has presented a new and interesting challenge. In the past, computer generated paper reports were used by planners to help them make engineering decisions. Today, a series of properly designed and color coded displays can convey the information more readily and successfully. Marie is interested in this concept and was involved in generating awareness and support for its application in other departments such as marketing and sales.

Marie holds an undergraduate degree in Sociology and a teaching certification from Boston University and a Masters Degree in Industrial Psychology from Stevens Institute of Technology. She is a member of the Human Factors Society and has presented a paper entitled "Color Issues in Computer Graphics" at the 1982 American Psychological Association Convention. Marie has recently completed a Masters degree in Business Administration—Marketing Management from Pace University. She continues to make Human Factors her area of expertise and has broadened its scope of application by accepting a position in the Marketing Department.

8   Color Computer Graphics in Military Cockpits

JOHN M. REISING
Flight Dynamics Laboratory
Wright-Patterson Air Force Base, Ohio

ANTHONY J. ARETZ
Department of Behavioral Science and Leadership
United States Air Force Academy, Colorado

Abstract

This chapter discusses the application of color computer graphics to information display in military cockpits. The use of color pictorial display formats, which can provide simple and intuitive information that allows for a potential reduction in pilot workload is strongly advocated. This chapter reviews past use of color in military cockpits, presenting research examples to show how color computer graphics can be used to display information to the pilot, and describing potential applications in future aircraft. Also, a discussion of color-coding techniques and human decision-making behavior is included as a basis for supporting the advantages of color pictorial display formats.

Introduction

The use of color cathode ray tubes (CRTs) in the Boeing 757/767 and the Airbus A310 has created a revolution in cockpit design. Flight-worthy color CRTs, coupled with advances in computer graphics, have freed the cockpit designer from the constraints of traditional electromechanical instruments and monochrome CRTs. The display designer can now use color pictorial techniques to create new display formats that present information in a more efficient manner. The purpose of this chapter is to show how this revolution is affecting the presentation of information in military cockpits now and for the year 2000.

Background

Although color CRTs have already appeared in commercial transport aircraft, they have yet to make their debut in military cockpits. The main reason for the delay is that only now are color CRTs being constructed to withstand the adverse nature of military fight. For example, a CRT has to be able to withstand up to 9 g in a fighter aircraft, whereas commercial aircraft are very seldom exposed to more than 2 g. Price is another reason; a color CRT built to meet military specifications can cost up to sixty thousand dollars. The thrust of this chapter is to show that color CRTs are necessary in military cockpits and worth the expense.

The reason color CRTs are necessary is their potential as a tool to help reduce pilot workload. The requirements of military missions put tremendous stress on the pilot, especially the missions of fighter and attack aircraft. For example, in order to attack and survive in a combat environment, fighter aircraft have to fly very near the ground (100 to 200 ft.) at close to the speed of sound. During an attack, the fighter pilot must decide what weapons to deliver, plan his flight routes into and out of the target area, monitor aircraft performance, listen for radio communications, and most importantly, monitor enemy activities to prevent being shot down. To make matters worse, attack missions must be performed in all kinds of weather from sunny days to foggy nights. Accomplishing this mission imposes a tremendous workload on the crew—obviously, it is even greater if it is to be accomplished by a single pilot. As a result, it is crucial that pilot workload be reduced to an optimal level.

In order to reduce pilot workload, design engineers will extensively use digital avionics in future aircraft. The value of digital avionics lies in its ability to monitor and control lower-level functions of the aircraft, thereby allowing the pilot to concentrate on higher-level decision-making functions. For example, digital avionics can consistently monitor the health of hydraulic, electrical, and fuel systems better than the pilot. In a typical visual scan of the cockpit instruments, a pilot may be able to monitor systems once per second while the avionics can monitor the same systems at a rate of thirty times per second. By releasing the pilot from these lower-level "housekeeping chores," digital avionics allow the cockpit design to be based on a management-by-exception philosophy. That is, systems information is only presented when called up by the pilot for examination, or when a system manfunction requires corrective action. Therefore, the pilot is able to concentrate on higher-level tasks related to the successful completion of the mission.

These digital avionics advances, while increasing the potential for reducing pilot workload, have also increased the amount of information that can be presented to the pilot. If the information available from all the avionics were displayed to the pilot in alphanumeric form, the pilot could easily face a situation of information overload, and mission performance could suffer rather than be enhanced. For example, the information required by a fighter pilot to perform a mission falls into several main categories: primary flight (attitude), engine status, navigation, communications, weapons systems tactical situation, emergency procedures, sensors, and systems status (e.g., fuel). In order to prevent possible overload, this information must be presented to the pilot in an easily understood and interpreted form.

Color pictorial coding techniques can present information in a simplified, more efficient form, hence the necessity for color CRTs in military fighter and attack aircraft. Since these aircraft stand to benefit most from the application of color Computer-Generated Imagery (CGI), they will be used in examples throughout this chapter.

Color in Military Cockpits

The use of color in military crew stations is not new. As far back as World War II color can be seen in the crew station of the P-51 where colored tape was used on engine instruments to indicate normal, caution, and emergency states. Traditionally, this use of color has been accepted with little controversy. Even in today's aircraft, warning/caution/advisory systems make use of red, amber, and green to portray information on electromechanical instruments. Generally, red is used to denote emergencies that require immediate action by the pilot; amber is used to show emergencies that are not immediately life threatening and can allow the passage of a certain period of time before they are remedied; and green is used to convey a safe condition. Blue, while permissible in military aircraft, has primarily been used for advisory conditions in commercial aircraft. In few of these applications, however, has the use of color pictorial presentations been considered. Usually, a colored light by itself has been the only indicator of the warning, caution, or advisory state. For example, an amber light was often used to inform the pilot of a caution state. In some instances, letters or words were added to the caution light so that the word "CAUTION" appeared in amber. Color has also been used for other purposes such as the blue sky and brown ground coding of altitude director indicators.

These uses of color on warning lights, messages, and altitude director indicators are well established in tradition. As mentioned earlier, however, in the revolutionary state of crew station information display technology, the role of color in advanced cockpits is not bound by tradition and consequently is not easy to define. This problem is just surfacing in today's military aircraft, which are in transition from electromechanical displays to CRTs—as exemplified in the Navy's F-18 and the Panavia's Tornado. These state-of-the-art military cockpits use monochrome (green) CRTs to present information to the pilot. Much of the information is displayed in alphanumeric text, similar to that seen on video display terminals. Use of CGI to portray information is limited, and as a result, pilots can easily become overwhelmed by the amount of alphnumeric data presented.

But military cockpits do not have to be limited to monochrome, alphanumeric display formats. The Boeing 757/767 and the Airbus A310 have already shown that color CRTs can be used to portray display formats, or pictures, of traditional electromechanical instruments. These traditional display formats were used to ensure an easy transition for the new technology into the airborne environment and to aid pilots accustomed to flying with electromechanical instruments. However, applying the new technology in this manner does not exploit the full capabilities of color CGI that can be obtained by combining both color and pictorial coding to create new display formats. Color pictorial CGI display formats can provide information and reduce pilot workload by minimizing information processing requirements. The following research examples illustrate how color and pictorial coding techniques can be used to help achieve this objective.

Research Examples

In a series of studies conducted at the Flight Dynamics Laboratory at the Wright-Patterson Air Force Base in Ohio, potential applications of monochrome and color display formats in fighter aircraft have been evaluated. Three specific applications of monochrome and color CGI have been examined in a fighter cockpit simulator:

1. A tactical situation display format.
2. An engine status display format.
3. A store's management display format.

During the evaluations, pilots were required to fly the simulator and answer questions concerning the display formats. The specifics for each research effort are discussed in this section.

Tactical Situation Display Format

A tactical situation display format provides the pilot with information concerning the location, type, and affiliation of possible threats such as other aircraft, missile sites, and anti-aircraft artillery in the aircraft's tactical airspace. The format used in this study was presented on a cockpit color CRT that also contained navigation information (Kopala, 1979). The symbols used in the display format represented aircraft, surface-to-air missles, and anti-aircraft artillery. In addition, placed above each symbol was an affiliation designator: hostile, unknown, or friendly. Figure 8-1 shows all possible combinations of the symbols and affiliation designators. The symbols were evaluated under three different density levels (10, 20, and 30) using both monochrome (black-and-white) and redundant color-coded versions of the display format. Figure 8-2 (see color insert) shows the color version of the display format with a density level of 30 symbols. In the color display format hostile symbols were red, unknowns were yellow, and friendly symbols were green. Pilots were required to answer questions concerning locations, quantities, and affiliations of the symbols. The statistical analysis revealed that pilots were able to answer questions faster at each density level with the color display format. Also, the difference between the response times for the two display formats increased as a function of density level. Clearly, a color-display format has a high payoff in displaying threat information.

The reasons that the color-coded format was so clearly superior in this application are alluded to by Krebs, Wolf, and Sandvig (1978). The authors state that color coding will probably improve operator performance when the display has the following characteristics:

1. Unformatted.
2. High density.
3. Search requirement.
4. Degraded legibility.
5. Logical relationship between the colors and the task.

The tactical situation display format satisfied all these criteria, so the benefits of color coding could be expected.

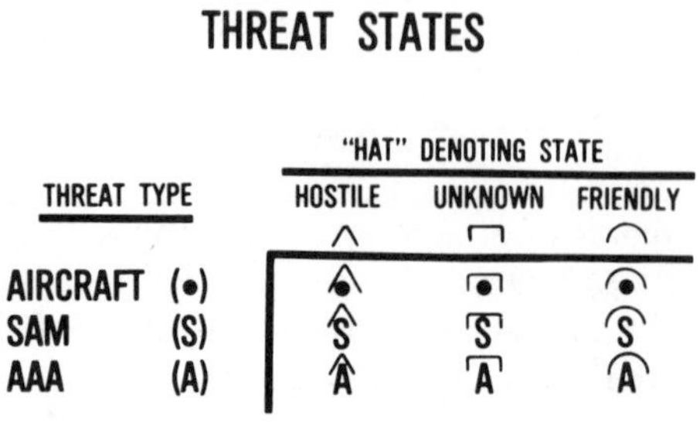

THREAT STATES

Figure 8-1 Possible combinations of symbols and affiliation designators.

Engine Status Display Format

In another study, color versus monochrome coding of aircraft engine status information was evaluated (Calhoun & Herron, 1981). The color version of the display format is shown in Figure 8-3 (see color insert). The square boxes represented the midpoints of the normal operating ranges for each engine parameter and contained digital readouts of the current parameter values. Vertical rectangular bars extended from the top or bottom of the boxes as the corresponding parameters deviated from the normal operating range midpoints. White reference lines were presented at the extreme ends of the bar ranges and represented the maximum and minimum points of the normal operating range. All the parameters were scaled so that the normal operating ranges were represented by the same bar length.

Normal, caution, and emergency states were indicated by shade and flash codes on the monochrome display format and by color codes on the color display format. For normal conditions, the bars consisted of empty rectangles in the monochrome display format and solid green rectangles in the color display format. A caution state was indicated by a solid white bar in the monochrome display format and by a solid amber bar in the color display format. If an engine parameter was in an emergency state, the white bar flashed and the color bar turned red. The task of the pilot was to fly the simulator and identify engine parameters that entered either a caution or emergency state.

In contrast to the tactical situation display format findings, the results of this study showed no significant improvements in performance when the color version of the CGI engine display format was used. Going back to the Krebs et al. (1978) rules, these results are probably due to the fact that the CGI engine format had low density, required little searching, and the legibility was not degraded. The pictorial coding by itself, therefore, was sufficient to present the information in an efficient manner. The ability to use a monochrome CRT to display this information also indicates an area of potential savings since monochrome CRTs are less expensive to incorporate in the design of a system.

Stores Management Display Format

The final evaluation to be described examined the feasibility of applying pictorial and color-coding techniques to display formats that present information pertaining to the stores being carried by an aircraft (Aretz & Calhoun, 1982). Four methods of presenting stores information were evaluated:

1. Alphanumeric display format.
2. Monochrome pictorial display format.
3. Color pictorial display format.
4. Alphanumeric/color pictorial display format.

Figure 8-4 (see color insert) shows the color version of the pictorial format. The shapes on the aircraft outline indicate the types of stores currently on board. For example, a Mark 82 bomb was represented as a rectangle with a round nose and distinct tail.

The Mark 82 will be used to describe the additional types of information presented for each weapon: inventory, selected, fuzed, armed, and emergency. A Mark 82 available in the inventory was represented by a dashed outline in both the color and monochrome versions of the display format. If the bomb was selected for delivery the dashed outline became solid and the center portion of its body became yellow (white in the monochrome condition). Weapon fuzing was indicated by coloring the nose and/or tail of the pictorial symbol green (black in the monochrome condition). Finally, when the bomb was armed, the center section turned green (black in the monochrome condition). Therefore, the entire bomb would be green (black in the monochrome condition) if all the steps had been completed properly for delivery. In addition, if an emergency condition occurred with the weapon, the Mark 82 turned red (flashed in the monochrome condition). Similar information was displayed for all types of weapons. The alphanumeric format presented the same information in alphanumeric form (e.g., "N FUZE" for nose fusing). During the evaluation, the pilots were required to fly the simulator and respond to several questions concerning the type, state, fusing, quantity, etc. of the stores displayed on the CRT. The statistical analyses indicated that pilot response time for the alphanumeric, color pictorial, and alphanumeric/color pictorial display formats was not significantly different; however, the performance for the monochrome pictorial format was significantly worse than these three.

An interesting point about these results is that there was no performance difference between the color pictorial format and the alphanumeric format. If a color pictorial format is supposed to display information in a more efficient manner, it would seem that the pilots should have performed significantly better with this type of display format. Krebs's rules really do not help in an attempt to explain these data, since the information displayed does not fall neatly into the extremes of each of the rules. That is, the information is not highly formatted nor is it unformatted; it does not have a high symbol density nor does it have a low density, etc. As a result, a follow-up evaluation of the stores formats was conducted to find a possible explanation.

The results of this follow-up study (Stollings, in press) indicated that when the pilot had as much time as was required to answer questions from the same display formats (up to 30 seconds), no performance differences were found; however when the exposure time was controlled to allow only short durations (50–750 milliseconds), pilot performance with the color pictorial format was significantly better than that with the alphanumeric format. Therefore, it appears that in displays of moderate complexity, when the Kreb et al. rules do not apply, one key to potential benefits of color coding lies in the time constraints placed on the operator. Therefore, in a fighter cockpit environment where pilot workload tends to be high, color pictorial formats may increase the rate at which information color in the cockpit can been used to convey information by itself or has been used to code relatively simple geometric symbols and alphanumerics.

Future Applications of Color CGI

The final research example, stores management, is a portent of the kinds of display formats that will be used in future military aircraft crew stations. Based on the kinds of information the pilot needs to complete his mission, the following are prime candidates for future applications of color CGI: primary flight, tactical situation, systems status, and engine health. The next few sections describe advanced concepts that use color pictorial CGI to present this information.

Primary Flight Display Formats

The pilot's primary flight display has been called the attitude director indicator (ADI), a display typical of the traditional computer-generated display. Its major purpose was to show the aircraft's orientation in space (attitude) and to direct the pilot back to his correct navigation path if he deviated from it. With CGI, the designer is not restricted to presenting traditional looking instruments but is free to present primary flight data in a novel manner.

For example, a driver going along a highway has a perception of speed based on the rate at which the broken lines between the lanes pass beneath the car. In addition, the sides of the road and the lane markings aid the driver in positioning the car laterally. Since virtually every pilot is also a driver, a number of primary flight displays have been designed to present a roadway in the sky. Some of the roadways have been turned into channels with the addition of side walls, or into tunnels with the addition of sidewalls and a roof. A channel-in-the-sky display format is shown in Figure 8-5 (see color insert). The use of color in this format also provides an easy means of judging whether the pilot is looking at the inside of the channel (green) or outside (orange).

Tactical Situation Display Formats

Probably the most challenging format to design represents the tactical situation in which overall navigational and threat status is presented to the pilot. Unlike the tactical situation display format discussed in the previous section, the observer's viewpoint does not have to be constrained to looking down on his aircraft but can be translated to assume any viewpoint relative to the aircraft—the viewpoint illustrated in Figure 8-6 (see color insert) is 7000 feet behind and 1000 feet above the aircraft. In addition, the display format includes not only the geographical terrain information needed for the pilot to navigate properly but also features such as towns and rivers and threat and target information. The challenge in designing this display format is that the designer must (a) take into account the geographical codes already presented on paper maps, (b) be familiar with the symbols for target and threats used in tactical planning documents, and (c) incorporate depth cues in the perspective mode so that the picture appears to have a third dimension.

Figure 8-6 shows an example of a tactical situation display format combining symbolic information, in the form of ground gridlines, with pictorial information illustrated by the aircraft and geographical features. This picture points out that it is not necessary to illustrate every feature in detail if the pilot's objective is to navigate and maintain awareness of the general situation. Obstacle avoidance, for example, can be shown very stylistically, and the level of detail required is quite minimal. For instance, the brown hills do not represent each valley and ridge line in the actual terrain, but detail is sufficient for the pilot to avoid running into the hill when flying low and fast. This illustration suggests a general principle in the use of color display formats in the cockpit: The goal is not to create high fidelity replications of the real world, but to represent the outside world adequately enough that the crew can complete their mission. Therefore, while the pilot is flying toward the target, the amount of detail on his displays may be quite modest, but when the pilot gets to the target area, a much more realistic view of the situation may be required. Also, since the high level of resolution needed in the target area is required for only a very small portion of the mission, the computer requirements for this type of display format can be minimized. With current hardware, the likelihood of displaying the type of display formats described in this chapter is probably slight. On the other hand, the air force is engaged in an encouraging program to develop very high speed integrated circuits (VHSIC), which promises to allow for the type of computational power that will be required of airborne computers to present color CGI display formats.

Systems Status Display Formats

In addition to showing the pilot his stores status, pictorial display formats can also show the status of such things as hydraulic and electrical systems (Jauer & Quinn, 1982). Future military aircraft will employ the concept of management by exception when dealing with these systems, which means that their status would be displayed only when called up by the pilot or when a failure had occurred. If a pilot exercises the option of viewing a particular system's status, either normal or failed, the pilot probably would not wish to see a detailed hydraulic system diagram or a complex electrical system schematic. Instead, the pilot is interested in learning if the systems are operating normally, and if not, what impact the failures have on the ability to perform the mission and what corrective action should be taken. For example, Figure 8-7 shows the hydraulic circuit 2A has failed and has caused a loss of nose wheel steering, main landing gear brakes, and hydraulic operation of the refueling probe.

A shaded or cross-hatched border on the display format could also be a convention used for immediate indication that an emergency condition exists or is impending. Once the pilot is aware of the problem, the action items to remedy the situation can be displayed (Figure 8-8). In this example, the pilot is directed to reduce airspeed to 200 knots and pull down, twist, and pull out his landing gear handle. The refueling probe can be extended by the emergency extender, and upon landing, aircraft braking is available through the emergency brakes.

The same information coding technique can be used for electrical failures except that it is a bit more difficult to show the exact part of the airplane that is affected. A view

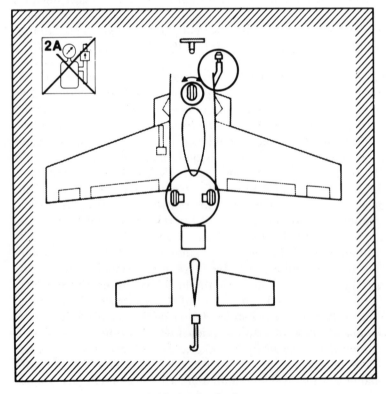

Figure 8-7 Effects of degraded hydraulic circuit.

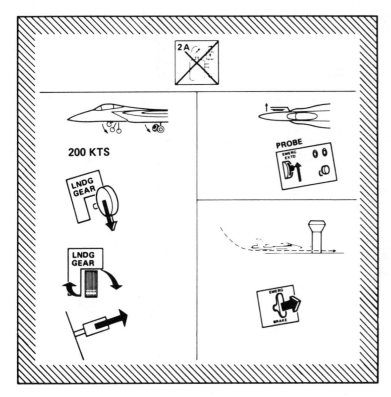

Figure 8-8   Hydraulic emergency actions.

of most avionics bays would depict numerous black boxes. Figure 8-9 is one attempt
to show the impact of a generator failure, which places the aircraft on battery power,
and the corresponding emergency procedures. Briefly, the crew is being shown that
both generators have failed and that electrical load, aircraft trim adjustments, and UHF
radio transmissions should be minimized. Also, on-board stores can be jettisoned, fuel
transfer to the wing tanks has been lost, and the crew should select the option indicated.
This selection may be made via a push-button switch on the periphery of the display
or, in the case of a touch sensitive display, the desired option may be selected by
merely touching the arrow shown.

Fuel Status Display Formats

Fuel status is another type of information required by the pilot. In a pictorial display,
format fuel status can be shown in one overall view that indicates the tank location,
level of fuel in the tank, and the tanks that are transferring fuel. Fuel status information
can be combined with a navigation display to provide available flying range information
(Figure 8-10). The white area of this format indicates the destinations the pilot can reach
easily under current wind conditions and fuel consumption. The circle bounding the
less densely shaded area describes the maximum range points, and the more densely
shaded area is beyond maximum range.

A considerable amount of detailed information is also shown on the format through
the use of alphanumerics. Reading clockwise starting at the upper right corner of the

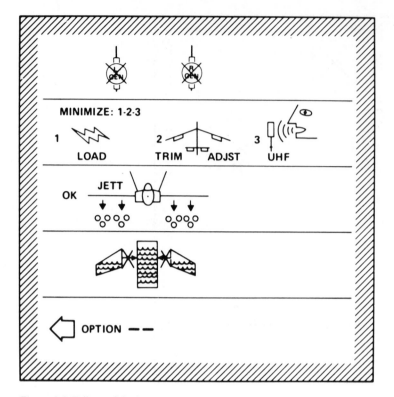

Figure 8-9 Failure of dual generator.

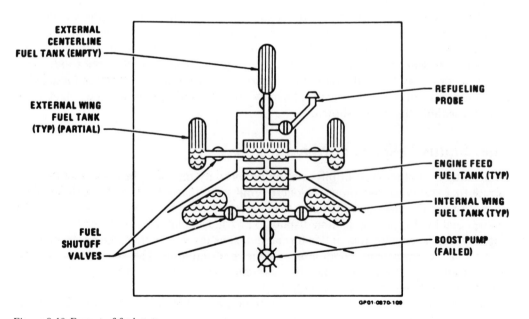

Figure 8-10 Format of fuel status.

format: destination selected is 100 nanometers away, and the estimated or computed time of arrival is 12:40. Present time is 12:27, the aircraft is using 7385 pounds of fuel per hour, and 25 minutes of flying time is available. Finally, 3590 pounds of fuel remain, and 1540 pounds of fuel are required to reach Destination 5. The pictorial format gives the pilot an excellent perspective of the overall situation; the alphanumerics provide specifics.

Engine Health Display Formats

Status, both normal and failed, has been illustrated for hydraulic and electrical systems, but in order to give the reader a deeper understanding of the simplicity in which pictorial formats can convey information, a step-by-step sequence of an emergency in the aircraft's engine is shown. The first scene (Figure 8-11) shows a two-engine aircraft and the status of its engines.

Starting at the top, a thermometer is used to indicate turbine inlet temperature. The shaded area shows the normal operating range and the top, or upper limit of the normal operating range, is shown by the two horizontal lines. A thermometer also shows exhaust gas temperature. N1 and N2 are compressor stages; their performance is shown by the hashed blockeds, and again the double horizontal line is the limit of the normal operating range. The amount of fuel going into the engine is shown by pipes with small circles of bubbles; the radiating lines, or flame, in the exhaust indicate a normal condition. In the next view (Figure 8-12) one engine is in afterburner and the fuel flow is increasing dramatically. Figure 8-13 shows that there is an overspeed of the compressor, and the exhaust gas temperature has reached a dangerous level.

In Figures 8-13 the shaded border indicates an emergency situation. The operator is being directed to reduce the left engine throttle setting to "off" and push forward on the control stick. The format also contains a "clock" in the lower left corner indicating the amount of time the troubled engine can operate under various conditions. Figure

Figure 8-11 Nominal display system.

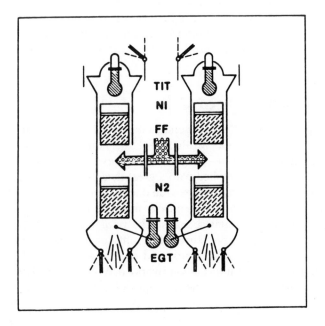

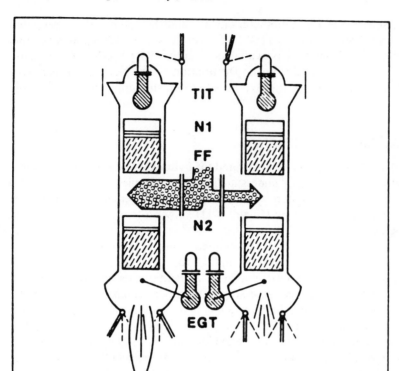

Figure 8-12 Abnormal engine status.

8-14 shows a fire, the upper right symbol telling the pilot to use the fire extinguisher to put out the fire. Again, the desired throttle settings are included. In the next display format (Figure 8-15) the pilot has successfully put out the fire, the right engine is still operating normally, and the pilot is being advised to land the aircraft. Figure 8-15 also presents a suggested course of action if the pilot had not been successful in putting out the fire.

Complex Airborne Display Formats Need Color

As the airborne system operators hand over their "housekeeping chores" of basic system monitoring to the computer, they will be free to concentrate their efforts on maintaining a higher level overview of their mission sitiuation. In order to achieve this level of thinking, however, the operators will have to be supplied with a great deal of information from the aircraft's sensors that their own senses cannot provide due to constraints such as weather, altitude, etc. The data from these multiple sensors must be presented to the pilot in an organized, composite display format, because the pilot will not have time to integrate the information from, for example, three different sensors and still perform all other tasks. Therefore, it appears that complex CGI display formats such as those just described will need color to prevent information overload. Within a display format of this complexity it is very important to examine the types of color codes that can be used.

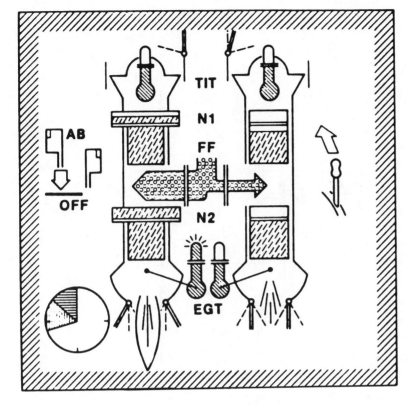

Figure 8-13 Emergency engine status and corrective action.

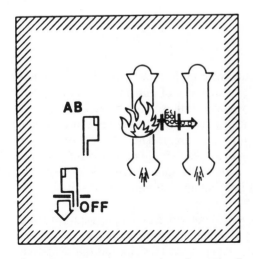

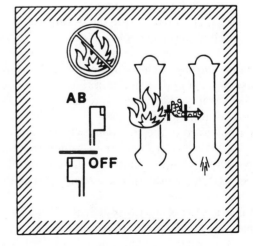

Figure 8-14 Emergency procedures for engine fire.

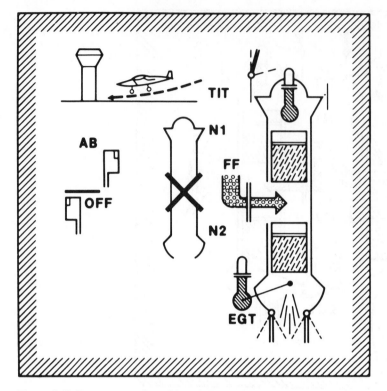

Figure 8-15 Emergency action with extinguished engine fire.

Color Coding Information

Based on the examination of advanced color display formats, color coding techniques can be divided into three categories:

1. Single purpose codes.
2. Color as part of the environment.
3. Dual purpose codes.

Single Purpose Color Coding.   A single purpose color code represents the traditional use of color coding in that a single color portrays one piece of information. Traditional codes will be used extensively in complex CGI formats like those seen in tactical situation display formats. For example, red will be used for enemy missiles and aircraft, amber for unknown or medium danger levels, and green for safe areas. This use of color coding is a further extension of the warning/caution/advisory philosophy in that it still encompasses these states, but now the colors reflect dangers or safe conditions imposed by the external world on the aircraft, rather than internal aircraft subsystem status.

Color as Part of the Environment.   This application of color does not depict information; instead, it adds fidelity to a scene so that it reflects the reality of the world. For example, the sky could be colored blue, and a brick wall or barn could be colored red. Relative to the latter two objects, there is nothing hostile or dangerous about either the barn or the brick wall (unless one crashes into them); their red color merely reflects their natural appearance in the environment. Similarly, the blue color is not an advisory state but reflects the natural color of the sky. The use of color in this manner has been found to be beneficial. Christ (1975) states that "using color in a pictorial display to provide a 'natural' representation of the real world has also been shown to decrease search time." Photographs were the medium referred to in this quote, but one could hypothesize with a fair degree of certainty that color used for natural representation of the environment would also be of value on a CRT.

Dual Purpose Color Coding. The single purpose code, which is an arbitrary use of color without relation to real world cues, and the natural use of that color in the environment can be combined to form a dual purpose code. For example, in a terrain avoidance display, the ground below the aircraft's current altitude can be shown as green, whereas the ground above the aircraft's current altitude can be shown as brown. In a purely arbitrary code sense, brown is used as something one could run into, whereas green indicates a safe area; however, this code serves a dual function in that its choice was based on the color shading of topographical map.

All three types of color codes (single purpose, environmental, and dual purpose) will be needed in a display format that provides combined information from several sources. The challenge for the display designer is to combine all three uses of color carefully so that a synergistic blending results. These "information rich" display formats will exploit the advantages of each type of color code in order to provide a clear, intuitive picture of significant mission and aircraft events.

Why Color Pictorials?

A major theme of this chapter is that information presented to the pilot must be simplified, and that color coding combined with pictorial information is the solution to the information overload problem. Why are color pictorial displays so ardently supported as the solution? The answer to this question is based on the characteristics of human decision making behavior.

Both Rasmussen (1980) and Hofstadter (1979) characterize human decision making as containing three levels of behavior. Rasmussen calls these levels skill-based behavior, rule-based behavior and knowledge-based behavior. Skill-based behavior is defined as an action in which a sensory input signal is received and results in the appropriate response. An example of skill-based behavior occurs when an aircraft suddenly banks left and the pilot's response is to bank the aircraft right to achieve wings level attitude.

Rule-based behavior is defined as an action in which a sensory input signal or series of signals is recognized in memory as applying to a specific set of rules. An example of rule-based behavior occurs when an engine fire-warning light illuminates in the cockpit and the pilot carries out the rules applying to the situation; that is, the appropriate emergency procedures.

Knowledge-based behavior is defined as an action applied to situations in which no set rules or procedures exist but must be created. In knowledge-based behavior, sensory inputs first have to be combined or chunked into symbols that are used to formulate new rules. Once the problem is formulated in this manner, the human resorts to rule-based behavior and applies the appropriate actions indicated by the rules. An example of knowledge-based behavior is a pilot becoming aware of an unexpected threat to his aircraft, such as a surface-to-air missile site. The first thing the pilot has to do is to formulate the problem by gathering data from his displays. In this scenario, the problem formulation process involves assessing the lethal potential of the threat site and determining the appropriate tactical strategy (avoid or destroy the threat) to handle the situation. Once the problem is formulated, it can be solved by applying the appropriate rules.

Hofstadter's (1979) three levels of human decision making are similar to those of Rasmussen. Although Hofstadter does not name his three levels he describes their characteristics when he talks about the flexibility of human intelligence:

> The flexibility of intelligence comes from the enormous number of different rules, and levels of rules. The reason that so many rules on so many different levels must exist is that in life, a creature is faced with millions of situations of completely different types. In some situations, there are stereotyped responses which require "just plain" rules. Some situations are mixtures of stereotyped situations—thus they require rules for deciding which of the "just plain" rules to apply. Some situations cannot be classified—thus there must exist rules for inventing new rules . . . and so on.

In combining Hofstadter's and Rasmussen's descriptions of human decision-making behavior, skill-based behavior corresponds to the "just plain" rules situation; rule-based behavior corresponds to the situations requiring rules for the application of "just plain" rules; and knowledge-based behavior is akin to situations requiring rules for inventing new rules.

These two theories of human decision-making behavior apply directly to the situation in fighter cockpits. In these cockpits, as in any human-machine system, the behavior that is easiest (skill-based) does not solve the most complex problems. Most problem-solving situations require the formulation of new rules. Unfortunately, humans are poor at processing data from several sources and making decisions. In fact, human decision-making behavior is best in situations containing moderate levels of complexity (Benbasat & Taylor, 1982). Therefore, the ideal human-machine interface would allow the operator to work in a rule-based behavior environment. Given current fighter crew stations, pilots are forced to work in a knowledge-based environment. If data are preprocessed and presented properly, rule-based behavior can be applied to a knowledge-based problem—but the key is that the information presented must aid in problem formulation, and it is precisely in the problem formulation process that the benefits of color pictorial displays are realized.

Color pictorial formats aid in problem formulation because information is processed by the avionics before it is presented to the pilot. In current systems, the data the pilot must employ in problem formulation are in raw form and require functioning at a lower cognitive level than is really necessary. The pilot is required to acquire the raw sensory data from several displays and to process the data further by grouping them into chunks that can be handled in memory. Normally, a pilot can handle from five to nine chunks of data at a time (Miller, 1956; Simon, 1974). While color alone can be used for chunking, color plus pictorial coding is even more effective (Teichner, 1979). Color pictorial formats provide processed data already grouped into manageable chunks that pilots can use at once—they are not required to preprocess or chunk the data. Therefore, they can operate at the middle cognitive level of rule-based behavior where the capabilities of humans can be exploited, rather than at the skill-based behavior level of raw sensory data processing or at much more difficult knowledge-based behavior level.

An example of a color pictorial cockpit based on this level of decision making is shown in Figure 8-16 (see color insert). The right outboard display (engine health) illustrates how pictorial color formats provide chunking at the lower end of decision making complexity. For instance, an engine may have seven parameters to monitor, each parameter being a single chunk of data. Since there are only seven chunks, the pilot is in the middle of his processing capacity. For two engines, fourteen chunks result and the pilot has exceeded the upper-end of this processing capacity. However, in a pictorial display format presenting an overall picture of the health of the engine, the data to be processed are reduced to two chunks, one for each engine.

The tactical situation display in the center of the cockpit illustrates how the chunking provided by pictorial formats can aid decision making at the highest level—rule formation. The complexity of the tactical environment, as discussed earlier, requires the pilot to navigate in all types of weather, fly very low and fast, avoid enemy threats, and hit the target. The formulation of the proper rules to accomplish this task is very difficult. Presentation of a single display format of chunked, pictorial data reduces the rule formulation task of selecting from a series of "just plain" rules, because different choices of action (e.g., alternate paths around the threat) can be presented clearly. Thus, preprocessing and displaying information to the pilot in a color pictorial format are of benefit in fighter cockpits—they provide information in a form that allows the pilot to work in a rule-based behavior environment more efficiently.

Conclusions

The use of color CGI in military cockpits is not a simple issue; rather, it is very complex due to the different types and quantities of information that pilots require to maintain awareness of the aircraft's status and the tactical situation. The issue is further clouded by lack of adequate rules to guide the crew station designer in applying color coding and advanced CGI techniques in new situations. In cases at the extreme ends of display complexity, rules exist to determine when color will help performance. However, in the large area between these two extremes, there are few rules or guidelines. Unfortunately, most of the pictorial display formats being designed for military aircraft fall into this gray area. As a result, potentials of color CGI can only be derived empirically to determine what type of color display format or level of abstraction (alphanumeric, schematic, or pictorial) is needed for the pilot's specific information requirements. One thing to keep in mind, how ever, is that increased performance is not necessarily the only justification for the use of color. If cost is not an overriding factor, aesthetic qualities alone can support the use of color in display design. People like color displays whether or not they improve performance.

The main advantage of the color CGI revolution is that it has removed the constraints on the display designer by allowing the application of color pictorials in the cockpit. The display designer is now primarily limited by his own creativity. It is the coupling of the high resolution shadow-mask CRT with CGI that will enable the crew station designer to produce displays that will dramatically improve the pilot's ability to obtain clearer, yet more complete, situation awareness data. Pictorial formats will enable the pilot to "stay ahead" of the mission and allow him to act as a fast-time information processor. The chunking capability of color pictorial formats is probably the most important attribute contributing to this ability. For example, Badre (1982) has shown that color pictorial formats can be used to increase the situational awareness of army battlefield commanders. Color's major role in pictorial formats is clear because the scenes shown to the pilot will be very complex, dynamic, and , in some cases, will have degradation of symbology. These are the conditions under which color has its maximum payoff in performance. Through very careful blending of single and dual purpose color codes within the context of the pictorial display format, it should be possible to provide a simple, clear, and intuitive presentation of information to the fighter pilots of the year 2000.

In fact, the pilots of the year 2000 are already going through extensive "training" in using color pictorial formats through exposure to video games located in every community in the United States as well as throughout Western Europe. Several of these video games simulate fighter attack missions in which the pilot (the player) has to navigate close to terrain and through extensive enemy threats to survive and destroy the target. The players of video games are very enthusiastic concerning these devices (they pay to play), and the more challenging and complex games are, the more they attract the expert players. By designing the information display technology in this manner and by taking advantage of this "training," designers can enhance the transition from video games to the color pictorial crew station. It is even desirable that formats similar to those being used in video games be adapted to the unique requirements of both military and civilian system operators. By developing and testing alternative color pictorial formats now a smooth transition of pilots into future generation fighter aircraft can be assured.

References

Aretz, A. J., & Calhoun, G. L. Computer generated pictorial storesmanagement displays for fighter aircraft. *Proceedings of the Human Factors Society 26th Annual Meeting*, 1982, 455–459.

Badre, A. N. Selecting and representing information structures for visual presentation. *IEEE Transactions on Systems, Man, and Cybernetics*, 1982, *12*(4), 495–504.

Benbasat, I., & Taylor, R. N. Behavioral aspects of information processing for the design of management information systems. *IEEE Transactions on Systems, Man, and Cybernetics*, 1982, *12*(4), 439–450.

Calhoun, G. L., & Herron, S. Computer generated cockpit engine displays. *Proceedings of the Human Factors Society 25th Annual Meeting*, 1981, 127–131.

Christ, R. E. Review and analysis of color coding research for visual displays. *Human Factors*, 1975, *17*, 542–570.

Hofstadter, D. R. *Gödel, Escher, Bach: An Eternal Golden Braid*. New York: Vintage Books, 1979.

Jauer, R., & Quinn, T. *Pictorial Formats, Vol. I: Format Development*. Air Force Wright Aeronautical Laboratories Technical Report (AFWAL TR-81-3156), Wright-Patterson Air Force Base, Ohio, 1982.

Kopala, C. J. The use of color-coded symbols in a highly dense situation display. *Proceedings of the Human Factors Society 23rd Annual Meeting*, 1979, 397–401.

Krebs, M. J., Wolf, J. D., & Sandvig, J. H. *Color Display Design Guide*. Office of Naval Research Report (ONR-CR213-136-2F), 1978.

Miller, G. A. The magical number seven, plus or minus two: Some limits on our capacity for processing information. *Psychological Review*, 1956, *63*, 81–97.

Rasmussen, J.U. What can be learned from human error reports? In Duncan, K., Grumeberg, M., & Wallis, D. (Eds.), *Changes in Working Life*. New York: John Wiley, 1980, 97–114.

Simon, H. A. How big is a chunk? *Science*, 1974, *183*, 482–488.

Stollings, M. L. *Information Processing Load of Graphic Versus Alphanumeric Weapon Format Displays for Advanced Fighter Cockpits*. Air Force Wright Aeronautical Laboratories Technical Report, Wright-Patterson Air Force Base, Ohio, in press.

Teichner, W. H. Color and visual information coding. *Proceedings of the Society for Information Display*, 1979, *20*, 3–9.

Biography

Anthony J. Aretz is a lieutenant in the U.S. Air Force and has been assigned to the Flight Dynamics Laboratory, Wright-Patterson Air Force Base, Ohio since graduating from the US Air Force Academy with a B.S. in human factors engineering in 1980. He has also earned a M.A. from Wright State University in human performance. His primary research interest involves crew system design and evaluation with specific interests in visual displays and speech recognition. He is currently detailed to the Aerospace Medical Research Laboratory as the Deputy Technical Director for the Cockpit Automation Technology program.

John M. Reising received his B.S. in Psychology (1964) from Xavier University in Cincinnati and his M.A. (1967) and Ph.D (1969) in Industrial Psychology from Southern Illinois University, Cabondale, Illinois. Since joining the Flight Dynamics Laboratory in 1972, Dr. Reising's primary research efforts have been in the area of crew system development. His early efforts involved designing fighter cockpits concentrating on the application of cathode ray tubes as multifunction controls and displays. His recent research efforts have been concentrated in developing full-color, pictorial display formats for fighter aircraft cockpits. Dr. Reising has also begun to examine the use of artificial intelligence software to make some of the lower-level systems management decisions for the pilot.

9 Color Displays Applied to Command, Control, and Communication (C³) Systems

PAUL T. BREEN and P. E. MILLER-JACOBS

The Mitre Corporation,
Bedford, Massachusetts

HAROLD H. MILLER-JACOBS

Sperry Corporation
Waltham, Massachusetts

Abstract

Color displays are becoming more prevalent in command, control and communication (C³) systems. The wider use of color in C³ systems is due in part to the belief that color, as compared to monochrome displays, aids in differentiating among different types of data and enables the presentation of a larger volume of data. There is, however, only limited research supporting this increased use. When the use of color is determined to be warranted, guidelines on color selection have been generated that can assist in display design.

Introduction

Command, control and communications (C³) systems are used to gather, store, and distribute the information needed to accomplish both military and civilian missions ranging from military air traffic control and air defense, to the servicing, launching and retrieval of the NASA space shuttle.

In the 1950s, when the computer and display industry was still building capabilities and developing economical manufacturing methods, military development programs led the state-of-the-art in computer and display products. The initial computerized command and control systems developed in the 1950s, such as the Semi-Automatic Ground Environment (SAGE) and the Navy Tactical Data System (NTDS), are examples of government sponsored development programs that provided industry with viable commercial products—including the digital computer itself. Today, the commercial market has achieved awesome growth while the military market has been beset by relatively little growth.

The application of color displays to C^3 systems has been examined many times in the past two decades. Until recently, the use of color displays has been deferred because of poor technical performance, poor reliability, and high costs. Furthermore, there has been an ongoing concern that the use of color displays may not offer significant performance advantages in C^3 applications.

Over the past five years, color display technology has improved, display equipment has become more reliable, and display costs have been reduced (for those products having wide application in the commercial market). While the question of utility remains in many cases, new C^3 applications are being developed for which the use of color is appropriate.

Systems that provide battlefield surveillance, threat assessment, weapon allocation, interdiction planning, and attack control are typical of today's military C^3 task requirements. These tasks require pattern recognition, track monitoring, and—of primary importance—selective information gathering for decision making.

To support this decision making, system operators typically will be supplied with detailed topographic maps (including information such as primary and secondary roads, terrain and elevation) that will show the operator which areas, for example, are screened from radar visibility. Color terminals will be used to display this information effectively. The use of color to code this typed of information is an accepted technique in C^3 systems, as evidenced by its use in topographic maps.

Because C^3 applications call for components that have been proven and are economical, the component choice for color displays is presently limited to cathode ray tubes (CRTs). Figures 9-1 through 9-4 (see color insert) illustrate several applications of color CRT displays on C^3 systems. In the next five to ten years, color displays may well use flat panel devices such as LEDs, plasmas and electroluminescent panels.

This chapter discusses CRT technologies and both the hardware and operator requirements for utilizing color displays in a C^3 environment. The results of an opinion survey on the use of color displays is presented as well as some guidelines for choosing color.

Performance Requirements
CRT Technologies

For many years, C^3 tasks have been accomplished using high resolution monochrome displays with random deflection systems, known as strokers. These displays provide fine grain images with moderate luminance. Because of their excellent performance, monochrome stroker systems are still widely used in C^3 systems. Familiarity with monochrome strokers has tended to promote the use of color penetrons in which the electron beam penetrates lasers of phospor to activate the desired color. However, the limited luminance on the display surface is a problem with color stroker, especially for red images and symbols in ambient illumination that is typical in most offices. Additionally, color penetrons provide a small number of discernable colors—four are advertised but only two or three are actually usable.

Raster displays have been slow in reaching the C³ community because of the high cost of the memory component and control units and also because of poor resolution— it has only been in the past few years that monochrome raster systems have been employed in C³ applications. This is a result of the explosive growth of the business, personal computer and CAE/CAD/CAM (computer-aided engineering, design, and manufacturing) markets. With the drive towards high definition TV by commercial display vendors in the next few years, economical high resolution color raster displays with resolution in the order of 1200 or more lines will be available for C³ applications.

Hardware Performance Requirements

The majority of commercial data processing and display equipment is designed to provide satisfactory performance in a benign environment with a controlled atmosphere; in other words, a home or business office. The warranties of commercial data processing and display equipment specify operating temperature and humidity limits of 40 degrees Celsius and 90 to 95% relative humidity (noncondensing), which is relatively restricting for military applications. Nonoperating temperature and humidity limits are representative of those encountered in commercial transport or in a warehouse with a controlled atmosphere. Shock and vibration levels are consistent with those encountered in commercial transport.

Some C³ applications take place in environments identical to commercial offices while others take place in extreme environments. Military applications often require exposure of equipment to a wide range of temperature and humidity and to the shock and vibration of transport over unimproved roads or on airborne and naval platforms. Military programs that provide benign environment can employ commercial display equipment. Where a benign environment cannot be assured, commercial equipment will not function properly.

Military standards thus exist for these extreme conditions. For example, military equipment provides typically higher (10°C) operating temperature than commercial equipment and close to 100% relative humidity (noncondensing). The humidity standard for the storage of military equipment is similar to the operating requirement, while the temperature standard for storage is increased to 70 degrees Celcius.

A number of recent military programs have specified high resolution color raster scan displays that (a) will survive in applications where transportation over unimproved roads and/or airlift is required and (b) can provide an operational display when contained within an airborne or mobile ground-based platform.

For ground based systems, color display equipment has been fabricated to provide satisfactory operation. Both penetrons and shadow-mask color displays have been employed.

Regarding airborne applications, resonance problems have been noted with the use of large diameter (19 inch) high resolution shadow-mask CRTs. This results because the standard commercial shadow-mask CRT provides insufficient isolation of the mask and electron gun from resonance effects. Work has recently been accomplished to correct this deficiency.

Military standards cover electromagnetic compatibility; that is, the risk of interference with or from surrounding equipment. Military standards exist for a related problem—the unauthorized access to the information on the display screen through the receipt of information radiated from the terminal. Lastly, there is the matter of damage to the terminal electronics from exposure to the electromagnetic pulse (EMP) and nuclear radiation associated with a nuclear burst.

Commercial equipment has recently been required to certify compliance to an electromagnetic compatibility standard promulgated by the Federal Communications Commission. If commercial equipment is used in C^3 applications, equipment must also conform to the requirements of military standards for unauthorized access.

While the use of qualified military equipment and components extends its ability to withstand temperature, humidity, shock, and vibration, it is more expensive. Using available data on representative display systems, military equipment carries a premium varying from two to five times the recurring cost of its commercial counterpart. It is reasonable to assume that this premium will be applicable in the area of color display systems.

Operator Performance Requirements

Color perception depends on each operator's ability to make wavelength discriminations of the light energy falling on the retina. The trichromatic theory of color postulates that there are three types of cone receptors in the normal retina, each containing a different photosensitive pigment. These pigments are sensitive to a Gaussian distribution of wavelengths, with each curve peaking at a different portion of the spectrum. These peak sensitivities have traditionally been labelled as "blue," "green," and "red" representing cones most sensitive to short, medium, and long wavelengths respectively (Mollon, 1982). The names given to colors are culturally learned, and therefore only loosely related to the wavelengths.

Individuals' abilities to discriminate light based on wavelength vary widely, making the concept of "normal" color vision a relative term. In addition, fine wavelength distinctions are difficult even for the person with so-called normal color vision. For example, a checkerboard pattern of 3 millimeter red and green squares is indistinguishable from a gold color when viewed from across a room.

Certain individuals have difficulty making wavelength discriminations that the vast majority of people are capable of making. The three major classifications are:

1. Anomalous trichromats—Individuals in this category have only a color "weakness." The three color systems appear to operate, but the sensitivity in at least one of the three is abnormal in its spectral response. The incidence of this type of deficiency is estimated at 5.9% of the male population and 0.4% of the female population.
2. Dichromats—Individuals in this category appear to have only two of the three color receptor systems functioning. They confuse red and green, seeing both as poorly saturated yellow. They have, however, normal visual acuity. An estimated 2.1% of the male and 0.03% of the female population have this type of deficiency.
3. Monochromats—Very few people (0.003% males; 0.002% females) fall into this category, where there is essentially no wavelength discrimination.

Since most C^3 installations are part of organizations where routine visual examinations can be given (e.g., military services), color deficiency can easily be detected. In those applications in which color display are being introduced, a screening program should be used for selecting operational personnel.

Within some military services, individuals found to be anomalous trichromats are subdivided into categories of mild or more severe deficiency. Approximately 2 ½% are in the "mild" group, and since their vision is very close to normal, few occupations are closed to those people. Chemists and electricians must have perfect color perception because these jobs involve making some fine color distinctions, such as that required during chemical titration or in identifying color-coded wiring. At present, jobs involving the use of color displays are available to persons who are mild anomalous trichromats.

Individuals in the more severe anomalous trichromat group, and those found to be dichromats (or monochromats) may have difficulty in discriminating shadings and colors close in wavelength, and so are considered to have severe deficiencies. They are restricted from certain occupations, such as satellite imagery operator and C³ analyst, that require operations involving color displays.

To insure success when introducing color displays even to screened operators, display should be selected in accordance with the guidelines discussed below. Finally, there is one surefire method of eliminating any potential problem associated with color deficient operators: use female operators, as color deficiency in females is extremely rare.

Color Utilization
Opinion Survey

Extensive reviews and experiments conducted several years ago brought about mixed conclusions on the utility of color (Christ & Teichner, 1974; Teichner, Christ, & Corso, 1977). Color was found to be an effective performance factor under some conditions but detrimental under others. This research may not be directly applicable to today's C³ requirements because most of the research was conducted with earlier generation CRT technology.

In contrast to the equivocal studies of years ago, some recent studies have found substantial performance improvements using color. A recent study of color coding in tactical displays found that when color was used for initial classification, errors and processing time were both substantially reduced. Information portrayed by traditional shape coding required 75% more processing time and produced 200 to 800% more errors than color coding (Sidorsky, 1982). In a study of highly dense aircraft situation displays, redundantcolor coding significantly reduced both response time and error rate (Kopala, 1979).

Irrespective of the positive or negative findings, color is being used on more and more systems. To determine just how widespread the use of color was in C³ systems and why color was specified in those systems, an informal survey of C³ developers was conducted to identify those systems that were either using color displays or specifying the requirement for color.

Survey Respondents and Results.   The sources used for this survey include project offices within the U. S. Air Force's Electronic Systems Division and display vendors and system contractors of the MITRE Corporation. Since this was an informal survey, personal communication was the primary mode of obtaining information. The survey results are not intended to provide quantitative measures of color utility in C³ systems;

rather, these results should be used to indicate if a trend exists in the use of color in C^3 applications.

Twenty-nine systems were identified as potential or actual candidates for the use of color, and they were categorized by primary mission (Table 9-1). The following information was collected for each system:

Prime contractor and responsible agency.

Display vendor and type of display (i.e., shadow-mask or penetron).

Status of the system in terms of its procurement development or operation (as of approximately October 1982).

Primary use of the system.

Rationale that was stated for selecting color displays.

It should be noted that the rationale stated for the use of color was the individual statement of the person being interviewed. It does not represent an official statement of the prime contractor, the responsible agency nor of the display vendor.

Air traffic management systems.   Five systems were primarily used for air traffic management, and four of the systems were made by one vendor. Both raster scan and penetron technology were used. Since the primary mission of air traffic control is maintaining seperation between aircrafts, color was chosen to better differentiate information on the display, with the goal of reducing display ambiguity and, thereby, human error.

Tactical C^3 systems.   Thirteen systems were used for tactical C^3, wherein the basic function is to be provided detailed information on the military situation for detection, threat assessment, and potential engagement. In this category, the primary reasons for selecting color were to provide an alerting capability for changes in the tactical situation, to differentiate various categories of targets and data, and to identify particularly high priority signals in a dense environment.

Satellite control systems.   Satellite control was the primary function of two systems. In these systems, color was used in three ways:

1. Text editing—In this application, color was used to differentiate various types of data, such as edited text from unedited text.
2. Status monitoring—The relative age of status information was shown by changes in color.
3. Telemetry analysis—Color was used to differentiate various types of data.

Management information systems.   Four systems were classified as primarily management information systems, which the display of status information for decision making is the primary function. Color was chosen for one system because of its alerting capability, another because of the high volume of data. In one system, color was mentioned as a specified requirement, the rationale of which was not stated. Finally, one system used color because it was considered appropriate for the state-of-the-art in office automation.

Image analysis systems.   Five systems were categorized primarily as image analysis systems. In these systems, data presented on the display must be interpreted to obtain information on such items as weather and geologic formations. It should be noted that

Table 9-1 Color Displays Applied to C³ Systems

Air Traffic Control (ATC) Systems

System	Prime Contractor/ Agency	Vendor & Display	Status	Used For	Rationale For Color
Advanced Enroute Traffic Control	Sanders/MITRE, METREK	Sanders Graphic 7 (penetron) and recently Graphic 8 (raster scan)	Operational evaluation facility	ATC for 1990 and beyond to enhance traffic safety	To reduce display ambiguity and thereby human error
ATC Digital Simulation Facility	Sanders/FAA, Technical Center, Atlanta	Sanders Graphic 7	Operational	ATC for Human Factors Evaluation and Training	Differentiate critical information in dense environment (e.g., weather)
FACTS (FACSFAC AIR CONTROL TRACKING SYSTEM)	Sanders/Navy Fleet Air Control and Surveillance Facility	Sanders Graphic 7	Operational at several sites	Navy Air Traffic Control	To differentiate: —background and target —ships and aircraft —classes of targets
MATCALS (Marine Air Traffic Control and Landing)	Sperry-Univac/Marines	Sperry-Univac (1657)	Prototype complete and demonstrated September 1982, Production first of 1983	Aircraft landing (in particular, glide/scope) ultimately "pilot hands-off" landing capability	Highlight target in color against background
Tempelhof Automation System	Sanders/ESD	Sanders Graphic 7	Contract Awarded	Upgrade Air Traffic Control	Proposed by vendor as no-cost option

Table 9-1A

Tactical C³I Systems

System	Prime Contractor/ Agency	Vendor & Display	Status	Used For	Rationale For Color
AEGIS (CC-47 Class)	RCA/Naval Sea Systems Command	OTI (Video generator) (Militarized RAMTEK)	Contract Definition	Being defined (likely candidates: Geographical Data, Battle Doctrine)	Primarily: Alerting capability
AN/UYQ-21 (Shipboard System)	Hughes/Navy	Hughes (Stroke Writer)	Updating to color	Sensor and Weapons Control	Alert operator to Control changes in situation
AWACS E-3A	Boeing/ESD	Hazeltine	Shock Mounted Color CRT in development	Airborne Surveillance and C³	Improve detection, reduce errors
BETA	BETA Joint Project Office/TRW	Aydin 5216	Test-bed, for possible deployment as JTFS (Joint Tactical Fusion System)	Automated fusing of intelligence fragments into a battlefield picture	To provide background maps and large volumes of data
E-2C HAWKEYE	Grumman/Navy	Hazeltine	Considering upgrading to color	Airborne C³	Differentiate target classes
Mobile Sea Range IDER (Integrated Data Extractor)	Sanders/Navy Fleet Analysis Center	Kratos (now Display Systems, Inc.)	Operational for 4 yrs Being replaced by Sanders Graphic 7	Mobile Navy C² Range Instrumentation and Control System	To differentiate: —background and foreground data —primary and secondary data

System	Prime/Service	Display	Status	Application	Benefit
Staff Planning and Decision Support System	BDM/Defense Nuclear Agency	Hazeltine	Evaluation stage using commercial equipment	Dispersed Command Post	Differentiate classes of data on map background
TCAC (D) (Tactical Control Analysis Center and ASAS SEWS (C) (All Source Analysis System, SIGINT, and EW System)	RCA/Army	RAMTEK (commercial monitor) used in test bed	Proposed color upgrade for graphics (in competition)	Tactical Ground C³	Reduces error and speeds operators' perception by a factor of 4:1
WMCCS (World Wide Military C² System)	Aydin/ESD	Aydin 5216 (Special)	Partially delivered	C² situation display at WWMCCS sites	High volume of data
MCE (Modular Control Element)	Litton/AF	Litton (penetron)	Full scale engineering development. Deliveries spring and summer of 1984	Tactical Aviation	Target sorting. C² Alerting mechanism.
TAOC-85 (Tactical Air Operations Center)	Litton/Marines	Litton (penetron)	Full scale engineering development. Deliveries spring and summer of 1984	Tactical Aviation	Target sorting. C² Alerting mechanism.
Joint STARS	(No prime yet)/AF and Army	RAMTEK 9400 and AYDIN 5216 used in Brassboard	In Definition	Tactical ground C³	High volume of data
Over-the-Horizon (OTH)	General Electric/AF	Aydin	Preliminary design	Early tactical warning	Complexity and quantity of data

Table 9-1B

Satellite Control Systems

System	Prime Contractor/ Agency	Vendor & Display	Status	Used For	Rationale For Color
Data System Modernization	IBM, Gaithersburg/AF Space and Missile Systems Office	Sanders Graphic 8	Prototype shipped	Upgrade satellite control facility	Text Editing: Background color to differentiate various types of data (e.g., edited and unedited) Status Monitoring: (e.g., color indicates age of status information) Telemetry Analysis: To differentiate types of data
Global Positioning Satellite	IBM, Gaithersburg/AF Space and Missile Systems Office	Sanders Graphic 8	Prototype shipped	Satellite positioning	Text Editing: Background color to differentiate various types of data (e.g., edited and unedited) Status (e.g., color indicates age of status information) Telemetry Analysis: To differentiate types of data

Table 9-1C

Management Information Systems

System	Prime Contractor/ Agency	Vendor & Display	Status	Used For	Rationale For Color
ACCESS (Automated C² Executive Support System)	AFCAC (AF Computer Acquisition Center) for SAC	No vendor yet	RFP released	Management Information System for SAC	Color considered appropriate for state-of-the-art office automation system
AEGIS DDG-51 Class	RCA/Naval Sea Systems Command	In completion	Definition phase	On-board ship diagnostic for battle readiness (e.g., damage control)	Primary: Alerting
Graphics Teleconferencing	Aydin/DCA Commander Caribbean Joint Task Force	Aydin 5216	Awaiting Award	Graphics teleconferencing between command centers	(Unspecified)
Shipboard Five Control Simulation and Training 942 Class Destroyers	Litton/Navy	Aydin 5216	Being installed	Shipboard Fire Control simulation training	High volume, divergent types of data

Table 9-1D

Image Analysis Systems

System	Prime Contractor/ Agency	Vendor & Display	Status	Used For	Rationale For Color
Airborne Weather Radar	Smith Industries and Bendix	Smith Industries and Bendix	Available	Weather data plus: —map data —synthetic aperture radar	High density, multiple overlays
AWDS (Automated Weather Distribution System)	(No prime yet)/Army and AF	No vendor yet	RFP in preparation	Prepare weather reports and predictions	Delineate differences in weather information
Cruise Missile Planning System	McDonnell-Douglas and ESL/Defense Mapping Agency	Aydin 5216 (variant)	Functional prototype delivered	Flight planning for cruise missile	High volume data
IDMS (Interactive Digital Image Manipulation)	ESL Inc./Department of Interior	Comtal	Operational	Geological data	Greater image spectral depth Greater feature identification
Tactical Environmental Support System	(No prime yet)/Naval Air Development Center	Ramtek for software development and proof of principle	Engineering development	Air/surface Oceanography (also C^3 application)	High density

in many of the above categories and, in particular this category, many systems are not listed because of security restrictions.

Discussion of Survey Responses.   The reasons stated for the use of color are listed in Table 9-2 in the approximate order of the number of times an item was mentioned. The most frequently mentioned item was that color facilitates the differentiation of targets from either background targets or noise. A related reason was that color enables the display of a large volume of data considered to be beyond the capability of monochrome displays. Opponents of "color-for-color's sake" and those awaiting research data to support the selection of color, question this reasoning. They argue that target differentiation can potentially be obtained using other data coding dimensions, such as shape and/or size.

Another reason given for the selection of color was its ability to provide an alerting mechanism that facilitates a quick reaction time. Flashing of symbols on a particular portion of the display and indicator lights have traditionally been used as an alerting capability.

It was also stated that color provides greater spectral depth and feature extraction capability. Although this item was further down the list, it is significant in that it may be an area where color can provide information that may not be available with a monochrome display.

Guidelines for Color Use

The primary question to be answered when considering the use of color displays for C³ applications is, "Will the use of color aid the operators in performing their duties?"

A functional analysis of the application is required to answer this question. A key consideration is the display environment. Will the display be subjected to extreme climatic conditions or be positioned in a cockpit or in a low ambient light environment? Have the operators been screened for color-deficiency? How much training and experience do they possess? It is also important to determine any time, accuracy, or other constraints imposed on the system. The responses to all these questions must be factored into the color decision equation. When the functional analysis indicates that color is

o To differentiate between background noise and targets (or foreground).	*Table 9-2* Rationale for Use of Color
o To display a large volume of data.	
o As a quick-response alerting mechanism.	
o To differentiate types of textual data.	
o For greater operator accuracy and speed.	
o For greater image spectral depth and feature extraction capability.	
o Considered appropriate for a "state-of-the-art" system.	

required for system performance, implementation questions arise. This discussion presents some of the relevant research.

Krebs, Wolf, and Sandvig (1978) consider color coding to be helpful under the following conditions:

When the display is unformatted.

When the density is high.

When the operator must search for relevant information.

When symbol legibility is degraded.

When color code is logically related to the operator's task.

Teichner (1979) offers four situations in which color could be effective for display:

In designating a specific target in a crowded display.

In demarcating an area of a display.

For warning signals or commands that have a limited number of possible alternatives.

For classifying or grouping data in which the number of classifications are small.

Although he notes that these applications are well suited for color, Teichner believes that color is not uniquely better than other coding devices and that other coding methods could do the same job. There is, however, one area in which color is unique—in coding map areas, such as terrain changes on a map. In C^3 systems that require the use of map data, color provides a coding dimension not otherwise available.

Number of Colors.   The question most commonly asked by those considering color display is how many colors to use. The answer to the question depends on the application. A multitude of colors may be valuable in an imagery system, while in text and graphic application too many colors, can result in an overwhelming and potentially confusing presentation.

The optimum number of colors recommended for cockpit applications is three or four (Krebs & Wolf, 1979). When redundant color coding is employed (for example, hostiles as red, with hostile airplanes as red diamonds and hostile ballistic missiles as red triangles), six to seven colors may be effectively used (Merrifield & Silverstein, 1982). For air traffic control applications, the use of orange, green, and a broad-band white (that is, having a fairly uniform spectral energy distribution) are recommended to avoid any color-blindness limitations in the controller population (Kinney & Culhane, 1978). Some systems presently under development are specifying eight colors (black, red, amber, green, purple, magenta, cyan, and white).

These suggestions pertain to systems involving search and identification tasks, where each color represents a unique class of information that must be discriminated. For application in which colors have a relative rather than an absolute meaning (such as in the coding of map and terrain data) these limitations are not relevant, and many more colors may be effectively used.

Color Specification.   Since there are individual differences in the way people perceive and label color, even among people with normal color vision, colors cannot be accurately specified by their common names. Colors are usually specified for display applications either by spectral energy distribution or by chromaticity coordinates of the Commission Internationale de l'Éclairage (CIE) system. Spectral energy distribution refers to the relative distribution of light energy among the wavelengths in the stimulus, and is com-

Color Name	Munsell Notation	Chromaticity Coordinates	Dominant Wavelength (nanometers)	Federal Spec 595 Equivalent (paint chips)
Purple	1.0 RP 4/10	X - .2884 Y - .2213	430	27144
Blue	2.5 PB 4/10	X - .1922 Y - .1673	476	15123
Green	5.0 G 5/8	X - .0389 Y - .8120	515	14260
Yellow	5.0 Y 8/12	X - .5070 Y - .4613	582	13538
Orange	2.5 YR 6/14	X - .6018 Y - .3860	610	12246
Red	5.0 R 4/14	X - .6414 Y - .3151	642	11105

Table 9-3   Recommended Colors for a Six-Color Code

monly referred to by the dominant wavelength in that distribution (e.g., a discriminable shade of green is 515 nanometers). The CIE method describes each color in terms of the three primaries (red, green, and blue) and specifies the color in terms of x and y coordinates on the diagram.

Other standards for specifying color are by the Munsell notation and by Federal Specification 595 (for U.S. government work). Six discriminable colors are listed in Table 9-3, along with their specification in each of the above color systems (Cook, 1978). These colors, particularly those at the extremes of the spectrum, are not all applicable to C³ systems without adequate test and evaluation.

Color Verification.   Color verification tests under the condition of the application should always be made before colors are specified. An example of such a verification was conducted for the airborne displays used on Boeing's 757/767 jetliners (Merrifield & Silverstein, 1982). This study examined color discrimination over a wide range of ambient lighting conditions (0.1 to 8000 foot candles). It was found that the color pairs of red-magenta, magenta-purple, and cyan-green were confused more often than other pairs of colors. Modifications in the final set of verified colors minimized the confusion.

It is also important to verify the potential color choices to avoid specifying colors that will create display and visual anomolies that have been noted in the use of color displays. For example, certain people see an unintended three-dimensional effect called chromostereopsis. This effect can be eliminated by avoiding the use of highly saturated colors and providing sufficient ambient illumination.

Color Codings.   The matter of what information should be represented by each color has been the subject of much discussion. Some have advocated that the decision as to which color to assign to a particular type of information should be left to the user to decide. Others maintain that this is a potentially dangerous practice because each operator could assign a different color to the same information. Indeed, in one air traffic control system that was installed in several locations, targets were coded in green in one location and background data in red; at another location the coding was exactly reversed.

A handbook for the design of army material maintains that color codes used on CRT displays be compatible with color stereotypes and conventional usage (red is considered an alerting signal, yellow advises of a marginal situation, and green indicates a satisfactory or "go-ahead" condition). In addition, white is used for indications that do not have negative or positive implications. Blue may be used for an advisory light, but it is not a good choice because the eye is not very sensitive to blue. The convention in military aircraft is essentially the same for red, yellow and green, but white is used to denote abnormalities of lower priority than red or yellow, and black denotes an "off" or not ready condition (Oda & Barker, 1979).

With the proliferation of color displays in C^3, simple and uniform color codes may not be feasible. On the one hand, if color is to provide an additional coding dimension, restricting the coding to overly specific conventions can limit its utility and versatility. On the other hand, using unconventional coding (e.g., red for friendly aircraft) could be potentially confusing. Display designers should use conventional coding wherever applicable and should conduct extensive tests before using newer colors such as orange and magenta. Also, the definition of the color code should appear in the appropriate actual color (e.g., "RED = hostile" in red).

Color and Other Dimensions.   Another aspect of color coding is the question of how color should relate to other coding dimensions. It is generally agreed that random or irrelevant coding should be avoided (i.e., coding not functionally related to operator's tasks or to other coding dimensions). Redundant coding, where information can be extracted from the display either by color or some other coding dimension such as shape (e.g., all hostile airplanes are red diamonds), is generally recommended. Redundancy may only be partial: if red is used to represent all hostiles—hostile airplanes may be red diamonds, hostile ballistic missiles may be red triangles. The use of completely redundant codes is recommended in the military handbook, MIL-HDBK-759A (1981) to ensure that color deficient personnel will be able to use the display. Other reasons for redundancy are for the preservation of information during color shifts due to display instability and aging or in case of color component failure (Silverstein, 1982).

Several other factors must be considered in the application of color to C^3 systems. Symbol size for critical data should subtend at least 20 minutes of visual arc, and should have a luminance of at least 1 Foot-Lambert (Silverstein, 1982). To minimize flicker, refresh rates should be in the range of 60 to 80 Hertz (Silverstein, 1982). The absence of flicker must be verified through testing because size, luminance, retinal position, and phosphor all impact percieved flicker. The color blue should be avoided, and for air traffic control applications, spectral energy distribution should be shifted more toward the middle of the visual range of wavelength making "red" appear as an orange or yellowish red (Kinney & Culhane, 1978).

Conclusion

Since the use of color displays in C^3 systems is still relatively new, there are few relevant standards or specifications. Some guidelines can be found in the references cited, but it is ultimately the responsibility of the display designer to keep abreast of advances in display technology and to research human performance with actual color displays to be used.

In conclusion, although the research justifying color is not overwhelming, there is the perception that it is valuable and its use is therefore increasing in many C³ systems. As the price of color equipment decreases with increased growth of related markets such as CAE/CAD/CAM and the personal computer, color displays will become even more prevalent.

References

Christ, R. E., & Teichner, W. H. *Color Research for Visual Displays.*(NMSU - JANAIR-FR-74-1, JANAIR Report 741103), Las Cruces; New Mexico State University, Department of Psychology, July 1974.

Cook, T. C. Color coding—A review of the literature. In M. J. Krebs, J. D. Wolf, & J. H. Sandvig. (Eds.), *Color Display Design Guide.* (Report ONR-CR213-136-2F), Minneapolis, Minn.: Honeywell Systems & Research Center, October 1978.

Kinney, G. C., & Culhane, L. G. *Color in Air Traffic Control Displays: Review of the Literature and Design Considerations.* Mitre Report (MTR-7728), McLean, Virg.: The MITRE Corp., March 1978.

Kopala, C. J., The use of color-coded symbols in a highly dense situation display. *Proceedings of the Human Factors Society 23rd Annual Meeting*, October 1979, 397–401.

Krebs, M. J., Wolf, J. D., & Sandvig, J. H. *Color Display Design Guide.* Honeywell Report (ONR-CR213-136-2F), Minneapolis, Minn.: Honeywell Systems & Research Center, October 1978.

Krebs, M. J., & Wolf, J. D. Design principles for the use of color in displays. *Proceedings of the Society for the Information Display*, 1979, *20*(1), 10–15.

Merrifield, R. M., & Silverstein, L. D. Color selection for airborne CRT displays. *Society for Information Display Digest*, 1982, 196–197.

MIL-HDBK-795A: *Human Factors Engineering, Design for Army Material*, June 1981.

Mollon, J. D. *Color Vision*, Annual Review of Psychology, 1982, *33*, 41–85.

Oda, D. J., & Barker, B. W. The application of color to ASW tactical displays. *Proceedings of the Society for Information Display*, 1979, *20* (1).

Sidorsky, R. C. *Color Coding in Tactical Display—Help or Hindrance.* Draft report, Army Research Institute, 1982.

Silverstein, L. D. *Human Factors for Color CRT Displays.* The Society for Information Display, International Seminar, San Diego, Calif., May 1982.

Teichner, W. H., Christ, R. E., & Corso, G. M. *Color Research for Visual Displays.* (Report ONR-CR213-102-4F), Las Cruces: New Mexico State University, Department of Psychology, June 1977.

Teichner, W. H. Color and visual information coding. *Proceedings of the Society for Information Display*, 1979, *20*(1), 3–9.

10 Color Displays for Medical Imaging

DANIEL L. M^cSHAN
University of Michigan Medical Center
Ann Arbor, Michigan

ARVIN S. GLICKMAN
Brown University
Providence, Rhode Island

Abstract

This chapter examines the role of color in the presentation of medical images. The important aspects of computerized medical imaging are introduced along with the general benefits and limitations of color in the presentation of medical images. An introduction is followed by a brief survey of the different computerized imaging modalities and their use of color in display presentation. Specific examples are presented on the implementation of color in the presentation of computerized tomography image data and derived three-dimensional anatomical data. The use of interactive computer-generated color graphics for radiation therapy treatment planning are also explored in detail. And finally, some speculations on the future role of color in medical imaging are presented.

Introduction

Computerized medical imaging refers to the acquisition and display of medical image data stored in digital form. The rapid growth in the use of digital imaging in the medical sciences can be attributed in part to the development of a number of new medical imaging techniques. The new imaging modalites of computerized tomography (CT), positron emission tomography (PET), and nuclear magnetic resonance (NMR) require numerical image reconstruction and thus inherently have digital image outputs. Other techniques such as ultrasound, nuclear medicine, and radiography have in the past utilized film or analog video displays but are now being converted to yield digital images. Digital imaging provides several advantages over conventional imaging because it allows a wider dynamic range in the acquired image, the ability to do image enhancements and feature extraction, and the capability to archive the images and recall them rapidly. Most of the digital imaging modalities utilize raster display technology. As a result, color, which comes more or less "hand-in-hand" with these displays, has been available for use in presenting digital medical images.

Early implementations of most of these new imaging techniques have attempted to use color to enhance the presentation of the data. The usual technique involved utilization of a look-up table (a hardware component on most color image display systems) to assign colors to the image values. This then forced all picture elements to have the same color if they had the same image value. A variety of color schemes have been reported ranging from a "hot-body" spectrum to a few discrete colors.

While the visual effects of these colored images were dramatic, the diagnostic usefulness often failed to materialize. For the diagnosticians who were accustomed to seeing monochrome images, color proved to be confusing and tended to obscure the important subtle aspects of the images. Many diagnosticians now feel that the trained observer can easily discern quite subtle changes using monochromatic displays and that color adds no new information. Some of the reasoning behind this attitude may be attributed to a lack of training in appreciating the color associations. However, their attitude is in some sense correct since in many cases the data content and resolution are often quite limited.

The primary image data are, in fact, monochromatic for many imaging modalities and thus yield only the spatial distribution of a single quantity without imparting any functionality that would distinguish different structures of similar image values. The viewer is left to interpret functionality of specific regions based on other factors, such as relative spatial locations, shapes, and texture. Color in many cases obscures this information, especially in areas where the background "noise" level is not constant, causing shifts in the color association. These changes in background are often unavoidable since picture elements normally represent a sampling of a finite volume that may include overlapping regions. An example of this would be a chest x-ray image where the ribs are superimposed on the lung image. Even subtle changes in the intensity of the data can cause dramatic changes in color and hue. The impact of a change in color tends to carry more weight psychologically than intensity changes. Therefore, artificially adding color to an image forces an association between image areas which in fact may be completely different.

In cases where noise or background activity is not a problem, the case for color can be argued. Wagner's (1975) book on nuclear medicine devotes a chapter to the subject and calls it "Color: Contribution or Camouflage?" Wagner makes the point that while the detection of subtle changes in grayscale is possible when two regions are adjacent, the determination of small changes in image content for widely separated regions is not always possible even for the trained observer. Color has the advantage of making these changes visible even to the untrained observer. Wagner points to this as another advantage of color, stating that it is often necessary to convey diagnostic information to the less experienced referring physicians and that color helps point out the important aspects of the diagnosis. Despite these advantages, at present color is not used extensively in presenting digital medical images.

A number of practical reasons have further limited the use of color. There is, for example, the need in medical practice to permanently record diagnostic information for continued care and legal reasons. The cost of permanent color hard copy (especially for life-size printouts) is more expensive than monochromatic copying; furthermore, color copies are not easily duplicated. The cost of publications using color is also prohibitive, thus limiting the exchange of professional experiences needed to establish widespread use of techniques employing color. In addition, color monitors require more attention to insure reproducible color and hue balancing. It is essential that consistent quality of output be maintained not only within an institution but also among different institutions. It is likely, that many of these technical problems will be resolved based on the current interest in color graphics in a number of fields and on the need to share these images. Nevertheless, at present these factors limit the use of color in medical imaging. As a result, when color is used, it is often limited to interactive uses not requiring hard copy or careful alignment considerations.

Despite these limitations and cautions, color is considered useful in a number of areas relating to the presentation of digital medical images. Holman and Parker (1981), discussing computer-assisted cardiac nuclear medicine, feel that color is most useful for functional images in which the functional components have been enhanced, as opposed to primary image data. An example is the display of a stroke volume image obtained by computing the differences (by subtraction) of two nuclear medicine images taken at the extremes of the cardiac cycle. Color in this case can help since there is a strong correlation between the generated image data and the functional characteristics of the spatial display.

A challenging area for the implementation of color lies in those imaging techniques that provide multidimensional data. NMR for example can produce spatial distributions of a variety of measurements. Unlike computed tomography, which measures only x-ray absorption data, NMR can provide tissue differentiation based on identification of atomic structure. Other examples of the use of color for multidimensional images are those techniques that allow real-time studies, such as nuclear medicine imaging for cardiac studies. The extra dimension of time and the ability of modern display equipment to present real-time replays, or even time-lapsed replays, provide diagnostic opportunities previously difficult to obtain. Color helps demonstrate the spatial-time relationships, since it provides locally functional (if not globally functional) landmarks that help track complex motions.

In addition to color's direct utility in enhancing the display of image data, color is an effective tool in conveying information about the image. Even with a grayscale image, color can be overlaid to present alphanumeric text and to display graphics. Text displayed in color is distinguished from the basic image and from other text contained within the same display. For example, color might be used to distinguish image identification data from a list of control commands. Graphics in the form of simple vectors or filled polygons can utilize color to highlight and functionally group graphical entities. The graphics can be plotted in the image coordinate system with geometrical correspondence to the underlying image, or it can be plotted as a separate graph.

A final area of color utilization is in the display of reconstructed three-dimensional images. Displays of anatomy based on precise data obtained from the new imaging modalities are now being effectively used for treatment design and evaluation. The methods are in some ways similar to the techniques of computer-aided design and manufacturing where colors help identify distinct structures. Color and shading provide valuable aids in quickly understanding complex three-dimensional images. The ability to generate and manipulate such displays is a major challenge even to state-of-the-art display systems. Examples presented in this chapter illustrate how color graphics are used first to visualize anatomical relationships and then to design appropriate radiation therapy treatments. The next section addresses different uses of color within the context of each of the specific areas of computerized medical imaging. Because of the similarities in the display aspects of many of these imaging modalities, only the unique aspects and specific examples are presented.

Medical Imaging Modalities
Nuclear Medicine

Nuclear medicine imaging is a well established diagnostic technique in which images are produced by measuring the spatial distribution of radiation emitted from injected radioactive tracer material. This technique is used to observe a variety of metabolic processes. Nuclear medicine studies are generally dynamic studies looking at rates of flow, rates of intake, rates of clearance, or changes in relative concentrations. The images produced are basically two-dimensional displays showing spatial distribution of radioactivity. The history of nuclear medicine dates back over fifty years. During these years, a variety of detection and display techniques have been used, ranging from direct exposure of photographic film recordings to sophisticated gamma cameras and raster display technology. A gamma camera is basically an array of radiation detectors with a corresponding array of collimators such that each detector "sees" a unique area. Events detected are accumulated into a digital array, which is then used to display the spatial distribution of activity. For examining large areas, the detector array (or the patient) can be moved to scan the entire body if required.

The use of color to display nuclear medicine images was first reported in the early 1960s using a simple printout of event counts, with counts above a certain value printed in a different color. A later effort utilized a color-filter wheel to generate color photographs from a monochromatic display. Modern systems allow direct viewing of color video monitors attached to raster display generators. The usefulness of color has been debated in almost every published comprehensive discussion of nuclear medicine technique. Interestingly enough, Wagner (1975), comments that failure of American nuclear medicine practitioners to readily accept the use of color is largely an American problem since the Europeans at least have accepted and practically demand that color be included with all new imaging hardware.

Color applied for nuclear medicine primary image data involves the assignment of color to relative activity. Figure 10-1 (see color insert) shows this use of color for a static series of orthogonal brain scans. In this figure, the red end of the spectrum relates to the high activity areas and blue indicates the low activity regions. Wagner feels that the color displays are generally best (or at least easier to understand) if reduced to a few colors, and his use of color generally is limited to four colors assigned to fixed ranges of activity. Some of the reasoning for this limit lies in the sometimes poor spatial resolution of nuclear medicine images (64-by-64 pixels) and the "statistical noise" of radiation detection. The use of smoothed image data can remove some of the problems of noise and poor resolution.

Beyond assignments based on activity, color can be used in nuclear medicine imaging in more complex and interesting ways. For instance, techniques have been developed that utilize multiple tracer injections using different radioisotopes. With pulse height analysis of the detected radiation, an identification of the activity from the different tracer sources can be made. The display for this study then uses color to distinguish the activity from the two injections. This technique is used, for example, to study myocardial perfusion by injecting different radioisotopes in the right and left coronary arteries. The results highlight collateral flow, which can be overlooked when the two images are examined separately (Wagner, 1975). An example of lung study entails the inhalation of a radioactive gas and an injection of a different isotope into the circulatory system. The combined picture, again using color to distinguish the two sources of radiation, provides a useful comparison of lung ventilation to pulmonary arterial perfusion. Similarly, use of color can be used to distinguish two images acquired at different times. An example is a study comparing the image of a heart at diastole to its image at systole. The changes and areas of overlap are of significant diagnostic value.

A different technique to examine the same cardiac problem is to generate a functional image by subtracting the two images; in other words, subtracting the end-systolic image from the end-diastolic image. The resulting image represents a stroke volume image and is often displayed in color. The image can be further manipulated by dividing by the end-diastolic image (background subtracted) to produce an ejection fraction image. Again, color is often used to display these images since the image values are functionally significant and the spatial distribution of these changes is of diagnostic value (Holman & Parker, 1981).

Computerized Axial Tomography

Computerized tomography has gained wide acceptance as a routine diagnostic tool for modern medical practice. This imaging technique produces high resolution cross-sectional images showing spatial distribution of x-ray absorption values, which are related to density. The raw data measured for CT are basically the same as conventional radiography; that is, the attenuation of x-rays passing through an inhomogeneous media. The measurement is in reality a summation of differential absorption along the path from the source to the detector. With CT, however, additional measurements are made along many intersecting paths taken at different angles, and the resulting data can then be used mathematically to solve for the absorption coefficients for a grid of small incremental volumes. The requirement that the paths be intersecting limits the measurements and reconstructed data to a slice or thin cross-sectional cut. A series of adjacent slices can, however, be acquired in a short period of time (well under a minute for modern scanners) and result in a complete three-dimensional picture of the scanned area (Cook, Dwyer, Batnitizky, & Lee, 1973; Moran, Nickles, & Zagzebski, 1983).

Probably because the characteristics of the measured and derived quantities are similar to conventional radiography, color has not played a major part in the routine use of CT imaging, although most CT scanners are equipped to produce pseudocolored images (Koeze & Meeks, 1983). The use of color is generally limited to enhancing images by comparing images before and after the injection of contrast media. The implementation of color in analyzing the CT image data and in displaying three-dimensional data obtained from multiple slices is discussed later in this chapter.

Positron Emission Tomography

Positron Emission Tomography is similar to x-ray tomography in that a reconstructed cross-sectional image is generated. PET imaging is also similar to nuclear medicine imaging in that it maps the distribution of radioactive tracer material injected into a patient's metabolic system. The technique involves the use of tracer materials tagged with a positron emitter such as 11_C, 13_N, 15_O, or 18_F. The emitted positrons are quickly annihilated by reacting with negative electrons and produce pairs of photons that exit the body in opposite directions. The patient is surrounded by a ring of detectors, and the detection of a coincidence event (i.e., two detectors on opposing sides detecting an event at the same time) defines a path. Again, the acquisition of thousands of intersecting paths enables a mathematical solution that identifies the spatial distribution of the tracer material (Moran et al., 1983).

The use of color in these systems is basically similar to that discussed for nuclear medicine. Like nuclear medicine, the studies tend to be dynamic studies and color is used in functional assessments of the metabolic processes. PET scanning has been used most successfully in looking at the brain and at cardiac functions.

Digital Radiography

Digital radiography is a rapidly emerging medical imaging technique. Effectively, digital radiography replaces x-ray film with a digitally stored image matrix. The advantages that make digital radiography attractive are primarily the greater contrast resolution available and the ability to review a sequence of images in real time. A number of techniques for digital radiography exist but the most common is the use of a digitized video signal taken from a video camera image of an x-ray intensifier screen (a fluoroscope). The typical resolutions of these systems is 512-by-512 pixels, but the demand is generally for higher resolution in an attempt to match the resolution of conventional radiography.

Because digital radiography replaces a previously monochromatic imaging media, color is not normally used in image displays. Color is sometimes used in digital subtraction angiography where a functional image is produced by subtracting an image taken before intravenous injection of contrast material from an image taken after injection. Similar to its use in nuclear medicine cardiac scans, color has also been used in real-time studies using gated heart studies to assess ejection fraction or wall motion abnormalities.

Nuclear Magnetic Resonance

Nuclear magnetic resonance is one of the most promising of the new imaging modalities. NMR imaging is similar to CT imaging in that cross-sectional pixel (volume elements) are measured. Unlike CT though, NMR has no preferred orientation and can easily measure data at any point within the volume. Also unlike CT, which measures only one quantity (an absorption coefficient), NMR can be used to measure a number of phenomena. The measurements depend on the density of the nuclei and the nuclear spin characteristics. NMR, therefore, has the potential for deducing the chemical compositions as well as the spatial distribution of nuclei. Because of this multidimensional nature of the data and because the measurements do not necessarily relate to physical density, it is anticipated that color will be utilized to a much greater extent than in digital radiography or CT imaging. Many of the images demonstrated to date have used color to successfully point out abnormalities or clinical findings. Since functionality can be deduced from the atomic compositions, color can in effect be assigned to different tissue types. It is the hope of many researchers in the field that NMR may eventually lead to identification of small tumor masses based on their characteristic signatures (Kaufman, Crooks, & Margulis, 1981).

Ultrasound

Ultrasound is yet another diagnostic imaging technique. One of the least invasive techniques, ultrasound generates normally two-dimensional images using a sound transducer to generate ultrasonic waves and then to detect the reflections. A measure of depth is obtained by measuring the reflection of echo times. Either by physically rotating the probe or through the use of a linear array of detectors, a two-dimensional image is acquired.

Color has not been used to any great extent in this area of imaging and in fact many of the systems still utilize storage scope displays that are inherently monochromatic. It can be anticipated that new techniques such as Doppler Shift imaging (using ultrasonics) and newer hardware will likely use raster displays and probably color. At least one manufacturer of Doppler Shift imaging equipment used to study the dynamics of cardiac blood flow (Carolina Medical Electronics, Inc. of Dopscan King, North Carolina) has produced an effective color display system to show both image data and analysis data in a composite image.

Other Imaging Modalities

A few miscellaneous imaging modalities use color. Thermography, which measures spatial distributions of infrared radiation, commonly produces color images (although not always stored digitally). Color seems to be a natural for thermography since heat and color seem to be associated. At least one talks of "cool" colors and "red hot" temperatures.

Another area that might be considered medical-related imaging (actually molecular chemistry) is the display of models of molecular surfaces. Displays of highly complex molecules such as the DNA molecule aid the medical researcher in understanding the spatial shape (classically) and the ways in which various molecules can be bound. Demonstrations using interactive color vector and raster graphics have shown simulation studies that allow the user to interactively "dock" one molecule to another. Of course, a large amount of computing is needed to determine if there is a stable minimum-energy binding configuration (Max, 1983).

Treatment Simulation

Computer-generated color graphics for treatment simulation is becoming an important area in medical practice. The input of three-dimensional information obtained from the new imaging modalities (CT, PET, and NMR) is making a significant impact on the physician's ability to carefully plan appropriate treatment. Recent reports have demonstrated the use of these data for presurgical planning, utilizing color graphics to present three-dimensional perspective plots of structural data obtained from CT data (Vannier, Marsh, & Warren, 1983).

The role of color as part of an interactive three-dimensional radiation therapy system is discussed in some detail later in this chapter. Briefly, for radiation therapy, treatment must be carefully planned before any radiation is applied. This planning involves defining the precise location and extent of the volume to be treated as well as the neighboring anatomy and then designing the most appropriate radiation dose delivery technique. The usual goal of this planning is to deliver a uniform dose of radiation to the target volume while at the same time minimizing the exposure and subsequent risk to surrounding healthy anatomy. The radiation modality most often used in treatment is an application of external radiation (Cobalt 60 or higher energy x-rays produced by linear accelerators). It is possible and necessary for external radiation applications to carefully plan the most appropriate placement of these radiation fields so that the treatment goals are achieved. For deep-seated target volumes, the planning requires the design of multiple radiation fields that overlap at the target volume. The establishment of the optimal arrangement is typically an iterative process in which the assessment of the geometrical convergence and uniformity of the radiation delivery to the target volume is balanced against the desire to minimize the dose to the surrounding anatomy, especially structures of critical sensitivity.

The design and assessment of these radiation fields is a complicated process. There are problems in visualizing and appreciating the three-dimensional extent of these volumes. There are difficulties associated with the proper geometric placement of the radiation fields. (Often the best positionings of these fields are at orientations that differ from the more conventional diagnostic radiographic views.) There are also significant problems in assessing the three-dimensional dose distribution relative to the patient's anatomy. Computer simulation using computer-generated color graphics plays an important role in overcoming these problems. Graphic displays of anatomical structures (as defined from diagnostic imaging) with color used to distinguish different structures are an important tool in appreciating the complex anatomical interrelationships. Interactive color graphics are used to design and to demonstrate the placement of proposed fields relative to the patient's anatomy. Color also is used in the presentation of dose distributions, helping to point out the important aspects of the dose delivery relative to the anatomical landmarks. The role of color in treatment simulation is to some extent similar to the other medical imaging areas discussed in that it helps convey functional descriptions of the data. Color helps the viewer to correlate the functionally distinct anatomical description with the proposed treatment descriptions and also with the descriptions of the final effects or results of the therapy. Extensions to both three-dimensional portrayals and to the extra dimensions of therapeutic parameters seem to demand the use of color in clarifying and highlighting the information to be conveyed (Goitein & Miller, 1983; McShan, Haumann, Reinstein, & Glicksman, 1976; McShan, Reinstein, Land, & Glicksman, 1983).

Applications of Color for CT-Based Treatment Planning
Uses of Color in Displays of CT Images

While color has been limited to diagnostic applications of CT, there are some other applications where color is an effective tool when working with CT images and derived data. The uses to be described reflect work done in the Department of Radiation Oncology at the Rhode Island Hospital and, as such, do not necessarily reflect routine practices in a diagnostic CT department. The use of CT data in a radiation therapy department is primarily to assist in treatment planning. CT data yield important geometrical information needed to establish the three-dimensional location and extent of cancerous tumors. In this section, the role of color graphics in analyzing and abstracting information from CT image data and in displaying three-dimensional anatomical pictures is discussed. The following section examines the role of color graphics in presenting these data for planning radiation therapy treatment.

As mentioned previously, color enhancement of the primary CT image data is rarely used; however, color is used for annotation and graphic overlays. Figure 10-2 shows an example of this use in which the underlying image is the result of a CT scan taken in the mid-thoracic region. The CT image is shown using a monochromatic grayscale. Color is added to the image through the text annotation on the border and with the color-coded contours used to identify anatomical boundaries. Color is also used for the graphic overlay, which is a plot of CT image values found along the red line that passes through the two lung cross sections. The horizontal axis of the plot represents distance along the line. The vertical axis represents the CT value magnitude. The two large dips in the curve profile are the intersections with the low density lung tissue. The horizontal green band superimposed is used to indicate a window on the range of CT values (vertical axis). The points along the line that indicates the cut are shown in yellow when the underlying CT values fall within the windowed range. This image is used to establish appropriate windows that will be used to define regions.

The displays in Figure 10-2 and the remaining figures (see color insert) are generated using a DeAnza ID-2212 image display system. This hardware displays a 256-by-256 square pixel image with 12 bits per pixel. Two of the bits are forced red and green overlay bits. The remaining 10 bits are mapped through lookup tables to regulate the 4-bit digital-to-analog converter analog output on each of the three color channels. Hardware text generation is provided at the bottom and right hand sides of the display, and each character can be displayed in one of four colors. While the particular hardware used is perhaps not important to the ensuing discussion, it is helpful to at least know the inherent capabilities of the display system. Often the attributes of a given computer-generated color graphics presentation are dictated more by features of the hardware than by design of the computer graphics programmer.

For example, in the system described the color selection and positioning for the text annotations are fixed by the hardware. The application software and interactive hardware interfaces have in this case taken advantage of this feature by providing a console with color-coded buttons and potentiometers. In Figure 10-2 and in the remaining figures, the text on the bottom row is a selection menu with each selection color coded to correspond to the appropriate button to be pushed to make the selection. While perhaps not as direct as a light pen or touch pad, this scheme provides a convenient technique for quickly making selections when buttons are the means of interaction. The technique allows the button functions to be programmable, and the limit of four colors is usually sufficient. Color coding of text is also used to indicate adjustable parameters.

In Figure 10-2, the grayscale for the underlying CT image is controlled by two parameters. The current values are indicated in the lower right-hand corner. Color-coded potentiometer control can be adjusted to make changes to the respective colored parameter. The use of color to annotate the variable parameters is an effective tool eliminating the need to remember the functions of numerous controls and avoiding extraneous labeling of commands such as "B1:" for Button 1.

In addition to the use of color for text annotations, color is used for graphic overlays. Figure 10-2 illustrates one example of how graphic overlays can be employed. Graphic overlays have the advantage of not destroying the underlying image and thus can be used to quickly plot temporary information. The graphic overlay may reflect a one-to-one correspondence to the underlying image or may represent a separate plot of data—both are used in Figure 10-2. The line intersecting the lungs is plotted in the image coordinate system while the profile plot is not.

A similar use of graphic overlay is presented in an associated histogram analysis program that allows the user first to define a region of the image using a rectangular window overlaying the CT image and then to see a histogram of the CT values for the pixels contained in the region. One of the applications of both the crosscut profiles and the histogramming program is to establish appropriate thresholds on the image data so that a region of similar density can be defined. If one can assume that the density within a structure is sufficiently uniform and distinct from surrounding tissue, then the anatomical structure can be isolated using simple thresholds. An overlay plot that highlights the pixels containing CT numbers falling within the chosen threshold provides a useful functional image. Often an image may contain many areas with similar density (the same problem in attempting to display primary image data in color). With the overlaid display of regions, the user can quickly isolate a particular region and, if desired, invoke an automatic boundary tracking routine that will track the edge of the region. The definition of regions is useful both for defining boundaries and for analyzing specific features of the underlying data. For example, cross-sectional areas can be measured and evaluations of density variations can be made for the regions enclosed. Similar measurements made on an adjacent set of scans result in a volumetric measurement.

The final use of color shown in Figure 10-2 is the outline plots indicating borders of relevant anatomical structures. Ideally, these would be plotted using overlay planes, but in fact they are written by overwriting the underlying image with values that map into an unused portion of the lookup table. (The reason for this is the limitation in the number of overlay bits available and the number of colors required to distinguish different structures.) The anatomical information is contained within the primary CT image, and identification of these boundaries is somewhat superfluous in the image shown in Figure 10-2.

Color identification and overlaying plots are, however, helpful in verifying the proper identification of these contours. The reason for making the identification is based on a desire to appreciate the entire volume imaged. In particular, for radiation therapy the user wishes to visualize the volume to be irradiated with respect to neighboring anatomy. One technique for visualizing the three-dimensional structure is to abstract anatomical boundary information from serial cross sections. With this information, anatomical surface descriptions can be made and plotted as a three-dimensional perspective projection. Manual identification of contours on multiple (20–30) CT cross sections is tedious and time consuming. Automatic boundary detection can be implemented for most of the gross anatomy with roughly 80% reliability. The problems in identification occur because of artifacts in the primary image data, partial volume effects due to finite slice thickness, or abnormal anatomical structures. Since the identification process is not perfect, it is generally necessary to verify and edit some of the contours. For this verification, a composite plot of all contours with color identification is helpful in quickly identifying erroneous boundaries.

With properly identified boundaries, the reconstruction and display of anatomical surfaces can be made. Figure 10-3 illustrates a reconstruction for the upper thoracic region. The surfaces of the external skin (back surface only) are shown in blue, the lungs in white, the spinal cord in green, and the esophagus in yellow. Actually, the esophagus is the target volume that for therapy treatment planning includes the immediately surrounding region. The definition for this boundary was made manually. The plotted surfaces are color coded and shaded, limited to ten gradations. While the image is quite abstract and seemingly removed from the detailed CT data, the viewer is reminded that the geometrical placements of the structures is based on precise cross-sectional information. The color coding is obviously artificial but has proven to be more effective than monochromatic images in helping the viewer appreciate the image.

Use of Interactive Color Graphics for Radiation Therapy Planning

Radiation therapy is a treatment modality that has proven effective in treating certain neoplastic or cancerous diseases. Radiation applied at sufficient levels is lethal to biological cells, primarily through damage to the DNA structure. While not particularly selective between healthy and abnormal cells, radiation can significantly reduce, if not eliminate, the bulk of the disease when concentrated at well-defined malignant tumor sites. Radiation therapy is most commonly administered using external beams of high energy photons or electrons. In some situations where the tumor is accessible, radioactive sources are applied directly to the tumor area. The prediction of the amount of absorbed energy deliverable by the different modalities can be made quite accurately. This capability allows the radiation therapist to preplan the treatments carefully, usually with the assistance of a computerized treatment planning system.

The computerized treatment planning system assists in the planning process by providing graphics to show the placement of radiation fields (or sources) in relation to the target area, by providing rapid calculations of the radiation dosimetry, and by displaying the distribution of dose delivery in relation to the patient's anatomy. This computer simulation is generally a highly interactive tool allowing changes to be made rapidly with quick calculations and interactive displays and evaluation of distributions. Computer-generated color graphics in these systems are of value in helping the planner to quickly understand and appreciate the geometrical relationships between target (tumor) volumes, nearby anatomy, radiation sources, and radiation dose distributions.

Basically, the goal of radiation therapy treatment planning is to maximize the radiation delivery to the target volume while minimizing the dose to the healthy surrounding tissue, especially to organs of critical sensitivity. In others words, the goal is to deliver a "tumorcidal" dose of radiation to the tumor while reducing the chance of complications caused by radiation-induced damage to normal cells. The first step in radiation therapy planning is to define the region to be treated and to appreciate its relationship to neighboring anatomy. As mentioned in the previous discussion on CT imaging, computerized tomography has greatly enhanced the accuracy of knowledge and appreciation of the three-dimensional structure of both abnormal and normal anatomy. The ability to precisely define and localize the regions to be treated now gives the radiotherapist much more confidence in designing treatments that tightly conform to the actual tumor volumes. Three-dimensional pictures, such as Figure 10-3, which are based on the actual patient data, are useful not only for appreciating the geometrical relationships but also for designing the actual treatment plan.

For external beam therapy applications where one is generally dealing with a diverging beam of radiation, a highly useful tool for planning is to simulate the view as seen by an incoming beam. This technique conventionally has been carried out using diagnostic quality x-ray imaging sometimes with direct fluroscopic television viewing. This same technique can now be done using computer simulations based on tomographic data. Figure 10-4 illustrates a simulation of this type. It portrays the same upper thoracic anatomy shown in Figure 10-3, but with the left lung and bronchus removed. The target volume shown in yellow is for an esophogeal tumor. The viewing angle is that of an incoming beam approaching perpendicular to the esophagus's long axis and at an anterior lateral angle. The rectangular graphic overlay, shown in red with gridded central axis, simulates the position and orientation of the incoming beam portal as defined by rectangular collimators. With this simulation, the beam portal graphics overlay can be interactively adjusted and quickly aligned to fit the tumor area. The cross-hatched areas shown in blue indicate regions where the radiation field is to be blocked, further refining the conformation of the field to the tumor volume. For this type of imaging, color is valuable in helping the user to quickly sort out the various features of the display. The use of solidly shaded surface displays of the anatomy is more generally acceptable to medical users than a wire frame or vector plot. Color vector plots are, however, used for the beam description and overlay the view of the anatomy.

Proper placement of the beams is only part of the requirements for radiation therapy treatment planning. One also needs to calculate the resulting dose distributions and to evaluate the radiation delivery with respect to the desired target volume and surrounding anatomy. Here again, computer graphics are commonly used to show the relationships. A common technique for viewing at the distribution is to plot isodose curves on top of a cross-sectional picture of the anatomy; similar in effect to weather maps showing isobar lines overlaying geographical maps. With CT or other cross-sectional image data available, an effective display is to plot isodose curves overlaying the primary image data. Figure 10-5 shows a cross-sectional slice through the center of the thoracic anatomy portrayed in Figure 10-3. With the dose normalized to 100% at a point in the center of the target volume, the 90, 50, and 20% isodose curves are plotted and labeled. A different type of labeling can be achieved by color coding the isodose lines. Color coding is convenient if standard color assignments are made and has the advantage that it avoids the need for labels which can obscure the underlying image.

Evaluation of the two-dimensional cross-sectional distribution must be extended to other cross sections in order to fully appreciate the three-dimensional dose distribution for the entire treatment volume. Figure 10-6 shows one type of display that can be used in an attempt to present a composite three-dimensional view of the dose delivery. Three cross-sectional planes taken through the midpoint and the two ends of the target volume are plotted in perspective with outlines for the external contour and important internal anatomical landmarks. The beam portal entry points are also plotted. The color coding of different structures as well as hidden line removal helps the viewer in visualizing the contour associations from one level to the next. Due to the low display resolution (for vector plotting) isodose curves are not plotted; instead, a pseudo color scheme is used by loading the display pixels (which project on to the calculational planes) with values proportional to the dose. The color lookup table is then used to assign color to different ranges of dose. This type of display is very effective. Since the lookup table can be modified quickly, selected ranges of dose can be highlighted and the range can be interactively adjusted. Because these modifications affect only the lookup table, the changes occur simultaneously for all planes displayed, giving a more "coherent feel" to the three-dimensional display. In addition, a cursor can be positioned at points on the display and a readout can be made using the image display pixel values. Readouts are shown for points in the region of the target and the spinal cord at each of the levels. This same display technique can be applied to orthogonal planes and to arbitrary cross-sectional cuts. When used with orthogonal planes, the dynamics of the highlighting option gives a good appreciation of three-dimensional shape of the dose volumes. Similarly, this technique has been applied to displays of anatomical surfaces where dose delivery has been computed from points on the surfaces and the results have been projected onto the surface display. Figure 10-7 demonstrates this for a treatment in the region of the cervix. It shows a portion of the bladder and rectum surfaces and the dose distributions on these surfaces. In this case, an intracavitary radiation application is used and the position of these sources is shown.

While perhaps some of the images demonstrated here for use in radiotherapy treatment planning could have been implemented using only monochrome display, color enhances the displays, helping the viewer to distinguish different structures in the display of multidimensional data. The primary purpose of graphic displays is to convey information, and color helps the user to rapidly understand complex displays. Color distinguishes primary image data, such as CT data, from generated data, such as radiation dose delivery. Used interactively, color highlighting of dose distributions especially with three-dimensional portrayals is a valuable tool for quick assessment of a particular treatment plan. In summary, the use of color graphics is of benefit to modern day radiation therapy treatment planning. It gives the treatment planner an added dimension in comprehending the complex geometrical relationships required to plan optimal radiation treatments.

Future Prospects

As newer imaging techniques prevail and the technology improves, the medical community will have a wealth of high quality images yielding not only descriptions of spatial extent but also important diagnostic information relating to pathology and metabolic processes. Undoubtedly, color will continue to find increasing utility in the presentation of these images. Color will likely find the important role hoped for by early researchers in computerized medical imaging.

The earlier difficulties with color are now being resolved. Higher resolution images now eliminate much of the color "artifacts" introduced by sudden changes in image content typical of low spatial resolution images. Cheaper and faster color hard copy is forecast for the future and will greatly facilitate the use of this diagnostic information in planning for appropriate care and in documenting the results for the patient's medical record. Color will continue to play an important role in displaying functional images obtained directly from the new imaging techniques or indirectly from sophisticated analysis. And color will find a much greater role in assisting the medical therapist in treatment planning and simulation.

The increased use of color graphics can be attributed to the system designers, researchers, and clinical users who are all becoming more experienced in the most appropriate uses of color in presenting the information needed. There is, of course, a continuing need to assess what is appropriate and to insure that the use of color does not overly enhance or obscure the findings required for proper medical assessments.

Exciting prospects exist for the role of color in future medical systems. The area of dynamic imaging, which is used to study real-time or time-lapse processes, is likely to increase dramatically with imaging devices that will allow, in effect, three-dimensional "movies" of biological systems (Wixson, 1983). The use of color in dynamic cardiac studies of blood flow and wall motion kinetics was discussed earlier. The extension of this using PET imaging will enhance these studies with demonstrations of the three-dimensional aspects. Similarly, dynamic CT scanners that can acquire real-time images are being built. These new imaging techniques coupled with new graphics systems that can perform real-time manipulations of complex space-filling structures will provide staggering amounts of data that would on their own overwhelm even the most competent viewer. Computer enhancements and color will be needed to assist the viewer in following and interpreting the complex spatial-time relationships.

Another area in which color will find increasing usefulness is in the realm of combining multiple imaging modalities. Most diagnoses are made on the basis of many sources of information. It is often necessary to physically relate information from multiple sources at one display station. The value of color in displaying multidimensional data obtained from different sources or different time frames has been discussed earlier. The same argument can be extended to the combining of images from different modalities.

The concept of multimodality imaging stations provides interesting challenges to medical system integrators. Problems abound in comparing images obtained from different techniques, ranging from differences in patient setup and orientations to differences in resolution and scaling of the data. A centralized way of collecting, archiving, and retrieving the data is also needed for such a system. There is a growing movement to create hospitalwide electronic networks that will provide this centralized service. The technology to provide both the high-speed data transmission and the massive amounts of data storage is now on the horizon with fiberoptic transmission lines and digital optical recordings capable of 2^{10} byte storage capacity on a single platter (McShan et al., 1983; Meyer-Ebrecht & Wendler, 1983).

With a further extension into the not-too-distant future, one can foresee these imaging stations possibly becoming part of a complete workstation. The workstation concept would allow not only image retrieval, but also access to library services, electronic mail, and patient data bases; and it would provide enough local computing power to analyze and display plots of medical results and statistics in color. Experiments in workstation concepts are being explored at a number of sites. One of the more ambitious efforts is being carried out at Brown University where a broad-band cable network has already been installed. A link to Rhode Island Hospital, a Brown affiliate, will be established in the future; and although the network will be used mainly for educational purposes, the lessons learned in the use of workstations that have access to centralized reference services and image and voice data will likely be applicable to the development of a physician's workstation. The examination of the role of color will be part of this experiment.

In summary, color graphics is likely to play an important role in the future of medical imaging. As new imaging modalities provide more noninvasive diagnostic insights into medical problems, the challenge to the medical community is to use that data in the most effective manner for the care of the patient. The use of color graphics is only a minor component in the overall process of health care and is not likely to revolutionize medical practice. Nevertheless, in a number of areas of medical imaging and medical planning, it does serve to enhance the ability of the medical practitioner to more fully appreciate the information needed to make sound medical judgments and in some areas can further aid in the design and evaluation of the best treatment possible.

References

Cook, L. T., Dwyer, S. J. III. Batnitizky, S., & Lee, K. R. A three-dimensional display system for diagnostics imaging applications. *IEEE Computer Graphics and Applications*, 1983, *3*(5), 13–19.

Goitein, M., & Miller, T. Planning proton therapy of the eye. *Medical Physics*, 1983, *10*(3), 275–283.

Holman, B. L., & Parker, J. A. *Computed-Assisted Cardiac Nuclear Medicine*. Boston: Little, Brown, 1981.

Kaufman, L., Crooks, L. E., & Margulis, A. R. *Nuclear Magnetic Resonance Imaging in Medicine*. New York: IGAKU-SCHOIN Ltd., 1981.

Koeze, T. H., & Meeks, D. R. Pseudocolor image processing of computerized tomographic scans. *Proceedings of the International Computer Color Graphics Conference*, March 1983, 171–177.

McShan, D. L., Haumann, D. R., Reinstein, L. E., & Glicksman, A. S. An interactive three-dimensional radiation treatment planning system. *British Journal of Radiology Supplement*, 1976, *15*, 144–146.

McShan, D. L., Reinstein, L. E., Land, R. E., & Glicksman, A. S. Automatic contour recognition in three-dimensional treatment planning. In *Computed Tomography in Radiation Therapy*, editted by Ling C. C., Rogers C. C., & Morton, R. J., New York: Raven Press: 1983, 167–173.

Max, N. L. Computer representation of molecular surfaces. *IEEE Computer Graphics and Applications*, 1983, *3*(5), 21–29.

Meyer-Ebrecht, D., & Wendler, T. An Architectural route through PACS. *Computer*, 1983, *16*(8), 19–28.

Moran, P. R., Nickles, R., & Zagzebski, J. A. The physics of medical imaging. *Physics Today*, 1983, *36*(7), 36–42.

Vannier, M. W., Marsh, J. L., & Warren, J. O. Three-dimensional computer graphics for craniofacial surgical planning and evaluation. *Computer Graphics*, 1983, *17*(3), 263–273.

Wagner, H. N. Jr. (Ed.). *Nuclear Medicine*. New York: H. P. Publishing, 1975.

Wixson, S. E. Four-dimensional processing tools for cardiovascular data. *IEEE Computer Graphics and Applications*, 1983, *3*(5), 53–59.

11 Color and the Computer in Cartography

JUDY M. OLSON
Department of Geography
Michigan State University
East Lansing, Michigan

Abstract

Color serves both aesthetic and functional purposes on maps. It is one of a relatively few symbol characteristics, or visual variables, that are available for graphically encoding information. There are a number of guidelines for using color on maps, and several color schemes are illustrated here including the monochrome, double-ended, and continuous-tone schemes for representing single sequences of values; the double-ended hierarchical scheme and its continuous-tone variation for showing values above, below, and near the average; two-variable and three-variable schemes; and shading schemes. While CRTs are probably the most commonly used computer device for color map display, other hardware offers additional opportunities for exploiting the computer in color map production. High quality computer-generated maps depend on appropriate equipment and a knowledge of maps.

Introduction

Cartography is concerned with the manipulation of spatial information for human comprehension. Most often, this manipulation results in a graphic product—a map. A map has certain characteristics that give it a unique position within the whole set of tools used by human beings for organizing and comprehending. It is a spatial representation of something that is inherently spatial and, as such, is an analogue of the original. It is also a symbolic representation on which the visual emphasis depends upon the map maker, who, within constraints to be sure, has the power to select what will be shown and how it will be represented.

When it comes to the choice of how things will be represented, color has long been used on maps and is undoubtedly one of the most noticeable symbols the user encounters on them. When employed carefully and knowledgeably it plays an extremely important part in the functioning of the map. The effectiveness with which map makers use color varies considerably, however, as one can readily observe in examining sample specimens from numerous sources.

The issue of effective use of color in mapping brings up several questions: What does the the the term "color" mean in conjunction with maps? Why use color on maps? What are the "rules" that are followed in using color effectively? What are the basic color schemes in a design repertoire? The answers to these questions will provide background for acquiring a facility in employing color on computer maps. The questions are also the backbone of this chapter, its purpose being to stimulate the reader to use (and see) color purposefully, for comprehending information, and not simply "because it is there." But the topic of color and computers in cartography also brings up a complementary set of questions: How are computers used to produce color maps? Are computers contributing to effective use of color on maps or leading to worse products? And is current technology a reason for great excitement or a source of frustration in maping? The answers to these questions provide a broader perspective on color mapping with computers.

The approach taken in this chapter is rather different from other expositions on color in cartography, and the interested reader may well wish to explore other works as well (e.g., Keates, 1962; Kimerling, 1980 and 1981; Olson, 1981; Robinson, 1967; Robinson, Sale, & Morrison, 1978; White, 1979).

Principles of Map Design with Color

An understanding of the basic rules associated with color use in mapping begins with some knowledge about characteristics of map content, or map subject matter, and the whole set of symbols used to represent map content. The subject matter portrayed on maps ranges widely and is limited only by the interests of human beings and by the constraint that the subject matter must be "mappable", i.e., spatially distributed and sufficiently concrete that definite marks can be used to represent it. Maps can also range from the very simple to the very complex. Only a few visual characteristics of symbols can be used to represent all these phenomena, and color is prominent among them—so prominent, in fact, that when color is used, the map is often referred to as a "color map."

Color Maps

What is a color map and why is color used on maps? Since the term "color" can have several variations of meaning, its use as an adjective with map requires definition. The terms "decorative" and "functional" will also be explained because they are keys to understanding the importance of color in mapping.

The term color, in its scientific sense, includes the dimensions of hue, value, and chroma; in this sense, every map uses color. Even the simplest monochrome map must have symbols that contrast with background, and this contrast is almost always established by differentiated value—normally black symbols on a white background. In this definition of color, all maps are color maps and the adjective does not narrow the term maps at all.

When the term color is used as an adjective with mapping, however, it is generally used in the vernacular sense of "nonmonochrome," or, more accurately, it is approximately synonymous with "chromaticity" (the combination of hue and saturation), and it implies that chromaticity is varied on the map. Even when defined in this narrower sense, color is so important in mapping that it has long been used despite the great expense it has added and despite the difficulties in producing it.

Color serves a number of purposes in mapping that can be divided into two broad categories: decorative and functional. The *decorative* category includes aesthetic use and the use to gain attention. Color has long been used for aesthetic purposes, and there no doubt will always be an aesthetic effect on maps when color is well used. It also invites attention; whether aesthetically used or not, color has a tendency to attract the eye and cause a map to be noticed and remembered, perhaps even if the memory is devoid of content. Who cannot remember the colorful maps on elementary or junior high school walls, for example, with little or no recollection as to what the colors represented?

But no doubt one of the most important reasons for using color on maps is to symbolize and to represent some defined component of content. This is what is referred to as the *functional* use of color. Green may be used to represent vegetation, red may be assigned to a specific class of roads, and blue may indicate water. On another map, red dots may represent out-migrants and blue dots in-migrants to an area. The functional use of color facilitates clear representation of relatively complex information and is often indispensable even when aesthetics are not a concern. Color may be indispensable even when a map has a captive audience whose attention will be directed to it whether it is colorful or bland or anywhere between. How, for example, could all the relevant information be recorded on a visual flight chart without the use of color? Or how could a complex land-use map be comprehensible in black and white?

Any purist will soon notice that it is almost impossible to put color on a map without its representing something, so the decorative/functional distinction requires some further examination. On a map with light green over the entire area within its borders, printed on a page that is otherwise black and white, is this light green decorative or functional? It means "map area" as oppposed to "margin of the map," and in that sense it is representational. On another map, a beige may be present within the black lines delineating blocks of a city, with streets remaining white. The beige stands for "nonstreet areas," so again it represents something. But are these uses of color functional? If so, how could color be put on a map such that it would *not* represent anything? Putting altogether extraneous pattern of color over a map simply is not done. The light green and beige *are* redundant symbols, however, since the black lines already distinguish map from margin area and blocks from streets. Take away the black lines and the green is truly functional as the only symbol for map area and beige as the only symbol for blocks (Pearson, 1980).

The implication is that a redundant symbol is a decorative one, raising the question of whether that notion is sound. It is well known, for example, that discrimination is often significantly improved by redundancy, hence it serves a representational purpose (Shortridge & Welch, 1982). It is also obvious that color on many maps, perhaps including the ones just described, is more dominant than the other symbolism that made it redundant! Even more complicated is the case of a map on which orange represents the low values (e.g., population density), green the medium values, and red the high values. Color certainly represents something, and it is nonredundant. But the map could just as well (and more effectively) have been mapped in monochrome (light, medium, and dark) tones. This use of color should surely be classified as "decorative" then, probably more attention-getting than aesthetic.

A more precise (though admittedly verbose) way of defining decorative use of color, then, is to say that it is either redundant to or a substitute for monochrome symbols without significantly increasing the amount, accuracy, or speed of information retrieval. Functional use of color, on the other hand, would imply not only that color represents something but that a monochrome representation of it would adversely affect amount or accuracy of information or speed of extraction.

Although categorizing each and every use of color as decorative or representational is difficult, the concepts are useful and the extreme cases at least, along what is undoubtedly a continuum, are recognizably different from one another.

Basic Rules of Mapping

Color (i.e., chromaticity) is an important way of symbolizing information for reasons that are found in an examination of the basic rules used in selecting map symbols. With the large, virtually infinite, variety of things cartographers might want to map, color is one of only eight visual variables, or symbol characteristics, that can be used (Bertin, 1967). The others are shape, orientation, grain, size, value, x-location (angle in polar coordinates), and y-location (radius in polar coordinates). Figure 11-1 (see color insert) shows examples of variations in each of the eight visual variables.

The eight variables are not necessarily used with equal frequency. The number of variations for each varies, and each of the variables is not equally noticeable on a map. More important, however, the variables are not interchangeable with one another except to a very limited degree. A coin toss might decide whether to use size or value to represent variations in the productivity of mines, but there are very good reasons for not considering shape for representing that feature.

Some visual variables readily suggest differences in kind while others suggest order and still others suggest not only order but also amount. Color and shape variations readily suggest differences in kind; orientation and grain evoke a sense of order; and size and value are the variables that readily suggest amount. The x- and y-location variables are generally used together to represent either a location in space or a combination of order and amount. Generally speaking, then, visual variables are used according to the nature of what is being represented. Cartographers usually do not use red, green, purple, and blue to represent a sequence of numerical values, nor do they normally employ symbols differing in size to represent items that differ in kind. They are much more inclined to use value (lightness-darkness) to represent, for example, varying temperatures, and differing shapes or colors to represent such objects as different types of buildings.

But how rigid is the application of such rules, or, rather, how rigid should they be? "Most of the time" would probably be the conclusion. Perhaps an even more interesting question, however, is how often is the map maker or designer aware of applying these rules? Although successful maps usually employ the visual variables according to the nature of the data, it is doubtful that memorization of the visual variables and their association with kind, order, or amount, leads anyone to be a good map designer. Rather, practice in good map design (or in looking carefully at maps) probably leads to the understanding or internalization of the visual variables and the types of data they can encode and convey most efficiently. (Compare this to learning languages: as an adult one learns a foreign language by memorizing grammer rules and trying to use them; as a child learning a native tongue, practice comes first and realization of the rules later.) Nevertheless, a look at the list of visual variables and their rules of application does at least instill a sense of the high degree of orderliness in mapping.

One must also realize that the choice of visual variables for specific phenomena on a map is only one (albeit important) component in choosing symbols. A map normally encodes several different things, and several different relationships must be maintained on a map. Rivers differ in size from one another; they differ in kind from roads and from forests. If enough relationships are combined, the cartographer may not be able to encode according to the rules. And some visual variables do not work as expected. For example, in making a black-and-white map showing land uses that differ in kind from one another, the cartographer may try to use patterns without varying value. It soon becomes apparent that patterns of equal value are much less visually different from one another than patterns of differing value (see Figure 11-1). Even if economics permits the use of color, the cartographer will probably find that value also must be varied to produce a reasonably successful map, that is, one with adequate contrast for reasonably efficient information extraction.

Other guidelines enter into map making that have nothing to do with whether data are differentiated on the basis of kind, order, or amount; and most of them relate to color rather than to other symbols. These rules are generally not in conflict with matching an appropriate visual variable with data type but are complementary or additional matters that enter into design decisions.

One of these additional rules states that because larger areas of color look more saturated than small areas, regardless of what certain bright colors might represent on a map, they are extremely dominating visually if they happen to cover large areas (Robinson, 1967). Bright yellow representing a land use that takes up most of the map is probably not a good choice, while it would be quite suitable for some land use that occurs in scattered small patches. A color that covers a very small area needs to be fairly bright and highly different from colors that cover other small areas if it is to be readily differentiated.

The size of area also enters in when using less bright colors that look unappealing over large spaces. One example is an experimental version of a map that I happened to seen in proof form. A seemingly suitable and logical scheme of colors had been chosen from small color chips, but when applied to the map, the dominant color gave the map an undesirable and uninviting look. The ugly color scheme was quickly abandoned.

Another color guideline is that certain colors are conventionally associated with certain phenomena (red with warm, blue with cold, green with vegetation, etc.). Cartographers should bear these associations in mind when choosing color for maps (Robinson, 1967).

When working with color CRTs to produce color maps, cartographers may well encounter the "advance and retreat" phenomenon and find it a problem. Different wavelengths of light come to a focus at different distances behind the lens of the eye; thus a patch of red may appear to be a different distance away from the observer than a surrounding field of blue. The more saturated (purer) tones on the CRT are probably more conducive to advance and retreat than the less saturated colors often associated with printing inks and paper. Hence, users of CRTs may have to be conscious of the need to tone down certain colors.

A completely different, but still important matter in examining the use of color on maps is that of color sophistication. Knowledge of color theory affects the way individuals use and see color. A spectral progression, for example, may look quite arbitrary to the novice and quite orderly to those with more knowledge of color. Avoiding use of a spectral progression in favor of a progression of some other visual variable is not always possible or desirable. Even with the risks of losing potential readers who do not understand color space, there is nothing inherently wrong with using the more subtle relationships in color space to represent analogous relationships among data.

Basic Color Schemes

Having considered the visual variables and their relationship to data type, having looked at other guidelines associated with color on maps, and having noted that color knowledge affects the way in which individuals are able to use and see color the question arises: Are there prototype color schemes to ease the problem of choosing and reading color on maps? Indeed there are; some of the major ones include the qualitative scheme, the single sequence, the double-ended sequence, the two-variable scheme, the three-variable scheme, and the shading arrangement. These are best explained by example. The maps illustrated have used the computer to varying degrees from not at all to direct preparation of the slide from which the printing materials were generated. While the primary purpose for including them is to discuss the color schemes, a brief summary of the degree of computer involvement in each is included in the next section.

Qualitative Color Schemes.   Figures 11-2 and 11-3 (see color insert) are of qualitative color schemes. The map in Figure 11-2 differentiates twelve different classes of land use that are essentially different in kind. Some land use types do bear more similarity to one another than others (wetlands and water, for example), and tones that are similar to one another have been chosen for these groups. The map in Figure 11-3 assigns various colors to different countries that have claims in Antarctica. The one departure from a simple qualitative scheme is that overlapping claims have been assigned colors that combine the hues representing the individual countries. Areas claimed by both Great Britain and Argentina, for example, are a combination of the reddish tone representing Great Britain and the bluish tone representing Argentina. Value has not been kept constant on these two maps, but the variation does not by itself represent anything; it simply aids in differentiating tones.

Single Sequence Schemes.   Figures 11-4, 11-5, and 11-6 (see color insert) are examples of single sequence schemes. Each scheme progresses from light to dark as represented values progress from low to high. The scheme in Figure 11-4 is a monochrome, or single-hue progression. The large number of tones of the single hue works well on this map of a continuous surface, i.e., a surface that progresses gradually from one value to another. On such a surface, the boundaries between tones can be labelled with numerical values and any given tone will be neighbored on the map only with the next lightest and next darkest ones. Hence, there is little chance of confusion as to the identity of the various tones on such a map.

A double-hue progression, but still representing a single sequence of values, is used in Figure 11-5. This allows greater contrast from one tone to another. Only four tones are used on this map, but longer sequences are quite possible when double-hue progressions are used. Note that the noncontinuous nature of the surface in this map would make large numbers of tones (especially if monochrome) more difficult to identify than on the previous map.

The scheme in Figure 11-6 varies continuously to represent the range of values. (Three alternatives to the browns appear in the upper left.) This variation of the single sequence scheme is becoming more common as more maps are produced on computer equipment, especially CRTs. It is not generally feasible to create this type of map manually, but computer production of them is quite straightforward (Sibert, 1980).

Double-Ended Schemes.   Double-ended schemes are represented in Figures 11-7, 11-8 and 11-9 (see color insert). These schemes actually make use of three psychologically distinguishable hues with the one in the middle of the scheme representing "the norm," and the other two representing "below the norm" and "above the norm." Thus, there is a hierarchy of categories with this type of scheme. In Figure 11-7, for example, there are nine categories present but one can easily group the greens, the yellows, and the reds into three visual categories. In Figure 11-8 the seven categories can be grouped into purples, grays, and browns. A fairly large number of categories can be represented with such schemes while retaining legibility. Interestingly enough, the color scheme in Figure 11-8, with its seven categories, was designed to accommodate the red-green color blind as well as those with normal color vision.

Figure 11-9 employs a double-ended scheme in which the tones vary continuously. Like the scheme in Figure 11-6, this variation is made feasible by the use of computers and appropriate peripherals (Sibert, 1980).

Two-Variable Schemes.   A two-variable scheme is used in Figure 11-10 (see color insert). There are many variations in the symbolism for this type of map and the example here has a spectral scheme, that is, one that uses all three primaries. The use of all three primaries results in four different highly saturated psychological hues in the four corners, with intermediate combinations in between them (around the periphery of the legend box) and less saturated colors in the center of the legend box. This two-variable map is a case where the structure of the color scheme is probably obvious only to the viewer who has a fairly solid knowledge of color space. Interestingly enough, the scheme also results in a qualitative representation, with regions of homogenous values easily distinguished from other regions of homogeneous values. The data encoded were sequences of amounts, however, and tones more or less varying in value (lightness-darkness) were used to encode each separate variable (Meyer, Broome, & Schweitzer, 1975).

Three-Variable Schemes.   Figure 11-11 (see color insert) shows an example, although a somewhat unusual one, of a three-variable color scheme. The three colors represent three different variables, in this case persons within three categories of length of residence. The color mixtures on the map give an indication of the proportion of residents in each neighborhood within these three classes of length of residence. Changes in the mixtures from place to place are distinctly visible with the largest proportions of short-term residents in the Fenway/Kenmore and Allston/Brighton neighborhoods (with their proximity to several universities), and high proportions of long-term residents in the southern neighborhoods and East Boston. A high degree of mixture in length of residence is clearly visible in all neighborhoods.

Shading Schemes.   Shading schemes are illustrated in Figures 11-12 and 11-13 (see color insert). In the map of Saguaro National Monument, the shading is a sort of natural rendering of the area and is superimposed with topographic information. The color scheme is continuous and represents a combination of lighting effects (it assumes a light source from the northwest) and the colors one would actually see in that area.

Figure 11-13 is a combination of tones representing various land uses with modulations of each to give the impression of superimposed shaded relief. The legend shows several tones for each land-use category because there are several possible tones per category on the map depending upon where a patch of land is located relative to the northwest light source. While it is obviously not possible to distinguish the category of every individual patch of land (there are 161 differently specified tones on this map), the general patterning and sense of terrain does come through. Like Figures 11-6 and 11-9, this map was created on a color CRT.

Computer Production of Color Maps

The examples of color schemes give at least a general idea of the ways in which color can be used on maps. Most of the examples used here were manually produced or were only computer-assisted, rather than produced by computer in final form. Any of the color schemes could be emulated on a computer, but there were three main reasons for using manually produced maps here: they were readily available; a computer-generated map is not necessary to illustrate most of these schemes; and it is still extremely expensive to produce computer maps comparable in quality to manually produced maps.

Figure 11-2 was manually produced, although the data were probably processed through a computer at one stage or another. Preparation of Figure 11-3 included computer plotting of the projection, the plot serving as the compilation that was then retraced with appropriate line widths and generalization. It is a classic example of a "computer-assisted" map, in that the computer was used only in selected parts of the mapping process. Here the computer enabled the student to choose the projection and its orientation according to the needs of the map rather than according to what was available. Figures 11-4, 11-5, 11-7, 11-8, 11-11, and 11-12 are all manual products; they could have been created on a computer but the quality would not be matched without a very sophisticated system. Figures 11-6, 11-9, and 11-13 were the ones produced totally on computer systems. None of these three would likely have been produced at all if manual methods had been necessary. Although the graphic quality is reasonably good for computer-produced products, it does not compare with the conventional products. Figure 11-10 is a computer-assisted product. Color separations were produced on a computer-output-on-microfilm unit, while subsequent steps in the process were conventional.

These examples provide only a limited representation of computer involvement in color map production, but they do raise awareness and suggest that computer production of color maps comes in great variety.

Equipment and Systems

Modern computer technology is giving more and more opportunity to exploit the use of color in mapping, but there is no single best device for producing a color map. The variety of ways of exploiting the computer usually involves variety in the hardware devices. While an individual's interest in color mapping may be spurred by a home computer or by some specific device at the workplace with color capabilities, any broad understanding of mapping in color by computer demands a broad look at devices and mapping systems.

The color CRT with an image that has been called up in one way or another to meet some immediate need is by far the most pervasive means of producing a color image at this time. A fair number of maps have been produced in this way. Such maps are often viewed only by a temporary audience, or they serve only as intermediate versions leading to a better final product using some other device.

The color CRT is not only the device that first comes to mind when computer maps are mentioned; it is also the one with the broadest applications. The image can be obtained quickly by processing through a mapping program, by displaying an already prepared picture file, or by displaying from some computer-accessed device such as a video disc. The technology is also going to be far more widely available than any other one that is useful for producing color maps. There are already numerous opportunities for obtaining color capabilities on home computers, and it is conceivable that maps will regularly be made available through video services to those with home computers (BYTE, 1983).

The CRT by itself produces only the temporary or soft copy image, a problem that may be of less and less concern as access to CRTs increases. A number of specially designed camera devices are available to preserve the imagery (Dunn, Matrix, Polaroid, Modgraph, Lang, and others). An ordinary 35-millimeter or other camera on a tripod can capture the display on the screen, but with the specially designed cameras, the signal is sent to a flat black-and-white screen within a closed box with a camera at the other end, and the primary color components (red, green, and blue) are successively exposed to the film frame through color filters. The resulting hard copy may be a slide, a print, or a transparency.

While this type of output does serve the purpose of preserving the image, it is not very useful for large-scale reproduction purposes. If the color image is subsequently to be reproduced as printed copy, it must be camera separated into component tones (the subtractive primaries this time, yellow, magenta, and cyan, plus black) and converted into a series of varying size dots (half-toned). Not only is this an expensive process but it also tends to degrade the image, if ever so subtly. Ordinary photographs consist of tones grading gradually into one another, which can be camera separated very successfully for printing. In contrast, a map is normally made up of discrete tones with distinct boundaries. The resolution of the screen and the film used to record the image from the screen has already decreased contrast and blurred boundaries, and the camera separation generally compounds the problems. (Figures 11-6, 11-9, and 11-12, which come directly from the CRT, were all continuous-tone maps.) The resulting printed image is suitable for illustrating papers concerned with mapping techniques, algorithms, and the like, but it is not generally suitable for production mapping. Such maps as U.S. Geological Survey (USGS) topographic maps produced in this fashion are unimaginable, and such a system is hardly the answer to the entire problem of producing maps.

Another way to capture CRT images on film is to use black-and-white film so that color separations can be produced directly without the color film image in between. Panchromatic continuous-tone film would pick up the varying tones as varying density on the film. The image could be enlarged to the desired scale and the images half-toned. The problem remains that half-tone screening of multitone images results in degradation. As a viable alternative, the U.S. Census Bureau (among others) has for several years used high-contrast film to capture the area of each separate tone in a map (Meyer, Broome, & Schweitzer, 1975). This high-contrast film results in crisp boundaries between the open areas and the opaque background of the film, and these frames serve as the open-window masks for tint screening when enlarged. The subsequent process of transferring the image to printing plates, then, is identical to that used in conventional mapping, and the resulting printed image is comparable in quality as well. In addition to Figure 11-9, the *Urban Atlas* series (U.S. Bureau of the Census, various dates in mid-1970s) and the *Atlas of Cancer Mortality* (Mason McKay, Hoover, Blot, & Fraumeni, 1975) serve as examples of such products.

Another device commonly associated with CRTs is the color plotter. Most involve ink-jet technologies (Applicon, ACT, Tektronix), but impact units with color ribbons are also popular (Tri-log), and a powder-based photo-charge unit has recently been introduced (Versatek). These devices are again more useful for single copies rather than for originals to be used in reproducing large numbers of copies through printing. The camera separation procedures must be employed if the image is to be printed, and again the results are not comparable in quality to methods involving high-contrast, high-resolution color separations.

In contrast to the CRT and accompanying camera and color plotter methods, pen plotters produce color maps by means of pens with colored inks. Until faily recently, the pen plotter was probably the most common means of producing single-copy color maps, rather than reproducible ones. Pen plotters with a selection of one to eight pens of various colors are common, and the color rendition is obtained by assigning different pens to different items on the map. The plotter is more suitable for drawing lines than for filling in areas and when maps are composed primarily of line symbols, the plotter is a very useful mapping device. Drawing lines close together fills areas, but the process is slow at best. Also, combinations of the pen colors to fill in area has extremely limited use; red and blue pens, for example, are not very useful for producing purple.

Open-window separations for printing can also be produced on a pen plotter, and lines or areas that are to be printed in different colors are plotted out as separate images. The biggest problem has been consistency of line quality as the pen plots. It requires a good technical pen or high quality felt tip (not the commonly used ballpoints) and high quality paper or inking film to produce separations in this manner. For accurate plots, flatbed rather than a drum plotter is desirable.

In conventional mapping, it has been common for many years to produce linework directly in negative rather than positive form. A slight variation in the plotting process (conceptually slight, but in practice demanding much higher quality equipment) allows this to be done by plotter as well. Rather than a pen, a scribing point is used, and scribing film replaces the inking surface. While the adjustments on the plotter become even more critical with this setup, the result is a plate-ready negative, generally of higher quality and with far finer (thinner as well as more even) linework. The negatively scribed sheet of linework is then used as the master for exposure of photosensitive peeling material, which is handled in conventional fashion.

The delicacy of hardware adjustment for scribing and the potential versatility in using a light beam and photographic material for plotting have resulted in the relatively widespread use of photo plotters in high quality map production. The processes of moving the light beam from point to point with the beam either off or on and sweeping out areas by successive plots of lines close together are essentially the same as the processes used in pen plotting. Both linework and open-window negatives can be plotted out automatically without changing materials or drawing tools, and plate-ready negatives of final size are quite feasible. With sufficiently detailed data sets and a well-adjusted plotter, the results can be impeccable. Until recently, the equipment required was very expensive because a flatbed plotter was needed (Gerber, Xynetics). With the introduction of drum plotters with light heads (Gerber), the cost has been reduced but is still relatively high compared to such methods as simple pen plotting.

For some applications, the variation in hardware is almost a cross between the photo plotter and the CRT that is photographed. In place of a light beam, a small CRT displays a small section of map. The section is exposed, and the map is built of a whole series of such exposures. Similarly, templates of, say, lettering can be exposed to film from devices that substitute for the lighthead on the plotter.

Another variation of the hardware that produces an image by means of a lighthead is sometimes referred to as a photowriter. This device is commonly used to plot out digital imagery (for example, Landsat scenes) and plots cell-by-cell (i.e., in raster format, rather than drawing lines between endpoints). It also varies the intensity of the beam and produces an image of varying density. As the definitional boundary between maps and images has become more and more hazy, this type of device must be included in discussions of automatically produced maps.

Laser platemakers are at the most sophisticated end of the scale of photo plotters (Scitex, Intergraph). This type of device can even eliminate the need for photographic materials intermediate to the plate that will be used for printing. The image, in the form of lines, solid areas, and even dot screens, is exposed by means of the laser either on photographic materials or directly onto the plates for color printing.

Two clarifying comments should be made before leaving the topic of hardware used to create color maps. First, the various pieces of hardware have numerous variations. Second, several methods of generating a color map image are possible for any given application. Modern customized systems (the so-called "turnkey systems" such as Scitex, Intergraph, Broomall) are using CRTs to allow working on the image and monitoring of progress and accuracy (King, 1981; Holomes, 1982). But the output may be via a camera, a pen plotter, a photo plotter, a laser platemaker, or a choice of more than one of them depending on the application of the system.

Effects on Quality of Maps

Map quality is greatly affected by just how a map is produced. There are at least two distinct influences on computer map quality—the system itself, which includes both the hardware and the software, and the way in which the system is used, that is, the human element in automated map production.

Hardware and software have certain inherent limitations, and no matter how intelligent the human beings are who are using them, they are inevitably constrained by these limitations. A character CRT (one that only produces characters in discrete spaces) can be used to create maps, for example, but these maps will inevitably be gaudy products. Questionable as the idea is of using such a device for mapping, a character CRT can produce maps quickly and cheaply, which could be the deciding factor in their favor for some applications. In this case, the quality of the product inevitably suffers because of the system.

It takes both a high quality system and appropriate use of it to produce good maps, and the process of accommodation between systems and mappers is still developing. Certainly the early days of computer mapping, when output was limited mainly to the line printer, were retrogressive from the standpoint of map design, and the constraint was primarily the technology. As devices became more varied and ideas for exploitation developed, the role of computers broadened to something more than merely faster production of maps. They made it feasible to do some things that were not feasible by hand—highly controlled continuous shading and timely series of maps of demographic distributions, for example. In a sense, then, hardware and software were beginning to affect mapping itself, not just speed, and as such were having a constructive effect on maps even if visual quality still did not come close to that of conventional maps. As hardware and software developed, the human side of the quality issue became at least as important as the hardware and software side. This was partly because the hardware and software has simply lost some of its extreme limitations, but also because the increasingly sophisticated technology has tended to encourage the technical expert instead of the cartographer to be the map maker. Hence, cartography went through a stage in which relatively fine systems were used to create low quality maps. More recently, however, the tendency is for equipment to be developed that truly suits the problems at hand (the turnkey mapping systems). At the same time, there is a tendency toward separation of the computer expert and mapping expert, who are linked by a dialogue as both become more conscious of the problems and unique contributions of the other. By no means has some ideal equilibrium been reached, but developments have taken place both on the hardware and software and the human sides of the problem, and computer maps are no longer inevitably recognizable by a crude electronic look. An outstanding example is the map called "History of Europe" produced using a Scitex system (National Geographic Society, 1973). It compares very favorably in quality to traditionally produced maps of its kind by National Geographic, and it demonstrates that computers in mapping have made strides of progress.

Problems, Frustrations, and Excitement

All this may sound as though cartography is at a stage of great flexibility in the employment of computer equipment for color map production. In one sense this is true—if one can afford the equipment. In another sense, color mapping by computer can still be troublesome in the extreme. Color CRTs are relatively inexpensive, but they produce softcopy that is difficult to share. Adding a camera requires introduction of the technician to handle the equipment, and there may be significant time required for photo development or a good size budget needed for fast developing materials. The hardware exists to make color separations for printing, but careful planning is required to obtain cost-effectiveness as opposed to intellectual and technical excitement, and the software must be structured for the output devices.

Even a process so seemingly "old hat" as plotting with a technical pen can cause hours of trial and frustration. For example, a cartography student recently attempted to produce sample maps using a form of dot symbolism being tested in her research. Ballpoint output was not entirely suitable due to unevenness in the area tones being created, but switching to technical pens and higher quality paper was disastrous when the slow drying liquid ink was smudged every time the next dot fell too close. In another example, a staff member of a production lab inked in by hand all the solid areas of several large cross-hatched plotter maps. His reason was that, while the coarser cross-hatching was very fast on the plotter, he could fill in the solid areas much faster himself and far more cheaply! What is more, his computer service center discouraged area filling because of the computer time consumed and the backlog of plots that can result.

It is also counterproductive to worry about two such divergent issues as looking for equipment for producing something printable and looking for equipment appropriate for a milieu that is increasingly electronic. Sometime in the future, when everyone can access from home or office a desired image from vast collections of some great electronic library, there will be little need to worry about how maps are processed in order to be printed. After all, if everyone could access maps at a terminal, printing would be an unnecessary process. But in the reality of today, if a cartographer puts together an interesting map that is to be shared with others, the opportunities for transmitting it electronically to the desired audience are next to nil. The map must be printed to be shared widely. In one sense, the separate concerns of mapping for electronic display and mapping for printing are not a waste of effort. Despite the rapid advances in technology and its distribution, paper maps as well as electronic ones are probably here to stay for a long while. But the balance is changing and the appropriateness of one or the other for specific applications is not very clear-cut, and the cost of equipment and software to be able to do both can very easily exceed the budget.

Despite the frustrations, there is ample reason to be excited about modern technology in the field of mapping. Perhaps the three most significant developments can be summarized as follows:

1. Use of computers by a wide variety of people is expanding. This means that there is far more flexibility in the mapping world than just a few decades ago.

2. The quality of color CRTs has increased greatly, permitting production of electronic maps that not only lacked feasibility under manual production, but are of decent visual quality.

3. The development of systems geared to high quality printing means that printed computer maps are now comparable in quality to manually produced maps. Even their cost-effectiveness is fast becoming a non-issue, and their products give hope that exploitation of modern technology will no longer be associated with poor quality products.

Summary

Color use in mapping is here to stay, and it did not take the invention of computers to make it viable. But with the increasing variety of computer hardware and software, much of which has color capability, the use of color is increasing and the need to understand its effective use on maps is also increasing.

A look at the visual variables shows how color fits in as one of only a few that are available. Numerous guidelines exist to aid mappers in using color appropriately, and several basic color schemes (qualitative, single-sequence, double-ended sequence, two-variable, three-variable, and shading schemes) serve well in mapping a wide variety of phenomena.

There are numerous ways in which computer systems are used in mapping, and developments in modern technology have been associated with a wide range of quality in the resulting map products. Both the equipment and the human beings using it affect the results, and both can impose limitations on map quality.

Computer use is far from free of frustration, but developments are at a point where the use of computers to produce color maps is also a source of excitement. With more people using computers, with higher quality and less expensive color equipment, and with systems capable of high quality printed results, a sharp knowledge of how to exploit the use of color on maps will find extensive use.

References

Bertin, J. *Semilogie graphique*. Paris: Gauthier Villars, 1967. (English version is entitled *Semiology of Graphics*, Berg, W. J. trans, Madison, Wis.: University of Wis. Press, 1983).

Byte. Special issue on Videotex. 1983, *8*(7).

Holmes, G. L. Computer assisted chart symbolization at the Defense Mapping Agency Aerospace Center. *Proceedings of AUTOCARTO V. International Symposium on Computer-Assisted Cartography*, American Society of Photogrammetry and American Congress on Surveying and Mapping, August 1982, 387–396.

Keates, J. S. The perception of colour in cartography. *Prodeedings of the Cartographic Symposium*, University of Glasgow, 1962, 19–28.

Kimerling, A. J. Color specifiction in cartography. *The American Cartographer*, 1980, *7*(2), 139–153.

Kimerling, A. J. Process color diagrams (follow-up note). *The American Cartographyer*, 1981, *8*(2), 180–181.

King, S. K. Achieving graphic-arts-quality color hard copy for thematic data. Presented at the Harvard Conference, Cambridge, Mass., 1981.

McKay, F. W. Automated cartography for cancer research. *Proceedings of the 1976 Workshop on Automated Cartography and Epidemiology*, U.S. Dept. of HEW, Public Health Service, Office of Health Research, Statistics, & Technology, National Center for Health Statistics. (DHEW Publication No. (PHS) 79-1254), Washington, D. C.: U.S. Government Printing Office, 1979.

Mason, T. J., McKay, F. W., Hoover, R., Blot, W. J., & Fraumeni, J. F. *Atlas of Cancer Mortality for U.S. Counties: 1950–1969*. (DHEW Publication No. (NIH) 75-780), Washington, D.C.: U.S. Government Printing Office, 1975.

Mason, T. J., McKay, F. W., Hoover, R., Blot, W. J., & Fraumeni, J. F. *Atlas of Cancer Martality Among U.S. Non-whites: 1950–1969*. (DHEW Publication No. (NIH) 76-1204), Washington, D. C.: U.S. Government Printing Office, 1976.

Meyer, M. A., Broome, F. R., & Schweitzer, R. H., Jr. Color statistical mapping by the U.S. Bureau of the Census. *The American Cartographer*, 1975, *2*(2), 100–117.

National Geographic Society. History of Europe: The major turning points. Map supplement. *National Geographic*, 1983, *164*(6).

Olson, J. M. Spectrally encoded two-variable maps. *Annals*. Association of American Geographers, 1981, *71*(2), 259–276.

Pearson, K. S. The nineteenth-century Colour Revolution: Maps in geographical journals. *Imago Mundi*, 1980, *32*, 9–20.

Robinson, A. H. Psychological aspects of color in cartography. *International Yearbook of Cartography*, 1967, *7*, 50–59.

Robinson. A. H., Sale, R. D., & Morrison, J. L. Color and pattern. In *Elements of Cartography*. New York: John Wiley, 1978, 299–319.

Shortridge, B. G., & Welch, R. B. The effect of stimulus redundancy on the discrimination of town size on maps. *The American Cartographer*, 1982, *9*(1), 69–80.

Sibert, J. L. Continuous-color choropleth maps. *Geo-Processing*, 1980, *1*, 207–216.

U.S. Bureau of the Census and Manpower Administration. *Urban Atlas*. (Multiple volume, GE80 series), Washington, D. C.: U.S. Government Printing Office, various dates, mid-1970s.

White, D. Interactive color mapping. *Proceedings of AUTO-CARTO IV*. American Society of Photogrammetry and American Congress on Surveying and Mapping, 1979, *1*, 272–277.

Credits

Figures 11-2 through 11-5 and 11-7, 11-8, 11-11, and 11-12 were prepared by students in my design classes at Michigan State University (MSU), the University of Minnesota (UM), and Boston University (BU). Credits are as follows: 11-2: Nan Miller (MSU); 11-3: Gustave Rylander (MSU); 11-4: John Simonson (UM); 11-5: George Martin (UM); 11-7: Anthony Goddard (UM); 11-8: Thomas Barrett (MSU); 11-11: Julie Matz (BU); and 11-12: Norman Meek (MSU). Figures 11-6 and 11-9 were provided by John Sibert of George Washington University; Figure 11-10 is from the U.S. Bureau of the Census; and Figure 11-13 was provided by Denis White of the Harvard Laboratory for Computer Graphics and Spatial Analysis.

Biography

Judy M. Olson is professor of geography at Michigan State University in East Lansing, MI 48824. She teaches various courses in cartography ranging from Introductory Cartography to Map Design to Uses of Computers in Cartography. Her research interests include not only the uses of color on maps and the uses of computers in her field but also quantitative mapping in general, the psychology of map, map production, and analytical cartography. Dr. Olson taught at the University of Georgia and Boston University before coming to Michigan State and has been a visiting faculty member at the University of Minnesota. She has published in a number of geographic and cartographic journals and has served as editor of *The American Cartographer*. She is a past president of the American Cartographic Association.

12   Color Hard-Copy Devices

MICHAEL A. ANDREOTTOLA
American Ink Jet Corporation
Woburn, Massachusetts

Introduction

Without question, we live in a world greatly influenced by color. Color is present every-where, from home video games to the most sophisticated computer-aided design and manufacturing (CAD/CAM) systems in the workplace. As the functional use of color in computer systems rapidly increases, so does the demand for a color hard-copy device to disseminate these applications. This has become a society dependent on fast, accurate information.

A rapidly growing number of problems in science, business, and industry is being solved faster, more accurately, and more economically through the use of computer-generated graphics. Raw data are converted into meaningful, decision-making infor-mation faster. Analyses of experimental data are more precise. Trend relationships among several complex variables are easier to spot. And all because people can look at pictures instead of numbers (Applicon, 1979).

For many applications, black-and-white vector graphics systems have provided a major improvement over traditional numerical analysis methods. Many other, more complex problems cannot be solved with conventional graphics methods and plotting equipment; for example, problems that require the accurate plotting of solid surfaces without perspective ambiguity, problems that require plots showing the interaction of more than two variables, and problems in which subtle changes within high density data must not go undetected.

Until recently, the most common computer graphics display was the direct-view, storage cathode ray tube (CRT). This is the device that made the field of computer graphics a reality by providing an inexpensive way to store large quantities of graphic data. With the advances made in semiconductor memory, it was possible to store

COLOR AND THE COMPUTER

graphics information electronically and give the conventional CRT new capabilities. It became possible to change the displayed image instantly and not wait for the picture to be repainted progressively.

Additionally, there was a significant reduction in resolution. A typical CRT displays approximately 512 lines of information while a storage tube displays 1024 lines. Once the change to conventional raster scan CRTs was made, it was possible to substitute a color CRT for the typical black-and-white CRT.

As it becomes available, color will be preferred for more applications because black-and-white graphics are used primarily for facsimile. Color is becoming a management tool for CAD/CAM in a variety of fields, from business graphics to cartography and solids modeling. The interest in color-copying devices will increase as more applications are introduced.

The factor that is the key in color hard-copy devices is the ease of information sharing. When output is limited to the terminal, it is very difficult to share ideas and accomplishments, so lack of suitable copiers is actually restricting the growth of color graphics.

CRTs and hard-copy unit products—art, two-dimensional and three-dimensional drawings, maps, cartoons, and digitized pictures—not only convey information but please the eye as well. These units are very much intertwined in many applications. Often a CRT is used for interactive manipulation of graphics data, in much the same way that one would prepare a rough draft of a document, and a plotter or other hard-copy device generates the final copy for permanent storage or publication.

Monochromatic CRTs have been used for over twenty years, and one-color plotters for almost as long. With the recent advent of color graphics displays, demand has risen for hard-copy devices that reproduce color graphics on paper, film, or other permanent media quickly and at a reasonable cost. Until very recently, no vendor saw a need for a unit that would print color alphanumerics alone with no graphics capability. Several printers with limited alphanumeric capabilities, and some alphanumeric printers with limited graphics capabilities (lines, curves) are now on the market. However, the consensus is that color CRTs will not gain wide acceptance without a companion color hard-copy device.

In a hard-copy device, the characters are usually formed using dot matrix techniques in which the horizontal and vertical placement of dots define the print window. Print quality is determined by the addressability, registration, resolution, and a spot size that is uniform throughout the plot. These parameters are dependent on the electronic components, the mechanics, and the interaction of the ink and paper. If these elements are precisely controlled, the resultant plot should be one of good print quality; that is, good edge definition, high contrast, and from any unwanted ink mist (Yamasaki, 1978).

Three terms that are part of the nomenclature often occur in discussions of hard copy. They are defined here to eliminate confusion:

1. *Addressability* refers to the number of positions per linear measure to which the printhead mechanism can be guided.
2. *Resolution* refers to the number of distinguishable dots per linear measure and is related to the size of the dot formed on the substrate. The dot size is primarily influenced by the ink/paper relationship.
3. *Registration* refers to the precision with which a dot can be placed on a given spot, critical in superimposing colors to form composite colors using subtractive dyes (Jaffe & Mills, 1982).

As more effort is put into color hard-copy output, it will be focused on improving the technology in two main areas. The first is print quality, which involves higher resolution, broader color gamut, and more fully saturated colors. There will be more need to go to raster-type output than vector-type output, which is associated with pen plotters. More work must be done with the ink/paper relationship to get more area fill and solid colors for a continuous file.

The second area concerns the time required to produce a plot. At this time, technologies offering very quick reproduction time are limited to ink-jet, laser, and electrostatic copiers.

The sections of this chapter provide descriptions of the currently available technologies of color hard-copy devices, color hard-copy applications, interfaces, and basic information on paper and ink requirements.

Available Color Technology
Dot Matrix Impact Printers

Dot matrix impact printers are the end result of applying color ribbons to the monochrome matrix line printer. Because the wire matrix printers had been the most common hard-copy device for small computer systems, it was obvious that this type of printer would be modified to produce color hard copy. The color system utilizes the same technique as that of black-and-white printers in that a ribbon is placed between the substrate and the small wires or hammers in the printhead. The ribbon consists of either three or four colors. Some colors are produced with a single strike on the ribbon while others are produced by multiple strikes blending additive or subtractive primary colors. The majority of the matrix printers available today use a 9-wire printhead which produce plots with a resolution of 50 to 100 dots per inch (Duffield, 1982).

Compared to other impact printers, dot matrix printers are versatile because they use wires to form a font or character. Nothing in the printhead resembles a formed character. The resolution of the plots is restricted to the size of the wires in the head. Primarily used to print alphanumeric characters, color matrix printers also produce various types of business graphics.

Vector Pen Plotters

Pen plotters are probably the most common technology for producing color copies, drawing vectors and text directly from computer output. The first vector plotters were introduced more than twenty years ago and have since remained relatively unchanged. The printing process is achieved by supplying vector data (e.g., x and y coordinates) to the driving motor, which in turn controls the pens. Changing pens permits varying or changing colors. Pen plotters produce plots of high quality with accurate placement of lines. They are relatively inexpensive, easily maintained, and simple to operate. Speed is limited because a pen plotter is basically an extension of handwriting. The rate of color plot production is dependent upon two factors: the speed and acceleration of the pen in its plot cycle, and the amount of filled area. Although pen plotters can output solid areas by filling in an area line-by-line, this is a time-consuming procedure.

The color quality of plots produced by a pen plotter is dependent on the ink/paper interaction. Each color must be distinct and not bleed when placed adjacent to another.

Pen plotters are capable of producing many of the graphics required today, from plots for reports and archiving to hard copy for CAD users. Colors are limited to the palette of pen plotters. For greater color variety, different saturation levels must be used.

Electrostatic Technique

The electrostatic technique has recently become available to produce color hard copy. Several plotters electronically produce a broad spectrum of color with translucent toners in magenta, yellow, cyan, and black. Some will plot on a roll up to 42 inches wide with length limited to the length of the paper roll. A 34-by-44 inch plot can usually be produced in about eight minutes. Programmed voltage is applied in an array of densely spaced writing nibs embedded in a stationary writing head. Upon digital command, the nibs selectively create minute electrostatic dots on the paper passing over the head. The paper is then exposed to liquid toner producing a permanent image.

A multiple pass technique is used. In the first pass, the paper is marked to "end of plot" to assure proper registration. Paper is then automatically rewound (at about 10 inches per second) to the plot starting position. With four consecutive passes, each pass putting down one of the colored toners from the toning station, a resolution of approximately 200 dots per inch is achievable. Electrostatic color plotters produce line graphics; however, there is a lack of color uniformity when it comes to fill-in on large colored areas.

Photographic Systems

Color hard-copy devices reproduce images from a CRT. The high resolution and color range of film enables high-quality color hard copy. The most highly developed material for color hard copy is film, and it is usually the standard of comparison for color quality. Film systems have also established themselves as the most reliable and versatile of the color hard-copy devices. The image input to the system is an analog red, green, blue (RGB) signal directly from the video source. The information is digitized and formatted into a color separation for output to a high resolution CRT. The film is then exposed to the CRT.

Development time can be substantial with film. Polaroid, however, has developed a system producing a relatively instant color print, a peripheral device used with medium to high resolution computer graphic systems and composite video sources (Polaroid Corporation, 1980). Hard-copy prints with good color quality and very high resolution are produced immediately, eliminating the distortion found in photographs taken directly from a video screen.

Film-copy devices produce quality line graphics and solid area coverage. The primary use of photographic devices is copies for presentation graphics for remote sensing imaging.

Laser Plotters

The computer printing market has recently been penetrated by laser printers. This has been achieved by combining the xerographic copier technology with easier scanning imaging systems. The process is accomplished by printing on a reusable photoconductor, sequentially transferring three toners to plain paper and thermally fusing the toner to the paper. The resolution of 100 dots per inch is similar to that of wire matrix printers but the print quality is higher. This is an effect of the thermal fusing process, which will cause the toner to flow to areas between the addressable points. Therefore, filled in regions are uniform, discrete dots and staircasing effects are not noticeable. The additive and subtractive primaries are precisely reproduced (Goren, 1976). The toner consists of transparent dyes and the color gamut is limited.

Ink-Jet Printers

Perhaps no other technology associated with printing and graphics has caused as much excitement and enthusiasm as ink-jet printing. Millions of dollars are being invested every year by many companies throughout the world on development of ink-jet printers. This year alone, it is estimated that as many as ten companies will introduce ink-jet printers using various technologies. These printers offer quiet operation, high speed, and compatibility of various substrates. Being programmable, the ink-jet technology is one of the most fitting for use in the production of color graphics. With its ability to reproduce video images quickly and with consistent color fidelity and fine detail, ink-jet technology is the best current candidate for use as a hard-copy device.

A variety of systems are available that produce a plot as small as 8½-by-11 inches to about 22-by-34 inches. The time to produce a plot varies from two to eight minutes depending on the size of the plot, drop ejection frequency, the number of nozzles, and the required resolution. Similar to dot matrix printers, ink-jet printers create graphics using groups of dots (pixels) comprised of colored inks. However, unlike matrix printers, they place dots on the paper by drops of ink that are emitted from an orifice at a very high velocity.

The ink-jet printers are divided into two basic groups, the drop-on-demand printers and the continuous flow printers.

Drop-on-Demand.   In the drop-on-demand technology, ink is emitted from the jet only when drops are required for printing. The printhead of drop-on-demand units uses capillaries or orifices that hold ink in a slight vacuum. The inks are supplied by separate reservoirs for each color. Behind the reservoir is a piezoelectric transducer that is separated from the reservoir by a diaphragm (Figure 12-1). The combination of surface tension of the ink and slight vacuum causes a concave meniscus to form within the orifice.

A binary voltage pulse is applied to the piezoelectric transducer to form an individual droplet of ink when a drop is demanded for printing. The vibrations caused by the transducer create shock waves within each capillary that first protrude and then rupture the meniscus, forming round, regularly spaced drops. When the diaphragm relaxes, the ink retracts into the nozzle without the drop. The orifice used with this technology is approximately 80 microns in diameter. Drop size can be controlled by varying the pulse amplitude—low amplitude pulses eject small drops while high amplitude pulses eject large drops (Heinz & Wehl, 1982; Lee, Mills, & Talke, 1982).

The drop-on-demand printers are simpler in design and operation than the continuous flow plotters. They offer smaller format reproduction and a smaller color gamut. This type of printer is used for production of business graphics and presentation plots. If cost is of importance, drop-on-demand may be more appealing than the continuous flow plotters.

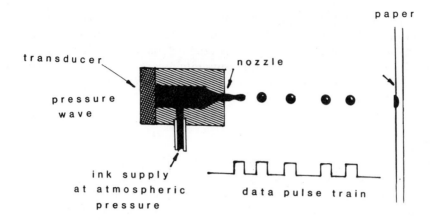

paper

transducer   nozzle

pressure
wave

ink supply
at atmospheric   data pulse train
pressure

Single nozzle impulse or drop on demand ink jet printhead

Figure 12-1 Drop-on-command ink-jet nozzle.

Continuous Flow Ink-Jet Printers.   Continuous flow ink-jet printing is attracting attention because of its ability to reproduce graphics at high speed with high resolution. This technology uses the principle of continuously emitting ink from a high pressure source through a capillary. As the ink leaves the opening in a stream, it will break off into small drops, as shown in Figure 12-2.

The ink stream undergoes a charge/no charge condition by binary switching. Drops that do not receive a charge pass through a high voltage electrode (2 kV) and onto the printing substrate. Drops that receive an electrical charge (200 V) are deflected from the high voltage electrode and into a porous deflection electrode (Figure 12-3). The Applicon Color Plotter has four nozzles, which emit four colored inks (magenta, yellow, cyan, and black). These nozzles are installed in a head that travels along a lead screw (Figure 12-4). A print medium is taped onto a rotating drum. The head moves a distance of .2 millimeters along the lead screw, which is controlled by a stepping motor. Increments of .2 millimeters are established around the drum circumference by an encoder attached to the drum, which provides clock-pulse for the control system. Depending on the speed of the drum, the number of drops to fill a picture element will vary. With the generation of multiple dots per pixel and the small orifice diameter (10 microns), some continuous flow ink-jet printers can print at 250 dots per inch (10 lines per mm).   Continuous flow ink-jet printers can be used for a variety of applications: seismic data, business graphics, medical scans, demographic data, and mapping charts. It is unsurpassed as a peripheral to a CAD/CAM system.

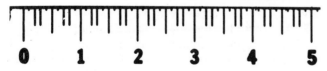

Figure 12-2 Droplet points from ink-jet nozzle.

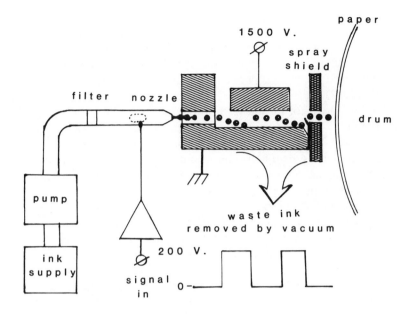

Components for a single nozzle Hertz continuous ink jet printhead

Figure 12-3 Continuous flow ink-jet nozzle.

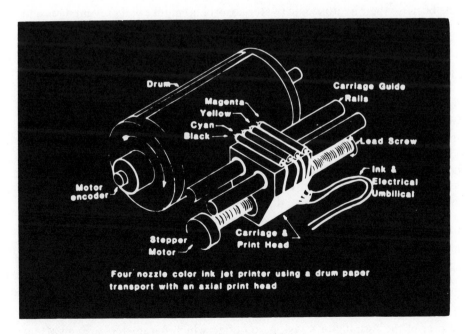

Four nozzle color ink jet printer using a drum paper transport with an axial print head

Figure 12-4 Mechanism of continuous flow ink-jet nozzle.

Inks

Neither the control aspects nor the mechanisms of the ribbon, printhead, or paper pose the greatest challenge in designing color printers. Surprisingly, the challenge is the task of formulating inks, toners, and associated paper with suitable chromatic and archival characteristics (Connolly, 1982).

When an ink is to be developed for an ink-jet printer, the formulator must keep in mind two sets of requirements. The first is associated with the quality of the resultant plot, which must be sharp, dense, and permanent. The second is the printer environment. A complete compatibility study must be undertaken to ensure that the ink is compatible with all materials it comes in contact with, and that the environmental parameters remain constant throughout the printing process.

Impact printers use pigments for colorants. Therefore, the color gamut is limited because pigments are opaque. It is very difficult to produce a composite by overlaying subtractive primaries. These inks are usually formulated with mineral oil vehicles of various viscosities and surface tensions to make them nonmiscible. Varying these parameters prevents colors on the ribbon from bleeding into one another.

Pen plotters and ink-jet printers use specially formulated inks according to their requirements. Inks are made up of a colorant (dye or pigment) and a vehicle to carry the colorant. Water is one of the primary components of a vehicle today for several reasons. It does not impose certain health problems associated with other solvents such as acetone, dimethylsulfoxide, low boiling point alcohols or other volatiles. Water is less expensive than these other solvents. Most specialty inks are formulated with distilled water because the physical parameters of water remain relatively constant over a wide temperature range.

A second component of the vehicle is a humectant, in the form of a high boiling point alcohol (glycerol, diethylene glycol, polyethylene glycol, etc.). Humectants are added to the vehicle because their hygroscopic (water absorbing) nature will prevent dyes and salts from precipitating and forming a crust that may clog the pen or orifice. If too much humectant is added, the viscosity will become too high, restricting flow rate from the nozzle or orifice. It will also greatly impede the drying of the ink on the printing substrate. If too little humectant is added, some type of clogging problem is certain to occur.

In addition to the colorant and vehicle, inks contain a bacteriacide/fungicide. The dyestuffs used for the colorants are organic and consequently an excellent growth and nutritive source for microorganisms. Once bacteria are introduced to and proliferate in an ink system, they can become a major source of filter and orifice clogging problems.

A fourth additive to the formulation may be various binders that would give the ink better water or fade resistance. Other dye solvents may be added as well.

After months (or years) of work have determined the proper components of an ink, the task is one-third completed. The next step is the development and testing of a filtration system. A nozzle to deliver inks in the continuous flow ink-jet printer is between 7 and 10 microns and requires that inks be filtered well below this level to prevent any type of clogging. The best approach is a filter network consisting of several depth filters, in series, with the larger pore-size filter first (approximately 10 microns) and going down to a final filter (submicron). All manufacturing, filtering, and bottling must be done in a clean environment.

The third part of the formulator's task is to define which parameters are important to the proper operation of the system. Six important parameters are considered in ink formulation.

Viscosity. The viscosity of the ink is of primary importance. As mentioned earlier, the humectant is the primary consistuent that affects this parameter. In ink-jet systems, the amount of humectant will affect the degree of crusting that may or may not occur. Too much humectant would make the flow of ink through a 7- to 10-micron nozzle very difficult. On the drop-on-demand printers, a thicker ink (12 centipoise versus 2 centipoise for continuous ink jet) is necessary. This is because, instead of high pressure, the drop-on-demand system uses an acoustic wave produced by a piezoelectric transducer to emit and propel an ink drop.

Specific Gravity. This parameter must be known because it is needed to determine the weight of the mass to be propelled (ink drops) for velocity studies, and to determine other physical constants.

Surface Tension. This parameter is one of the primary regulators of where the actual drop will form in continuous ink-jet printers. In drop-on-demand printers, it helps to regulate control of the concave meniscus to hold ink in the system. Once the ink is deposited onto the printing substrate, the interaction of the surface dynamics of both the ink and paper play a major role in how the final form of the dot will appear.

Optical Density. The optical density is used to determine a quantitative evaluation of the contrast of the ink against a known value; that is, the print medium.

Dielectric Properties. This parameter is important only to the continuous flow plotters. The ink drop must be able to accept an applied voltage that will determine where the drops are to be placed. In the Applicon Color Plotter, for example, drops not required to be part of a character receive a charge of 200 volts. On their way to the printing media they pass through a high-voltage field of approximately 2000 volts. Because like charges repel, these droplets are deflected into a waste receptacle. The drops intended to be part of the plot do not receive a charge; thus, when they go through the high voltage field there is no effect on their trajectory.

pH. The pH of the ink is critical for several reasons. Solubility is greatly affected by the dye used in formulation. Also, as most dies are pH indicators, the color of some dyes will change if they go from a low to high pH value. There must be a correlation between the pH of the ink and printing media; otherwise, the archival quality of the print may deteriorate. If, for example, the ink is acidic and so is the paper, this highly acidic state will cause degeneration of the paper and thus the plot. Therefore, it is advisable to use a high pH paper (or as close to neutral as possible) if ink is to have a low pH.

Another reason for controlling the pH of the ink is that the orifice of some ink-jet systems is made of metal. If this is the case, the pH of the ink should be close to neutral to prevent corrosion.

Lightfastness has been a problem in water-based systems using organic dyes. This is due to the effects of ultraviolet light on the dye, oxidation, pH of the ink, the paper and/or the environment.

Other Formulation Considerations

When formulating an ink, the chemist must be aware not only of the components of the ink but also of the materials in the components. Determining the compatibility of the ink formulation and the hardware is usually accomplished by immersing a representative sample of the hardware in the ink. The immersed piece is then placed in an oven and evaluated over a period of time. The heat will accelerate the development of any conditions that would occur during normal operation of the plotter.

The new ink-jet printers come equipped with four colors (magenta, yellow, cyan, and black) and four nozzles. Some of the key parameters for choosing the desired dye for an ink are the peak wavelength of the dye, the breadth of the absorption peak, and presence of any unwanted secondary peaks. If the parameters are optimized, the resulting color gamut can produce a wide range of brilliant, reproducible colors.

Several of the parameters are very difficult to control in an ink-jet system. Certain types of printers recirculate ink, causing evaporation of the vehicle, which may alter the pH. When this occurs, corrosion of parts of the ink delivery system, precipitation of dyes, and clogging of nozzles can result. Also, the ink may pick up paper dust and other impurities in the atmosphere, which can cause additional problems. For example, in the Applicon Color Plotter, large ink drops formed at the tip of the nozzle, after the plotter was out of plot mode (Figure 12-5). The drop electrostatically attracted paper

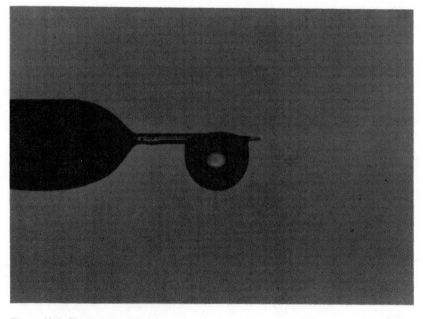

Figure 12-5 Clog-causing ink drop.

dust to it and formed a mixture. Because of the various polymers in the inks and in the paper coating, this mixture caused an insoluble precipitate that clogged the nozzles.

Paper

Once it is feasible to place an ink droplet on a determined spot, the resultant print quality is determined by the interaction of the ink and paper. The paper must absorb the ink drop with symmetric spreading and very little feathering, a problem associated with migration of the ink along the length of paper fibers. If paper has been produced with elongated or varied length fibers, spots or blotches may appear on the final print. Also, if there is too much migration of the ink through the fiber, the optical density of the particular area will be greatly reduced since the same volume of ink will cover a greater area.

Many of the printing devices use what is called "plain" paper—actually, there is nothing quite so simple as "plain" paper. Every paper is manufactured with specific qualities; for example, handling properties (strength, stiffness, and cure), print quality, and ink acceptance. The fiber composition and sheet formation is as important as the quality and quantity of any fillers or coatings used. Print can be on either the wire or felt side of the paper; however, for best color reproduction a smooth-surfaced paper is required (Leekley, Tyler, & Hutton, 1978). When the white light from an illuminating source penetrates the ink layers, portions of the spectrum get absorbed by the dyes while other parts of the spectrum reflect from the base sheet and travel back to the dyes for further absorption. With smooth paper, this reflected light will come straight back through the dye and give the observer a true characteristic of the dye hue. With rough surface paper, the reflected light will become scattered and thus degrade the quality of the print.

One paper selection method is to start with a good photographic quality paper for a base, and define the chemical properties intrinsically important to the application. For example, these properties might consist of the pH of the paper, trace metals, and the sizing element. As mentioned earlier, the pH effects the performance of the paper and the color characteristics of the dye. The chemical purity of the components of the paper is critical because many chemicals can adversely affect the permanence of the print.

The main material of photographic paper is a cellulose fiber produced from a highly bleached pulp (Kasper & Wanka, 1981). Blending various types of fibers and adjusting refining conditions can produce papers with a wide range of physical properties. Uniform fiber distribution is important in paper used for ink-jet printing because of its effect on the uniformity of the image layer. In a poorly formed sheet, uneven swelling and drying will cause surface distortions resulting in a cockled appearance of the paper and printed image, and a mottled effect.

Photographic papers also exhibit the machine direction of the fibers as well as the two-sidedness characteristic of sheets produced on Fourdrinier machines. When the paper is formed on the paper machine wire, the fibers have a tendency to line up in machine direction. This tendency is compounded in the subsequent wet-pressing and drying operation. Separation of the fibers in the vertical plane takes place due to the drainage on the paper machine wire. This leads to differences in physical properties such as tensile strength and stiffness, and dimensional changes with fluctuations in relative humidity. Paper absorbs and loses moisture readily as the humidity of the environment changes.

Applications of Hard-Copy Devices

Color hard-copy devices are helping to solve a wide range of research, engineering, and manufacturing problems. Complex problems (e.g., seismic data analysis, solids modeling, mapping, finite element analysis) are often addressed successfully.

Seismic Data Analysis.   Seismic analysis service organizations and major oil companies are using color plotting systems to enhance the value of seismic data plots. An example of color seismic plotting is shown in Figure 12-6 (see color insert). By adding color to these plots, the analyst can obtain a limitless variety of data displays. For example, the interaction of two variables (frequency and velocity) can be shown by black trace superimposed over a variable color-band background. Adding dimension to the background permits it to be viewed as a true contour, providing the analyst with a color picture of the strata being studied.

Mapping.   Both producers and users of contour maps benefit from color hard copy. A contour map produced on a color hard-copy device is easier to read than vector-plotted maps because color surface shading and raster patterning eliminate confusion in viewing elevations and contours. Topographic maps showing the relationship among variables, such as the presence of different minerals, can easily be produced by assigning a primary color to each variable. The color created by the combination of primary colors in any area indicates the relative presence of each variable while the intensity of the color indicates the concentration.

The pen plotter is the primary device used when cost is a major factor and simple line graphics are required. If, however, applications require solid area coverage (e.g., seismic plotting) film, electrostatic, or preferably continuous ink-jet is recommended (Figure 12-7, see color insert).

Computer-Aided Design.   Computer-aided design makes extensive use of electrostatic plotters and pen plotters for applications in which accuracy and high quality are critical. This had been limited to a black-and-white plotting, but recently the application of color has been gaining acceptance. The design of integrated circuits is now being accomplished with the assistance of color plotters. Production of check plots to ensure proper registration and alignment of layers in complex printed circuits is simplified. The addition of color to the plots improves quality control by making it easier to trace individual layers (Figure 12-8, see color insert).

Business Graphics.   Business systems are possibly the largest users of color graphics plotters. They are neither fully dependent on the colors of the CRTs, nor do they require the resolution needed of other applications. A pie chart or a bar chart commands more attention with the addition of color, with two important caveats: use of appealing colors and use of a good neutral black.

Large format charts (e.g., PERT charts) are primarily plotted with electrostatic plotters because speed and quality can be obtained at a reasonable cost (Figure 12-9, see color insert).

Graphic Arts.   In graphic design and large-scale printing applications, such as the production of wallpapers for interior decoration, an ink-jet system is most effective because of its fine resolution and area fill-in. Manufacturers can eliminate costly and time-consuming press setups and test runs. The advent of digital television and recording is a recent development that provides the capability of editing time sequential images (Yamasaki, 1978) (Figure 12-10, see color insert).

Medicine.   Many medical imaging systems offer color display capability, like the computer axial tomography (CAT) scanners. At this time, most of the medical community

	TRILOG C-100 IMPACT PRINTER	HP 7220C PEN PLOTTER	HP 7580A PEN PLOTTER	DUNN 630 SERIES FILM CAMERAS	GEO SPACE 6400 FILM PLOTTER
Technology:	dot matrix impact printer	mechanical fiber tip pens	mechanical pens	high resolution CRT color filtering film recording	CRT scanning film
Resolution:	100 dots/inch	.001 inch	.001 inch	1200 lines/frame	192 lines/inch
Colors:	cyan, magenta, yellow	8 pens	8 pens	red, green, blue	cyan, magenta, yellow
Speed:	Plot 3-1/4 min/ page Print 150 lines/ minute	slow 14 in/sec	slow 24 in/sec	1 minute	2-1/2 minutes
Image Size:	11 x 13.2 in.	11 x 17 in. A3	24.5 x 46.85 in. (D-size)	8 x 10 in.	42 x 60 inches
Quality:	medium	high line quality	high line quality	very high	very high
Versatility:	print & plot	limited	limited	line, solid area continuous tone	line solid area continuous tone
Approx. Cost: (1983 $)	$12,000	$5,000	$15,000	$16,000	$63,000

COMPARISONS OF HARD-COPY DEVICES

	XEROX 6500 CCP LASER COPIER	PRINTERACOLOR INK-JET PLOTTER	APPLICON INK-JET COLOR PLOTTING SYS.	VERSATEC ECP42 ELECTROSTATIC
Technology:	laser writing xerographic	drop-on-command ink-jet	continuous ink-jet	electrostatic charge coated paper liquid toner
Resolution:	100 dots/inch	100 dots/inch	125 dots/inch	200 dots/inch
Colors:	Cyan, magenta, yellow	cyan, magenta, yellow (7 color combinations)	cyan, magenta, yellow	cyan, magenta, yellow & black 512 combinations
Speed:	3 min/page	2 min/page 3 copies/min	8 min/plot bidirectional	8 min/E-size 34 by 44 inch
Image Size:	8.5 x 11.0 in.	11 x 15.7 in. fan-fold	22 x 34 in. D-size	42 in. x 500 ft.
Quality:	medium	medium	very high	very high
Versatility:	line, solid area, half-tone	print & plot	line, solid area, half-tone	line, solid area, half-tone
Approx. Cost: (1983 $)	$31,000	$6,000	$55,000	$98,000

COMPARISONS OF HARD-COPY DEVICES

Table 12-1 Hard-copy device comparisons.

is resistant to pseudocolor x-ray images, so most hard copy is reproduced in black and white. However, some work is being done in color using the Applicon Color Plotter (Figure 12-11, see color insert).

Data Analysis.   Data analysis includes applications in research, development, engineering, and production in all market sectors from education and government to manufacturing organizations. Copy in this category is usually produced in small format.

Raster Technique.   There is an inherent need for a plotter that can quickly produce a copy suitable for presentation or publication. An alternative to the vector method of plotting and its constraints is the raster technique.

A computer-generated raster image is based on a rectangular array of digital information (Jern, 1979). Each element of this array is known as a pixel. An example of a raster image is a black-and-white dot picture produced on a matrix printer. The digital information that defines a pixel in this case is a singlel bit. The two values of a bit, 1 or 0, will then correspond to the two possible natures of the dot (i.e., black and white), and these conditions can be extended by adding two variables—color and intensity.

Table 12-1 shows a comparison of characteristics available in hard-copy devices. The prices quoted are given in 1982 dollars.

Interface to Hard-Copy Devices

Peripheral suppliers usually furnish interface boards to tie their devices to other equipment. In most cases, the user will utilize the CRT for interactive manipulation of graphics data. Once the image to be copies is on the CRT, the interfaced hard-copy device generates the copy on a substrate. Many types of interfacing techniques can be employed. Most color hard-copy units accept separate RGB inputs on the three ports and produce output in three overlaid colors. This method is convenient for units that interface with terminals directly because most color terminals come with standard RGB output ports to drive remote monitors.

In some cases, the attempt to generate hard copies directly from a video screen may cause problems. A color CRT is a low resolution device with a limited number of picture elements while many of the latest hard-copy devices have a high resolution. For example, if the image to be copied is on a screen with a resolution of 6 pixels per millimeter and put on line to a plotter with a resolution of 6 pixels per millimeter, each screen pixel will have to be represented by a 3-by-3 printer pixel in order to retain scale. This leads to the "jagged edge" effect (Jern, 1979). Many hard-copy devices can approximate the color hues displayed by color terminals with point intensity variation by using dithering.

Dithering

Dithering is a technique to produce different intensity levels of the same color on raster scan devices in which the pixels can be one of two values (on or off). It was developed to create grayscales on devices that could only produce a black or white dot (Marston, 1983). Shading is obtained by repeatedly applying a dither matrix to define the pattern of dots making up the plot. Figure 12-12 shows a 4-by-4 dither matrix that can produce 17 levels of gray from white (0) to black (16). The scale is created by transforming the variable of interest into 17 values corresponding to the gray levels. White is obtained by leaving all of the cells empty, and black is obtained by filling in all of them.

The grayscale technique is extended to color by varying the proportion of pixels occupied by each primary or each two-way mixture of the subtractive primary colors (magenta, yellow, and cyan). When two of the colors are put in the same place, a mixed color results. For example, magenta plus yellow will give red. Black is realized by putting down equal amounts of the three primaries. The eye will combine the dots into a coalesced hue providing there is no obvious large-scale structure to the dither pattern.

To understand the mixing technique, think of an eight-color matching system like the one shown in Table 12-2. Colors other than the three primaries and the three pair mixtures (red, green, and blue) must be created by a mixture of different color dots that are blended by the eye. This is accomplished by using a dithering pattern. There

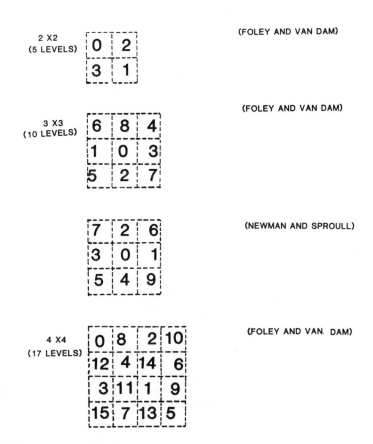

Figure 12-12 Dithering techniques.

EIGHT COLOR MATCHING SYSTEM

Table 12-2 Color matching system.

White = no pigment

Cyan = cyan pigment only

Yellow = yellow pigment only

Magenta = magenta pigment only

Blue = magenta and cyan pigment

Green = cyan and yellow pigments

Red = magenta and yellow pigments

Black = magenta, yellow, and cyan pigments

are three scaled values assigned to each point on the plot for the three subtractive primaries instead of using the single scaled value for each point as was done with the grayscale.

Each of these color levels is composed with the corresponding dither matrix value for the location, and if it is exceeded, a dot of that color is printed. For example, if only the scaled value for magenta at the point exceeds the dither value, then a magenta dot is printed. If both magenta and cyan exceed the dither value, then both are printed and a blue dot is obtained. If all three scaled values exceed the dither value, then a black dot results.

Usually, a separate color code is used for each point in the plot rather than three individual values. This particular code corresponds to an index table that contains a set of ascending values for the three primary colors. The user would choose the color set according to the required visual properties. For good flexibility, it is quintessential to have the dither matrix and color code table external to the plotting subroutine.

Software

One method of circumventing the interfacing problem is through host-resident software. One solution to the jagged edge problems associated with hard copy is the Universal Raster System (UNIRAS®), a raster-device independent software package for creating high resolution hard copies (Brown & Surprise, 1980).This software can be used with any device capable of accepting data in raster format. Rasterization is accomplished by the software and the resulting image is sent directly from the host computer to the hard copy device by way of a RS232 serial interface or a parallel interface. This package does not require any local intelligence in the output device. The resolution, number of colors, and number of picture elements are totally under user control in the UNIRAS® software.

This type of user control enables the creation of fast and inexpensive high resolution hard copy from low resolution screens. This particular software can also simulate screen color intensities with dithering techniques, obtaining the same number of color combinations.

UNIRAS® consists of a fundamental package and five high-level applications packages. This software performs the plotting primitives such as draw line, plot text, and fill-in area, and handles the raster data base. GEOPAK® is a mapping package for 2-, 3-, and even 4-dimensional presentations of grid and contour maps. GIMAGE® displays scanned data such as satellite or medical data. BIZPAK® produces business graphics such as bar charts in 2- or 3- dimensions, pie charts, etc. SEISPAK® displays seismic exploration data. KRIGPAK® produces a number of advanced KRIGING® geostatistical display routines including fault support.

Data Format

Data can be formatted according to the system, the hard copy device, and the type of output. The Applicon Ink-Jet Color Plotter produces full color images from binary, raster image data received from one of a variety of input interfaces (Brown & Surprise, 1980).Data formatted according to Type-I specifications contains a bit for each point on the plotting surface in each of the primary subtractive colors (magenta, yellow, cyan and black). The Type-I data may be written to tape or directly to the plotter by way of an online

Initially, data are blocked into records on a raster-by-raster basis. A single raster is put down for each revolution of the drum to which the printing medium is attached. For most plots, except C-size, the rasters run horizontal to the way the plot is normally viewed.

The first dot of the first raster appears in the upper right corner of the plotting surface viewed from the front of the plotter. Data are plotted starting with the most significant bit of the first byte of data received. Within each raster block, or tape record, data for each color of ink are grouped as a series of bytes describing the raster data according to color. This grouping corresponds to the same sequence as the alignment of the nozzles on the printhead (i.e., magenta, yellow, cyan, and black). To overcome the physical separation of 0.400 inch between the capillaries that deliver the ink, the data for each color, except the leading magenta capillary, are delayed within each raster block, as shown in Table 12-3.

With the exception of data for black, data for each color must be included in each raster block; that is, there is not provision for compressing or otherwise minimizing transfer of all zeros data in Type-I data format.

The length, in bytes, of each raster block identifies the plot characteristics as to size (A/B, C/D, E), colors and density (5, 8, 10 lines per mm) according to Table 12-4.

For particular cases in which the record length is an odd number, the length may be increased by one or three bytes to make the length even if required by the hardware generating the tape. If, on input to the plotter, the record length is one greater than required, the extra byte is assumed to be at the end of the record, and ignored. If the record length is three greater than required, an extra byte is assumed to follow each color block, and each of those three bytes is ignored.

Density	Yellow Delay	Cyan Delay	Black Delay
5 dots/mm	50 rasters	100 rasters	150 rasters
8 dots/mm	80 rasters	160 rasters	240 rasters
10 dots/mm	100 rasters	200 rasters	300 rasters

Table 12-3 Density vs color display.

Bytes	Size	Colors	Density (lines/mm)	
516	B	3	5	*Table 12-4* Plot characteristics.
688	B	4	5	
825	B	3	8	
1032	B/D	3	10/5	
1100	B	4	8	
1376	B/D	4	10/5	
1596	E	3	5	
1650	D	3	8	
2064	D	3	10	
2128	E	4	5	
2200	D	4	8	
2550	E	3	8	
2752	D	4	10	
3189	E	3	10	
3400	E	4	8	
4252	E	4	10	

Tapes can be formatted to contain partial plots and/or more than one plot. While the number of bytes per record identifies the plot characteristics as to size, density, and ink colors this is not to say that a B-size plot could not be plotted on a D-size machine with the resulting plot occupying a fraction of the total plot area. A B-size plot is equivalent to ll-by-17 inches; a D-size is 22-by-34 inches. The color plotter software interface formats are given in Table 12-5.

PLOT DATA CHARACTERISTICS FOR TYPE-I DATA

Table 12-5   Color plotter software interface formats.

B-size 5 lines/mm
4 colors -- magenta, yellow, cyan, black
172 bytes/color
688 bytes/raster
2,125 rasters/plot
1,462,000 bytes/plot

B-size 10 lines/mm
4 colors -- magenta, yellow, cyan, black
344 bytes/color
1,376 bytes/raster
4,250 rasters/plot
5,848 bytes/plot

D-size 5 lines/mm
4 colors -- magenta, yellow, cyan, black
344 bytes/color
1,376 bytes/raster
4,250 rasters/plot
5,848,000 bytes/plot

D-size 10 lines/mm
4 colors -- magenta, yellow, cyan, black
688 bytes/color
2,752 bytes/raster
8,500 rasters/plot
23,392,000 bytes/plot

Summary

The benefits of color hard copy are not extensively realized. The popularity of color hard copy devices will increase dramatically in the near future and the industries that use them will benefit from the easier interpretation of complex data and improved communications. With the numbers and quality of hard-copy devices being introduced every year, a hard-copy device as a peripheral to every graphics systems is possible. Although the cost of systems seems less each year, other criteria are also useful in choosing a system: color quality, resolution, plot production speed, and probable life of the technology.

References

Applicon. When the picture is worth more than a 1000 words. (Sales literature), Burlington, Mass.: Applicon, 1979.

Brown, J. L. & Surprise, C. Applicon color plotter tape formats, Type-I data. Burlington, Mass.: Applicon, 1980.

Connolly, E. Printers prepare for a colorful future. *Electronic Design*, 1982, 99–108.

Dawes, A. Color hard copy devices. Santa Clara, Calif.: Versatec, Inc., 1981.

Duffield, P. A new niche for ink-jet printers. *Mini-Micro Systems*, July 1982, 187–192.

Foley, J. D. & Von Dam, A. *Fundamentals of Interactive Computer Graphics*. Reading, Mass.: Addision-Wesley, 1982.

Goren, R. Problems of pictorial xerography. *Journal of Applied Photographic Engineering*, 1976, 2(1), 103–106.

Heinz, J. & Wehl, W. Drop-on-demand and acoustic drop shaping. *Society for Information Display International Symposium Digest*, 1982, 13, 152–153.

Jaffe, A. B. & Mills, R. N. *Color Hard Copy for Computer Systems*. Research report, San Jose, Calif.: International Business Machines Research Laboartory, November 1982.

Jern, M. *Hard Copy Alternatives and a Closer Look at Ink-Jet Plotters and Their Applications*. Product bulletin, Woburn, Mass.: American Software Contractors, 1979.

Kasper, K. B. & Wanka, R. Chemical formulations and requirements for photographic paper. *Journal of Applied Photographic Engineering*, 1981, 7(3), 67–72.

Lee, F. C., Mills, R. N. & Talke, F. E. Drop-on-demand ink-jet technology for color printing. *Society for Information Display International Symposium Digest*, 1982, 13, 156–157.

Leekley, R. M., Tyler, R. F., & Hutton, J. D. Effects of paper on color quality of printer. *Tappi*, 1978, 61, 108.

Marston, P. T. *Creating Various Colors Using a Four-by-Four Dither Pattern*. Unpublished paper, San Marcos, Tex.: Interactive Systems Laboratory, March 1983.

Newman, W. M. & Sproull, R. F. *Principles of Interactive Computer Graphics* (2nd ed.). New York: McGraw-Hill, 1979.

Polaroid Video-Printer. Product bulletin, Cambridge, Mass.: Polaroid Corporation, 1980.

Yamasaki, I. Quantitative evolution of print quality for optical character recognition systems. *IEEE Transactions SMC* 1978, 8(5), 371.

Acknowledgements

The author would like to thank Dennis Şurette, of Applicon, for his assistance in photography and mechanical illustrations associated with this chapter.

UNIRAS, RASPAK, GEOPAK, GIMAGE, SEISPAK, and KRIGPAK are registered trademarks of American Software Contractors, Inc., Woburn, Massachusetts.

Biography

Michael Andreottola received his Bachelor of Science degree in Biochemistry in 1971 from Georgetown College, Lexington, Kentucky, and a Master of Business Administration in 1980 from Northeastern University, Boston, Massachusetts. Mr. Andreottola was research associate at the Retina Foundation in Boston from 1972 to 1974. From 1974 to 1977, he held various positions with the Mead Corporation in Dayton, Ohio. His major accomplishments at Mead were involved with the isolation and identification of microbial growth which contaminated inks used for ink jet printing. Holding the position of Staff Scientist, he worked extensively on the formulation and manufacturing processes of ink jet fluids. He was also responsible for manufacturing processes of minute electrical components which relied on his expertise as a microscopist.

In 1977 he accepted a position with Applicon, Incorporated, the Burlington, Massachusetts based CAD/CAM manufacturer. As the manager of ink and paper development, he has formulated inks for the Applicon ink jet printer.

Mr. Andreottola has performed extensive experimentation on the mechanism of the liquid jet i.e., pressure vs. piezoelectric transducer and glass capillary vs. orifices.

In 1983, he founded the American Ink Jet Corporation in Boston, Massachusetts. Here, inks for various types of pen plotters and ink jet printers are formulated and manufactured. Specialty papers and clear films are also available which compliment the inks. Some of these inks are considered the standard of the industry.

Mr. Andreottola enjoys many outdoor activities in the New England area. He holds a trainers license and owns and trains thoroughbred race horses at Suffock Downs in Boston. He is also a part-time karate instructor.

13 Color and the Instructional Use of the Computer

H. JOHN DURRETT and D. THERON STIMMEL
Interactive Systems Laboratories
San Marcos, Texas

Introduction

Computers are being used to accomplish instructional objectives in a wide range of situations. They are used to help kindergarten students learn the alphabet, provide remedial reading training to adults, and aid physics professors in demonstrating complex models of physical processes during a lecture. Several years ago Licklider (1979) pointed out:

> Information technology is flourishing. It is providing business, industry, the professions, and government with marvelous new tools and techniques to help them acquire, process, store, transmit, and use information. But the field of education is not taking much advantage of the new technology.

Today this statement is less accurate. A veritable explosion of materials and computers have been developed purporting to solve a wide range of problems in education and training.

Computers and Instruction
A Brief History

The post-Sputnik period of the late 1950s and early 1960s saw an increased concern for subject matter learning in our educational systems. Programmed instruction was widely hailed as a new era in education. Carefully programmed material was widely developed, and the notion of individualized learning became quite prevalent. Dr. William

Uttal (1967) headed a development group at IBM that pioneered the use of a digital computer as an instructional device. Some of the programs developed by this group were simply elaborate programmed instruction devices. Some, such as a program to teach college statistics, actually simulated a tutor; the students performance dictated the next step in the presentation of materials.

Neither programmed instruction nor computer-assisted-instruction (CAI) developed as fully in the 1960s as their proponents had hoped. As people became aware of the great explosion of new information, educators became more concerned with teaching children how to learn about new events probably at the expense of learning factual material. At the time, CAI required a very high cost per student hour because the students each had to have a bulky and often unreliable typewriter terminal hooked into a large central computer. If the student was not able to work directly at the computer site, a dedicated telephone line was required between remote terminals and the central computer. The expense of the lines plus the high cost of control computer time made CAI economically impractical except as a research effort.

A combination of two trends has now made CAI acceptable, feasible, and even compelling. First of all, trends in education have moved toward increased concern with fundamental competencies. The need for individualizing instruction so that more students are able to achieve competencies has become a central theme in education. Large classes make it difficult for the teacher to work with each student on an individual basis. Declining SAT and ACT scores in science, mathematics, and reading and verbal skills dictate a need for concern.

The computer represents an infinitely patient adjunct to the development of basic competencies. An excellent project at Stanford University exemplifies what might be done with the computer in the elementary school (Atkinson & Fletcher, 1972; Atkinson & Paulson, 1972).The Stanford educators showed that CAI increased performance of students in mathematics and reading at inner-city Oakland schools. Their remarkable results, along with many other developments beyond the scope of this chapter, drew serious attention to CAI.

CAI has allowed teaching to extend beyond the traditional classroom to a wide variety of other settings and milieus. This second trend is reported in some detail in a recent report by the Educational Testing Service, in which the implications of the recent developments of computers in instruction is discussed in depth. An important final section of this report brings home the fact that the computer has allowed much of instruction to be moved from a physically limiting environment, such as a public school or university, into practically any environment in which clients wish to receive instruction. Large corporations such as ITT, IBM, and Control Data are in the business of providing instruction in a wide range of skills and subject matters (Educational Testing Service, 1983).

Color Computer Graphics

Color computer graphics is an area in which capabilities are being increased at a rate so rapid that it is becoming feasible to generate color graphics on systems selling for $100 or less. At the high end of the financial scale, such systems as the DICOMED "Imaginator" could allow the kind of color graphics used in "Star Wars" to be available for instructional use. Unfortunately, society has not provided the financial means to employ "Star Wars" color graphic technology to widespread educational use! At the less expensive end of the spectrum, increasing color graphic capabilities at lower cost and greater ease of use is a pervasive trend.

Although color computer graphic systems are becoming increasingly easy to use, it still requires considerable training for an instructor to generate and store color graphics on a computer. Adding color to a graphic increases the amount of memory needed to store the graphic for later use. Such expenses in time and memory dictate that color be used judiciously in computerized instruction. Durrett and Trezona (1982) give a brief survey of how to use color effectively in computer graphics.

Access to Other Media Materials

A very important instructional capability of the computer is in its ability to access and control devices such as slides, tapes, and videodiscs. A great deal of proven instructional material already exists and can be stored external to the computer. This allows fairly simple computers with limited memory and processing speed to access material by simply issuing control commands that will bring the material to the student. A particularly important development in this area is the videodisc. Over 50,000 images can be stored on one side of a videodisc and accessed by a computer with a maximum latency of .5 seconds. Up to 30 minutes of motion pictures is available on 1 side of a videodisc. The difficulty and cost of making videodiscs is rapidly declining. Erasable discs and discs with write-over capabilities are in the near future. Media materials can be easily placed on a videodisc. This allows actual photographs to be used, which are far more realistic than even the best computer graphics. Figure 13-1 represents a schematic outline of a computer as a central component of an audiographics and/or videographics instructional system. The text entry can be handwritten, typed, or read from tape, videodiscs, or any of a number of devices. Likewise, the graphic entry device can come from a wide range of sources including graphics developed on a computer. In this type of instruction, the computer can best be described as a technological manager of instruction.

The next section discusses the things a person should consider in deciding how to use color effectively in the instructional use of a computer. Since traditional media as well as computer graphics are involved, research on the effects of color in media is applicable as well as the research on the influence of color on learning and comprehension.

Human Information Processing and the Instructional Use of Color

In the most comprehensive review of the literature pertaining to the use of color for visual displays, Christ (1975) examined forty-two studies published between 1952 and 1973. He quantitatively analyzed the results of these studies in order to compare the effectiveness of color codes and achromatic codes. His analysis indicates that color may be an effective performance factor under some very specific conditions, but that color can be detrimental under other specific conditions. Furthermore, he found that the nature of these conditions can be revealed through experimental modelling.

Three generalizations can be made in regard to the use of color in instruction. First, when color is used selectively to direct attention to novel material, increased learning of that material will occur. Second, the use of an excessive amount of color does not

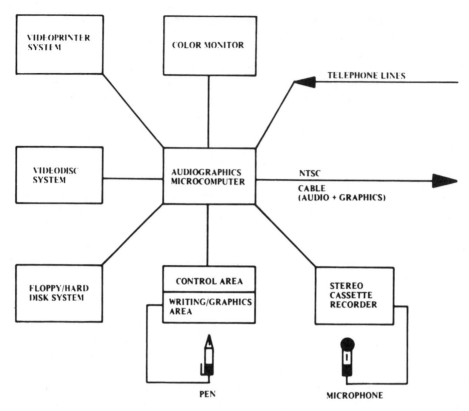

Figure 13-1 Schematic outline of computer as central component.

serve to direct attention, and no improvement in learning is observed. In fact, excessive amounts of color have a negative influence on learning. Third, when color is presented in its richest form, such as in pictorial material, that material is recalled more accurately than if it were portrayed solely in black and white.

This chapter focuses on some of the specific conditions where color has an influence on instruction. We will consider the influence of color on (a) learning and comprehension, (b) the attention process, (c) coding, cues, and contest, (d) release from proactive inhibition—a case study of how to look at color in relation to other variables, and (e) instructional media.

Learning and Comprehension

Farley and Grant (1976) tested the hypothesis that memory for learned material after one week is greater for color than for black and white presentations. They conducted their study on 52 undergraduate nursing students between the ages of 19 and 25. The students were randomly assigned to either a color or black and white slide-tape presentation. Retention was tested 7 days after the presentation. Farley and Grant found support for their prediction of significantly greater memory for the material presented in color compared to the material presented in black and white.

The conclusions of Farley and Grant contrast sharply with results of previous research, which showed little or no observable influence of color on complex learning tasks. Farley and Grant argued that the present approach to color and media influences, emphasizing arousal in information processing, may be extended to individual difference analyses. They proposed that individualization in instruction through specific arousal and treatment conditions may lead to improved performance.

Other research that seems to indicate that color can have a significant effect on the learning of information was conducted by Wong and Yacoumelos (1973). In their study of the resolution capability of television displays, they asked nine ROTC students to distinguish details from pictographic and line-graph maps. The researchers concluded that a color display has some advantage over a black and white system of equivalent resolution. In addition, they found almost perfect identification of alphanumeric symbols for all map and display types at an image resolution of nine television lines per millimeter. Thus, under specific conditions, it appears that color displays are superior to black and white displays in presenting detailed graphic information.

In addition to the study of color for use in presenting graphic information, it is important to look for research dealing with the recall and recognition of words or pictures under various conditions of color. In a study by Borges, Stepnowsky, and Holt (1977), it was found that recall and recognition performance for three different modes of presentation (written words, black and white pictures, color pictures) varied considerably between children and adults. Results of their study revealed a developmental trend of increasing recall performance with age. In addition, whereas adult performance was significantly affected by the mode of presentation (such that color pictures were recalled and recognized more readily than words), the performance of children did not vary with the mode of presentation. The data indicate although that both children and adults do have pictorial and color cues available in memory, children apparently are not able to utilize this color information as quickly as adults can. The researchers suggested that it is the cognitive structures of children that retard their utilization of stored color information, but that children can be trained to use this information effectively.

In a more specific comparison between color and black and white presentations, Katzman and Nyenhuis (1972) conducted two experiments in which they paid undergraduate students to look at nine slides of posters and ten slides of comic book stories at a self-determined rate. The first three slides were the same for all of the students in the study. The remainder of the presentation was shown in color to one group of students and in black and white to the rest. Learning was assessed by recall of material from the comic book story and opinions of the material. Katzman and Nyenhuis found that color increases the recall of peripheral visual material (media content irrelevant to the plot or theme), but not of the central material. There was mixed support for the proposition that color increases the liking of and attention to the material presented.

Clearly, there is a need to conduct additional research. The results from studies dealing with color are not unanimous in their support for its enhancement of learning and comprehension. Reid, Croft, and Jackson (1977) found that when color was incorporated into printed stimulus material in order to analyze students' study skills (comprehension and learning of map, graph, and diagram reading), no difference could be found in the interpretation of black and white versus color material. Perhaps the issue is not one that is so clearcut as color versus no color resulting in changes in comprehension and learning. Dwyer (1971) may have a better view in analyzing the influence of color. She found that the use of visuals does not automatically improve student achievement and that different types of color and black and white illustrations differ in their effectiveness at improving a student's learning and comprehension. Clearly, the informed, selective use of color must be based on empirical research before it can be said unequivocally that color is effective and in which ways it is effective.

Color on Attention

It has been known for some time that when the attention mechanism is devoted to an item for an extended time, that item will be learned to a deeper level. Thus, one of the major results of the use of color may simply be to direct an individual's attention to the material to be learned, thereby causing the individual to spend more time with that stimulus so that it will be learned to a deeper level. To study this effect, Cunningham and Odom (1978) investigated the ability of 64 children 6 and 11 years old to solve problems which required the analysis or synthesis of salience-assessed stimulus relations. They found that the relative salience of the relations of form, color, and position could be assessed, and that a salience hierarchy could be determined for each individual. Following this individual assessment of salience, the children were given special recall problems in which the salience of the relations and the type of evaluation required for solution were varied. In analysis problems, the relative salience of the irrelevant relation was either higher or lower than that of the relevant relation. In synthesis problems, the two relations to be evaluated were either more or less salient. Both younger and older individuals were able to solve problems that required the analysis or synthesis of the relations involved; however, the speed of solution was affected by the children's initial salience hierarchy. Where hierarchy and problem solution were consistent, the children's rate of problem solving was faster; otherwise, their rate of solution was slower. Thus, color may be more important for some children and may serve to either assist or hinder problem solution.

In another study dealing with the use of color in manipulating the attention mechanism, Cahill and Carter (1976) found that for both undergraduate and graduate students the influence of color can be either positive or negative, depending on the number of colors involved in a stimulus display. They tested normal-vision students in their ability to search for 3-digit numbers on a display. The density of the display ranged between 10 and 50 sets of 3-digit numbers. These numbers were coded in from 1 to 10 colors. Cahill and Carter observed that search times increased linearly with density of the display, but showed a curvilinear relationship to the number of colors used. While there was an initial decrease in search times as the first few colors were added to an uncoded display, this was followed by an increase in search times as still more and more colors were added. Cahill and Carter found that minimal search times at different display densities were associated with different code sizes, and that search times increased as more colors were added to the code, even when the number of items per color category was kept constant. The researchers observed the detrimental influence of color on search times for larger code sizes. Clearly, it appears that when a limited amount of color is used in a graphics display, the subject is able to locate key points that can then be used to partition the material to be searched. However, any relative advantages to searching given by this partitioning appear to decrease as the number of partitions increases.

Color on Coding, Cues, and Context

Color appears to affect the coding of information in human memory. Ceci, Lea, and Howe (1980) found this to be true when their subjects acquired information regardless of whether this information was related to the semantic category. They found that older children (10 years) tend to be able to use the color and spatial information more effectively than young children (4-7 years). Thus, color can serve as a redundant cue for relevant information to be remembered.

Shontz, Trumm, and Williams (1971) found that color coding for information location can effectively improve overall visual search performance. They investigated visual search performance as a function of color-coded and uncoded information location, number of categories coded, number of objects per category, and background clutter. Thirty-three undergraduates searched 12 areas of modified, sectional aeronautical charts for a total of 48 checkpoints. The identification of checkpoints was established with labels plus geographical context information. They found that color served as a partially redundant code for information location. In general, their findings indicated that color coding for information location is most effective when (a) many categories of information can or must be coded, (b) highly distinguishable colors and peripheral vision are used, and (c) the number of objects per category is kept reasonably small.

Color also has a powerful effect on context when learning material. Elio and Reutener (1978) investigated the effect of color on the encoding and organization of word lists. They presented 120 female undergraduates with hierarchically organized or randomly arranged color patterns. They determined recall scores for each of the individuals. It was found that these recall scores were significantly higher with the hierarchical color pattern than with a random color pattern. This facilitating result occurred for both hierarchically organizations and random assignments of word lists. Elio and Reutener concluded that individuals may use context as both a cueing or a differentiating factor when encoding, and as an organizational device for retrieval. Thus, color can be a useful technique allowing instructors to make use of the context factor to enhance recall and retrieval.

Perhaps the most important results pertaining to the use of color for improvement of comprehension and learning within a context are the findings of Hinds and Dodds (1968). In their studies, they used color as an added or redundant dimension for the coding of information for beginning level reading. They found that primary school children had significantly superior scores in vocabulary and spelling when keywords and concepts were presented in color. These results can be generalized to the improvement of vocabulary and comprehension for adults. Clearly, when a limited amount of color is used to serve as a context in a redundant cue for material to be learned, significant improvements in learning occur.

The results of Kroll (1977), however, indicate that we must be careful in the use of color. It appears critical that both the original stimulus and the choice of responses be coded in the same color, otherwise significant decreases in learning can occur. In a precise test of this phenomenon, Kroll had 20 undergraduates decide whether two letters, presented simultaneously, had the same name. Whether the letter was capital or lowercase and its color were logically irrelevant to the classification. They found that classification responses were slower when the two letters were in different colors than when they were in the same color or than when one was white. When one of the letters was white, the color of the other letter did not appear to affect decision latencies.

Release from Proactive Inhibition—A Case Study of How to Look at Color in Relationship to Other Variables

The introduction of new material is a major source of forgetting old information. In other words, memory for previous learning often competes with the retention of new learning. When old learning lowers the retention of new learning, learning psychologists refer to it as *proactive inhibition*. A schematic diagram showing a typical proactive inhibition experiment is presented in Figure 13-2.

If the experimental group in Figure 13-2 retains less of the B list, then proactive

Proactive inhibition.   The experimental design for *proactive inhibition (PI)* is as follows:

	Step 1	Step 2	R	Step 3
Experimental Group:	Learn A	Learn B	E	Test B.
Control Group:	Put in time	Learn B	S	Test B.
			T	

If, when the material of Task *B* is tested, the control group does better than the experimental group, it may be concluded (assuming no experimental flaws exist)tht PI has taken place.   That is, the Task *A* materials interfered with the later retention of Task *B* materials.

Figure 13-2   A typical proactive inhibition experiment.

inhibition (PI) may be said to occur if other differences between the experimental and control group are held constant. This paradigm may be used to study variables such as types of materials to be retained.

It has been demonstrated in the psychology laboratory that PI may build up very rapidly over a period of minutes when repeated learning trials are presented (Wickens, 1972). If some relevant aspect of the material is changed for one group on fourth trial, quite often the effects of PI are greatly diminished relative to a group that continues to receive material in the same manner. This phenomena is called "release from PI." The release from PI technique has been widely used to study the way in which people encode and retain information. Presumably, if changing some aspect of the material to be remembered releases PI, then that aspect of the material is crucial to the way the material is being encoded. Zechmeister and Myberg (1982) provide an excellent summary of this area. The theoretical implications of release from PI is perhaps best developed in the cited Wickens (1972)

The reader might well ask at this point: What has release from PI to do with the way in which color effects the encoding and retention of materials? Two experiments by Gardiner et al. (1976) show how the release from PI technique can be used to understand the role color might play in the way people encode and remember information. In both experiments, materials were either presented in black print for 3 trials and changed to red print on the fourth trial. If color was an integral part of the way in which the subjects in the experiment encoded the information, there should have been a significant improvement on Trial 4 for the groups for which the color of the print was changed. In contrast, the control group which received the same color print on the fourth trial as they had received on the previous 3 trials should not have shown an improvement.

In Experiment *A*, subjects learned groups of familiar words. In Experiment *B*, subjects learned groups of consonant trigrams. The results are presented in Figure 13-3. Note that for Experiment *A* there is a steady decline in percent recalled, presumably due to the steady buildup of PI. If only this experiment had been done, it would have supported the assertion that color of print plays little role in the encoding and retention of verbal materials. Experiment *B*, however, shows a classic example of release from PI obtained by changing the color of the print. Note that on Trial 4 of Experiment *B* the experimental group performed almost as well as they did on Trial 1. This is a very strong recovery from PI and shows that changing colors had a dramatic effect.

Remember that in Experiment *A* familiar words were the materials to be recalled. Color was probably not encoded as an important cue because highly over-learned semantic features were readily available for coding. For the consonant trigrams of Experiment *B*, more superficial aspects of the stimuli, such as the color of print, might

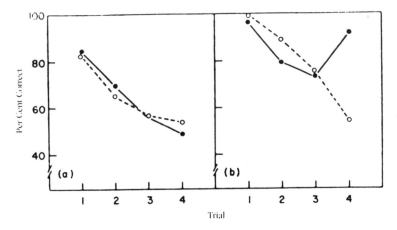

Figure 13-3   Results of Gardiner experiment.
—— Experimental group
- - - Control group

be part of the encoding process. In any event, such research certainly shows us that: (a) it is possible to obtain measures showing whether or not color is a key part of the coding process; and (b) one must be careful to state what kinds of materials a person must encode and remember.

This discussion of the release from PI research can begin to give the reader some idea of the manner in which research on questions of color in coding and learning is conducted. Practical implications of the research of Gardiner, et al, indicate that in situations where people need to learn fairly meaningless material or very new, unfamiliar material, changing the color in which material is printed could result in considerable improvement in retention. The generality of these results, of course, would have to be carried out in a range of situations analogous to the actual instructional situation that would occur.

In concluding this section, a paradox has been made apparent to the authors. The amount of research done on color as a variable in learning, attention, and coding reached a peak in the late 1960s and early 1970s, declined slightly during the 1970s, and declined dramatically between the late 1970s and the present. This is paradoxical because the use of color in the media of instruction and the potentials for use of color in instruction has grown dramatically. The problems of the decline in the quantity research on color in instruction is discussed more fully in the last section of this chapter.

Instructional Media

Films.   There is fairly consistent evidence that there is no measurable learning benefit from using color instead of black and white films. Hoban and Van Ormer (1950) reviewed the literature from 1918-1950 and came to this conclusion, based on research conducted through 1950. Johnson and Roberson (1979) conducted a fairly extensive experiment on subjects ranging from first graders to adults. Using a multiple choice test as their measure, they concluded that there was no immediate benefit following a six-week period of using color film. Recently, Chute (1980) found that color in a film helped fourth and fifth grade students of all ability levels learn incidental information; the amount of benefit depended on ability level. Additional evidence that color may be more effective than previously thought comes from a study by Spears (1976) on black and white versus color television. He found that color was more effective for visual-modality preference learners.

Slides, Photographs, and Transparencies.   Zimmerman (1977) compared recognition memory for color versus black and white slides and transparencies. Superior recognition memory was found for the color slides and transparencies. Scull (1975) found that in geography instruction color photographs did not result in better recall or comprehension of processes than black and white line drawings. His study indicated that well-written descriptive materials may have neutralized the effects of the photographs. O'Connor (1980) compared the effectiveness of black and white and color transparencies in college biology learning and found no benefit from using color.

Textbooks.   Morgan (1971) compared color with black and white textbook photographs and found no benefit of color. A study done in New Zealand by Reid (1977) considered the effects of coloring the portion of the text that included study skills material and found this to have no instructional benefit.

In conclusion, it seems that research on instructional media has not yet shown color to be of great benefit. Given its lack of proven efficacy, why has the use of color in instructional media seen such a great increase? The answer seems to lie in the affective realm. For example, Johnson and Roberson (1979) relate that when they told some of their older subjects that the study had shown no advantage of using color, the subjects were concerned because they liked the color presentations better. Moser and Kondracki (1977) studied color versus black and white instructional television in nursing education and found students preferred the color presentation. Reich and Meisner (1976) found that, while color had little learning advantage over black and white television, the emotional impact of the color television, as measured by the semantic differential, was greater. These affective results point to a probable justification for the continuing and even increasing use of color in instruction.

Integrating Color into a Computer Instructional System

When considering the introduction of any feature into a computer instructional system, one must be aware of: (a) the capabilities and limitations of the computer instructional system available, (b) the characteristics of the material to be used in the system, (c) the power and sophistication of the computer software designed for the system, (d) the characteristics of the instructors who are going to use the system, and (e) the characteristics of the students who will presumably be instructed by the system.

Since most courseware designed for computer instruction will have color capability (especially if it wants to have commercial viability!), the question of integrating color into the system needs to address the last two items—instructor characteristics and student characteristics.

Instructor Characteristics

We believe that in most cases, computer instructional systems will be used in adjunct with other methods of instruction—at least in the immediate future. A human instructor will usually be involved in such systems and will often decide the extent to which the computer will be used in the instructional system. This is probably wise in that most computerized instructional material is fairly primitive. Computer technology has far outstripped the sophistication of educational theory and practice necessary to take full advantage of it. Instructors should maintain an open-minded but skeptical attitude towards computer instructional sytsems.

There is an attitude that can block the critical trial and error processes necesary to develop better computer instructional systems. This attitude has been variously referred to as "cyberphobia" or "computerphobia"—the irrational fear of using computers. While not discovering a great fear of computers, recent research by Stimmel, Connor, McCaskill, and Durrett (1982) found considerable evidence of negative feelings towards computers and using the computer in instruction on the part of preservice elementary school teachers. These teachers showed a feeling of oppressiveness about using computers, seeing the computer in terms of such descriptors as "heavy," "dark," "powerful," and "dirty." To the extent that these teachers are representative of the teachers who will be instructing children in the future (and they probably are a representative sample), it is important to realize that their negative attitude may affect their willingness to meaningfully incorporate computers into their future instructional efforts. As seen in Chapter 4 of this book and the preceding parts of the present chapter, the presence of color is usually a factor conducive to more positive affective responses. Thus, effective use of color may not only be important in making computer instruction systems more palatable to instructors as well as to students. If instructional materials are not pleasant and comfortable for instructors to work with, they will not be as widely used as possible.

Student Characteristics

We have established that students ranging from elementary school children to adults generally prefer to receive instructional materials in color. In the consideration of exactly where and how to use color, however, it should be kept in mind that from 6 to 8% of males and .4 to .6% of females have some type of color deficiency (Raphael, 1966). In one study of learning, disabled children (a population where computerized instruction shows great promise as an infinitely patient instructional tool), 13.5% showed color deficiency (Litton, 1979). Thus, if hue alone is used as a critical coding feature of material, the instructor risks losing some effectiveness on a portion of his or her students. Litton feels that the number of color-deficient children in the study cited above was sufficiently large that teachers should exercise control over the use of color-coded materials and color-related materials.

Student characteristics will also interact with task characteristics. The instructor who is going to do instruction with the computer needs to thoroughly understand the perceptual and cognitive factors of color of the present volume. Although we know of no research that is directly related, we suspect that students who matured without the general presence of color television (those 30 years and older) may find heavy use of color in their instructional material less desirable than do younger students.

Conclusion

It is fair to say that color has an important role to play in the instructional use of computers. Although good instruction can be carried on without using color at all, color is an additional feature in human encoding processes and can serve as an attention-getter. Perhaps the strongest reason for using color in instructional computing is affective. People generally like to work with materials that are in color.

A word of caution needs to be entered here. We have mentioned that research on color as a learning and instructional variable had all but ceased by the late 1970s (if published results are valid indicators). This is unfortunate. We are far from a complete understanding of how color ought to be used in a computer instructional system. The role of color is just a small part of the total needed research on computer instructional systems. Perhaps as a more complete conceptual framework for computer instructional systems develops, the role of color may become more clearly defined.

Summary

Computers are being used in a wide variety of instructional situations. After a laborious start, the instructional use of computers has grown rapidly in the past decade. Computers have been shown to be effective instructional devices when properly used.

Computers accomplish instruction both by directly presenting materials and by providing access to other media such as videodiscs. A review of the research literature on color, human information processing, and their joint relationship to computer instructional systems revealed that (a) color is at best a weak aid for memory, (b) if misused, color can hinder learning and retention, and (c) the main advantage of color is in the affective domain; that is, people generally prefer instructional materials to be in color. Additional discussion was directed towards the problem of using color to enhance instructor acceptance of computer instructional systems and being sensitive to problems of visual color deficiency in using color in such a system.

References

Atkinson, R. C., & Fletcher, J. D. Teaching children to read with a computer. *The Reading Teacher*, 1972, *25*, 319–327.

Atkinson, R. C., & Paulson, J. A. An approach to the psychology of instruction. *Psychological Bulletin*, 1972, *78*, 49–61.

Borges, M. A., Stepnowsky, M. A., & Holt, L. H. Recall and recognition of words and pictures by adults and children. *Bulletin of the Psychonomic Society*, 1977, *9*(2), 133–144.

Cahill, M. C., & Carter, R. C. Color code size for searching displays of different density. *Human Factors*, 1976, *18*(3), 273–280.

Ceci, S. J., Lea, S. E., & Howe, M. J. Structural analysis of memory traces in children from 4 to 10 years of age. *Developmental Pychology*, 1980, *16*(3), 203–212.

Christ, R. E. Review and analysis of color coding research for visual displays. *Human Factors*, 1975, *17*(6), 542–570.

Chute, A. G. Effect of color and monochrome versions of a film on incidental and task relevant learning. *Educational Communication and Technology: A Journal of Theory, Research, and Development*, 1980, *28*, 10–18.

Cunningham, J. G., & Odom, R. D. The role of perceptual salience in the development of analysis and synthesis process. *Child Development*, 1978, *49*(3), 815–823.

Durrett, J., & Trezona, J. How to use color displays effectively. *BYTE*, April 1982, 83–86.

Dwyer, F. M. Color as an instructional variable. *AV Commumication Review*, 1971, *19*(4), 399–416.

Educational Testing Service, 1983.

Elio, R. E., & Reutner, D. B. Color context as a factor in encoding and as an organizational device for retrieval of word lists. *Journal of General Psychology*, 1978, *99*(2), 223–232.

Farley, F. H., & Grant, A. P. Arousal and cognition: Memory for color versus black and white multimedia presentation. *Journal of Psychology*, 1976, *94*(1), 147–150.

Gardiner, J. M., Redman G., & Ball M. The role of stimulus material in determining release from proactive inhibition. *Quarterly Journal of Experimental Psychology*, 1976, *28*, 395–402.

Hinds, L. R., & Dodds, W. G. Words in color: Two experimental studies. *Journal of Typographic Research*, 1968, *2*(1), 43–52.

Hoban, C. F., & Van Ormer, E. B. Instructional Film Research, 1918-1950. Naval Social Devices Center, 1950.

Johnson, B., & Roberson, J. Color in instructional films: Does it still make no difference in learning achievement? *Educational Technology*, 1979, *10*(1), 32–35.

Katzman, N., & Nyenhuis, J. Color vs. black and white effects on learning, opinion, and attention. *AV Communication Review*, 1972, *20*(1), 16–28.

Kroll, N. E. Effects of irrelevant colour changes on speed of name decisions. *Quarterly Journal of Experimental Psychology*, 1977, *29*(2), 277–281.

Licklider, J. C. R. Impact of information technology on education in science and technology. In D. K. Deringer and A. R. Nolnar (Eds.), *Technology in Science Education, the Next Ten Years: Perspectives and Recommendations*. Prepared for the National Science Foundation, July 1979.

Litton, F. W. Color vision deficiency in learning-disabled children. *Academic Therapy*, 1979, *19*, 437–443.

Morgan, R. L. The effects of color in textbook illustrations on the recall and retention of information by students of varying socioeconomic status. *Dissertation Abstracts International*, 1971, *32*(3-B), 1892–1893.

Moser, D. H. & Knodracki, M. R. Comparison of attitudes and cognitive achievement of nursing students in three instructional strategies. *Journal of Nursing Education*, Juanuary 1977, *16*, 14–28.

O'Connor, P. J. A comparison of three forms of AV presentation in general science lessons. *Graduate Research in Education and Related Disciplines*. 1980, *6*(1), 67–82.

Raphael, M. Color: A new dimension in teaching reading. *Catholic School Journal*, 1966, *66*, 56–57.

Reich, C., & Meisner, A. A comparison of colour and black and white television as instructional media. *British Journal of Educational Technology*, 1976, *7*(2), 24–35.

Reid, N. A., Croft, A. C., & Jackson, P. F. The effects of coloured stimulus material on study skills achievement. *New Zealand Journal of Educational Studies*, 1977, *12*(1), 66–71a.

Scull, R. C. Instructional effectiveness of two types of visual illustration in facilitating specific geographic learning at the college level. *Dissertation Abstracts International*, 1975, *35*(2-A), 7038–7039.

Shontz, W. D., Trumm, G. A. & Williams, L. G. Color coding for information location. *Human Factors*, 1971, *13*(3), 237–246.

Spears, R. E. The effects of color versus black-and-white television on learning for college students with auditory or visual modality preference. *Dissertation Abstracts international*, 1976, *37*(5-a), 2588.

Stimmel, T., Connor, J. L., McCaskill, E. O., & Durrett, H. J. Teacher resistance to computer-aided instruction. *Behavior Research Methods and Instrumentation*, 1981, *13*, 128–130.

Uttal, W. R. *Real-Time Computers*. New York: Harper & Row, 1967.

Wickens, D. D. Characteristics of word encoding. *Coding Process in Human Memory*, 1972, p. 16.

Wong, K. W., & Yacoumelos, N. G. Identification of cartographic symbols from TV displays. *Human Factors*, 1973, *15*(1), 21–31.

Zechmeister, E. B., & Nyberg, S. E. *Human Memory: An Introduction to Research and Theory*. Monterrey, Calif.: Brooks/Coles, 1982.

Zimmerman, D. P. The effect of color on recognition memory for selected pictorial material. *Dissertation Abstracts International*, 1977, *37*(8-a), 4798.

14   *Color Text Display in Video Media*

CHRISTOPHER SCHMANDT

Massachusetts Institute of Technology
Cambridge, Massachusetts

Introduction

The use of color as a component of computer output raises particular problems with cathode ray tube (CRT) displays. Color often necessitates use of nonstandard computer terminals, and color further complicates the display process that transforms digitally encoded text or graphics into an electrical video signal. With an expanding home computing market and a variety of teletext experiments, interest is rising in displaying color on either National Television System Committee (NTSC) or NTSC-resolution monitors. Through a tutorial analysis of digital and analog video technologies, this chapter explores techniques to facilitate this display. An understanding of terminal limitations, grayscale technique, and the utility of conventional displays will aid the discussion.

Terminal Limitations

For applications requiring text only, such as word processing or computer programming, a range of standard terminal displays is quite adequate. These terminals are limited in several ways including that they generally do not have the capability of displaying text in multiple or arbitrary colors; there is little provision for the mixture of text and graphics; and their video format is incompatible with off-the-shelf color video components. For these reasons, it is necessary to consider alternative arrangements for color text display.

A number of video formats may be used, with a wide range in cost and similar range in text quality. If text could be portrayed adequately with lower resolution components, even conventional broadcast standard (NTSC) home televisions might be suitable. Many visual artifacts are associated with such a display format; in general, video text is relatively poor, even compared to inexpensive hard-copy output.

Grayscale Technique

An improvement can be made using a technique called grayscale. In the case of black and white text, this involves inserting gray fringes around the characters. Although the character is thus blurred, it will in fact be better transmitted and rendered in video, as it requires a lower band-width signal. The same principle applies to color; with red text on white, the fringes would be intermediary in both luminance and saturation (i.e., pink). We will refer to this as color scale, although luminance is in many ways the predominant component. This band limiting is even more useful in encoded color displays, which allocate proportionately less band-width for chrominance than luminance.

Grayscale is, in fact, a general-purpose tool for display of arbitrary color graphics; it implies a continuous transition between the foreground color and the background. It is natural to utilize grayscale when variable luminance display capability is built into CRTs. From the typesetting viewpoint, one might assume that since the original (or ideal) text is one bit (black or white), the same should be sufficient for display. In fact, that is not the case.

In a wide range of applications, it is desirable to display text on general-purpose graphics displays, and in some instances there may be no alternative for use of color. Cost is definitely a factor; standard video components will always be less expensive than specialized formats. Recently, bit-mapped displays have become more popular—text is generated by copying a master character, pixel by pixel, into video display memory. This allows placement of characters at arbitrary points on the screen, in multiple fonts and sizes. If the video processor generates color, several colors can be displayed simultaneously. Most notably, text and graphics can be mixed on the same screen.

Utility of Conventional Displays

Many television sets already in American homes are being used extensively in the lower cost home computer world. Text and graphics display hardware, combined with local storage and intelligence linked to remote databases via telephone, is an obvious next step for home computer applications. Both teletext and video text assume display on home television; although text may be in red, green, blue (RGB) format locally, it must use the same resolution and frame rate as NTSC.

Another motivation for use of conventional displays is the desire to mix text with graphics, either within the frame store or as an overlay. In the consumer electronics world, the economy of scale gained with NTSC is significant; video discs, tape decks, switchers, keyers, cameras, etc. are all readily available for a variety of interactive video systems, while alternative technology is either expensive or nonexistent.

Video Systems
Rendering Text in Video

Several techniques are used to produce text in the form of video output. A common one is the concept of a digitized version of each character—a font is represented as an array of discrete points, each of which is either foreground or background. Grayscale simply allows each point to be one of some greater number of colors; that is, foreground, background, and some colors in between.

Character Generator. A generator requires a region of memory in which the textual contents of the screen are stored as encoded characters (e.g. the American Standard Code for Information Interchange, or ASCII). Another region holds the pixel-by-pixel array values for each possible character. As the electron beam moves across the face of the CRT, the character generator calculates which character to display and which line of the array for that character is currently being illuminated; it then produces the proper electrical signal as it reads out the value of each pixel from the stored array.

Digital Frame Store. The digital frame store is an alternative approach. A region of memory holds a pixel-wise image of the screen; each memory location is one pixel. A video processor reads these locations sequentially, producing a signal appropriate for the values found there. More memory holds the bit maps for each character. Writing text to the screen consists of moving a copy of the character from this part of memory to the display memory.

Text Display Problems. The root of the problems associated with text display are the point-by-point digital representations of characters found in both approaches. Consider an "abstract" character, as perhaps conceived by a typographer. This character is crisp, with precise edges and a single uniform color; its outline is smooth, of infinite precision and resolution. Somehow this character must be scan-converted, or sampled, into an array of discrete points of comparatively low resolution.

Clearly, detail must be lost simply because much less information is stored in these coarse arrays of pixels. But the process of sampling a continuous analog signal at discrete points, and later reproducing another continuous signal from that information is used in a wide variety of areas, including video cameras. A body of knowledge called sampling theory describes the proper procedure to minimize information loss. We draw on sampling theory in our analysis of the display of color video text to help explain why a camera works better than a frame store and how to emulate the camera for text display.

Video Display Parameters

There are a number of video display formats with varying band widths and transmission schemes; it is important to understand the parameters that indicate how much information these formats can transmit. The information capacty of a video channel is a function of the number of lines on the screen, how rapidly the signal can change along a line, frequency of refreshing the screen, and the method of encoding the three-dimensional color vector between light and electricity.

Vertical Resolution. The most common issue in today's computer graphics markets is the number of display lines, or vertical resolution of the monitor. In general, the greater the number of lines, the higher the information content of the screen. NTSC and encodable RGB both use 480 visible lines. With the screen's 4:5 aspect ratio, this necessitates a scan line divided into 640 pixels for a frame store. In an effort to render smaller detail, some display systems now use upwards of 1000 lines. Many home computer systems use much less resolution in the frame store; they must display the same line several times, however, because they are generally viewed on televisions with 480 lines.

Frame Rate.   A second parameter is the frame rate and display scanning sequence. Video is inherently a dynamic medium. An electron beam scans a phosphor coating on the screen, which produces light; the light emission decays rather rapidly and must be refreshed. How often this occurs is the frame rate, which can be increased to transmit more information and result in a more stable image. Interlace is sometimes a component of the scanning rate. It is a scheme wherein all the even scan lines are displayed sequentially, followed by all the odd lines. Two passes, called fields, make up a single frame. Visual effects of interlace become noticeable when very small horizontal objects are displayed.

NTSC is 30 Hz (hertz) interlaced; that is, 30 times a second the entire screen is refreshed in two vertical sweeps. Other, nonstandard formats refresh the screen at 60 Hz (usually not interlaced) or higher. Clearly, a 60 Hz refresh must be driven with twice the band width of an otherwise comparable format.

Another parameter of the frame store is the number of bits per pixel, or the degrees of freedom in representing the value of each point on the screen. One bit per pixel means objects must be rendered with each point either on or off (e.g., black or white). More bits would allow points to be one of some number of gray values, or perhaps other colors.

National Television System Committee

In discussing display of color, it is particularly valuable to mention the NTSC video standard because it was developed particularly for color transmission and is the most commonly used format for inexpensive computer displays (Conrac, 1980).

NTSC was developed under two important constraints: The band width of the broadcast television channel had been determined previously, and new color broadcasts had to be viewable on older black and white television sets. Meeting the latter constraint meant continuing to transmit a luminance-only signal that could be received properly on monochrome receivers. The former constraint required that the additional chrominance information somehow be interleaved with the existing luminance and audio signals, as band width was not increased.

Color space is three-dimensional; a vector in color space can be represented as coordinates on a variety of axes. A camera, like common frame store output, uses red, green, and blue axes (*RGB*). Painters usually think in terms of intensity, hue, and saturation (*IHS*). With NTSC, one axis was constrained by compatibility to luminance. Two additional color axes were selected, called in phase (*I*, an orange-cyan axis) and quadrature (*Q*, a magenta-green axis). This coordinate system is referred to as *YIQ*.

YIQ Problems.   The problem is to transmit the *I* and *Q* components within the existing band width. To do this, a 3.58 MHz (megahertz) subcarrier is superimposed on the luminance signal. The *I* and *Q* components contribute to this subcarrier so that its amplitude corresponds to saturation, and its phase is a measure of hue. Although amplitude may be absolute, phase must be determined by comparison with some reference; for this reason, nine cycles of phase reference subcarrier (the "color burst") are transmitted during of each horizontal retrace.

Chrominance band width.   Problems arise from this sharing of band width on a single channel instead of sending three separate signals, as with unencoded RGB video. The first is simply that relatively little band width was allocated for chrominance. The eye is much more sensitive to small spatial variation in luminance than chrominance, so just enough band width to allow for perception of color detail at normal viewing distance was allocated. This concept of "proportional band width" may be adequate for watching broadcast television, but proves insufficient for the detail required to render color text on a screen that will be read from a distance of two feet.

Although the band width of the luminance signal may be as high as 4.2 MHz, the *I* signal is limited to 1.3 MHz and the *Q* signal is only 0.5 MHz wide. This proportionality can be measured to some extent by observing that although one would expect 640 pixels across a scan, there are only about 200 cycles of subcarrier during the same time. It implies that even less detail can be displayed with color text than black and white; this is only partially true, however, as most of the visual information used to distinguish between characters arrives as luminance.

Signal crosstalk.   The second problem with interleaving luminance and chrominance is that there may be crosstalk between the two signals. For example, physical objects being displayed as black and white may be of the proper spatial frequency (the distance between objects) to result in a luminance signal very close to 3.58 MHz. In fact, the chrominance decoder circuit will detect this luminance and display it as spurious color.

Digital Video Display Artifacts

Some factors degrade the quality of digitally generated images, and must be overcome to display higher quality, denser text. The first three artifacts are inherent in conventional raster graphics and NTSC video. The last three artifacts are unique to NTSC. These artifacts are at their worst in the case of binary value text, because of its high contrast and information content (i.e., spatial frequency). Also, these same factors affect alternative video technologies (e.g., 60 Hz or 1000 line displays) to different degrees.

Stairstep Lines.   The most noticeable artifact in frame-store-generated video is the "jaggies" of computer graphics parlance (i.e., the stairsteps along curved or slanted lines). Observed in a thin line slightly skewed from horizontal, the "line" consists of a series of steps, its length inversely proportional to its slope. This is due to the inability of the frame store's array of points (pixels) to render the continuous "ideal" line properly. This phenomenon is best understood in the context of sampling theory discussed in the next section. Sampling theory will also show that increasing display resolution does not eliminate jaggies, but may make them a little less troublesome.

Image Flicker.   Another potentially disturbing effect is scintillation, or image flicker. It can be seen in a display of a thin (one pixel wide), horizontal white line on a dark background; the line appears to flicker or move. This is the result of interlace, the sequential display of alternate fields consisting of either the even or odd scan lines. The line falls on only one field, and hence is displayed only every thirtieth of a second, a rate at which flicker is perceptible to the visual system under normal viewing situations. A wider line falls on both fields, because it contains two or more vertically adjacent pixels, and hence at least a part of it is illuminated every sixtieth of a second.

Resolution.   Video resolution is seen as inadequate by those familiar with hundreds of points per inch typesetting fonts in hard copy. Video resolution is usually determined by the number of scan lines, which determines pixel size. There is clearly some minimum size character detail, the width of one scan, which can be displayed. This is usually insufficient detail for fine character elements such as serifs or stroke-width variation, a fact which partially explains the visual monotony of video text terminals.

Encoding Artifacts.   Encoding artifacts, particularly luminance to chrominance crosstalk, are also serious limitations to use of NTSC. Luminance to chrominance crosstalk is seen as colored fringes on the borders of sharp edged objects or small image detail. This noise may appear to vibrate or crawl up the screen, as chrominance alternates phases on successive frames. In the encoded video signal, chrominance information quadrature modulates a 3.58 MHz carrier, which is transmitted in the same signal as luminance information. Any luminance that happens to have a spatial frequency in this range will get decoded and appear as spurious color information.

Band Width Limitations.   Several band width limitations are inherent in NTSC. With a digital frame store and digital-to-analog converter, one may generate a signal requiring an instantaneous transition from black to white by storing certain values in adjacent pixel memory locations. But this sharp signal must thereafter pass through real physical components, such as encoders and distribution amplifiers, all of which are intrinsically band limited, causing ringing in the signal as it passes through them. This ringing is a function of both filter and signal sharpness, but only the signal can be controlled. Ringing will have various effects on components such as monitors, depending on what filtering is employed in their input stage.

Chrominance Band Width.   A last consideration is the still more limited chrominance band width of NTSC. Limited chrominance band width is necessary to avoid crosstalk into luminance, and is partially based on the physical size of differentiable colored regions perceivable by human eyes. Comparing an encoded picture of colored lines to an unencoded one illustrates that we can perceive color details much smaller than the smallest colored area displayable in NTSC. Hence, we have difficulty displaying horizontally small colored objects, including text, in NTSC. The assumptions that lead to this "proportional band width," or lower broadcast band width for color information apply for normal scenes and normal viewing situtations, neither of which is true of the text environment.

Analog Camera Comparison

The discussion of limitations and artifacts associated with display of text from a digital frame store might lead to the conclusion that video is simply an unsuitable medium. That conclusion can be disproved by focusing a video camera on a page of text and observing its ability to display it significantly better than most computers can. Since the camera does so much better a job, it is worthwhile to discuss its signal generation process and then to argue that digital display algorithms modeled after camera behavior will result in noticeably better text display.

Camera as a Sampling System

It is useful to study the camera as a sampled system; sampling theory is itself an extensively utilized analysis tool (Oppenhiem & Schafer, 1975). The camera must convert an optical image, focused onto a photo-responsive target, into an electrical signal. It does this by scanning the target in a continuous horizontal line, then sweeping back across and down to the next line. Thus, the image is continuous in the horizontal direction, but sampled (measured at discrete locations) vertically.

Sampling theory indicates that a signal can be sampled and faithfully reproduced only if it contains no components above half the sampling rate (the spatial frequency determined by the distance between centers of scan lines). Low-pass prefiltering is necessary to eliminate "alias" components above half the sampling rate, and a filter with the same cutoff is required at the regeneration stage. Sharp edges (high contrast boundaries) have significant high frequency image components, while more gradual shading variations have lower frequency. Moiré is a good example of aliasing resulting from improper filtering (Shroup, 1973). It is the high frequency, sharp edges of the digital video signal that cause the problems discussed in the previous section.

Vertical Sampling. As the camera samples the light image in the vertical direction, dividing it into scan lines, the operator must insure that the image contains no high frequency components either by defocusing the lens or by filtering the sharp image during scanning. The latter technique is actually used. The camera filters the image by defocusing the electron beam scanning the target so that it is just under twice the width of a scan line (Figure 14-1). This insures that even if an object is only one scan line thick optically, it will have an electrical effect on two or more adjacent scans. In effect, a low-pass filter band limits the input to the sampling system, coincidentally minimizing scintillation by precluding the appearance of objects on only one field.

Horizontal Sampling. The image is also filtered in the horizontal dimension, even though it is scanned continuously rather than sampled. The intersection of the beam with the target has a nonzero area. As the beam sweeps across the image, the resulting signal is in fact the convolution of the two (Figure 14-2). If the beam were an infinitely small point, the signal could change instantaneously as the point crossed a sharply focused edge. In fact, however, it takes some time for the entire beam to cross; the rise time and therefore the frequency responses are limited.

This effective smoothing of sharp edges in the horizontal direction (i.e., limiting the frequency of the video signal) is in fact desirable for video transmission. The ringing introduced into the signal as it passes through a band-limited system is lessened if the frequency of the signal is already limited. Luminance to chrominance crosstalk is reduced, since it is caused by high frequency luminance information interfering with the color decoders in receivers.

Figure 14-1 Overlapping camera scans.

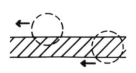

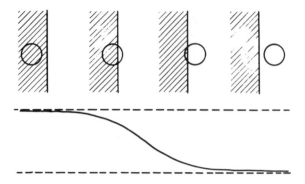

Figure 14-2 Convolution of the beam and image.

Spatial Effect.   The signal produced from a camera is the convolution of the optical image and the electron beam as it scans that image on the target. It is useful to understand the spatial effect of this convolution origin of the video signal. High frequencies in the video are responsible for detail and sharp edges in the image, in both luminance and chrominance. The camera beam limits response time both vertically and horizontally, effectively blurring the image and thus eliminating broadcast and NTSC artifacts—a picture too sharp to be transmitted is softened. Blurring spreads out an object visually, dovetailing well with the limited band width of the chrominance signal, which is unable to display very fine color detail.

A corollary of this image blurring is lower resolution; thus, we must also consider, for the first time, a resolution/luminance tradeoff. Because the beam has finite area, a vertical dark line against a lighter background will cause the video signal to drop to full black only if it is wider than the beam, because only then can the entire beam area be filled by the dark region of the image. A line thinner than the beam can still be displayed; the signal just will not go all the way down to black (Figure 14-3). In fact, an arbitrarily thin line can be displayed, although the lack of contrast between the thinnest lines and the background will eventually render them invisible. Thus, the design of the camera trades off contrast (dynamic range) for reduction of artifacts.

Other Components.   Illuminance in filtering and blurring is emphasized here simply for ease of explanation—all chromaticity components of the image apply equally well. If we had been considering saturation instead of luminance, we could have referred to a saturated red line on a white background. As such a line becomes thinner, the beam

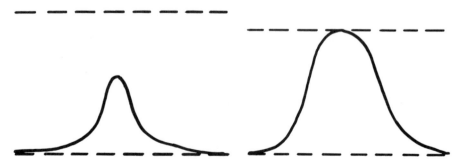

Figure 14-3   Video signals resulting from scan of vertical line.

would be filled by less red and more white as it sweeps across, and the line would appear an increasingly less saturated pink on display.

The Monitor

Considering the camera as a sampling system, it is also important to understand the reconstruction stage; this is, the video monitor recreating an optical image from the electrical signal. As noted previously, beam defocusing in the camera acts as a low-pass prefilter in the sampling process. Similarly, reconstruction requires a low pass filter on the output stage to limit the signal to half the sampling frequency, in order to avoid aliasing. This is also accomplished in the monitor by defocusing its beam, a duplicate of the camera sampling scheme.

As the camera beam is defocused, a very thin horizontal line midway between two scan lines will be detected equally on both scans. The beam is also defocused on display; hence the line will appear on two adjacent, overlapping scans. In fact, the light is additive, and the visual effect will actually be brightest midway between scans, accurately rendering the sampled image (Figure 14-4). If the original line were higher or lower, one scan would be affected more than the other, and the "center of moment" of the additive light regions would accurately move up or down (Figure 14-5).

Thin vertical features will be displayed in various gray levels, where the size of the original image will influence the level of illumination. But observers of the display on the monitor tend to see thinner lines, not grayish lines. In visual perception, a similar size/luminance interchangeability seems to occur when objects are very small (Cornsweet, 1970).

Consequences for the Frame Store

The camera displays detailed images fairly well, but the one bit frame store does not. The preceding section argued that since the camera and monitor make up a sampled system, it is important that both stages obey the filtering rules of sampling theory. A digital frame store is even more clearly a sampled system; it too must obey these rules. This implies the need to filter the data in the frame buffer, or rather generate appropriately prefiltered data. The algorithm that fills image memory locations is the parallel to the electrical scanning of light in the camera.

A consequence of low-pass filtering in the camera is smooth transitions in luminance

Figure 14-4 Superposition of light from two adjacent pixels of equal intensity.

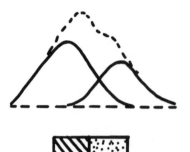

Figure 14-5   Superposition of light with unequal pixel intensity.

along sharp image boundaries in both dimensions. A parallel digital algorithm requires at least some gray levels. The intermediate values are necessary even for an image to be perceived as only black or white (Crow, 1977).

An illustration is a camera that has an extremely small, highly focused beam. If this beam were a point, and the image on the target were high contrast and also well focused, the beam could change from minumum to maximum intensity nearly instantaneously. The resulting signal would alias, producing moirés, for example, if the camera were pointed at a window screen and stairsteps as object boundaries suddenly sloped into the adjacent scan. It would contain high frequencies, due to sharp edges, and hence be susceptible to encoding artifacts and ringing. As sampling is being done in the vertical direction only, this system could still position an object arbitrarily in the horizontal dimension, but not in the vertical.

The black and white frame store suffers identical limitations, with the additional one that it is sampled in the horizontal dimension as well. Hence, it may be thought of as an array of points to be filled with information about the original image and displayed in some manner. From the camera discussion, we saw that the image could be properly sampled, and high-frequency related artifacts minimized, by low-pass filtering. This can be done easily with a frame buffer, provided some added luminance information is provided.

Multi-bit Fonts

Implementation of these ideas introduces grayscale to fonts during low-pass filtering (Warnock, 1980). Instead of forcing each pixel in the character to be either on or off, we assign it several bits of luminance information. In our experience, a carefully designed font can generally be well represented by two or three bits per pixel, provided they are designed by hand (Schmandt & Kobayashi, 1980). These additional gray levels are introduced in the process of reducing and filtering a large, one-bit character master. The result is a solid black core (if the character is large enough) surrounded by a thin band of gray (Figure 14-6, see color insert); the character has effectively been blurred.

Legible Color Text

It certainly is counterintuitive that blurring text makes it more readable. But in fact the character is simply modeled so that the digital video generated from it will behave more like the camera analog. Avoiding the more extreme artifacts under discussion makes text in fact considerably more legible, allowing higher density. Although the discussion focuses on grayscale, similar improvements can be seen with color text, where the intermediate pixel values represent intermediate luminance and saturation between the text and background colors.

Faithful Rendering.   Filtering allows more faithful rendering of the desired character image. Sampling artifacts (i.e., jaggies) are reduced as the introduced grey levels appear along the stairsteps to smooth them visually. Gray pixels allow thinner vertical lines and finer character details to be displayed, just as the camera can display lines thinner than the beam through luminance cues.

Scintillation Reduction.   The low-pass filtering in the vertical direction tends to force horizontal character elements to spread over adjacent scan lines. This reduces scintillation, while simultaneously allowing display of thinner lines. Recall from the discussion of the monitor that two adjacent grey pixels will not display as a gray rectangle; they display as small overlapping areas, with additive light output causing the apparent object to appear centered between them. This analog of beam defocusing in the camera similarly takes advantage of overlap in the display monitor. This process does not simply repeat the even field on the odd; a line may appear on two scan lines, or three if it is thick enough, and the actual distribution of luminance among those scans will determine where the line appears to be.

Reducing Crosstalk.   The video signal from grayscale fonts has lower frequency than one-bit text, as intermediate gray level pixels in the horizontal dimension slow transition time. As discussed, artifacts result from unduly sharp edges, and grayscale smooths them. This reduces both ringing (Figure 14-7, see color insert) and luminance to chrominance crosstalk. Figure 14-8 (see color insert) displays chrominance detected in a monochrome signal (i.e., any visible chrominance is crosstalk), showing the improvement between grayscale and single-bit text.

An interesting note for display of colored text is that, given NTSC spatial chrominance resolution, it is beneficial to spread out the character luminance through this blurring. Most of the character information is in the luminance, which is perceived properly even though spread out. When these wider regions are colored, their larger size is more closely matched to the smallest areas of chrominance that can be displayed in NTSC.

A Font Implementation

Analysis of the artifacts associated with digital video and the transfer function of camera sampling suggested the use of grayscale or color scale to emulate the camera, applying a spatial low-pass filter. The Architecture Machine Group of the Massachusetts Institute of Technology has experimented with various styles of type and number of bits per pixel in both unencoded and NTSC video. To invite comparison, fonts generated in the laboratory were modeled after popular Futura, Clarendon, Courier, and Helvetica fonts.

Font Design.   For our purposes, we found that two bits per pixel were sufficient for a significant image improvement; however some clarification is required. In general, quality continues to improve as luminance information is increased, at least up to five or six bits per pixel. Since our applications usually involve fonts as overlays to other graphic information or as multiple pages of text buffered in the same frame store, it was desirable to minimize text memory depth allocation. Because the font pixel data must be moved into frame store memory by block data transfer, fewer bits per pixel allow faster image access.

Of course, the font design task is much more difficult with fewer bits devoted to luminance, and indeed our fonts required much careful hand editing. With more bits per pixel, much of that could have been done automatically. Once the time investment is made, however, a complete font requires no additional work and can be used for multiple applications. Most significant is the vast improvement gained by adding only the first bit of grayscale.

Summary

This paper examined the process of converting color text from computer memory representations to video output. To obtain high quality text display, it is necessary to consider features and limitations of the various video media. This is particularly true with color text because color users are more likely to utilize conventional raster displays.

After analyzing the process whereby the camera samples an optical image and the monitor subsequently recreates it, we suggest that spatial low-pass filtering is necessary for faithful rendering of digital display output. Since the algorithm that writes to pixels in the frame store is the parallel to a camera scanning light focused on its target, that filtering must be internal to the character generation system. Grayscale and color-scale fonts are a special case application of this analysis to particular display requirements.

References

Conrac Corporation. *Raster Graphics Handbook*. Covina, Calif.: Conrac Corp., Conrac Division, 1980.

Cornsweet, T. *Visual Perception*, New York: Academic Press, 1970.

Crow, F. The aliasing problem in computer generated shaded images. Communications of the Association for Computing Machinery, 1977, (*20*)11, 779–805.

Kobayashi, S. C. Optimization algorithms for greyscale fonts. Bachelor of Science thesis, Massachusetts Institute of Technology, 1980.

Leler, W. J., Human vision, anti-aliasing, and the cheap 4000 line display, *Proceedings of SIGGRAPH*, 1980, (*14*)3, 308–313.

Oppenheim, A. V., & Schafer, R. F. *Digital Signal Processing*, Englewood Cliffs, N.J.: Prentice-Hall.

Schmandt, C. Soft typography, information processing '80, *Proceedings of International Federation of Information Processing Societies*, 1980, 1027–1032.

Shroup, R.G., Some quantization effects of digitally generated pictures. *Proceedings of the Society for Information Display*, 1973 .

Warnock, J. The display of characters using grey level sample arays, *Proceedings of SIGGRAPH*, 1980, (*14*)3, 302–307.

15   *Color and Business Graphics*

HOWARD A. SPIELMAN

Digital Equipment Corporation
Marlborough, Massachusetts

The term "business graphics", in its broadest definition, reflects the use of charts and graphs to represent data. Such graphics are used in many fields of endeavor, not only business, in which there is need for a visual display of quantitative information. There seems to be no easy answer to the question of why the graphical representation of data, using computers, is known as business graphics, other than the fact that it is business people who are willing to spend money on business graphics hardware and software. The name also helps to segment the market as distinct from areas such as Computer-Aided Design/Computer-Assisted Manufacturing (CAD/CAM), computer-automated cartography, and computer-aided graphic arts/design.

The marketing of business graphics hardware and software is typically aimed at middle or upper level management decision makers. This raises two interesting observations:

First, these business people must expect an appropriate return on their investment to go ahead and purchase the available hardware and software. They feel that the introduction of business graphics into their portfolio of management tools adds enough value to warrant its cost.

Second, the graphic representation of data, as a subject of academic study, is part of the professional training in the fields of drafting, cartography and graphic arts/design. Scientists and engineers also have professional training in this area and prepare reports and publish journals replete with the most sophisticated graphic representations of data. But the business people, the management decision makers to whom "business graphics" are now being actively marketed, typically have no professional training in its structural fundamentals or its practical applications. The purchase of these business graphics systems indicates that there is a tacit assumption, made by almost all business graphics users, that they fully understand the meaning of bar charts, line charts, pie charts and, of course, the implications of color, in their graphic output. In fact, this assumption is rarely true. The field of business graphics is in urgent and critical need of research, teaching, and close international and cross-cultural communication.

Various answers are given to the question of why people need business graphics. They range from "a productivity enhancement" to cutting down the information overload of computer printouts of tabular data, to "an attention-getter" to wake up an audience and impress upon them a conclusion based upon the data. The notion of communication is a common denominator of almost all reasons for using business graphics.

The subject of this chapter is less color and business graphics than it is color and data communication. Communication, as it pertains to data, can be either of two major types: communicating the information contained in the data, or communicating a perception of the meaning of the data. Using a parallel from linguistic communication, the first type is a factual report and the second type is an editorial opinion. The linguistic parallel provides a way to learn much more about business graphic communication.

The Graphic Language of Communication

A factual report and an editorial are both printed with the same symbols. In many languages, these symbols are called an alphabet and are the primary structure of the language. Combining these symbols into words gives a secondary structure, and grouping the words into sentences gives a tertiary structure. Each language has rules for these combinations (spelling) and groupings (grammar). If these rules are not followed, the result could range from miscommunication to no communication at all. There is also a quarternary structural level to language. This is the series of subtle cues that helps in discriminating between sentences of fact and those of opinion. Only extensive practical experience teaches discrimination between these two types of linguistic communication. In recognition of this difficulty, most newspapers assist their readers with this discrimination by putting editorials on a separate page known as the editorial page.

Business graphics communication is very much like written linguistic communication. Both are built from a finite set of symbols, with increasing levels of structural complexity, until it is possible to produce factual reports and editorial opinions using graphic imagery.

For each of the languages of the world, the rules for each of the levels of linguistic structure (spelling and grammar) have been established over long periods of time. These rules are taught over many years in the schools of every country. This is not true of the study of the meanings of the graphic symbols used to represent data and the images formed by the combinations and groupings of these symbols. This study is minimal.

With this state of affairs, many business graphics users are very much like primary school students in their lack of ability to easily discriminate a factual report from an editorial opinion when it is expressed in the graphic language. This immediately raises a key issue in regard to color and business graphics. When we were trained in these linguistic skills back in our own primary school training, how many of us recall being exposed to text that had multicolor letters or words, or three-dimensional symbols often from varying perspectives? If our child's elementary school textbook were printed this way, how would we react? Would this be a good pedagogic approach for the lessons of linguistic communication? Remember, even color comic books have the words of the text printed in black.

Could it be that we adults of the late twentieth century are just biased against color in linguistic communication? After all, if our local newspaper began to print its front page news, or its editorial page, with multicolor and three-dimensional words, would we believe it as much as the old black and white edition? But what is our view toward color in graphic communication? Surely, many of us have seen color graphic presentations, sometimes even nationally and internationally televised, where we are led to believe that a multicolor and possibly three-dimensional graphic image is giving a factual report of some data. In fact, though, the image may have been designed with a purposeful editorial slant to help shape our opinion. Does this bother us as much as a ''colored'' editorial in our newspaper?

Once the structural fundamentals of the graphical representation of data are known, and we can read graphic communication as well as linguistic communication, it is quite remarkable to see the large proportion of purportedly factual images that are in fact just editorial comments. It is also surprising to realize the large proportion of graphic images that are no more than amateurish exercises in graphic design—for they are unintelligible in terms of true data communication.

The primary function of management decision makers in many organizations is to make unbiased decisions based upon a careful review of the facts reflected in the data. How successful can they be if they are not fluent in the language in which the data are presented—the graphic language? The most difficult aspect of this situation, though, is the fact that most business graphics users assume that they fully understand the meaning of the language. It is true that they may have had some training in a secondary school mathematics course (possibly in algebra), but as in most fields, we often find that a little knowledge can be dangerous.

Data—The Base

Computer graphics would have nothing to communicate to management decision makers if there were no data to be graphed. When we think of computer graphics we very often forget this and take the data for granted. If we take the foundation of a building for granted and do not build it in accordance with the environmental conditions of the site and carefully established engineering standards, we run the risk of having the building come crashing down on us at some point in the future. So too in business graphics. The data defines the environmental conditions for our graphic structures. We must understand these conditions, the conditions that impact the structural foundation of our images, before we launch into a study of the superstructure—the bar charts, line charts, and pie charts, much less the color of these structures.

The data reflect some of the vital signs of an organization. The archetype of today's organizations is, in many respects, the biological organism. To use a human analogy, data such as blood pressure readings reflect a vital sign of the human organism. To a business manager, a table of blood pressure readings may have little meaning and so will a graphic image of them, whether produced by computer or not. Surprisingly, though, such a table or graphic image may also contain little meaning for medical decision makers. What, we may then ask, are the criteria for ''meaningful'' data?

The first criterion must be that the data are relevant to a real, significant, issue. There must be a clear purpose for delving into the data. Without this context for data analysis the data cannot possibly become meaningful information. With our table of blood pressure readings, for example, is there any purpose for a medical doctor or business manager to focus attention on this data? For some further examples of this, we may look at many of the images in the advertisements of graphics hardware and software vendors. We may ask what real business issue the images were designed to illuminate?

The other criteria are not easy to identify. To understand the concerns, though, let us pursue our blood pressure example for medical doctors. Of course they will understand how the data were collected and what they represent, but they may ask some questions before concluding that the data are "meaningful" and then beginning their analysis. Are the data all from the same person? Were they taken from the same arm? How often was the blood pressure taken? If taken on different days, was it the same time on each day? What were the environmental conditions? Was the person at work or on vacation? Did the person eat, exercise, or have medication before the measurements were taken? Only after carefully answering these and other questions about the data will doctors be prepared to let the data impact their decision making. It is only after understanding the background and veracity of the data that it is appropriate to study a table or graphic image of the data. The issues raised here may not identify altogether sufficient criteria for meaningful data. Having raised these issues, though, we may note that they are typical of a number of issues in the field of the graphical representation of data. There is much need for further research.

While this concern has been a problem throughout the history of tabular data analysis, it has been even more of a problem throughout the history of the graphical representation of data since its beginning in 1785.

Historical Precedent

Most users of computer graphics have no knowledge of the history of the graphical representation of data. They realize that it predates the era of the computer, but how did it begin? While the ancient Egyptian surveyors of 3000 years ago used hieroglyphic symbols to indicate a coordinate grid, it was not until 1637 that the French philosopher and mathematician René Descartes (1596-1650) formalized the relationship between a mathematical function and the coordinates of each of its points. The graphical representation of data, though, is not directly related to Descartes' work on analytic geometry. Descartes began with a mathematical function and then graphed the numerical values of its coordinate points; in contrast, graphical representation of data begins with numerical data resulting from empirical observation and then graphs it on a coordinate grid. This is a subtle, but critical, difference.

Almost 130 years later, Joseph Priestly (1733-1804), an English chemist and theologian, developed the notion of considering time as a line (Priestly, 1765). His chart was rather large (about 1 m by .6 m) and represented the time interval between 1200 B.C. and 1750 A.D. Across the top of the chart he placed the time scale with vertical lines at fifty year intervals. He represented the life span of two thousand famous individuals by using solid horizontal black bars in their proper chronological position. When dates of birth or death were not exactly known, he indicated this with a series of dots either before or after the solid bar. While this was only a one-dimensional chart, it was a major step towards today's business and scientific graphics, where we regularly graph time series of data in a two-dimensional format with time across the horizontal axis just as Priestly did in 1765. The true beginnings of modern business graphics, though, were still twenty years away.

In 1785, William Playfair (1759–1823) engraved the plates in a volume containing forty-three charts of the type now called line charts or surface charts and one horizontal bar chart. *The Commercial and Political Atlas* went through three editions (1786, 1787, and 1801) and represented "by means of stained copper-plate charts the exports, imports and general trade of England . . ." (1st and 2d ed.). The third edition was subtitled "representing . . . the progress of the commerce, revenues, expenditures, and debts of England, during the whole of the eighteenth century." In the same year that he published the third edition of his *Atlas* (1801), Playfair also published the first known use of the circle graph and pie chart, "The Statistical Breviary; shewing [sic] on a principle entirely new, the resources of every state and kingdom in Europe; illustrated with stained copper-plate charts, representing the physical powers of each distinct nation with ease and perspicuity."

Playfair was the first person to use the two-dimensional graphical representation of data as we know it today, and he clearly charted the type of data that produced business graphics. In fact, most of his graphs in the 1786 and 1801 editions were done in hand-washed watercolor over the engraved lines. It seems he tried to save money in the 1787 edition and use only black and white with texturing effects, but he returned to the color in 1801. William Playfair can truly be called the "father" of business graphics. It is quite amazing to note how his explanation of the method of "lineal arithmetic," as he called it, although written almost 200 years ago, sounds so utterly modern:

> The advantage proposed by this method, is not that of giving a more accurate statement than by figures, but it is to give a more simple and permanent idea of the gradual progress and comparative amounts, at different periods, by presenting to the eye a figure, the proportions of which correspond with the amount of the sums intended to be expressed.
>
> Suppose the money received by a man in trade were all in guineas, and that every evening he made a single pile of all the guineas received during the day, each pile would represent a day, and its height would be proportioned to the receipts of that day; so that by this plain operation, time, proportion, and amount, would all be physically combined.
>
> Lineal arithmetic then, it may be averred, is nothing more than those piles of guineas represented on paper, and on a small scale, in which an inch (suppose) represents the thickness of five million guineas, . . . as much information may be obtained in five minutes as would require whole days to imprint on the memory . . . by a table of figures.

Some interesting observations can be made in Figure 15-1 (see color insert). Aside from the style of the lettering and the date in the lower right corner, it is hard to identify that this image is almost 200 years old. Today we would call this a line chart, or possibly a surface chart due to the colored surfaces between the lines. It uses a full title, a subtitle, and footnotes, just as we find on contemporary charts and pays particular attention to the use of capitals versus lowercase letters, as well as character size and the centering of the text on the layout. The grid for the field is not overly busy, especially considering that Playfair used four bold scale lines at multiples of one million pounds and the axes are appropriately labeled. He has used color very effectively. The bold red line, the color of greatest intensity, is used to draw the viewer's attention toward the "Line of Exports."

Following Playfair's analogy above, we can almost see the pile of "five million guineas" representing the value of these exports under that red line. Most viewers immediately make the assumption that the red line is representing the revenues accruing to England, especially as they see the "Balance in Favour of England" legend in the large blue shaded areas. Using the pink color in the area labeled "Balance Against England" graphically represents the accounting notion of a "loss in revenue" as "a sea of red ink." To further exhibit the thorough care with which Playfair designed his charts, we may note that the proportions of the entire grid field are exactly in the ratio of 5 to 3. This, of course, is the proportion of the "golden rectangle" which, since before the time of the ancient Greeks, has been recognized as having great appeal to the eye and supposedly eliciting increased visual perception.

Did Playfair commission a number of research studies to identify all these parameters for his charts? It seems not. He did, though, take a lot of time in thinking about these issues, for it was a major effort to prepare copperplate engravings with handwashed watercolor tints, in his time. It was not quite as simple as punching a few buttons on his business graphics computer terminal. One wonders if chart makers today would prepare better charts if they had to reflect longer on the major resources they were about to bring to bear on the preparation of a graphic image of their data.

But do chart makers of today have to be concerned at all with these isssues? Could we not now commission the research studies to identify all the parameters that go into preparing quality graphic images and then prepare our software with all the proper defaults to automatically respond to this knowledge base? Here, again, is a golden opportunity for scholarly research with major practical applications. A thorough literature search, in the English language, will find several score excellent papers, primarily from the fields of cartography, psychology, and audiovisual communication. But clearly more work needs to be done, especially in the area of international and cross-cultural visual communication. For example, in a non-English-speaking country, do people associate the pink color on Playfair's chart with the idea expressed by the English phrase "a sea of red ink?" Aside from this linguistic overtone, there are many cultural or religious overtones to the use of color that can seriously impact international graphic data communication. This should be of particular concern to multinational corporations, where this can greatly impact their own internal communication. There are many significant issues to be investigated in this area, hopefully with a large measure of international cooperation and support from the computer graphics hardware and software vendors.

Historical Accident

For all of Playfair's genius in his "lineal arithmetic," now known as "the graphical representation of data," he fell prey, as we still do today, to the success of his technique. Despite the needs, as mentioned above, for further research on the perceptual issues of graphic communication, charts such as Playfair's are powerful communicators. Truly, he must have wanted his image to "imprint on the memory" the results of his research in the archives of "the Custom House Books." It is these books that were the source of his data. But was he successful? Is Playfair's communication to us—the image that is imprinted on our memory—a true reflection of that data?

We may have seen the untrue reflections in the fun house at a carnival when looking in the curved mirrors that make us look taller, fatter, or otherwise more garish than in reality. What must we do to prevent our computer graphics for management decision makers from becoming such untrue reflections of reality? A review of Figure 15-1 may help to answer this question and illuminate a critical problem persisting in today's use of computer graphics in business. A brief historical excursion may be appropriate here. If we do not learn lessons from the mistakes of the past, we may be doomed to repeat them.

The first question we may ask is: What issue was Playfair trying to address? It seems that he was attempting to show what we would call today the "balance of trade." The blue coloring on the chart indicates a surplus in the value of the English goods crossing the Atlantic Ocean heading west, as compared to the value of North American goods heading east to England. If all of these goods were paid for, in a hard currency, the blue shaded area would be a true reflection of this balance of trade. Further investigation into the meaningfulness of the data would have us enquiring into its background and veracity. In this regard, let us assume that the eighteenth century English Custom House books are complete and accurate.

But there is more to the meaning of the data. In Playfair's commentary on this chart he raised the issue of many speculators shipping cargoes on consignment and often failing in their business ventures. The chart is thus not an image of the flow of accrued revenues across the sea. It is just what it is clearly described to be: a "Chart of Imports and Exports of England to and from all North America." It is the implied value of the cargo as it passed through the English Customs House, not the value of the revenue that should have passed, in the opposite direction, across the ocean.

Let us review our history just a bit further to more fully understand the implications of these issues for today's management decision makers. In Playfair's chart, North America includes the lands that are now Canada, the United States, and the English-speaking isles in the Caribbean Sea. The precipitous drop in the "Line of Exports to America" (red line) begins early in 1774, following the Boston Tea Party on December 16, 1773. It may be seen to increase its rate of decline even further after an act of Parliament closed the Boston seaport to commerce on June 1, 1774. The marked drop in the "Line of Imports from America" (yellow line) during 1775 is clearly related to the beginning of the American revolution on April 19, 1775. The base "Line of Imports" from 1776 through 1780 is the value of goods shipped from Canada and the Caribbean, since the revolutionaries in the thirteen American colonies would not be shipping goods to England during that period of war.

The blue shading and the legend "Balance in Favour of England" between 1776 and 1780 is most amazing to observe. Could the English have been selling so much to the Americans during the American war for independence? Here is where Playfair seems to have read too much into his data. Most of those "exports" were probably military supplies and the salaries for English soldiers in America. The fact that the "Line of Exports" abruptly changes slope and rises in the second quarter of 1775 strongly supports this, as the British would have been earnestly reinforcing their positions during the siege of Boston following the battles of Lexington and Concord in April of that year. The exports counted in Playfair's data were not being paid for by the country receiving them. They were being paid for in the tax burden of the English, who were sending them. No revenue was accruing, and thus no "Balance in Favour of England." Surely, Playfair intended this chart as a true reflection of the data in the Custom House Books, the text of his title is a true reflection of the data in those books and on his chart. But his chart communicates, or imprints on the memory, an image of the balance of trade, that is different from the text of his title. Clearly, the communication of this image does not seem to be a true reflection of reality.

Now, 200 years later, if one of today's computer graphics exhibited similar data for the period 1970 to 1982, how important would such a misperception be to the leaders of government who may imprint the image on their memory? Would this image affect their decisions? What can we do today to prevent these historical accidents from repeating themselves?

History Repeats Itself

The history of statistics, or the development of data analysis techniques, is generally tied to the history of empirical data collection. In the eighteenth century, during William Playfair's life, there was very little empirical data collection, so he had to use what little data he could find. Unfortunately, his purpose for delving into the data, the real, significant issue he was trying to address, was not fully supported by his data. In times of social, political, and commercial peace, it may be plausible to equate exports with accrued revenue, as Playfair tried to do. As we have seen, though, that assumption did not hold during years of social, political, and commercial strife.

How many management decison makers of today, though, are just like William Playfair? They have a purpose for delving into data, but they do not have the appropriate data to address their issues. We, in the twentieth century, have massive databases. Often they are "on-line" on our computers. Still, we must assess if the available data are appropriate to the significant issues we wish to address. All too often, business graphics presentations are built upon inappropriate data, yet they survive solely on the reputation of their high-tech imagery and attention-getting pizzazz. It is a common observation that data on a computer graphic output are perceived to be even more believable than tabular computer printouts. This is a heavy responsibility that must be borne by those who design business graphics software and graphic output.

Our high-tech capabilities are also impacting the history of statistics or data analysis. There are many graphics software packages today that come full circle to the work of Descartes. They take the empirically observed data points and calculate a mathematical function that will best describe the data. This is often done with linear regression or other higher order smoothing algorithms. These capabilities are very easy to invoke and are often used by management decision makers with access to computer graphics. The line of the best-fit equation is then drawn accross the data, often in a contrasting color. Here too, we can learn a lesson from history.

What would a linear regression of Playfair's "Line of Exports" look like? It would be a straight line starting at the upper left of our chart and descending to the lower right. Would it tell us anything about our data? Would it offer any predictive value for future years? Clearly, the answers are "No." Regression, or any other smoothing algorithm, is inappropriate to use when the data are so violently impacted by unnatural phenomena, such as a war. It seems so obvious here, but unfortunately, all too often we see people misunderstanding the details of their data because they do not step back to get an overview of the environmental background. Computer graphics makes us even more vulnerable to this problem, since it allows us to delve so deeply into our data so quickly that we may easily miss the external environmental concerns.

In both of these examples we must beware of the seductive power of high-tech. On the one hand, it allows us such easy entry to our data and data analysis, and on the other it allows us to be impressed, and to impress others, with the polish of its output, especially graphic output. Just as each generation must relearn the lessons of history, so too must each generation of management decision makers relearn these lessons. There is no simple software solution to remove this burden from our shoulders because there are no simple rules for determing the appropriateness of the data or the appropriateness of the statistical analytical tool to the problem at hand. This is the responsibility of the human brain, and not the computer brain.

There are areas of data analysis for management decision making where we can define rules. Two key applications are in the development of a data dictionary and a graphic dictionary—a color dictionary should be sure to follow.

The Data Dictionary

It is easy to be critical with the luxury of almost 200 years of hindsight, but where did William Playfair err? He erred in the use of his data dictionary and in his ensuing use of a legend on the data. The value of exports recorded in the Custom House Books is not the same as the value of revenue accrued for those exports, thus he did not consistently define his data elements. He used data elements of one type, exports, with the intention of drawing a comparison between data elements of another type, revenues or balance of trade. Once he misapplied his data definitions, whether he planned to or not, Playfair imprinted an editorial opinion on our memory. He may have planned to prepare a factual report on true and meaningful data, but his misinterpretation of the true meaning of the data allowed him to create an image that communicated misinformation. What began as a straightforward effort in factual reporting produced a product, possibly unknowingly, of editorial opinion.

In business, the concept of balance of trade could possibly be translated into the term "net operating revenue" or NOR. Could the type of problems that Playfair confronted occur in a chart of NOR? "Probably not," we may answer, because today we have rules or standards in our data dictionary.

The concept of NOR is precisely defined in the dictionary mandated by the accounting profession. All business data reported in tabular form relies on this dictionary to define part of its meaning. Therefore, all business data reported in graphic form must rely on the accounting definitions. In fact, we may now see how useful it could be if the graphical structures, and the use of color, were also based upon such well thought out dictionary definitions and standards.

The Graphic Dictionary

As we have seen, an appreciation of the meaning of data is more than an esoteric subject to be studied by scholars. It is critical to every decision maker who may ever attempt to use data in a constructive manner. Any graphic superstructure we may build will come crashing down upon us if it is not built on a firm footing of meaningful data. Furthermore, the type of graphic structures that are available to us when we build our charts , the engineering standards for construction, and the graphic dictionary are also defined by the type of data with which we are working.

A simple example of this can be seen in business graphic output distributed at a recent trade show. The exciting feature of the software is that data residing on the accounting system were easily displayed on a word-processed document (see Figure 15-2). The intent seems to be to compare the financial results of two succeeding years. What is being communicated? Were the 1982 results of 5, 10, or 20% better than those of 1981? Ask this question of several of your colleagues and see what response you get. A little arithmetic on the raw data (6221 and 7462) shows the answer to be 20%! Did this graphic communicate a true reflection of reality? Was it a productivity enhancement? Would color, instead of black and white, have helped?

The problem here is that a pie chart, as this is called, should only be used to show component parts of a whole. Two succeeding years of financial results are not parts of a whole. The engineering standards for graphic construction were violated here— miscommunication was the unfortunate result. It would seem that if humans could not remember the definitions in a graphic dictionary, then at least the software could be made intelligent enough to identify the type of data with which we are working and prevent such output from being created. Here, again, is a fertile field for further development.

One other example will illustrate the need for a graphic dictionary with data represented on a coordinate grid. When one reads the title "Price vs. Resolution/Pixel" at the top of the chart, one expects to find a scale of "Price" rising from zero up the left-hand vertical axis and a scale of "Resolution/Pixel" extending to the right across the

Financial Highlights   *Figure 15-2*   Financial highlights.
      in thousands u.s. $

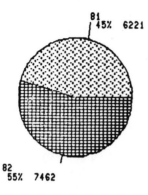

81
45% 6221

82
55% 7462

Thousands

horizontal axis. This expectation is based upon the definitions in our inherent graphic dictionary that we may be recalling from a high school course in algebra. From the field of statistics we may know that each of these measures are known as a ratio level of data. This means just that the scales are built from a continuous series of uniform intervals and that they each have a discrete zero point. We might expect to see a line chart not unlike Playfair's chart of "Imports and Exports vs. Time." Figure 15-3 (see color insert) appeared in a recent advertisement for hardware to produce presentation-quality slides. The image quality seems excellent. The colors draw the viewers' attention, even with a red line just like Playfair's. But what is being communicated?

The chart does not match my expectations and I am greatly disoriented. "Price" is not where I would expect it to be from my inherent graphical dictionary. Instead "Pixel Resolution" has replaced it. This is a new term, not the same as that in the title. In fact, on the horizontal axis there is an altogether new scale. This is not a ratio scale. It is a nominal level scale, since it reflects just names of things. It has no relation to a continuous scale of real numbers. Why then, is a continuous red line drawn across it? On further examination, the pixel resolution scale is a true ratio scale, rising from an implied zero at the origin. But on the right of the chart there is a "Recorder System Price" scale that is neither linear nor logarithmic. It is not a scale, but rather a list of numbers arrayed according to the unwritten algorithm of their relationship to pixel resolution.

A number of basic standards from the universal graphic dictionary have been violated here. The graphic image has not been built with proper regard for the types of data it is representing. The effect is much like that caused by using words in violation of their definitions in the linguistic dictionary. Reliable and expeditious communication has not occurred. It remains unclear what people will take away from this image, and a decrease in user productivity has been caused by the additional time it takes to attempt to decipher it.

What was the intent of that image? It seems the message is: "Our recorder gives the same resolution as the high-priced system, for one tenth the price!" In this case, it seems that those sixteen words may have been worth more than one multicolor picture because the graphic image does not seem to communicate as clearly. Sometimes the enthusiastic use of the high-tech capabilities of three-dimensional bars with dropped shadows, overlaid lines, and inset legends may not communicate as well as a few well chosen words.

It is important to realize that as Playfair was developing his lineal arithmetic at the end of the eighteenth century, the other modes of graphic communication were already fairly well developed. Engineering drawing, the precursor of CAD/CAM, had been used by ancient civilizations and was already highly developed to serve the needs of the industrial revolution. Cartography, also having its roots in ancient civilizations, had been established as a discipline for well over two hundred years serving the sixteenth and seventeenth century navigators. The use of graphic arts/design for communication goes back to prehistoric cave paintings, and by the end of the eighteenth century many of the world's classics in graphic arts/design had already been created. For these other modes of graphic communication there has been a long period of time to develop and refine the symbolic language used for this communication. Has the history of business graphics been long enough for us, in the late twentieth century, to feel that the symbolism has reached a steady state? To judge by the increasing capabilities of our computer graphics system, it would seem that we are in a most unsteady state at the present.

The increasing capabilities are typically brought to us by experts in the technological fields of hardware and software, and not necessarily in data analysis, accounting, or graphic arts/design. As we further develop these technological capabilities we must return to our historical sources to not only build upon a firm data dictionary, but to also establish a sound graphic dictionary.

Currently, there is ongoing research in the United States on a taxonomy of graphic structures. This is much like the eighteenth century work of Linnaeus, who proposed a taxonomy of organisms based upon biological structures. A part of this taxonomy of data representational graphics is based upon the statistical definitions of nominal, ordinal, interval, and ratio levels of data. This holds promise for establishing the sound graphic dictionary, which is needed in this field, upon the firm base of statistical data definitions. When this work is soon published, it will be critical to elicit a broad base of international review, for there may well be some graphic structures that do not easily cross cultural or linguistic borders.

One example of this may be the common time-line chart. Since Joseph Priestly's *Chart of Biography* in 1765, Western cultures have graphed time on a horizontal axis, reading from left to right. In the Nagoya City Museum in Nagoya, Japan, a beautiful time-line chart describing the volume of the rice harvested and the percentage given to the government is displayed showing time plotted on the vertical axis, increasing from top to bottom (Figure 15-4, see color insert). Since the Japanese language can be read from top to bottom, does this graphic image communicate the data any better to a Japanese person than Priestly's or Playfair's structures? Can a person from a Western culture understand this graphic language? This is but a sample of the type of issues to be addressed in developing an international language of graphic communication.

We have seen that the accounting profession has accepted the charge to give a factual snapshot, or true reflection, of the reality of a business concern. To achieve this end, they have mandated a well defined data dictionary and a structural layout of their tabular representations of data. Upon this background, it seems this may be a fertile area to begin to build a well defined graphic dictionary.

Computer Graphics and Reporting Financial Data

The role of accountants in business is typically to analyze real business issues using data of high veracity recorded in well-defined elements. These data are usually of the snapshot variety; that is, they are a reflection of a state of affairs at a particular point in time. The Statement of Income and Balance Sheet are examples of these snapshots. The structure of financial statements are usually well defined in tabular form, and thus the same should hold true in graphical form. Accountants, by profession, do not want to analyze or report editorialized data; therefore, a graphic image in this environment must factually communicate the information contained in the data. Accountants are also exposed to massive amounts of data. They should thus have a simple graphic system through which they can visually see, instead of read, thus enhancing their potential productivity.

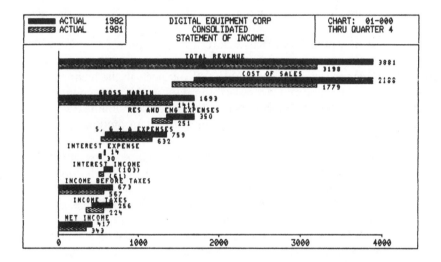

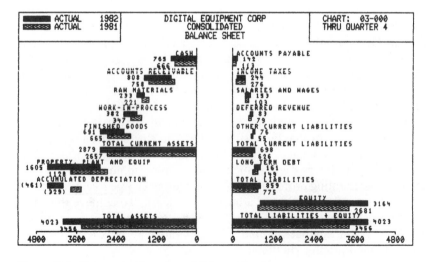

Figure 15-5   Statement of Income and Balance Sheet.

An American accountant Irwin M. Jarett has developed such a system (1983). In response to the above mentioned constraints, he does not use many different basic graphic structures. In fact, he only uses bar, no line charts nor pie charts. While he uses vertical bars for time series charts, he represents all other financial statements with horizontal bars. He also refrains from using color on his charts, except as a sort-key on the outer borders to allow for easily finding a particular chart from within a stack. Two examples of these are a Statement of Income and Balance Sheet, with actual data taken from a recent annual report (see Figure 15-5).

On the Statement of Income it is easy to see the relationship between the Cost of Sales and the Total Revenue (Equip Sales, Service & other). Backing the Cost of Sales off the Total Revenue gives the Gross Margin, a subtotal with its base on the vertical axis. Other expenses are then backed off the Gross Margin, and Interest Income is added back, until Income before Taxes is arrived at as a subtotal. Finally, backing off Income Taxes yields the corporation's Net Income.

On the Balance Sheet, it is easy to see that Total Assets equal Total Liabilities and Equity. Moving up the right side, the relationship between Total Liabilities and Equity is clear as are the component parts of the Total Liabilities (Long-Term Debt and Total Current Liabilities). The component parts of Total Current Liabilities can also be seen. On the left side, from the top down, one sees the component parts of Total Current Assets, a subtotal. The relationship between these Current Assets and Long-Term Assets (Property Plant and Equipment, less Accumulated Depreciation) is also clear as the Total Assets line is achieved.

Dr. Jarett (1983) developed this system based upon his years of experience as a certified public accountant and financial consultant, as well as his study of much of the existent literature on graphic communication. The graphic structures that Jarett has developed reliably hold the same formats every time data are entered into them. They are not cluttered with three-dimensional shadings, dropped shadows, or distracting grid lines. They are also not confused with different colors. The data always shows up in the same expectable place, with the same expectable simple shadings and labels, and the same expectable color. These standard formats allow the user to learn the vocabulary and sentence structure of this financial graphics language. While standardization may be a clear virtue in graphic communication, it raises critical concerns in the introduction of this system into an organization.

The Introduction of a Financial Graphics Reporting System

Jarett's software, known as Fingraph™, was first installed over three years ago in the controller's office of Digital Equipment Corporation's Educational Services in Bedford, Massachusetts. It is still in use, and throughout this time its impact on management decision makers has been studied through five different levels of management and financial analysis support staff. It is used to produce standard monthly manangement reports, as well as for ad hoc analyses, especially disaggregations.

All levels of management are generally quite satisfied with these graphic formats and some managers are rather enthusiastic. After several months of use, the highest level manager remarked, "I like them. Once you're used to them, you can see what you want. There's far more information on one page of graphics than with text." This is a rather amazing comment, as most chart makers often get frantic over what tabular data they must cut out in order not to clutter a graphic chart. We must notice that the user found more information, not more data. The fact that someone, in this case through using the predefined graphic structure, selected only certain specific, well-thought-out pieces of data, is a key to this user's comment. Specific data elements in the proper context are percieved as "more information."

Regarding this information, the manager continued, "Some things I was really impressed with, for example ROA [return on assets] I found extremely useful. It also worked great for the balance sheet" (see Figure 15-5). When queried further as to why he liked them, he replied, "They are very useful to quickly see what's happening. I can identify problems as I switch from one organization to another." This is, from a high-level business manager's point of view, one of the key virtues of business graphics. It lets managers identify problems. It distills the data down and communicates them as information that can stimulate action to solve the problems.

Should this graphic output have high quality to achieve these results? "Absolutely, yes," asserted this manager, "It's important to have high quality ouptut without high cost." His notion of quality related to clear legibility of text and image, but he wanted to try to have his cake and eat it too, since he was not willing to pay too much for this quality. In fact, though, he felt that he had reached this happy state, for he had a high quality and low cost black and white graphic printer. When asked if he'd like to see his output in color, he replied, "No, color drives up printing costs." Technological advances are steadily bringing down the hardware and production costs of color output and thus slowly negating this concern. As we shall see, though, there are other even greater potential costs associated with color output.

Was this just a flash in the pan, a hot new idea that would fade in a few months? This manager felt convinced that graphic reporting would be fully integrated into the decision-making process. He asserted, "We've got to use it to run the business." Another member of the management committee, representing operations in Europe, also commented on the graphics: "This is really superb. This is probably the best new management tool I've seen since I've been on the committee." The fact that the tool is still being actively used, and further proliferated throughout the company, more than three years later, is testimony to the impact it has had.

Much behind-the-scenes preparation took place, though, before these managers could feel this strongly about the graphics reporting system. Lower level financial managers and analysts had to be trained in the use of the software to generate the charts, as well as in the use of the charts themselves in financial analysis. Hardware resources also had to be distributed so that all supporting staff and managers could have as much access as they needed to generate the required graphics. Throughout the organization a clear message was heard that all should be prepared for a change. All this preparation was critical to the success of the program. There needed to be strong conceptual support from the top of the organization and strong technical support from the lower level staff.

After one year, the study found that all managers had ceased wrestling with the graphics issues. The training and year's experience had addressed the initially critical, and sometimes negative, concerns regarding the graphics standards. By the end of the first year, managers and analysts felt they were constructively using computer graphics as a transparent tool to truly understand business issues and offer strong support for their decision making capabilities.

Now in its fourth year of using this financial graphics reporting system at Digital Equipment Corporation, further research is being conducted in an effort to quantify the impact of computer graphics on management decision making. When this experimentation is completed, the results will be published and available to the public, worldwide. From this base of data on black and white graphics, comparisons are also being made with color graphics. Surely, though, today we find color business graphics used on the highest levels of corporate management without any data on its impact on management decision making.

Executive Decisions and Color Business Graphics

There are many corportations now using color business graphics and many of them claim much success for their programs. The standards by which this success is measured are not always clear, but it is interesting to observe that the higher the resolution of the output, the more frequently the users seem to perceive their program to be a success.

While in this one chapter we cannot review all the types of output formats used in these systems, we can become sensitive to some of the issues that need to be addressed when designing or using these systems.

Though based on entirely fictitious data, the images in Figures 15-6 and 15-7 (see color insert) are similar in design to those used in the boardrooms of a number of multinational companies. They are commonly called "bubble charts." The axes are precisely defined in the context of the accounting definitions for data from each European subsidiary. The vertical axis measures Net Operating Revenue (NOR) of each subsidiary as a percentage of the Gross Domestic Product (GDP) of that subsidiary's country. Since this would typically be in thousandths of a percent, the scale is marked in exponential notation. The horizontal axis measures Profit Before Taxes (PBT) of each subsidiary as a percentage of their NOR. The vertical axis is thus a measure of market penetration and the horizontal axis is a measure of profitability. Each circle represents one of the ten color-coded countries of Europe, and the size of each circle is proportional to the NOR of that country's subsidiary.

Managers who use these bubble charts assert they understand these axis and can make sense of this image. With our concern for color and data communication in mind, let us look at two particular issues.

A member of the technical staff creating the true versions of these charts (not Figures 15-6 and 15-7) was asked, "To what is the size of the circles proportional?" His immediate response was, "The area is proportional to the NOR of that subsidiary." He was reminded that people really have difficulty discriminating areas, especially in circles, and then he responded, "Oh, let me check in the algorithm." After checking the software he remarked, "It's not the area. It's the radius." Either way, he has a communication dilemma.

If the area of one circle was to be twice that of another, then according to our high school algebra, the radius of the larger one would be 1.4 times larger than the smaller. This is the square root of 2. If the radius of one circle was twice that of another, then of course the area of the larger would be 4 times that of the smaller. When people look at these circles, they cannot discriminate area measurement from linear measurement. If one does the empirical, psychological research, it is found that most people perceive one circle to be twice the size of another when the radius is 1.7 times larger. This is clearly halfway between 1.4 and 2.0 and shows how these two types of measurement get homogenized in our perception. Does this mean we should change our algorithm to reflect this research finding? Remember that, for a doubling of the data, most people respond at a factor 1.7, and there are of course other people on either side of this peak on the normal distribution curve. What if the chairman of the board is a 1.5 person, and the chief executive officer is a 1.9 person? Should we have seperate algorithms for each of them? Extensive experience in the use of these charts and training through simulations may be the answer to this concern. Our second concern arising from these charts may be more difficult to resolve with training.

Look at the circles in Figures 15-6 and 15-7, and find the ones in each figure that are the same size as others in the figure. Are they the same size in both figures? Figure 15-6, with its dark background, was designed for 35mm slide presentation, and Figure 15-7, with its light background, was designed for overhead transparency use. In responding to these questions, we are now in the realm of figure-ground relationships, and may be beginning to be aware of the myriad of issues to be addressed in fully implementing color in business graphics. Have the designers, or users, of the charts addressed the perceptual attributes of color? A concern for these attributes of hue, saturation, lightness, and brightness should be a precursor to the more advanced issues of figure-ground relationships, or the contextual effects of color. It is often very difficult to predict the context in which these colored circles will be found. Yet, the contrast, size, and visual location of these circles greatly impact the perception communicated to the user.

Those of us who may have a developing sense of frustration at these issues should just think of the executives who use these charts. They allocate many millions of dollars in resources drawing upon these for decision support. It is here that we can see the great potential costs associated with a misperception of the graphic output.

Change

The transition from the use of tabular data representation to the use of graphical data representation, and then on to the use of color, is a major change for many individuals and organizations. In the mid-1980s it is a change we are actively going through and will continue to go through for a number of years. This is typically not an easy change, for change is often hard to accept, much less adapt to. It is interesting to note that as revolutionary as William Playfair's charts were to the communication of information, it took another 128 years before the first book on the subject of graphic communication was published in the English language. In 1914 Willard C. Brinton published his now classic text, *Graphic Methods for Presenting Facts*. Change certainly came slowly in that era, but we seem to be making up for it in the present day. With the current speed of development of computer hardware, software, and databases, we must pause from the dizzying pace and establish a perspective for the future.

Business Graphics - Flying by the Seat of the Pants

Before taking off in the new Boeing 767, one would hope that the manufacturer of the aircraft has based the design of the color graphic cockpit displays on a thorough program of sound research into the most effective and reliable methods for communicating in-flight data to the pilot. One would also hope that the pilot has gone through rigorous training and simulation in the use of the color graphic cockpit displays. Based upon the data communication from those displays, the pilot makes decisions that impact the lives of all persons on board and protects an investment in a valuable piece of equipment. Of course, the thorough program of sound research was conducted along with the rigorous pilot training and simulation. We, therefore, fly contented.

How different are business managers from pilots? They, too, make decisions that impact the lives of all of their employees. Many business managers, not wanting to be left behind in the 1980s are installing color business graphics systems. Has the manufacturer of the hardware, and of the software, based the design of the color graphic displays on a thorough program of sound research into the most effective and reliable methods for communicating data? Such thorough research is only now beginning to be done, with some of the most notable work coming from the Interactive Systems Laboratories of San Marcos, Texas. In general, though, the answer is unfortunately, "no." Has the business manager gone through rigorous training and simulation in the use of the color graphic displays? Unfortunately, the answer here is also almost always, "no." If pilots did this, could it be said that they were "flying be the seat of their pants"? Would you want to fly in their plane?

When discussing this issue with a high-level manager in a Fortune 100 company, he replied, "Yes, but, business managers do not have to respond as quickly as pilots in a jet plane cockpit. Besides, we also have the tabular data to fall back on." This manager, formerly an officer in the air force, and also possessing a doctorate in physics, commented from a very interesting vantage point.

Regarding the issue of response time we may note that business managers do not sit in the boardroom as continuously as pilots sit in cockpits. We must also consider the responsiveness of the environment. A jet plane can respond much faster and more reliably than a business organization. To compensate, business managers need a continuous stream of reliable information to keep on top of their organization. We have seen that it is specific data elements in the proper context that are perceived as more information. What the buyers of today's business graphics systems are really looking for are the well researched color graphic business cockpit controls that they may have tomorrow.

Regarding the "data to fall back on," the physical sciences have made major advances in the past several generations. These advances have been based to a great extent on the analysis and interpretation of data. Can we rightfully compare the background of a typical user of business graphics systems with the academic preparation, the dissertation research and the post-doctoral rigors of a career in the physical sciences? It is just because of this distinction, in training and application of quantitative methods for the analysis of data, that designers of business graphics systems must carefully design the "cockpit controls" of the color business graphic boardroom of the future. As this careful design is being developed, both industrial and academic management training programs must also begin the training of users with some theory and much practical simulation just as rigorous as that required of our pilots. Organizations managed by individuals with knowledge of color business graphics and a background in such training and simulation will truly command a most distinct market advantage.

The Future of Color and Business Graphics

The future of color and business graphics rests not in the development of the technology, for surely that will advance on its own. The future of color and business graphics rests in the development of an international graphic language of data representation and communication. To achieve this end, there must be on-going research in colleges, universities, and industries. The results must be published and shared, and there must be a forum for international dialogue on the issues. This should attract experts from the fields of graphic arts/design, statistics, semiotics, linguistics, cartography, and psychology, among others. It is hoped that computer hardware and software vendors will be in the forefront of supporting and fostering all these activities and enhancing their products with the result of the research.

If business graphics, in black and white or color, is going to be effectively used, there must be large-scale training in theoretical issues as well as simulation in practical experience. This must not only be in the use of hardware, software, and databases, but in:

1. Identifying significant issues and relevant data,
2. Structural and functional issues in the actual graphical representation
3. Analysis of data.

We have clearly seen that a little knowledge can be dangerous—thus, it is critically important to gain a firm base of both knowledge and experience.

We must become graphically literate, or "graphicate" as the literature is now using the term, if we are to truly realize the vast potential of color and business graphics.

References
Contemporary

Bertin, J. *Graphics and Graphic Information Processing*. Berlin:Walter de Gruyter & Co., 1981.
Bertin J. *Semiology of Graphics*. Madison, Wisc.: University of Wisconsin Press, 1983.
Jarett, I. M. *Computer Graphics and Reporting Financial Data*. New York: John Wiley, 1983.
MacGregor, A. J. *Graphics Simplified*. Toronto: University of Toronto Press, 1979.
Schmid, C. F., & Schmid, S. E. *Handbook of Graphic Presentation*. (2d ed.) New York: John Wiley, 1979.
Schmid, C. F. *Statistical Graphics Design Principles and Practices*. New York: John Wiley, 1983.
Spielman, H. A. Computer Graphics for Management: Prerequisites for an Effective Introduction. In Tosiyasu L. Kunii (Ed.), *Computer Graphics: Theory and Applications*. Tokyo: Springer-Verlag, 1983, 300–309.
Spielman, H. A. The Impact of Computer Graphics on Decision Making. Unpublished doctoral dissertation. Boston College, Chestnut Hill, MA, 1985. University Microfilm #85–22291.
Tufte, E. R. *The Visual Display of Quantitative Information*. Cheshire, Conn.: Graphics Press, 1983.

Classic

Arkin, H., & Colton, R. R. *Graphs—How to Make and Use Them*. NewYork: Harper & Brothers, 1936 (1st ed.), 1940 (2d ed.).
Arnold, S., & Smart, L. E. *Practical Rules for Graphic Presentation of Business Statistics*. Columbus, Ohio: Bureau of Business Research, Ohio State University, 1947 (1st ed.), 1951 (2d ed.).
Brinton, W. C. *Graphic Methods for Presenting Facts*. New York: The Engineering Magazine Company, 1914.
Brinton, W. C. *Graphic Presentation*. New York: Brinton Associates, 1939.
Carroll, P. *How to Chart Data*. New York: McGraw-Hill, 1960.
Haskell, A. C. *How to Make and Use Graphic Charts*. New York: Codex Book Company, 1919 (1st ed.), 1920 (2d ed.).
Haskell, A. C. *Graphic Charts in Business*. New York: Codex BookCompany, 1922 (1st ed.), 1926 (2d ed.), 1928 (3d ed.).
Lutz, R. R. *Graphic Presentation Simplified*. New York: Magazines of Industry, Inc., 1949.
Playfair, W. *The Commercial and Political Atlas*. 1786 (1st ed.), 1787 (2d ed.), 1801 (3d ed.).
Priestly, J. *A Chart of Biography*. London: 1765.
Riggleman, J. R. *Graphic Methods for Presenting Business Statistics*. New York: McGraw-Hill, 1926 (1st ed.), 1936 (2d ed.).
Spear, M. E. *Practical Charting Techniques*. New York: McGraw-Hill, 1969.

16 The Executive Decision: Selecting a Business Graphics System

NANCY E. JACOBS
Indiana University
Bloomington, Indiana

Abstract

Evaluating the wide variety of business graphics systems available can be a baffling experience. This chapter introduces DIAD, a systematic approach to selecting a business graphics system. Organizational needs and resources are determined before characteristics of individual systems are considered. Finally, each system is evaluated for ease of operation, product quality, design flexibility, adequacy of documentation, vendor support, cost, and overall suitability.

Introduction

Ultimately, there is very little mystery to the decision to purchase—or not to purchase—a business graphics system. Like many other actions taken daily by business executives, the investment is influenced by organizational context—what demands are made on a firm and how well a system meets those demands; the costs and benefits of upgrading performance; the availability of resources for improving organizational resources.

For many firms, purchasing a business graphics system is an important part of a larger commitment to improved organizational communications. But the investment is not appropriate for every business, and the same system will not serve every owner equally well. The question then remains: "Is business graphics right for the organization?"

Finding the answer is not always easy. The computer graphics market continues to expand as new products and capabilities debut almost daily. The potential buyer can quickly become deluged with promotional literature and can spend hours talking to vendor representatives. But acting on these sources of information involves a major, possibly unwarranted, assumption: that you need a business graphics system in the first place.

To determine whether your company should purchase a computer graphics system, start your investigation where your expertise is greatest-by assessing your own business. This chapter introduces DIAD (Definition, Inventory, Assessment, Decision)—a systematic approach to the selection of a business graphics system (see Figure 16-1). DIAD is based on the philosophy that any significant decision concerning business operations should rest equally on (a) an understanding of the organization's internal requirements and resources and (b) an analysis of external capabilities to match those requirements and resources. For the executive, decision making involves discovering the overlap of these two areas.

As the DIAD model suggests, it is best not to look at hardware until you have identified your organization's graphic needs. It is far better to find a solution to fit your needs—not to find the needs to fit a solution. As you proceed, cultivate a skeptic's eye. Assumptions can be expensive. Unless you have carefully investigated a system before you purchase it, you can not be confident about its capabilities or compatibility with your requirements.

DIAD: BUSINESS GRAPHICS ANALYSIS FORM

System Name:

Vendor:

Lease/Purchase Price:

Product Turn around Time: Fee for "Rush Job":

Product Formats: Service Charges:

1.   EASE OF OPERATION is:

Unacceptable   Excellent

        0   1   3   3   4

Checklist:

_____ Convenience of system startup and use.

_____ Ease of creating and manipulating files (saving, editing, copying).

_____ System responsiveness (e.g., time taken to display image).

_____ Amount of training required.

Figure 16-1

Figure 16-1   continued

2.   **PRODUCT QUALITY is:**

Unacceptable   Excellent

     0   1   2   3   4

Checklist:

_____ Quality of final product.

_____ Legibility of text in the product.

_____ Range of products produced.

_____ Ease of obtaining proofs (e.g., paper hard copy).

3.   **DESIGN FLEXIBILITY is:**

Unacceptable   Excellent

     0   1   2   3   4

Checklist:

_____ Convenience of modifying a design.

_____ Range of colors, patterns, and text fonts.

_____ Types of input accepted (e.g., tablet, keyboard).

_____ Usefulness of special features (e.g., contour mapping).

4.   **DOCUMENTATION is:**

Unacceptable   Excellent

     0   1   2   3   4

Checklist:

_____ Suitability of user's guide format.

_____ Usefulness of information presented.

_____ Clarity of information presented.

_____ Incidence of errors in the documentation.

5.   **VENDOR SUPPORT is:**

Unacceptable   Excellent

     0   1   2   3   4

Checklist:

_____ Adequacy of warranty protection.

_____ Convenience of maintenance/repair.

_____ Adequacy of procedure for updating software.

_____ Time required to receive final product.

_____ (Optional) Quality of production center's service.

Figure 16-1 continued

6.   SYSTEM COST is:

Unacceptable   Excellent

　　　0　　　　　1　　　　　2　　　　　3　　　　　4

Checklist:

____ Cost of acquiring the system.

____ Associated costs (training, environmental changes).

____ Cost of obtaining output (labor, materials, service charges).

OVERALL RATING

7.   For my organization, this system would be:

Unacceptable   Excellent

　　　0　　　　　1　　　　　2　　　　　3　　　　　4

Step 1—Definition

Questions: Does my organization need a business graphics system?
What features should the system have?

Should you buy a business graphics system? The answer probably is not as clear cut as you think.

Your first step in dealing with the question requires you to make some carefully considered projections about the volume and types of products you will need. If your business has a graphics department, or if your visuals are produced by an outside service, gather information about your needs in recent years. Ask for the volume and costs of original visuals only—traditional means of generating duplicates are usually less expensive than producing computer-based visuals.

If you are investigating business graphics in anticipation of increased reliance on audio-visual products, old usage statistics may be of little value. Instead, you can make necessary projections based on some creative fact finding. Ask for input from the departments within your organization that are most likely to benefit from a computer graphics system. What type and volume of products do they anticipate using?

Once you have the figures in hand, look for patterns of use in the data. Has the trend been to rely on a particular format (35mm slides, paper copies, etc.) or visual content (words only, charts and graphs, etc.)? Consider whether anticipated developments within your organization are likely to have a serious impact on your need for graphic materials. For example, is your organization embarking on a new training program or introducing a new product line that will require audio-visual materials?

If your company is sufficiently large, you may benefit from a further breakdown of figures by department. This will be particularly useful in making projections based on future needs in specific departments.

If, as with most businesses, the art you require consists of words, charts, and graphs, you are in luck—this is the visual content produced by less expensive graphics systems. More complex drawings, however, will require you to consider more costly, sophisticated systems.

The range of media formats you will require will have an important impact on the hardware and software you should consider. Business graphics systems most commonly produce slides, but many can also provide a variety of other formats (overhead transparencies, video, 16mm film, paper hard copies). Multiple formats mean increased costs, though. Expect each new option to add anywhere from a few thousand to more than a hundred thousand dollars to the total cost.

You can use your volume and format projections to determine just how effective a business graphics system will be for your organization. If you use the system to produce only one format, annual volume can be as small as a few hundred originals. That figure rapidly rises into the thousands if multiple formats are required. Unless you anticipate production at this minimum level, in-house business graphics is probably not a cost-effective investment.

System Characteristics

Your data gathering should have paid off in a clear indication of what materials your company uses and to what purpose. For internal activities, such as training or brainstorming sessions, image clarity is generally more important than aesthetic value. A relatively inexpensive, low resolution system (fewer than 1000 lines) will meet those needs. Be aware, however, that the output of such systems has the jagged appearance often associated with computer-generated products.

If, on the other hand, you are presenting your corporate image along with the information (e.g., marketing presentations, stockholders meetings), appearance is as important as the data communicated. High resolution output has the slick look of professionally prepared art—but its cost can be many times higher than that of a lower resolution product.

Step 2—Inventory

Question: Can my company afford a business graphics system?

Support for a business graphics system will come in three forms: facilities, funding, and personnel.

Facilities

Resources available to you include both obvious and less apparent considerations. An example of the former is the availability of appropriate space for equipment (i.e., humidity and temperature-controlled). Required support services more often fall into the latter category. For example, if you choose not to buy a film recorder, can nearby computer graphics service centers support your production needs? Or, if you do purchase a recorder, are there external facilities to process those materials? If you need to provide for in-house film processing, what will that capability cost and what facilities will it require?

If your company already uses a computer for other applications (payroll, database management, spreadsheets), you will want to investigate software designed for that computer. At best, you may be able to use the same machine. At worst, you will benefit from software compatibility among your organization's computers.

Funding

Assuming you have a finite sum to commit to business graphics, you may need to consider ways of boosting that expenditure. If your organization is large, pooling departmental funds may be the answer. However, this option can be risky if the needs of the different departments differ radically. You may find it necessary to return to the definition stage of the DIAD model to modify your statement of system requirements.

Alternatively, you may argue for increased funding on the basis that it can be less expensive to establish a computer graphics facility than to rely on a large traditional graphics department. Before making such an argument, consider two caveats. First, it is unlikely that you can abolish existing graphics services. Business graphics is unlikely to meet all your requirements, although you may be able to reduce dependence on traditional processes.

Second, recognize that staff reduction is the most likely source of savings. Although private organizations usually have greater freedom to reduce staff than public agencies, the effect on employee morale can be devastating in either case. A much more positive approach is to document the need for expanded service, utilizing business graphics rather than additional staff.

Personnel

Employee considerations can significantly affect the implementation of business graphics in an organization. The number of personnel needed and the skills they must possess will depend on the quality and quantity of materials needed, as well as the type of system purchased.

Remember that business graphics simply reduces the repetitive steps in graphics production. Those using the system must still have some knowledge of effective design. Individuals assigned to operate the new system should be enthusiastic about computer-generated graphics and be efficient learners. Such characteristics will reduce training time and increase production efficiency.

Step 3—Analysis

Question: Which systems meet my company's requirements?

By documenting your organization's anticipated needs and resources, you have a clear picture of the ideal business graphics system for your purposes. Finding that system—or even a close approximation—is another matter.

As a first step, differentiate between required features and those you would like to have but can live without (call them "attractive" features). As you examine the many products on the market, you will frequently revise your list of attractive features. The core of required features should remain clearly constant because it reflects your organization's needs, as identified in the definition stage of DIAD.

Information Gathering

Your skeptic's eye will be important to you as you differentiate among the many sources of business graphics information. Other users of computer graphics systems and reviews in computing periodicals, particularly those devoted to computer graphics are among the more objective sources. Trade shows enable you to see several products and talk to vendor representatives in less time than would otherwise be possible. Take advantage of these contacts to expand your knowledge of what is available. Ask specifically about the features on your required list. If the answer seems incomplete or unclear, rephrase it and try again.

As a general rule, don't purchase a system you haven't seen in operation—preferably in a setting similar to your own. If you do not know current users of a system, the vendor can provide a list of names you can contact. You should at least call to the check performance claims; in many cases, a visit will be worth the time and expense.

By this time, you may feel overwhelmed by the volume of information you have acquired. Categorizing the strengths and weaknesses of a system and rating its appropriateness for your organization's needs is simplified through use of the analysis form, presented in this chapter. Orderly comparisons are facilitated by dividing information into descriptive and evaluative components. Evaluative data are then further divided.

System Description

Descriptive information is the easiest to obtain, but do not let its availability blind you to its usefulness. To help you differentiate between objective and subjective information, keep the source of your information in mind. Armed with such information, you will better understand which products warrant further investigation. A word of warning, however: Computer graphics is a constantly changing market. Use the information you have gathered to guide your investigations, but remain alert to new developments.

In each case, you will want to know the name of the system and the vendor, and the purchase or leasing price. In the case of some microcomputer-based systems, the software may run on more than one brand of computer. Find out what system components are provided, which additional ones are required, and what optional components are available.

If you have decided to use an external service center, you will want to determine the standard charges for products and handling, as well as any additional fee for a rush job. Time required for processing and delivery of the finished product is also an important consideration.

Consider how information is entered into the computer and in what form the output is produced. Input may require a keyboard, digitizing tablet, or data files created for use with spreadsheet or database programs. Output often takes the form of simple text display, and tabular text is commonly provided. What types of charts and graphs are possible? Can you include more than one chart in a design? Does the system produce only simple geometric shapes or does it provide for free-form design of more complex images?

System Evaluation

You can summarize a business graphics system's effectiveness with one question: How well does it fit my organization's requirements? Your evaluation should focus on six important predictors of user satisfaction: ease of operation, product quality, design flexibility, documentation, vendor support, and cost. The form on page 000 provides checkpoints for each of these areas, plus an overall rating of the system. Based on an analysis of the unique requirements and resources of your organization, your evaluations of available products can prove your most valuable resource in making a decision.

The form is designed to be used as you become familiar with a system. Answer the items in whatever order seems appropriate, returning to those you have omitted later. You may find that your impressions change as you learn more about the system.

The scales for these items range from 0 to 4, with high marks indicating a positive rating. In general, a mark of 4 should indicate that the system meets your needs and expectations very well; a 2 means the product's performance is acceptable, but that there is room for significant improvement. A zero rating should be assigned if an important feature is absent, or if some aspect of the system could seriously hinder its use.

Feel free to add comments or expand on items in the form. The characteristics of any one system tend to become increasingly difficult to recall with each new system you consider. A word or two explaining each rating or recording important strengths or weaknesses can bring those perceptions into sharp focus again.

Ease of Operation

A business graphics system should provide for improved organizational communications without undue expenditure of resources. To obtain optimum productivity with minimum frustration, look for a system that allows you and your staff to go about the business of creating graphic materials without learning computing.

Because first impressions play an important part in gaining employee acceptance, requirements for getting the system running should be examined. Start-up can be as easy as flipping a switch or as complex as juggling several disks and entering a series of complex commands. If the user encounters trouble, provisions for correcting problems (prompts, command summaries) should be readily available.

Saving or recalling a file should be a simple, straightforward process. If the results of an editing session prove less desirable than expected, the user should be able to abandon those changes and return to the original design. Finally, a user should feel comfortable operating a system after a reasonable training period. While there may be more complex techniques that will take longer to master, basic operation should be transparent enough that the novice is quickly able to feel productive.

Product Quality

Quality should be measured in terms of the appropriateness of the final product for the setting in which it will be used. Arrange to use sample products in settings that are characteristic of your operations. While they are in use, examine the products for legibility of text and aesthetic quality.

The image you see on the monitor screen should be a reasonable representation of the product that will be delivered. Insufficient feedback about the image may mask unexpected results in the final product. Yet this preview function varies from a low resolution, monochrome image in some systems to a full color display in others.

Design Flexibility

Freeing the user from repetitive tasks is an important function of business graphics. A flexible system will enable you to choose the size, color, and placement of graphic elements—and to change any part as needed.

During the definition step you determined the range of colors required. Similarly, you will want to consider the number of text fonts (type styles) needed. If you will require more than one, be sure the system provides it.

Depending on the applications you anticipate, special functions may prove useful. Some systems have standard symbol libraries or allow the user to create them so that symbols may be stored for use in future designs. Contour mapping or animation is available in the more sophisticated systems.

Documentation

In a very few cases, business graphics packages are so well designed that the user's guide is seldom needed. Chances are, however, that you'll need documentation that is as well organized and error-free as possible. For the novice, a step-by-step lesson on system operation can ease those "getting started" jitters. The more experienced user does not need hand-holding, but appreciates a good index for locating specific information quickly.

The manual should be clearly written and contain enough information to help the user solve those problems that can be anticipated. This may include explanations of error messages or hints for avoiding common mistakes.

View documentation errors as a warning. Under pressure to market a new product, a vendor may try to rush testing procedures. Mistakes in the user's guide may foreshadow other problems that can arise with system use.

Vendor Support

Distributor concern for customer satisfaction is reflected not only in the product you buy but in the quality of service that comes after the sale. Product warranties, the convenience of system maintenance and repair, and the ease of getting information and advice are important factors in the vendor-client relationship.

As noted earlier, the business graphics market changes almost daily. The vendor should have a mechanism for informing customers of changes and making it possible for them to update their systems.

System Cost

This category evaluates the various costs of ownership. The price of acquiring hardware and software is only the beginning. Producing and handling charges are a major expense, and eventually may total more than the system price. Less obvious, but no less important, are staff training, time required to operate the system, changes in facilities, and eventually, the cost of updating as the vendor modifies the system.

Overall Rating

Because you have rated the system on a number of characteristics, you may find it difficult to compare it to other systems. Comparing overall sytsem scores should help you identify appropriate alternatives and eliminate inappropriate ones.

If all categories are equally important to your organization, average their ratings for the overall score. Usually, however, you will place greater emphasis on some features than others. Take care that a strong reaction to one category does not influence other scores.

Step 4—The Decision

Question: Which system is best for my organization?

By this time, you have probably discovered that ideal system—one that does everything you could ever want. You have probably also checked its price tag and winced. In business graphics, as in most other areas of business, the cost of a solution increases dramatically the more nearly it approximates the ideal. Although the "perfect" business graphics system may be unaffordable, one that meets most of your needs may still be within your means.

If you can not justify purchasing the system you want, start by eliminating a few of those attractive features. For example, using an external service center to generate the final product is often more economical than purchasing a film recorder. By using an external service and restricting output to simple computer art (words, charts, and graphs), you can purchase a high resolution, microcomputer-based design station for approximately $10,000. Such an arrangement may prove more desirable than facing the problems associated with maintaining in-house output devices.

Instead of buying a less expensive system, you may delay the purchase, waiting for competition to drive prices down while capabilities improve. If recent trends hold true, the currently unaffordable system may be more reasonably priced within a year or so.

Alternatively, you may decide on a compromise of these strategies: beginning operations now with a less sophisticated system and upgrading later. Such a choice minimizes risks and offers the opportunity to explore business graphics firsthand before making a larger commitment. Consider a microcomputer-based system that can be networked with more powerful equipment, thereby protecting your original investment.

Conclusion

A cost-effective business graphics system must not only be affordable, but appropriate for the requirements of your company. Although making a selection will involve several compromises, systematic evaluation using the DIAD model can result in the best possible match between organizational needs and the capabilities of business graphics.

Acknowledgment

The author would like to thank Dr. Deane K. Dayton for his assistance in clarifying many of the concepts discussed in this chapter.

Index